A HISTORY OF ZAMBIA

A History
of Zambia

ANDREW ROBERTS

Lecturer in African History
School of Oriental and African Studies
University of London

AFRICANA PUBLISHING COMPANY
A DIVISION OF
HOLMES & MEIER PUBLISHERS
NEW YORK

First published in the United States of America 1976 by
Africana Publishing Company
a division of
Holmes & Meier Publishers, Inc.
101 Fifth Avenue
New York, New York 10003

Library of Congress Cataloging in Publication Data

Roberts, Andrew.
A history of Zambia.

Bibliography: p.
Includes index.
1.   Zambia--History.   I.   Title.
DT963.5.R62   1976   968.9'4   76-40923
ISBN 0-8419-0291-7

PRINTED IN GREAT BRITAIN

Contents

Maps

Table

Illustrations

ix

ACKNOWLEDGEMENTS

Plates
Plates I(b), VII(b), VIII(a): Roan Consolidated Mines, Ltd.
Plates III(b), IV(b), VI(a, b), VII(a): National Museums of Zambia
Plate IV(a): National Archives, Rhodesia
Plate IV(d): Pitt-Rivers Museum, Oxford
All other photographs were taken by the author.
Plate V(a) from V. Giraud, *Les Lacs de l'Afrique Equatoriale* (Paris, 1890),
p. 255
Plate V(b) from E. Holub, *Von der Kapstadt ins Land der Maschukulumbe*
(Vienna, 1890), II, p. 57

Line drawings
1–3: Messrs. Thames and Hudson (from J. D. Clark, *The Prehistory of
Africa* [1970], pp. 92–93, 130, 177)
4: Cambridge University Press (from J. D. Clark, *Kalambo Falls*,
II [1974], p. 291)
5–7, 8a: British Institute in Eastern Africa (from *Azania*, V [1970],
pp. 85, 99; VII [1972], pp. 102–3; VIII [1973], p. 17)
8b: The Prehistoric Society (from *Proceedings of the Prehistoric Society*,
XXXV (1969), p. 188)
9a, 10–14: National Museums of Zambia (from *Zambia Museums Journal*, vol. 2 [1971], p. 55; J. O. Vogel, *Kamangoza*, pp. 12, 44, 61;
B. M. Fagan, *Iron Age Cultures in Zambia*, I, pp. 99, 101, 143; B. M.
Fagan *et al.*, *Iron Age Cultures in Zambia*, II, pp. 119, 123)

The cover design shows a Lunda policeman; Kazembe IV holding
audience in 1831; David Livingstone and Kenneth Kaunda.

Preface

This book tries to survey the whole span of human history in the territory which in 1964 became the independent state of Zambia. There are obvious objections to such an enterprise. It was not until the very end of the nineteenth century that this territory became a single political unit, the British colony of Northern Rhodesia. Its frontiers, like so many colonial frontiers, bore little relation to previous political, economic or social divisions. The colony comprised a variety of political and cultural groups, whose histories had linked them to peoples outside the new frontiers as well as within them. Clearly, the discussion of Zambia's pre-colonial history cannot be confined to events which simply happened to take place within its present borders. The historian of Zambia must constantly adjust his perspective to fit the actual spheres of human activity which he is studying, whether these are kingdoms, religious cults, trading networks or language groups. Indeed, this point applies with special force to the colonial period: as a source of both labour and copper, Northern Rhodesia was simply part of the vast mining complex of southern Africa.

This is therefore a study of history in Zambia, rather than a history of Zambia. None the less, it can be argued that modern frontiers can provide quite as good a basis as any other criteria for an overall survey of the human past in any one part of Africa. No one geographical area would be equally appropriate for discussing the Late Stone Age, the Early Iron Age, and the brigand kingdoms of the nineteenth century. And in the case of Zambia it can be claimed that this is as yet one of the few parts of Africa for which such a survey is possible. Modern frontiers in central Africa may be highly artificial, but they have greatly influenced the course of historical research. Scholars working in Northern Rhodesia, and then in Zambia, have built up a body of knowledge about the country's past which is perhaps more comprehensive than that for any of the numerous surrounding territories.

This knowledge has been gathered in a number of different ways. For all but the past century, written records are few and far between. In Zambia, as in most of the rest of Africa, reading and writing was virtually unknown before colonial rule. Oral traditions take us back a century or two, but for earlier periods the historian is almost entirely dependent on archaeology. Since 1939, numerous excavations have been conducted on behalf of the Museum and the Monuments Commission at Livingstone. In its earlier stages, this research was primarily concerned with the hunting and gathering cultures of the Stone Age, but over the past twenty years there has been a strong emphasis on the farmers and herdsmen of the Iron Age. This work is now supported by a large number of radio-carbon dates, and it is clear that Iron Age cultures were fairly widespread in Zambia by about AD 500. There have been few dramatic discoveries, and no spectacular monuments have come to light: Zambia has no Great Zimbabwe. But it can be claimed that we now have a fuller picture of changes in everyday life during the first 1500 years or so AD than is available for almost any other country in black Africa. We know a good deal about related developments in Rhodesia, and Malawi has not been neglected, but Iron Age archaeology in Zaïre is very patchy; in Angola and Mozambique it has hardly begun, and it has only recently been given proper attention in South Africa.

Archaeology in Zambia has thus made a major contribution to our understanding of the Iron Age throughout central and southern Africa. Nor does this work simply concern peoples and cultures that have long since disappeared: it throws light on the earliest history of people who live in Zambia today. Until quite recently it was supposed that the ancestors of the country's modern inhabitants had all settled there within the last three or four centuries. But it now seems clear that at least some of these ancestors were living in Zambia almost a thousand years ago, while there are a few groups of people who have probably been there since the Early Iron Age. So if we look at history in Zambia in a very broad perspective, we must think in terms of continuous developments within more or less settled communities since at least AD 1000.

Inevitably, archaeological research has told us most about changes in material culture. The main outlines of social and political change only begin to come into focus some time around the sixteenth or seventeenth century. From this period, increasing light is shed by evidence preserved by the people of Zambia themselves, especially their own historical traditions and social institutions. We also begin to learn something from literate visitors. From the end of the seventeenth century there are occasional reports by traders based on Portuguese settlements in the lower Zambezi valley. Between 1851 and 1873 David Livingstone travelled extensively across the country; he wrote three books about his travels; and he was followed by other European explorers and missionaries. From the 1890s the historian's main sources are the records of government officials. Written African records are unfortunately very scarce; reading and writing was introduced only at the end of the nineteenth century, and African education made slow progress under colonial rule.

Compared with that for other African countries, this body of historical evidence for the last few centuries is not particularly impressive. On the other hand it has received much expert attention. The Rhodes–Livingstone Institute was founded in Northern Rhodesia in 1937, and this sponsored a series of studies by social anthropologists in several parts of the country. Together with the work of a few earlier scholars these studies provide an invaluable ethnographic basis for historical research. Some indeed were specifically concerned with historical problems, and several shed light on the social effects of modern labour migration and the rapid growth of the Copperbelt towns from about 1930. In 1953 Northern Rhodesia became part of the Central African Federation, and one of the few unqualified achievements of this misguided experiment was the development of a National Archives service; this also sponsored the first comprehensive study of the country's colonial history by a professional historian, Lewis Gann.[1] Since Independence, there has been a great deal of research into the Zambian past, by Zambians as well as by foreigners, and much of this work has been based on the University of Zambia.

There has thus been no lack of material for the present book: rather, the problem has been one of balance and proportion. In facing this I have been guided mainly by the nature of the existing literature. It seemed worth while to attempt a fairly comprehensive account of Zambia's archaeology; our knowledge has grown enormously since the last survey of this kind was made.[2] For similar reasons I have devoted a good deal of space to more recent pre-colonial history. On the other hand, there seemed no need to provide more than a brief outline of the colonial period. This is of course of immense importance for understanding Zambia today, but it is also relatively accessible. Gann's monumental history remains the leading authority on the period up to 1953, and though this is more illuminating on European than on African society it is balanced in this respect by the work of Robert Rotberg and Richard Hall, who were able to take the story up to Independence.[3] Much more has been done since these authors wrote, but any adequate synthesis of this research would require a book to itself; it would certainly far outrun the space available here. Instead, I have made room for some account of the main economic and political changes since Independence, though there are important themes in the social and cultural life of modern Zambia which I have totally ignored.

Whatever the merits of this design, it may still be doubted whether an overall survey of history in Zambia can be anything more than the sum of its parts. Even if the origins of the present population can be traced back a thousand years or more, it remains very difficult to see their history as a coherent whole. The political unification of the country is not only an extremely recent event; it cut short the growth of quite different patterns of domination. It would thus be very misleading to present the whole span of history in Zambia in terms of continuous political change. Yet it would be equally misleading to consider it as simply an agglomeration of separate histories, concerning groups of people who until recently had little or nothing to do with each other. Research on all fronts is throwing increasing light on processes of economic and religious change which cut across small-scale political divisions and do give coherence and continuity to our knowledge of large areas and periods.

In this book I have tried especially to stress the broad patterns of change in production and trade which underlie the confusing variety of pre-colonial political groupings. For this the archaeological evidence provides an invaluable foundation; in particular it enables us to see how from early times trade in copper and other metals has played a part in linking different communities. The modern copper mines, of course, are based on a wholly alien technology; in this sense their development constitutes a completely new chapter in Zambia's history. But this industry posed fundamental economic problems which were by no means new. In earlier days the main exports from Zambia to the outside world were ivory and slaves rather than copper, but such commerce raised many of the questions which worry Zambia today: the economic and political role of foreigners; the effects of external trade on local production and also on moral values; the use of manpower; the consequences of dependence on a single commodity for export, or on a single trade route. The fact that Zambia is a land-locked territory far from any coast has meant that it has always been on the periphery of international and intercontinental trade and prone to domination by traders with greater access to the world's markets. As yet, there is still much work to be done on such themes. It is astonishing that there is still no detailed economic history of a country which has been of major importance to the industrialised world for the past forty years.[4] Fortunately there are signs that this neglect is being repaired.

This book owes a great deal to the work of many scholars. I must also acknowledge the help and stimulus I received when working in Zambia, first as a research student in 1964–5 and then as a research fellow at the University of Zambia from 1968 to 1971. Several friends have given advice on different parts of the book; I am specially grateful to David Phillipson for his comments on the first five chapters. Parts of Chapter VII appeared in *African Social Research*, no. 10 (December 1970). Various passages in Chapters IX, X and XI are taken from my contributions to *Aspects of Central African History*, edited by T. O. Ranger (Heinemann Educational Books, 1968).

A.D.R.

1. L. H. Gann, *A History of Northern Rhodesia: early days to 1953* (1964).
2. B. M. Fagan (ed.), *A Short History of Zambia* (Lusaka, 1968 – second edition).
3. R. I. Rotberg, *The Rise of Nationalism in Central Africa – the making of Malawi and Zambia, 1873–1964* (Cambridge, Mass., 1966). R. Hall, *Zambia* (1965; revised edition, 1976).
4. Economists have shown greater interest than historians (see, e.g. R. E. Baldwin, *Economic Development and Export Growth: a study of Northern Rhodesia, 1902–1960* (Berkeley and Los Angeles, 1966).

NOTE ON PRONUNCIATION

African words cited in the text are spelled in accordance with the orthography of the International African Institute. The letter *c* is pronounced 'ch', as in 'chair'. Vowels are pronounced as in Italian. Thus *citemene* is pronounced 'chitéméné'.

Aerial view of the Victoria Falls: the gorges immediately below the Falls indicate their earlier positions.

(b)
Open-cast copper mining at Chambishi in 1966: this shows how the crust of the earth buckled and folded some 600 million years ago, after the ore-bodies underneath had been formed.

II(a)   *A Lozi homestead built on an artificial mound on the upper Zambezi flood plain; in the foreground is an artificial channel and a fish-dam.*

(b)   *A* citemene *garden near Chitimukulu's village, in Bemba country; the clearing is covered with fine ash from burning piles of branches.*

Kalemba rock-shelter:
excavations in progress, 1971.
There are faint traces, not
visible here, of red schematic
paintings under the white
figures.

(b)
Grave of a young man at Ingombe
Ilede; there are lengths of copper
wire above his head and copper
bangles on his right arm. Beneath
his chin is one of the nine conus
shell discs suspended from his
necklace

IV(a) *Kansanshi copper mine in 1901: a team from Tanganyika Concessions, Ltd., exploring an old African working.*

(b) *Copper cross found in one of the graves at Ingombe Ilede (length c. 12″/30 cm.). (below)*

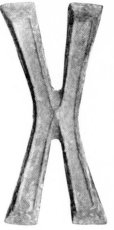

(c) *A double iron bell, flanged and clapperless, belonging to the Shila chief Mununga, near Lake Mweru; it was made by Luba craftsmen to the north-west. (left)*

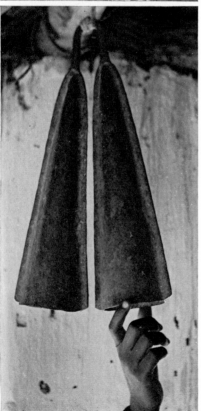

(d) *Iron-smelting furnace in Mambwe country, four miles east of Mbala, in the 1920s (height c. 7′/2·3 m.).*

V(a)   *The fortified capital of the Bemba king, Chitimukulu, as seen by the French explorer Victor Giraud in 1883: note the inner trench and stockade (crowned with skulls) round the royal enclosure. A tall granary, with a ladder, is visible near the centre.*

(b)   *A labour dispute in 1886, at the village of the Toka chief Musokotwane: Subiya porters hired by the Czech explorer Emil Holub argue over the amount of cloth due them as wages. Holub's wife is on the far right.*

VI(a) *An ABC lesson in 1887 at the Paris Mission's newly-opened school at Sefula, near the Lozi capital. The teacher is Aaron Mayoro, a catechist from Lesotho; the photograph was taken by François Coillard.*

(b) *An early but undated picture of L. W. G. Eccles, who came to Northern Rhodesia as a surveyor in 1912 and in 1948 introduced the Urban African Housing Ordinance.*

VII(a)
*Grave of a migrant
worker, around 1931:
the place is not known,
but he was on his way
home to Nyasaland
from the Copperbelt.*

(b) *Married quarters in the African compound at Roan Antelope mine in 1927; such
huts were eventually replaced by more substantial houses.*

VIII(a)
*The underground
training school at
Roan Antelope mine,
1967; the African
instructor shows how
a rock-face is charged
for blasting.*

(b)
*Church at Katondwe,
near Feira; this was
designed by a Jesuit
missionary to recall
the onion-domed
churches of his native
Poland. It was
opened in 1938.*

I

The Natural Setting

Zambia's best-known physical assets are its copper mines and the Victoria Falls. The visitor who arrives at Lusaka, the capital, will at once see signs of the wealth produced by the copper industry: the grandiose international airport, the opulent, copper-sheathed Parliament building and the tall office blocks in the city centre. Five hundred kilometres to the south-west the wide Zambezi river suddenly drops into an abyss, forming the largest waterfall in the world. Elsewhere the visitor may well find the landscape monotonous and lacking in human interest. Little of Zambia's best scenery is visible from the main roads, and it often seems that uninhabited woodland stretches everywhere to enormous flat horizons. In fact the woodland is neither empty nor endless. Within it, and beyond it, most of the population still makes a living from the soil. This varies greatly in quality, and in contrast to most British farmland it has been little altered by the hand of man. Like the copper ore-bodies and the Falls, the soil of Zambia is essentially a residue of more or less distant geological events. A study of human history there may properly begin with a brief history of the country itself. We shall therefore consider the origins of Zambia's minerals and land-forms, its soils and vegetation, before turning to see what man has made of this environment.

Geology

Zambia lies in the southern tropics, a huge butterfly shape sprawled across one and a half thousand kilometres of the great inland plateau which forms the spine of Africa. This plateau is mainly based on very old crystalline rocks, rich in minerals but making for soils of low fertility. In these respects, indeed, Zambia is typical of the tropical world in general. The oldest rocks in the country are classified as the Basement Complex and correspond to an early phase in the pre-Cambrian geological era. The lower, and earlier, layers in this Basement Complex may be as much as 2,000 million years old. Upsurges of volcanic activity far below the earth's surface caused folds and faults in these rock layers; the heat affected the mineral composition of the rock and in places formed granite. Other typical early Basement rocks are gneisses, micaceous quartzites and schists such as mica and hornblende. These can be seen outcropping on the surface, mainly in the east and south-east. The upper Basement layers – known on the Copperbelt as the Muva group – are very much younger rocks. They are mostly quartzites, schists and conglomerates, usually visible near the surface outcrops of the lower Basement. The whole Basement Complex contains various mineral ores: gold at Sasare and Chakwenga; a small copper deposit near Chakwenga; tin near Choma; and manganese at Kampumba, Chiwefwe and near Mansa.

The Basement Complex was considerably eroded and overlain with later rocks. Sea covered much of what is now west-central Africa, and as it retreated it left sedimentary deposits, classified as the 'Katanga System'. These rocks were laid down between 1000 million and 620 million years ago, and all Zambia's most important minerals derive from them. The Katanga sediments cover much of central and north-eastern Zambia, but the copper minerals are mostly concentrated in deposits on the Copperbelt and around Mumbwa. The main ores are malachite, azurite, chalcopyrite, bornite and chalcozite; they occur in sedimentary layers of shale, sandstone, dolomite and quartzite. The large iron ore-body exposed at Sanje, west of Lusaka, and the lead and zinc deposits at Kabwe, also belong to Katanga sediments. Elsewhere, as in the north, they are very little mineralised. Here and there – as near Mumbwa and Mazabuka – granite outcrops testify to volcanic intrusion into Katanga sediments. There are also numerous granite outcrops in the north, but it is seldom clear whether these were formed by volcanic intrusion before or after the Katanga sediments were laid down.

The next series of rock-formations, the 'Karroo system', began to take shape rather more than 300 million years ago, in a near-Arctic climate. For a time ice-sheets covered part of Zambia, and their retreat caused rock fragments to cement into tillite. Water then deposited the main Karroo sediments – sandstone, mudstone, conglomerate and coal – along the line of the Luangwa and middle Zambezi valleys. The largest coal deposits are in the lower Gwembe valley, at Maamba and Nkandabwe, but there are thinner coal seams elsewhere along the middle Zambezi, and also in the Luangwa valley. Fossil tree-trunks in Karroo sandstone can be seen near Chirundu, just above the confluence of the Zambezi and Kafue. Reptile fossils have been found in Karroo sediments in the middle Luangwa valley. The last phase in the Karroo sequence corresponds to the Jurassic period, about 160 million years ago. Molten rock seeped up through cracks in the earth's crust and formed a basalt-type lava which spread over much of western Zambia;

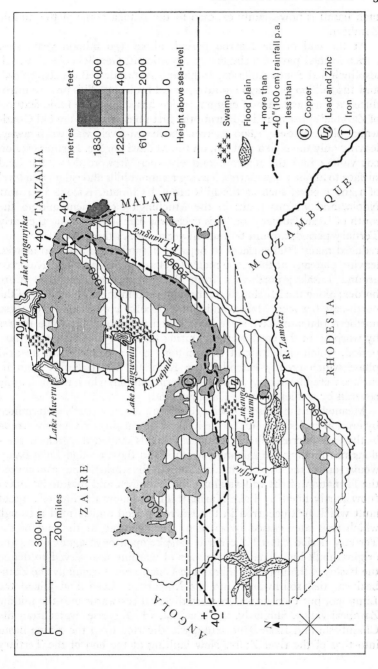

such basalt is now mainly exposed in the Batoka gorge of the middle Zambezi.

At the end of the Karroo period, about 150 million years ago, Africa formed part of a single super-continent, Gondwanaland, which also included South America, India and Antarctica. But between 130 and 120 million years ago Gondwanaland broke up. This process introduced a long sequence of erosion, which has shaped the basic features of Zambia's present relief. During the first phase most of the old Gondwana plateau, over 1,800 metres above sea-level, was worn away, leaving only the Nyika plateau, on the Malawi border. Further erosion cut valleys into the plateau, and elsewhere it wore down the land surface to about 1,300 metres, leaving remnant hills and ridges at a level of 1,400 metres, such as the hills around Chipata, Kaloko Hill near Ndola, and various peaks in the Muchinga escarpment and to the south of Lake Tanganyika. This cycle was completed during the early Tertiary period, around 60 million years ago. A third cycle of erosion reduced many land surfaces to between 1,150 metres and 900 metres, leaving plateaux at the 1,300 metre level around Choma and Kalomo; around Lusaka; north-west from the Copperbelt along the Zaïre border; along the Muchinga escarpment; and in the granite areas of the north-east between Mansa and the Tanzania border. Some of these northern plateaux have since been raised to as much as 1,500 metres by warping in the earth's crust. During the latter part of the Tertiary period, which ended about two million years ago, there was an arid phase which greatly extended the Kalahari desert. Sands from its surface were blown over much of western Zambia, which is thus largely covered by a thick layer of Kalahari sand.

Meanwhile the present drainage system, already partly determined by erosion cycles, was further defined by upwarping and downwarping in the earth's crust. Such gradual upheavals shaped the great depressions surrounding the Lukanga swamps and those around Lake Bangweulu (one of the largest inland swamps in the world). They also caused the formation of rift valleys along the Luangwa and middle Zambezi (now partly filled by Lake Kariba). These follow the line of a great fault which first occurred in the Karroo period and formed a trough which was later erased by erosion. The warping at the end of the Tertiary period caused the earth to split open once again along the original fault-line. The same process of warping also served to define the basins of the upper Zambezi and Chambeshi. Originally the Zambezi emptied southwards into the Makarikari Lake, and joined the Limpopo, but then its waters were diverted eastwards into the middle Zambezi valley. Similarly, the Luapula, which carries water from the Chambeshi and Lake Bangweulu, was diverted from the Kafue basin into that of the river Zaïre. New faulting at the end of the Tertiary period created the rift valleys of Luapula-Lake Mweru and of Lake Tanganyika.

During much of the Pleistocene period, which began some two million years ago, the climate was relatively wet, and the action of flowing water further shaped the course and nature of river valleys. The prevalence of flat land surfaces, as a result of repeated erosion and warping, impeded drainage: instead of flowing steadily down a single channel, river water was often spread out over large flat basins – not only the swamps of Bangweulu and Lukanga, but the flood plains of the middle Chambeshi, middle Kafue and upper Zambezi. Such areas were covered with thick sediments of silt and gravel carried down by the river waters. At present, during the dry season, the waters retreat from the flood plains, leaving them open for human and animal use.

Where rivers flowed down from plateaux into rift valleys, they created scenery of a very different kind. Fast-falling water eroded the lip of a waterfall and eventually gouged out deep new channels throughout the escarpment rocks. Such gorges can be seen on the middle Luapula, tributaries of the lower Luangwa, and northern tributaries of the middle Zambezi, especially on the lower Kafue. One particularly fine example is the Kalambo river, which now drops 221 metres from the high plateau near Mbala and runs through a correspondingly deep gorge before flowing into Lake Tanganyika: this is the second highest waterfall in Africa and the twelfth highest in the world.

But the most famous and impressive gorges and falls are of course on the Zambezi itself. At one time, perhaps a million years ago, the Zambezi flowed down a broad valley which continued over the plateau surface to the head of the middle Zambezi Rift, at the mouth of the Matetsi river. Here the Zambezi fell about 250 metres from the plateau escarpment. But these original falls steadily retreated upstream as the river cut into the lip and wore down into long fissures in the river bed. These cracks had appeared at the end of the Karroo period, during the cooling of the basalt lava which had covered this area. Since the cracks ran mostly along an east–west axis, and since this was roughly the axis of the upper part of the middle Zambezi, there was no broad fall of water extending across the valley: instead, the water cut deep channels along its own line of flow. Towards the end of the Middle Pleistocene, probably less than 40,000 years ago, the Batoka Gorge had been carved out to a point ninety kilometres above the original fall.

At about this point the pattern of erosion changed abruptly. For here the river valley followed a north–south axis, cutting sharply across the lines of faulting. This meant that the water now eroded the rock into great walls running across the valley, over which the river spilled in broad curtains of water. Once one new fall had been formed, the river began to wear down on the lip until it found the line of weakness immediately behind it; in due course the rock along this line would collapse, and the rear wall of the resulting trough would become the new Falls. In this way, eight falls were formed one after the other in a space of only eleven kilometres, and this has caused the zigzag sequence of gorges below the present Victoria Falls. The retreat from the last line of the Falls has created two great promontories which run out immediately in front of the present Falls. These provide a ringside seat from which to admire a curtain of falling water over 1·5 kilometres wide and 110 metres high – the largest in the world.

This natural wonder is extremely recent. The lowest of the zigzag gorges below the Falls cannot be more than about 35,000–40,000 years old, for man-made stone tools of about this age were buried by gravels on the margins of the old river bed for nineteen kilometres below the present Falls. These gravels could only have been deposited by the river when it still flowed over the plateau and had not yet cut the whole sequence of gorges. As for the upper three gorges, and the Victoria Falls themselves, these have probably been formed within the last 10,000 years or so. Wind-blown sand thought to have been deposited within this period is found on basalt spurs downstream of the three upper gorges. Since it did not accumulate on spurs any further upstream, it is clear that there the Zambezi still flowed along its old river bed, over the plateau surface which is now so dramatically dissected by the last three gorges.

Climate, Soils and Vegetation

This rapid geological survey has served to introduce Zambia's principal natural features. But to appreciate the Zambian landscape as a setting for human and animal life we must also take account of the effects of climate. The Last Glaciation took place about 70,000 years ago. By the time the Victoria Falls had taken shape, the climate of Zambia was much as it is today. Owing to its location in the southern tropics, Zambia enjoys plenty of warmth and sunshine, but the tropical heat is moderated both by altitude, since most of the country lies well above 900 metres, and by rainfall.

Zambia's rainfall is concentrated in one rainy season, from November to March or April. This rhythm is determined by the convergence of three main airstreams – 'Congo Air'; the north-eastern monsoon; and the south-eastern trades. Towards the end of the year the belt of low pressure along the Equator moves south, so that the zone in which these airstreams meet also moves south. The crucial element is the Congo airmass, which carries the most moisture. This advances from the north-west so that the rains first arrive at places such as Mwinilunga and Lake Mweru in early November; they reach the southern and eastern borders in late November and early December. In most places the wettest month is January, though in some areas there are two peaks, in December and March. As the new year continues, the equatorial low-pressure belt moves north again, and with it the convergence zone. The trade winds from the south-east begin to prevail, and the dry season first arrives in southern Zambia in March; it usually reaches Mbala, in the far north, in early May. Rainfall is therefore heaviest in the north, where the period of air convergence is most prolonged. It ranges from 100 cm to 150 cm a year, north and west of a line running roughly east from the upper Zambezi and up the Luangwa valley. South and east of this line rainfall ranges from 100 cm to as little as 64 cm in the middle Zambezi valley. In this belt of lower rainfall, the total can vary from year to year by 20 to 30 per cent or more.

Sunshine and temperatures vary with the rainfall cycle. Towards the end of the dry season, during September and October, mean daytime temperatures rise to between 29°C and 32°C in the north and north-east, and to as much as 35°C over most of western Zambia; they rise still higher in low-lying valleys. Night-time temperatures during this hot season are 10°C to 16°C lower. With the arrival of the rains the weather becomes cooler and more humid, and daily sunshine is reduced to three hours in the north and five hours in the south. By May the rains have ceased, and a cool dry season begins – this is Zambia's winter. The sun is now overhead far into the northern hemisphere, and in June and July daytime temperatures in Zambia average less than 13°C in the north and east, and less than 10°C in the west; to the south and west, ground frost often occurs at night.

The interaction of rainfall and geology has affected patterns of human settlement in two ways: the means by which water is drained off the surface, and the formation of different soil types. Most parts of Zambia are fairly well watered. Not only are there several lakes, major rivers and flood plains; these large masses of water are fed by a multitude of small tributaries. As rainwater runs off the gentle slopes of the plateaux, it quickly forms numerous but shallow channels through which it flows relatively slowly: water is thus plentifully exposed over the land surface. The smaller streams are liable to dry up towards the end of the dry season, but meanwhile water has collected in long shallow depressions, known as 'dambos'. During the rains, these dambos become waterlogged or even flooded, but during the dry season they release their water and enable some streams to maintain a perennial flow. The one major exception to this pattern is that large region in western Zambia where rainwater percolates so rapidly through the Kalahari sands that there is little or no surface run-off, and consequently very few streams between the river valleys. Instead, the rainwater first accumulates beneath the sand ridges and then seeps away into dambo-like depressions called *milapo*: these may be permanently waterlogged, so that fertile peat is formed.

The variations in Zambian soil types are intimately related to variations in vegetation and human land-use, so it is convenient to consider these together. Over most of Zambia the soil is 'ferralitic', derived mostly from the weathering of very old rocks, including granite, in the Basement and Katanga series, but in places derived from Karroo sediments. Such soil tends to be sandy and unduly acid; it is deficient in the mineral bases needed for plant life, such as lime, magnesium, potash, phosphorus and nitrate. The quality of the soil is diminished by the nature of the rainfall; this is mostly concentrated in brief but heavy downpours which tend to wash away the mineral bases. (Where this leaching process is far advanced, the subsoil is transformed into hard infertile laterite, which may form a crust at the surface if the loose topsoil is eroded away.) The poorer soils are thus mostly found on the north-eastern and north-western plateaux, where the annual rainfall exceeds 100 cm. The typical vegetation cover is deciduous *miombo* woodland (comprising smallish trees of the *Brachystegia Isoberlinia* and *Julbernardia* genera) intersected by grassy dambos. The traditional form of agriculture is a type of slash-and-burn cultivation known as *citemene*. This is a 'bush-fallow ash culture': every year, trees are felled or pollarded over a wide area in order to fertilise small clearings with wood-ash; these are sown with finger millet, an unusually hardy cereal, or kaffir corn. Thereafter, subsidiary crops may be planted for a few years; clearings are then left fallow for ten to fifteen years.

In southern, central and eastern Zambia, also covered with *miombo* woodland, the ferralitic soils are less heavily leached and have proved better adapted to cultivation: maize is more easily grown and, in present times, hoe-and-plough methods have tended to replace slash-and-burn. On the major escarpments of the Basement rocks – above the middle Zambezi, Luangwa and Luapula valleys – the topsoil has been more heavily eroded, and laterite crusts often approach the surface. These shallow, rocky 'lithosols' are far from fertile. Where they are cultivated it is often because it is also possible to market products, such as charcoal, from the *miombo* woodland.

The best soils in Zambia are also derived from Katanga and Basement rocks, but they are relatively rich in bases and contain ferromagnesian minerals. Such 'fersiallitic' soils are found only in certain stretches of undulating country where the rainfall is less than 100 cm, in Central Province (Lusaka–Kabwe–Mumbwa); Southern Province (Monze–Mazabuka), and Eastern Province (Petauke and Chipata). The vegetation is distinctive, a mixture of *Acacia, Combretum* and *Afrormosia* trees known as *munga* woodland, standing in tall grasses suitable for cattle. The soils were traditionally cultivated with the hoe rather than by slash-and-burn methods, and in recent times maize has become the staple crop. As the water-table tends to be very deep in such areas, they were probably not especially favoured by African cultivators until recently, but they naturally attracted early European settlement. Other favourable soils are the result of seasonal flooding in depressions on the plateaux. The Kafue Flats and the upper Zambezi flood plains are enriched by alluvium deposited by these two major rivers. The annual flooding of the Kafue has proved an obstacle to cultivation, but both plains provide excellent grazing for cattle. The margins of the upper Zambezi plain, like those of the Bangweulu swamps, include patches of rich peaty soil which can support quite intensive cultivation: the same is true of many smaller waterlogged depressions. A further incentive to human settlement around the major lakes, swamps and flood plains is their abundant fish, especially bream and other *Tilapia*.

Along the middle Zambezi, the Luangwa and the lower Luapula valleys, the soils derive from Karroo sediments. In places, especially around the confluences of tributary rivers, they are enriched by alluvial deposits and intensive hoe-cultivation is possible. The more fertile soils of the lower Luapula support *cipya* woodland, a mixture of predominantly tall trees and grasses which is also found on the fringes of the Bangweulu depression: the staple crop in such areas is now cassava. The valley floors of the middle Zambezi and Luangwa are mostly covered with a canopy of *mopane* trees, which flourish on alkaline clay-flats. Among the least fertile soils are the Kalahari sands of western Zambia. These support a variety of grasses and trees including evergreen teak. Bulrush millet can be grown in these sands, but only if gardens are then left fallow for long periods. Slightly better conditions are found in the south-east corner of this Kalahari zone, where the sand layer is thinner and is probably derived in part from underlying rock.

Patterns of Human Settlement

Climate, soil and vegetation have been the main factors in determining the possibilities for agriculture in Zambia. But man's capacity to exploit these resources has depended on other factors: his success has been severely limited by disease, but also increased by his own ingenuity and innovation. Some of the commonest and most lethal tropical diseases are rife in Zambia. One of the worst is sleeping-sickness. Large parts of the country are infested by tsetse fly: one variety, *Glossina pallipides*, frequents shady river-banks, while the other main type, *Glossina morsitans*, prefers the more open woodland. The flies transmit parasites, called trypanosomes, from the blood of infected animals and humans.

Some parasites cause nagana in cattle and horses, while others cause sleeping-sickness in man. Wild animals are more or less immune, but for this reason they are all the more dangerous as hosts to the parasites. At present, tsetse fly is mainly concentrated along the Luangwa valley; west of the great bend in the Kafue river (the Kafue 'Hook'); and east of Lake Mweru. These areas are now mostly game reserves, but a few parts are inhabited, and there are smaller patches of tsetse fly along the Zambezi and Luapula valleys, and on the north-eastern plateau. To some extent, man can eliminate the fly by clearing bush and killing off game, and the present limits of infection are both cause and effect of human settlement patterns. But before the introduction of modern medical and other control techniques the fly was even more widespread than it is today. Over most of Zambia, cattle and draught animals could not be kept. Manure was seldom available, and in most areas, until this century, the only transport was human porterage.

The commonest tropical disease in Zambia is malaria; less common, but no less debilitating, is bilharzia. Both are caused by parasites whose hosts – the anopheles mosquito and a type of snail – breed in water. For most of the year there is a great deal of surface water throughout most of the country, so that both diseases are quite evenly distributed. They are relatively seldom fatal, but they are extremely enervating; they severely lower resistance to other diseases; and bilharzia can persist for long periods. Leprosy also occurs, but smallpox has now been virtually eradicated and yellow fever is unknown. Zambia is, however, considerably afflicted with diseases common to temperate climates. Of these, respiratory ailments are perhaps the most serious group; people are often inadequately protected against the damp and cold around the end of the rainy season and easily contract pneumonia, bronchitis or influenza.

Man made important advances in modifying and exploiting the Zambian environment long before European intervention began to alter the pace of technological change. This will become clear in later chapters: here it is enough to take note of a few major themes. One is the crucial importance of fire, and iron tools, in subduing woodland for cultivation; indeed, the present distribution of types of trees is to some extent the result of long and gradual adaptation both to spontaneous and accidental bush-fires, and to deliberate large-scale clearance. Iron tools were also vital for controlling water: instead of depending entirely on surface water, some people relied more on digging shallow wells, especially in dried-up dambos. In places, drainage was undertaken: the most striking example is the flood plain of the upper Zambezi, which was opened up to partial cultivation as well as seasonal grazing once canals were dug to direct the flow of flood-water, and once mounds were built to rise above it.

Man's ability to wrest a living from the soil has been still further enlarged by the introduction of new crops. Most of the food crops now grown in Zambia are native not to Africa but to America: as elsewhere in Africa, contacts with Portuguese traders and settlers promoted the spread of maize, cassava (manioc), sweet potatoes, groundnuts and sugar cane. Cassava is especially well suited to the poor soils typical of much of Zambia, and in some areas, as in the north-west and along the Luapula, it has replaced the original staple. It is a root crop which can be harvested as desired and has therefore been very important in reducing the risk of famine during the 'hunger months' preceding the main cereal harvest, which is usually early in the dry season. Since it can be stored in the ground it is immune from the pests which make heavy inroads into household granaries. On the other hand, cassava is seriously deficient in vitamins and is a major factor in the malnutrition which is perhaps more widespread in Zambia than any other disease.

Throughout most of human history in Zambia the density and distribution of population have been determined by man's capacity to produce food for himself and his dependants. Within the past century, trade in foodstuffs has reduced the need for subsistence cultivation, while modern medicine and hygiene has made possible a rapid growth in population. The present total is rather over four million, and more than a million people live in or around towns. Even so, the distribution of the rural population still reflects fairly closely the country's agricultural resources. Less than one-fifth of the total land-surface can be cultivated according to indigenous land-use methods. Outside the towns, the average density is only four people per square kilometre. Large regions are uninhabited – the tsetse-ridden game reserves of Luangwa and western Zambia, and much of the sand belt west of the upper Zambezi. A few areas are quite thickly populated: in the most fertile parts of the Southern and Eastern Provinces, on the upper Zambezi flood plain, on the lower Luapula and around Lake Bangweulu, the density rises in places to well over 40 per square kilometre. In such areas the staple crop, maize or cassava, is cultivated more or less intensively, and cattle-keeping or fishing helps to enrich the diet.

Elsewhere, in the vast *miombo* woodlands of the north-east and northwest, the density ranges between two and ten per square kilometre. Cattle-keeping is impeded by tsetse or lack of pasture; opportunities for fishing are limited; and much space is needed to practise *citemene* cultivation. In such regions of inferior soils the vital factor is 'carrying capacity': the number of people who can be supported by a given area during the whole period needed for the complete regeneration of woodland after clearing, pollarding and cultivation. In north-eastern Zambia this probably averages well under four per square kilometre. If population density in a given area much exceeds its carrying capacity, land will not be left fallow long enough; it will eventually cease to be cultivable and the natural vegetation may take a very long time to recover its original size and variety. The obvious alternative, especially in pre-colonial times, has been to cultivate new tracts of woodland, which may be plentiful; but they may also be tsetse-infested, or lack perennial surface water, or be too remote from other human settlements and communication routes. For these and other reasons, even the sparse woodland populations are unevenly distributed, with long-term effects on the woodland itself.

It is not, of course, enough to consider the Zambian environment in isolation, if we are to appreciate its importance for human history. The present international frontiers are no more than eighty years old and only in the last decade have they become in themselves a major constraint on human movement. Zambia forms only a part, albeit a large part, of the whole central African plateau, and its social and economic history can only be understood in the context of this broader geographical unit. Contacts between what is now Zambia and the surrounding areas have been fostered by basic similarities in the natural environment, which have encouraged broad similarities in social and cultural development. The natural features typical of Zambia – old rocks, eroded relief, extensive woodland, a relative abundance of surface water – are also typical of much of south-eastern Zaïre, eastern Angola, Rhodesia and western Mozambique, and also the Transvaal. In all these regions it is generally possible to make a living from the soil, but seldom very easily, and the real wealth of the land lies less on the surface than in underground mineral deposits. In recent times these common factors have served to involve Zambians in the whole mining complex of southern Africa – from Shaba to Kimberley. In earlier centuries, the unbroken woodland of the Zaïre–Zambezi watershed was the scene of prolonged migration, and also trade. Much of north-eastern Zambia lies within the Zaïre basin, and the whole complex drainage system has tended to facilitate human settlement and intercourse throughout this vast region.

 On the other hand, natural barriers to human movement have also played an important part in Zambian history. Most obvious is its distance from the sea, which is of critical importance at the present day. The rugged escarpments above the Luangwa and the middle Zambezi have impeded (though by no means prevented) communication between what are now Zambia, Malawi and Rhodesia. Rivers, like swamps, may be both help and hindrance to travel; in practice, water transport has been unimportant in Zambia except on the upper Zambezi, the lower Luapula and Lake Bangweulu. Finally, the very sparseness of population in so much of the country has tended to reduce the scale and frequency of internal communications. Where the rural population is comparatively dense, it is concentrated in a few clusters remote from one another. The importance of these different factors has varied considerably in the course of history, depending on the purposes of communication and the means employed. In Zambia, as in many other new nations, modern transport techniques have improved external communications but in some ways have been of rather doubtful benefit to internal communications. The railway from the south, and a tarmac road, span the Zambezi gorge just below the Victoria Falls, but thereafter they seek to avoid the scenic excitement of escarpments and valleys for the surer ground of the plateaux. Even here they closely follow the main watersheds, in order to minimise the risk of flash-flooding and subsidence from innumerable small rivers and gullies. Thus although the major modern routes link up industrial centres, they tend not to run very close to villages, which are seldom sited right on a watershed. And some of the major clusters of the rural population occur in country much better suited to cultivation than to road-building, such as the fertile depressions of the upper Zambezi, the Luapula and Lake Bangweulu. The desire for easy access to the towns and to modern facilities has thus drawn many people away from the environments most favourable to subsistence, while modern imports have undermined older networks for the exchange of local products.

There is, then, no close correspondence between Zambia's modern transport routes, the distribution of the rural population and the incidence of major scenic attractions. The monotonous appearance of the plateaux is indeed deceptive; the grey-green woodland canopy on either side of the road is a dusty veil which obscures most of the country from casual view. The natural variety of Zambia, scenic, human and animal, is scarcely evident to the traveller until he leaves the roads for rough tracks and footpaths, or ventures out into swamp and open water. And in a country without grandiose ancient monuments such exploration is vital to a sense of the past that extends back beyond our own century. Not only does the past survive more obviously off the beaten track, in the rhythms and rituals of village life – which are often less 'traditional' than they seem. In Zambia as elsewhere, there are abundant traces of man's handiwork in earlier times. The scatter of stone tools; the painted cave; the deserted village mound; the ruined furnace; the crumbling stockade round the ditches of an old chief's capital: these are still visible reminders of the work of earlier generations in meeting the varied challenges of the Zambian environment. We shall now see what history can be written from such remains.

II

The Stone Age

The Early Stone Age

The history of man in Africa may be traced back to types of early man whose remains have been found in Ethiopia, Kenya, Tanzania and South Africa; these have been dated to between four million and half a million years ago. There are no known sites in Zambia which belong to this earliest phase in human history, but thereafter the archaeological record is comparatively rich. The oldest signs of human activity in Zambia are stone tools – cleavers and chopping tools known as 'hand-axes' – found in the valley of the Kalomo river and in gravels which once formed the bed of the Zambezi, above and below the Victoria Falls. These tools represent the 'Chelles-Acheul' phase of Early Stone Age technology in the Old World; their makers probably belonged to the species *Homo erectus* (upright man), who made 'hand-axes' at Olduvai Gorge, in northern Tanzania, over half a million years ago. The oldest of the Zambian hand-axes may be well over 200,000 years old.

Stone tools of this 'Acheulian' type have been found all over Africa, especially in the Sahara and southern Africa. In Zambia they have been found to the south of the lower Kafue, and on the Copperbelt, as well as at the Victoria Falls, but the most interesting Acheulian collection in Zambia comes from near the Kalambo Falls, at one of the most important archaeological sites in Africa. Throughout much of the Stone Age and early Iron Age, men made settlements beside the Kalambo river, just above the Falls. The earlier levels of human occupation were each covered by the waters of the river which then deposited a fine layer of sand. In this way, each layer of tools and other remains was sealed off and preserved, thus forming a vertical sequence which is an invaluable guide to changes both in human skills and in climate and vegetation. Much later the river cut deeply into the original layers of sand deposit, thus exposing to view the sequence of human artefacts. The earliest tools from Kalambo actually come from below the present water-level and may be well over 100,000 years old.

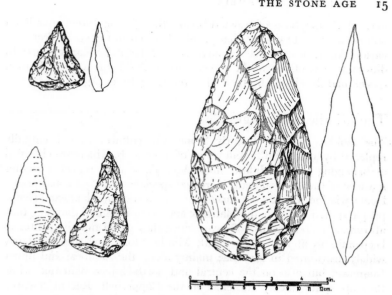

Fig. 1. Early Stone Age tools of 'Acheulian' type from Kalambo Falls
Two small scrapers, in chert, and a quartzite 'hand-axe'.

The makers of these Acheulian tools lived by gathering wild vegetable foods, perhaps also by fishing, and certainly by hunting wild animals. These would have included the main species found in central Africa today. No bones are preserved at Kalambo, but the gravel beds in the Victoria Falls area have yielded bones of warthog and hartebeest, and also of extinct varieties of elephant and giraffe. Man probably still obtained a good deal of his meat by scavenging, but he was slowly increasing his ability to kill game. His main weapons would have been natural stones suitable for throwing; these are often found in Acheulian camping sites. But by late Acheulian times man was also making simple wooden spears and clubs, and he had made a new discovery of immense importance: the use of fire. The earliest evidence of fire in sub-Saharan Africa comes from Kalambo Falls, where charred logs, ash and charcoal have been preserved at the lowest, waterlogged levels. Fire not only enabled man to cook food and warm himself; it also scared away wild animals and could be used in hunting, by burning grass and driving game through the blinding smoke. The stone tool-kits – flake knives, scrapers, choppers and cleavers – were used to skin and carve up animal carcases, and to collect and prepare vegetable food from trees and bushes: various edible fruits, nuts and seeds have been found on the Acheulian levels at Kalambo. A semicircle of stones at the same site may mark the base of a wind-break, though the three grass-lined hollows at this site suggest that people slept out in the open. From the various kinds of evidence we have about later Acheulian cultures in different parts of the world it seems likely that some form of human speech had developed by the end of the Early Stone Age.

The Middle Stone Age

The tool-kits typical of Early Stone Age cultures were eventually replaced by a rather different range of stone tools, which are classified as belonging to the Middle Stone Age. These tools reflect a greater mastery of the environment, increased specialisation and considerable local variation. Instead of concentrating near the main lakes and rivers, people spread out over the plateaux and occupied small dambos; they also made increasing use of caves, since they could now light fires to keep animals at bay. As a result, Middle Stone Age sites are fairly widely distributed in Zambia: mainly along the Zambezi and upper Luangwa, but also on the central and north-eastern plateaux, while they are quite thickly clustered on the Copperbelt. Recent research suggests that in southern Africa the transition to the Middle Stone Age was under way at least 125,000 years ago, and perhaps much earlier.

The sequence at Kalambo Falls helps to illustrate this transition. The uppermost Acheulian levels are overlain by tool-kits of a some-what different kind. These later tool-kits belong to an intermediate type known as 'Sangoan' which is widespread in sub-Saharan Africa. It may have been an adaptation to the growth of thick forest and bush in many regions; large pick-like chopping tools tend to replace the hand-axe as the typical heavy-duty implement. Sangoan tools often appear rather crude by comparison with the best examples of late Acheulian industry, but this is misleading: in fact, they may indicate greater sophistication in exploiting the resources of the forest, for the cruder Sangoan tools were most probably used to make a variety of other tools from wood which have not survived.

Regional variation within Zambia became quite pronounced during the Middle Stone Age. At Kandanda, on the upper Zambezi, small picks and hand-axes were evidently retained throughout the Middle Stone Age. In contrast, the Zambezi gravels near the Victoria Falls provide much clearer signs of development from Sangoan techniques in a type of tool-kit misleadingly called 'proto-Stillbay'. The main feature of this type is the making of tools from stone flakes rather than cores. Earlier tools, whether choppers or scrapers, were largely made by paring stones down to a core, and the resulting flakes were little valued. The typical proto-Stillbay tool is a flake carefully obtained from the outside of a stone: the flake would then be retouched to form a scraper, a cutting edge, or even a spear-point, while the remaining core might well be thrown aside.

The most interesting proto-Stillbay collection in Zambia was obtained from a small hill or *kopje* near the town of Kabwe (formerly Broken Hill). In the course of mining operations from 1907 onwards a large cave was revealed, and above its floor were found stone tools, a few simple bone tools and fossil bones of various animals. The latter included certain species, such as giraffe, wildebeest and gazelle, which suggest that the area was a much more open, grassy savanna than it is today. This would certainly reinforce the impression that 'proto-Stillbay' tools were the work of people who relied heavily on their efficiency as hunters.

The most spectacular discovery at Kabwe was made in 1921, when an almost complete human skull was unearthed at a depth of twenty metres. This skull, and a few other human bones found near by, are the oldest human skeletal remains which have so far come to light in south-central Africa. Their age is not known exactly, but they can fairly safely be associated with the stone tools and animal bones found near by. According to the most recent analysis, these suggest that 'Broken Hill Man' may be over 125,000 years old. To scientists he is known as *Homo rhodesiensis*, a type which has also been found in East and South Africa. This closely resembles the Neanderthal Man of North Africa, Europe and western Asia, who became extinct around 35,000 years ago. It is not quite certain whether Broken Hill Man, like Neanderthal Man, belonged to the species *Homo sapiens*, or whether he was a late survival of *Homo erectus*, who made the hand-axes of the Early Stone Age. It is at any rate likely that during much of the Middle Stone Age Zambia was populated by more than one type of man, and it was only around 20,000 BC that *Homo sapiens sapiens*, modern man, prevailed everywhere in Africa at the expense of other types.

The most widespread industry of the Middle Stone Age in Zambia is the Stillbay. This is evidently derived from the proto-Stillbay tradition: flake tools and fine points predominate and core tools are virtually absent. The best Stillbay collections in Zambia come from the Younger Gravels of the Victoria Falls region, a cave near Mumbwa and Twin Rivers Kopje, overlooking the Kafue Flats south-west of Lusaka. Twin Rivers also revealed a rich variety of animal bones, in which those of warthog and zebra predominate; and it is the only Stillbay site in Zambia which has so far yielded radio-carbon dates: about 31,000 BC and 21,000 BC. Collections of apparently late Middle Stone Age industries have recently been recovered from sites on the upper Zambezi, near the Angola border; from Mandenga, near Chirundu; and from Kalemba rock-shelter in eastern Zambia: the latter collection has been dated to between 35,000 BC and 23,000 BC.

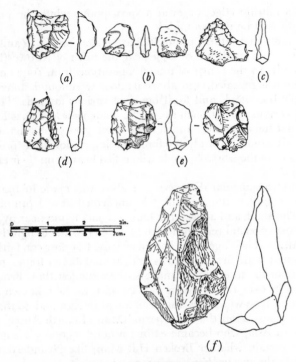

Fig. 2. Middle Stone Age tools of 'Stillbay' type from Twin Rivers Kopje
(a) Angled scraper; (b) Used flake; (c) (d) and (e) Scrapers; (f) Hand axe.
All quartz except for (c) chert and (f) dolerite.

At Kalambo Falls, the Sangoan industry had been succeeded by about 29,000 BC by a distinctive regional variation known as the Lupemban. This type is mostly found at sites in the lower Zaïre basin and in forest areas north of Lake Tanganyika. This distribution confirms the impression that Lupemban tool-kits, like those of the Sangoan, were extensively used for working wood: they too include many core tools, such as axes and adzes, although the Lupemban tools are usually more finely trimmed. Flake tools similar to those of the Stillbay industries are also found, but the most characteristic Lupemban tool is a large blade-like point, shaped like a long leaf. Such tools were the result of a meticulous process of flaking and they are technically superior to the much smaller Stillbay points. They may have been used for cutting wood, but it also seems likely that they were hafted for use as spear-points. Some insight into the actual manufacture of Middle Stone Age tools is provided by a large 'workshop' on Liamba Hill, about forty-eight kilometres east of the Kalambo site: the hillside has been quarried for its chalcedony, and the rubble is strewn with cores and flakes which are presumably the debris left by generations of workmen who took only their best work back to their camps.

The Late Stone Age

The Late Stone Age is marked by a major advance in technology. Hitherto man had relied largely on tools made from either stone or wood, but not both together. As we have seen, there are hints that some Stillbay and Lupemban tools were combined with wooden handles. But it is only in later industries that we find unmistakable evidence of a general reliance on composite tools formed by hafting and gumming together separate parts fashioned from stone, wood and also bone. Usually only the stone and bone parts of such tools have survived, but these are easily distinguished from earlier tools. The stone blades and points of the Late Stone Age are typically much too small to have been used in the hand; they were clearly made to be fitted to knives, digging sticks, spears and also arrows. For the outstanding invention of the Late Stone Age was the bow and arrow, which enormously increased man's capacity to survive and multiply at the expense of his fellow creatures. And Late Stone Age man was everywhere modern man, *Homo sapiens sapiens*. In interpreting his remains, the archaeologist can legitimately and fruitfully compare them with Stone Age techniques which survive today, as among the few remaining bands of 'Bushmen' in the Kalahari desert south-west of Zambia.

The Late Stone Age may be said to have begun around 15,000 years ago, both in Africa and elsewhere in the Old World. Like earlier phases in stone technology, it was the result of a quite gradual process of transition, but by this relatively recent point in time man's advances in technical skill were taking place at least as rapidly as major changes in climate and environment, and to some extent independently of them. In Zambia, Late Stone Age sites have been located both beside lakes and rivers and at numerous caves and rock-shelters on the plateaux. Thus, as one would expect, there are regional variations in tool-kits which may be attributed to differences in environment. At the same time, it is also possible to recognise certain distinctively local features in Late Stone Age collections which may simply be due to the strength of local cultural traditions among different groups.

At a few sites in Zambia there are remains of industries, sometimes called 'Magosian', which were clearly transitional between the Middle and Late Stone Ages. At Kalemba rock-shelter, in eastern Zambia, a transitional industry of this kind has been dated to about 23,000 BC and at Leopard's Hill Cave, about forty-eight kilometres east-south-east of Lusaka, a similar industry has been dated to around 20,000 BC. At

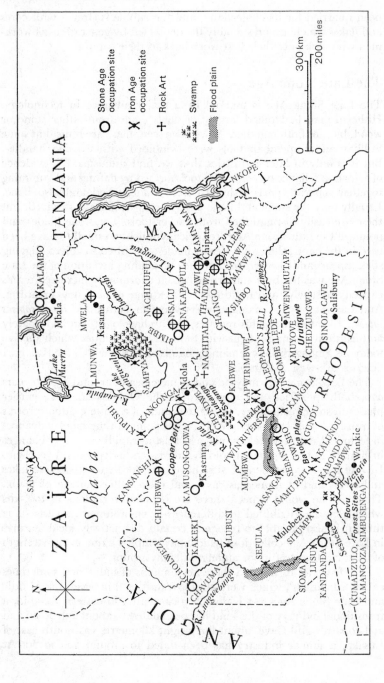

about the same depth, a fragment of a human skull was found which resembles that of a modern 'Bushman'. At Kalambo, a Magosian industry appears to have persisted as late as 7500 BC, but in certain other areas Late Stone Age industries had been established long before this.

By about 15,000 BC, distinctly Late Stone Age industries had been developed both at Leopard's Hill Cave and at Kalemba rock-shelter. These closely resemble the earliest phase of the 'Nachikufan industry' which has been found at many sites in central, northern and eastern Zambia. Nachikufu itself is a cave to the south of Mpika, and most Nachikufan sites are caves or shelters in rocky outcrops rising slightly above the *brachystegia* woodland of the northern plateaux. This was if anything rather thicker than it is today, and it probably included patches of evergreen forest, of which there are now only a few isolated remnants. Such terrain is not well suited to big game, and while the makers of Nachikufan tools used the bow and arrow, they probably relied still more on trapping and snaring the smaller animals and on

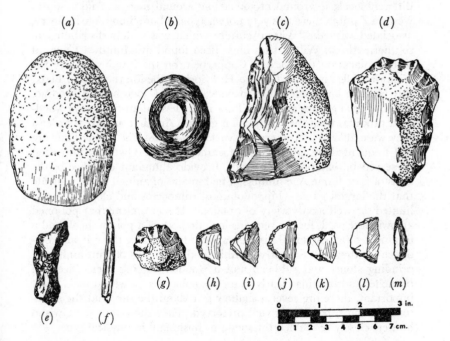

Fig. 3. Late Stone Age tools of Nachikufan type from Nachikufu Cave
(a) Polished axe (diorite); (b) Small bored stone; (c) and (d) Scrapers (quartzite); (e) Hollow scraper (chert); (f) Polished bone point; (g) – (l) Microliths (arrowheads?) (quartz); (m) Micro-drill (chert).

exploiting the varied resources of the woodland. Among their most characteristic stone implements are arrowheads, barbs and drills; bored stones, which were perhaps used to weight digging sticks for unearthing edible roots and tubers; grindstones, for preparing wild foods; scrapers, for fashioning wooden game traps and fences; and edge-ground axes, probably used to strip off tree-bark and to hack out bees' nests. The Nachikufan industries were by no means identical; during the last 10,000 years or so BC several local variations were developed. Such changes can be traced at Mwela Rocks, near Kasama; Nakapapula, near Chitambo Mission; and also at Kalemba, where the latest stone tools, from about 4000 BC onwards, belong to a distinctive 'Makwe industry', named after tools from Makwe rock-shelter, further west, which have been dated to between 3500 BC and 2500 BC.

In southern and western Zambia, there were other patterns of regional variation during the Late Stone Age. A distinctive industry at Kamusongolwa rock-shelter, near Kasempa, has been dated, at different levels, to around 11,500 BC and around 2000 BC. And in south-western Zambia there was yet another type of Late Stone Age industry, associated with the 'Wilton' culture which was widely distributed in southern Africa. Wilton sites have been found at Mumbwa Cave, at several places on the western Copperbelt, on the Zambezi above the Victoria Falls and near Gwisho Hot Springs, beside the Kafue Flats; this last site has been dated to between about 3000 BC and 1700 BC. These Wilton groups appear to have made less exhaustive use of woodland products than the Nachikufan groups. And in some areas at least they were able to hunt a greater variety of game. The Kafue Flats are still frequented by large herds of game, and the Gwisho camp sites, preserved in waterlogged mounds, provide abundant evidence of the skills of Late Stone Age hunters. The remains of animal bones indicate that the largest game – hippopotamus, rhinoceros and elephant – was hunted, as well as a variety of antelope. It seems clear that poisoned arrows were used, for the remains include pods of a poison shrub and a fragment of a bowstave. Fishbones were found, and there is also evidence for the collection of vegetable foods: remains of fruit and nuts, grinding stones and rubbers, and a wooden digging stick. Pieces of branches and matting clearly mark the collapse of a wind-break. Most important, there are several shallow graves on the site, and the skeletons, for once, have been well preserved. They show that the Gwisho hunters closely resembled the modern 'Bushman' in physical type.

III

The Iron Age in the North

Some time around the fourth century AD Zambia began to enter the Iron Age.[1] And here, as elsewhere in southern Africa, man's first use of iron tools was linked to his first efforts to produce food by deliberately sowing and harvesting food crops. There is no sign at all that Late Stone Age men in Zambia, for all their ingenuity in hunting and gathering, had made the great transition to agriculture; nor did they keep domestic animals. Further north, in parts of North and West Africa and in Ethiopia, Late Stone Age man had made this advance to food production: in these regions, both farming and stock-keeping can be traced back to 3000 BC and earlier. From 1000 BC, Stone Age farmers began to occupy the equatorial forests in the Zaïre basin and around Lake Victoria while herdsmen moved down the East African Rift Valley into northern Tanzania. But this southward spread of food-producing techniques did not extend very far south of the Equator until the coming of iron-working. This first reached Egypt from Assyria in about the seventh century BC. It seems clear that it was primarily the use of iron hoes and axes (together with the controlled use of fire) which first enabled man to cultivate the wooded plateaux of eastern and southern Africa.

There is now an impressive body of evidence to show that iron-working, stock-keeping and agriculture first penetrated these regions during the first few centuries AD. And it is also clear that these innovations came about as the result of major migrations. The few skeletal remains from early Iron Age sites in eastern and southern Africa indicate that the inhabitants were in varying degrees of Negro physical stock and thus distinct from the 'Bushman'-like hunters of the Late Stone Age. Moreover, we can also presume that these pioneer farmers spoke early forms of languages belonging to the great Bantu family, for the geographical distribution of their sites corresponds very closely to that of the Bantu languages today. It was, in fact, a 'Bantu explosion' which introduced the Iron Age in eastern and southern Africa. And a comparison of the different types of pottery found at early Iron Age sites throughout this part of Africa strongly suggests that the Bantu explosion radiated outwards, to the east and south, from somewhere to the north of the equatorial forest.

The commonest remains from Early Iron Age sites are sherds of earthenware pots, which in themselves are signs of a fairly settled way of life based on cultivation. Late Stone Age man tended to move his camps frequently in search of game; he thus travelled very light, and in any case he had no use for pots in which to cook cereal foods. At a few Early Iron Age sites carbonised cereal seeds – of millets and sorghums – have been found; while stone rubbers testify to the grinding of grain.[2] Wild foods were still gathered and hunting was still important: the bones of many game animals are found at Early Iron Age sites. But the keeping of livestock is attested by the bones of domestic animals, including cattle, sheep, goats and chickens, as well as dogs. The evidence for iron-working is also clear enough. Iron tools are seldom present, since iron quickly disintegrates in acid tropical soils; but iron slag is common, and pottery draught-pipes for smelting-furnaces are also found. Early Iron Age men presumably made much use of wooden tools which have seldom been preserved, but there is no sign that they used stone blades or points for their knives, spears and arrows. At some sites, the foundations of mud huts have been revealed, and it has been possible to form an idea of the layout of a whole household, or even a village. Charcoal fragments are quite common, and it is mainly these which have been used to obtain radio-carbon dates.

The settlement of Zambia, and east-central Africa in general, by Early Iron Age farmers took place remarkably rapidly. Their pottery is sufficiently alike to be grouped together as 'Early Iron Age' – a term which refers to a cultural style rather than a period of time. Nevertheless the replacement of Stone Age cultures was a very piecemeal process, and the immigrant farmers clearly belonged to a number of different groups, each with its own cultural tradition. Just as variations in the forms of stone tools enable us to distinguish different Stone Age traditions and cultures, so too variations in the shape and decoration of potsherds can be associated with different regions and periods. Pottery is in fact our best evidence for the social and cultural identity of Iron Age communities in Zambia for all but the last few centuries.

From an analysis of pottery types and related radio-carbon dates, we can now discern three main phases in the settlement of Zambia by Early Iron Age farmers. The first phase began with the southward expansion of farming (and presumably Bantu-speaking) communities through East Africa during the first two or three centuries AD. This led to a southward movement of farmers through the country east of the Luangwa valley. In the course of the fourth century AD, Iron Age farmers settled in south-eastern Zambia and Malawi, while others moved on into Rhodesia and the Transvaal. During the fifth century

AD much of the country west of the Luangwa, as far as the upper Zambezi, was settled by Iron Age farmers with a rather different pottery tradition. Their origins are still obscure, but they probably came from the Shaba region of Zaïre and represented a western stream of Bantu migration, distinct from the earlier movement through East Africa. Finally, during the sixth century AD, the country around the Victoria Falls was occupied by people who appear to have come from the south, introducing pottery styles which had been established for some time in Rhodesia.

The impact of these migrations varied a good deal from one part of Zambia to another. In the south the first farmers were relatively numerous and they seem to have quickly displaced or absorbed most of the Late Stone Age population. In the north and east, by contrast, the dense woodland probably discouraged farmers from large-scale settlement at this early stage. There are in any case relatively few known sites of the Early Iron Age in these regions, while there is plenty of evidence that they were inhabited by Late Stone Age hunters until quite recent times.

Soon after about AD 1000, much of central and southern Africa was settled by a new wave of immigrants. Their pottery has much less in common with the various Early Iron Age styles than with pottery which is made in the region today. For this reason it is known as Later Iron Age pottery, and the people who introduced it may be regarded as ancestors of many of the present inhabitants. Within Zambia, such pottery seems to have been introduced as a result of two different processes of migration. One was confined to the far south, between the Victoria Falls area and the lower Kafue; the other spread over most of central, northern and eastern Zambia and probably originated in Shaba.

From this brief outline of Iron Age settlement in Zambia we may turn to look in greater detail at the history of such communities, as it may be inferred from the more important sites. Rather than discuss them in strictly chronological order, it is more convenient to consider them in terms of developments within four main regions. This chapter will survey the north-east (including the country east of the Luangwa), central and western Zambia; the next chapter will survey southern Zambia, about which we know much more.

The North-East

The river bank above Kalambo Falls, which has provided so much information about Stone Age man in Zambia, has also yielded most valuable evidence of Early Iron Age settlement. The type of pottery found at Kalambo has also been found at several other places in north-eastern Zambia. We can distinguish a 'Kalambo tradition' which spread over the plateau between the Luapula and Luangwa rivers, and some makers of such pottery were clearly influenced by contact with the Early Iron Age cultures already established to the east of the Luangwa. But there are very few known sites in the north-east which were actually inhabited by Early Iron Age men: most of the Kalambo-style pottery comes from caves and rock-shelters which continued to be occupied by Late Stone Age people. These evidently obtained pottery from the incoming farmers, but equally clearly they maintained their own stone industries, and their own hunting-and-gathering economy.

It is not hard to explain why we can trace the persistence of these stone industries in the north more easily than the introduction of iron-working and food production. Although the Late Stone Age men were nomadic, they were in a sense short-term nomads. They might move camp several times a year in search of game and vegetable food, but they naturally tended to make their camps at particularly suitable places. In the north-eastern woodland, this probably meant that they moved, where they could, from one cave or rock-shelter to another. Over a long period, therefore, such places would be successively occupied, abandoned and reoccupied by the same or different groups. In this way, quite deep deposits of their remains might accumulate over the years at any one site, and be sheltered against erosion by rain or wind. By contrast, the Iron Age populations in the north-east were long-term nomads. They built their homesteads actually in the woodland, close to perennial water and close to land that could be cultivated. By carefully alternating their crops and making new clearings every year, they might be able to stay in the same village for ten years or more. Thereafter, however, they had to move their villages some distance, and begin a new cycle of shifting cultivation, just as people do in the area today. Thus at any one village site they would leave a relatively thin deposit, and since there might well be no reason to build a later village on exactly the same site, there would be no later remains – such as house mounds and floors or simply rubbish – to seal off and protect the original deposit against dispersal.

This is why the Early Iron Age site at Kalambo is so important. For the river bank was evidently one place to which farming communities did return from time to time. Just as it contains sequences of Stone Age occupation at different levels, so too there are layers of Early Iron Age occupation overlying one another, and several of these have been carbon-dated. As a result, we can see clearly that the first farmers to settle at Kalambo effectively displaced any Stone Age residents they may have found. There is in fact no evidence of Stone Age occupation at the site after about the eighth century BC, while there were at least four different Iron Age settlements at various times between about the fifth and eleventh centuries AD. Up to about the tenth century, at least, the pottery remained very much the same, which suggests that the Kalambo farmers were not much influenced by new contacts or migrations during the first millennium AD. Traces of pole-and-mud huts have been found, fragments of a few simple iron tools and also eight graves. The acidic soil has not preserved the human bones, but the dead were buried with a variety of goods, for the graves revealed animal bones, iron slag and a great deal of pottery. A copper bracelet and part of a copper ear-ring, datable to about the tenth century, may have come from copper workings in Shaba.

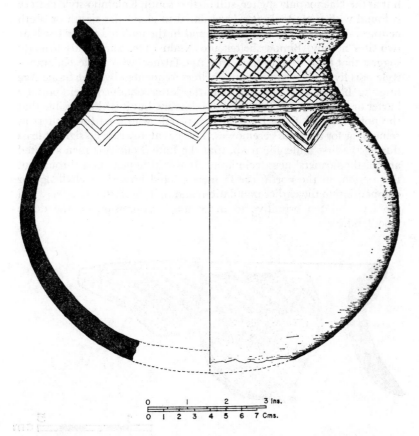

Fig. 4. Kalambo Group pottery
Early Iron Age pot from a grave at the Kalambo Falls site. The incised cross-hatching, the channelled lines and the bevelled rim are typical of this group; the last two features are also found at several other Early Iron Age sites in East and Central Africa.

There are a few other places at which Kalambo-style pottery has been found which may well have been inhabited by Early Iron Age men: two sites beside Lake Tanganyika, and one at Samfya, at the south end of Lake Bangweulu. But these sites have not been excavated and are thus undated. More interesting are the finds of Kalambo-style pottery in stratified deposits left by Late Stone Age people. One of these is at Mwela Rocks, where the pottery was found extending through the upper half of a deep deposit of stone tools. Further south, at Nachikufu, a similar deposit dated to the ninth or tenth century contains no pottery, but at the Nakapapula shelter, still further south, Kalambo-style pottery is found with stone tools at a level dated to about the eighth or ninth century. A similar combination is found in the undated upper levels at two sites nearby, Bimbe shelter and Nsalu cave. Such finds strongly suggest that from time to time Iron Age farmers who made Kalambo-style pots lived fairly close to the shelters frequented by Late Stone Age hunting bands. It is possible that the latter obtained their pots by barter or theft from their farming neighbours, but it is also possible that the pots were left there by Iron Age people who used the shelters as refuges, or for religious ceremonies. There is at any rate no sign, at least during the first millennium AD, that the Late Stone Age men adopted any of the farmers' new techniques. It would appear that throughout this period, in the north, the farmers offered no serious challenge or competition to the earlier population, and that their iron tools were still too few and too primitive to make much impression on the dense woodland.

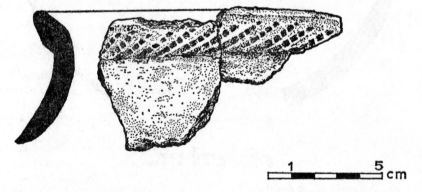

Fig. 5. Kamnama pottery
Early Iron Age potsherds from Kamnama; rows of dots have been stamped with the teeth of a comb. Horizontal bands of such diagonal 'comb-stamping' or incised lines are characteristic of the Early Iron Age at Kamnama.

East of the Luangwa river, the picture is much the same. As yet, only one Early Iron Age settlement has been found in the region: at Kamnama, beside a dambo near the Malawi border. The pottery there has been dated to about the fourth century AD, and it somewhat resembles pottery found at Nkope, at the south end of Lake Malawi. Pottery in the same general tradition has also been found among deposits of stone tools at a few rock-shelters in eastern Zambia. At Makwe, such pottery has been found at one level dated to about the third century, and at another of the tenth or eleventh century. At Thandwe, a level dated to the third or fifth century AD contains no pottery, but it is found at two levels dated to between the eighth and twelfth centuries. The topmost deposits at Kalemba shelter have yielded a few sherds which also belong to this eastern Early Iron Age tradition.

Rock Art

Besides preserving such stratified deposits, the rock-shelters of northeastern Zambia have another claim on the historian's attention. In many of them rock-paintings have been found, and these throw further light on both Late Stone Age and Iron Age communities in this part of the country. Indeed, such paintings are almost entirely confined to the north-east, for elsewhere paintable rock surfaces are very rare. Some of these rock-paintings are naturalistic representations of animals, such as have been found in many parts of southern Africa. The Zambian examples cannot compare in number, size or quality with those at such celebrated sites as the Matopo Hills in Rhodesia, but in their own way they are just as interesting to the historian. For the naturalistic paintings in Zambia are commonly found on the same rock surfaces as a quite different kind of painting, consisting of more or less abstract and schematic patterns and designs. Similar schematic paintings have also been recorded in Tanzania, Malawi, Mozambique, Rhodesia and South Africa, but it is only in Zambia that they have been carefully studied and related both to naturalistic paintings and to other archaeological evidence.

The naturalistic rock-paintings in north-eastern Zambia, as in other parts of southern Africa, are fairly clearly the work of Late Stone Age hunters. The pigments are mostly red or purple, though black was occasionally used. Various kinds of game are depicted, especially antelope, and these are occasionally accompanied by very stylised figures of men, sometimes with bows and arrows. The contrast between finely observed animal forms and distorted human forms is usual in the rock art of southern and eastern Africa, and it supports the theory that the paintings were intended as a kind of sympathetic magic; if man could summon up mysterious powers over an animal by accurately painting its likeness, he would obviously protect himself by not portraying his own likeness. The richest collection of animal paintings in Zambia is at Mwela rocks, near Kasama; they are scattered there over a wide area of rocky outcrops and boulders and there are probably many still unrecorded. Among the most interesting paintings at Mwela is a lifelike warthog with its characteristic erect and tufted tail and a group of fifty-six stylised human figures surrounding a large animal. Elsewhere on the northern plateau, animal paintings occur at Nachikufu shelter (two elephant), and at Nakapapula; there are also animal paintings around Nachitalo Hill, at the eastern end of the Copperbelt. East of the Luangwa valley there are a few animal paintings, mostly of antelope, at Zawi Hill and Katolola, near the Malawi border: these seem to belong to a rather different style.

There is no clear indication as to the age of any of these animal paintings. It is, however, unlikely that any paintings in Zambia are very old, since they all occur on surfaces which are close to daylight and are therefore subject to fading and weathering. (This contrasts with the many rock paintings of Europe which are located deep in tunnel caves and could thus have been preserved much longer.) The age of the oldest paintings in Zambia is thus to be estimated in centuries rather than millennia. And it is at any rate likely that an animal painting at Somena rocks, near Mwela, belongs to the Iron Age, for it shows a lioness standing over a supine horned animal which looks very like a domestic ox.

The schematic paintings at the rock-shelters present rather more complex problems of interpretation. They are painted in a variety of colours – yellow, red, orange, purple and white – and the designs include grids, parallel lines, concentric circles and arrangements of dots; and also crude shapes which are evidently modelled on human and animal figures (anthropomorphs and zoomorphs). At first glance, a richly painted rock surface such as the wall of Nsalu cave seems a bewildering and meaningless confusion of patterns and colours. On closer inspection, however, it becomes clear that some paintings have been superimposed on others, and that certain techniques are characteristic of particular regions. By analysing such superimpositions and regional variations, it has been possible to reach some general conclusions as to their relative age and authorship.

Whereas the naturalistic paintings may safely be attributed to Late Stone Age artists, the schematic paintings are clearly the work of Iron Age communities. In the first place, the schematic paintings are in general more recent: there are several examples of them overlying naturalistic paintings – at Mwela, Nachitalo and Nachikufu – but only one example of the reverse – at Katolola; and this is after all consistent with the archaeological evidence that Late Stone Age man inhabited eastern Zambia long after the arrival of Iron Age man. And the only piece of direct evidence for the absolute age of the schematic paintings at least places them well within the Iron Age; the red grid designs at Nakapapula were executed some time after a fall of rocks which can be dated to between the seventh and ninth centuries AD. Furthermore, there are broad regional variations in some of the schematic designs and these correspond quite closely to the main regional variations in pottery styles during the Early Iron Age: there are marked contrasts not only between the schematic paintings east of the Luangwa and those of the northern plateau, but also between the latter and the paintings from Nachitalo and other Copperbelt sites. This strongly suggests that some at least of the schematic artists belonged to the same cultural groupings as the makers of Early Iron Age pots in these regions.

But it is the superimposition of different kinds of schematic paintings on one another which most clearly shows that they are comparatively recent. At Nsalu cave a sequence of colours has been traced which closely agrees with the evidence from other sites west of the Luangwa. The earliest schematic paintings at Nsalu, apart from some fine yellow-brown scribbles, are in yellow; these are overlain by red paintings, which are in turn overlain by bichrome paintings, in red and white. The latest paintings are in a greasy white pigment and consist of anthropomorphs and sun motifs. The sequence from red to bichrome to white is largely paralleled in eastern Zambia (which really belongs to a separate rock-art zone extending into Malawi). At Zawi, Kalemba and Chaingo, the earliest schematic paintings are in red and the latest are in white. And at Sakwe we begin to find evidence, not only for chronological sequence, but also for continuous development from the red paintings onwards, suggesting that the different styles were due to gradual changes in cultural habits rather than to work by completely separate groups of people. The red grid designs at Sakwe and at two other sites are contemporary with red outline zoomorphs, since these overlie and are overlain by each other. Such red outline zoomorphs seem to have been imitated in the white outline shape at Chaingo; this looks rather like a leopard-skin, for it has been filled in with white finger dots, a technique which can be traced back to the red schematic art. At Thandwe there are no early red grids, but there is a red outline, like that at Sakwe, which has been filled in with greasy white paint, and is overlain by white paintings of hoes and objects resembling grain bins. There is also at Thandwe a leopard-like design of white dots without any outline, and this is overlain by two white paintings which link the sequence to our own times: three circular designs which the local people today associate with initiation ceremonies, and a crude but unmistakable motor car.

We can thus observe a gradual evolution from early red schematic paintings to late white paintings. East of the Luangwa, it can be shown that the white painting tradition persisted into the twentieth century. And since this most recent work was apparently the outcome of a continuous development from the early red paintings, it is reasonable to suppose that these too were the work of Iron Age people. We then may go still further and ascribe to Iron Age people the few rock engravings found in Zambia. The pecked designs at Chifubwa shelter, near Solwezi, and beside the Munwa stream in the Luapula valley, are very similar to certain kinds of schematic paintings; so too are the concentric circles at Munwa. The axe-shapes engraved at Ayrshire Farm, near Lusaka, closely resemble axes known to have been made by neighbouring people within the last two centuries.

If we conclude that the schematic rock-paintings were done by Iron Age people, it becomes somewhat easier to guess their purpose. They are unlikely to have been merely decorative, since there is no sign of Iron Age people actually inhabiting rock-shelters except for brief periods in time of war: the shelter at Simbo Hill, in eastern Zambia, is said to have been painted by refugees during the last century. But we do know that in recent centuries people regarded such rocky places with a certain religious awe, believing them to be the abode of powerful spirits. We also know that some Zambian peoples have used rock-shelters for initiation ceremonies; the designs at Thandwe bear this out, and there is a striking resemblance between the 'spotted leopard' at Chaingo and the spotted animal figures made for girls' puberty ceremonies both in eastern and northern Zambia. Thus it seems clear enough that the late white paintings played some part in ritual occasions, and it is therefore likely that the earlier schematic paintings also fulfilled certain religious or magical functions, perhaps including rain-making.

On present evidence, then, we may presume that, throughout much of the Iron Age, farming communities visited rock-shelters for specific social or religious purposes and painted on their walls; they may also have brought and left their own pots, perhaps when making offerings. Whether such Iron Age people made their visits when Late Stone Age people were in residence, we cannot say. The antelope at Katolola, superimposed on red grids, seems to be a clear example of Late Stone Age men painting on rock that had already been used by Early Iron Age men. Since such a superimposition is at present unique, it is possible that much of the schematic painting was done after Late Stone Age man had disappeared from north-eastern Zambia, but the local inhabitants today have so little to say about the paintings that most of them, especially to the west of the Luangwa, are probably some centuries old.

Central Zambia and Early Copper-Working

In the woodland between the lower Kafue river and the Copperbelt, the coming of Early Iron Age peoples made a much greater impact than in the north and east. Several of their settlements have been found and excavated, while there is little evidence for the persistence of Late Stone Age communities. To some extent, of course, the greater number of known Iron Age settlements in this region must be regarded as accidental, for most of them have been discovered in the course of modern building and farming operations. Nevertheless, some of the same factors which encouraged the growth of modern towns and large-scale farming in the region are also likely to have appealed to the pioneer farmers of the Early Iron Age. Around Lusaka and the head-waters of the Kafue on the Copperbelt, there are areas of relatively fertile soil, and there are also easily accessible mineral deposits. Iron ores around Lusaka, and copper ores in or near the Copperbelt, were clearly exploited from early times.

One of the earliest Iron Age sites in central Zambia is Kapwirimbwe, thirteen kilometres to the east of Lusaka. Here the remains of a small village have been dated to about the fifth century AD. The inhabitants lived in pole-and-mud huts, kept domestic cattle, made a distinctive kind of pottery and practised iron-working intensively. The site does not seem to have been occupied for very long, but several smelting furnaces appear to have been built on and near the site, and a great deal of iron slag and bloom was found. There is a rich deposit of iron ore a few kilometres to the east, and the area is known to have been a centre of iron production in more recent times. A number of iron objects were preserved at Kapwirimbwe, including a razor, a spear-point, a ring and what may be keys from 'thumb pianos' such as are still made in central Africa. A little pottery resembling that from Kapwirimbwe was found at Leopard's Hill Cave, not far to the south-east. This occurred in the most recent deposit of stone tools at the cave, dated to about the sixth century AD. A few stone tools of a similar type have been found at Twickenham Road, in Lusaka, but there is no reason to suppose that they are any more recent. It thus appears that a Late Stone Age way of life did not long survive the advent of people such as those who lived at Kapwirimbwe.

The cultural tradition represented by the Kapwirimbwe pottery continued in the Lusaka area for several centuries. The site at Twicken-ham Road, in Olympia Park, Lusaka, was occupied in about the tenth or eleventh century by people whose pottery was very similar to that at Kapwirimbwe. They kept goats, and they seem to have smelted iron near by. It is likely that these people, or others in the same

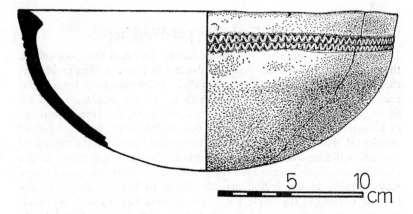

Fig. 6. Kapwirimbwe Group pottery
An open bowl from the Twickenham Road site, Lusaka. This shows the 'false relief chevron' motif typical of much Early Iron Age pottery in Central Africa; it was made by impressing rows of triangular shapes in the clay.

cultural tradition, traded or settled south of the Zambezi, for this later Kapwirimbwe-style pottery closely resembles pottery which has been found at Muyove and Sinoia Cave, north-west of Salisbury, Rhodesia; the latter site has been dated to between the sixth and eighth centuries AD.

On the Copperbelt, as in the Lusaka area, the Early Iron Age can be traced back at least as far as the middle of the first millennium AD. So far, two sites have been excavated and dated: Chondwe and Kangonga. These are both village sites, some kilometres to the south-east of Ndola. Chondwe was probably occupied several times by Early Iron Age peoples between about the sixth and ninth centuries. Kangonga was occupied only once, probably around the eighth century. The Early Iron Age pottery from these sites is very similar to pottery which has been recovered from the surface at a number of places throughout the Copperbelt. This pottery forms a distinct class of its own and is known as the Chondwe group. Most of the Chondwe-group sites are on the edge of dambos and were probably village sites, though a few sherds of Chondwe pottery have also been found in rock-shelters. At a few shelters and dambo sites (including Chondwe itself), Late Stone Age tools have been found, and it is likely that Late Stone Age industries persisted in this region, as in the north-east, rather later than in the country further south.

As yet we know relatively little about the way of life of the Chondwe-group people. There is no direct evidence of agriculture at their

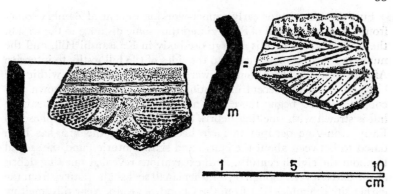

Fig. 7. Chondwe Group pottery

Early Iron Age sherds from Kangonga, on the Copperbelt. Chondwe Group pottery commonly displays such combinations of different decorative motifs – grooves, comb-stamping, incision and false-relief chevron.

sites, but they presumably settled beside dambos in order to exploit their fertile soils; they used grindstones; and they may have used grooved rocks for the same purpose. There is no sign of stock-keeping, but the inhabitants of Chondwe evidently practised hunting and fishing. There are a few remains of pole-and-dagga structures and at some sites iron smelting is attested by fragments of tuyeres and iron slag.

It is also clear that the Chondwe-group people made copper and traded it. Copper bangles were found in an early occupation level at Chondwe itself, and the copper could well have come from a source near by, such as the old workings at Bwana Mkubwa. At two other sites, Luano and Roan Antelope, bangle-impressions occur on Chondwe-group pottery, and Roan Antelope would have been close to the African copper working which was destroyed by the modern mine. At both these sites there were several potsherds which resembled Early Iron Age pottery from eastern, northern and southern Zambia. Such 'foreign' pottery may have been imported, or it may have been produced by immigrant potters; in any case, it strongly suggests that copper-working by the Chondwe group people stimulated contacts with other peoples some hundreds of kilometres away. This impression is confirmed by evidence from the Twickenham Road site in Lusaka. For here a second occupation, in or after about the eleventh century, left pottery very similar to that of the Chondwe group, and also a thin copper strip, the earliest dated copper in the Lusaka area.

Further evidence for early copper-working in central Zambia comes from Kansanshi, north of Solwezi and thus some distance to the west of the Copperbelt. There is a large ore-body in Kansanshi Hill, and the numerous deep trenches cut into the sides of the hill testify to intensive African mining. These trenches were probably mostly dug within the last 500 years, but recent excavations at Kansanshi have shown that copper smelting began there very much earlier. A large area near the hill is strewn with smelting debris, and within this area two phases of Early Iron Age occupation have been observed: the first has been dated to between about the fourth and sixth centuries, and the second to about the eighth century. Both excavations revealed smelting debris at the dated levels, though on a rather small scale. The pottery from the earlier site resembles that from the Chondwe group. Near this smelting area, there is a village site which has been dated to about the eleventh century. This yielded a wide range of domestic artefacts, including iron tools and copper ornaments. The pottery here bears most resemblance to roughly contemporary pottery from a site far to the west, Kamusongolwa, near Kasempa.

The overall impression left by Kansanshi and the Copperbelt sites is that throughout the second half of the first millennium copper mining and smelting took place on a rather small scale. But it is also clear that the skills of smelting both iron and copper were introduced more or less simultaneously in central Zambia. This is confirmed by evidence from early Iron Age sites in Rhodesia, while copper mining and smelting was practised in the eastern Transvaal by the eighth century.

The Luangwa Tradition

Early in the present millennium, parts of central and southern Africa were occupied by people quite distinct from the various Early Iron Age groups. At several sites in Zambia, Malawi, Rhodesia and South Africa, pottery dated to the eleventh or twelfth century AD seems to have much less in common with the Early Iron Age styles than with the pottery traditions of the present inhabitants. In Zambia, such 'Later Iron Age' pottery was introduced by two distinct processes of migration. One of these was confined to the south and will be discussed in the next chapter. The other migration spread over most of central, northern and eastern Zambia: its pottery has been classified as belonging to a single 'Luangwa' tradition. Pottery of this kind has been dated at Chondwe, near Ndola, to around the twelfth century. Elsewhere, the dating evidence is less conclusive, but it seems fairly certain that this was also the period during which Luangwa pottery was introduced at Twickenham Road, Lusaka; Nakapapula; Kalambo; and Thandwe.

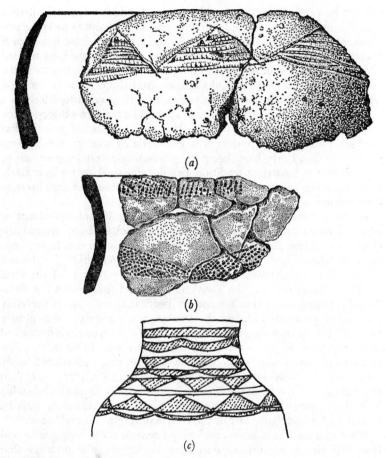

Fig. 8. Luangwa Tradition pottery
(*a*) Part of a pot found at Twickenham Road; the horizontal band of comb-stamped triangular blocks is common in pottery of the Luangwa Tradition.
(*b*) Sherds of comb-stamped pot found just below the surface at Nakapapula rock-shelter; they closely resemble pottery made by Lala women in the area today and were probably left by refugees from raids in the nineteenth century.
(*c*) A modern pot of the Luangwa Tradition, in the Livingstone Museum; this is also decorated by comb-stamping.

The differences between this Luangwa pottery and the Early Iron Age pottery strongly suggest that its makers belonged to a distinct group of people, who had entered the country from elsewhere. In view of the points of resemblance between the Luangwa pottery and modern pottery in central, northern and eastern Zambia, we can probably regard it as the work of people directly ancestral to some modern Zambians. It would certainly seem that in these regions there has been a broad continuity in traditions of pot-decoration over the past millennium or so, and this in turn would have involved some continuity in the actual physical stock of the inhabitants. And there is another reason why we may suppose that the Luangwa tradition was introduced as a result of a substantial process of migration. The modern pottery which resembles it is all made by women. It is thus reasonable to infer that the Luangwa-tradition pottery was also made by women. Yet it seems very likely that Early Iron Age pottery was made only by men (see p. 40). Since the Luangwa-tradition people managed to replace Early Iron Age styles of pot-making, we may well suppose that they brought their women with them.

We may thus conclude that there was a significant movement of people into central, northern and eastern Zambia from around the eleventh century. As yet, the archaeological evidence can throw little light on where they came from, or what they were like. The known distribution of Luangwa pottery indicates some process of dispersal from the Shaba region. The Twickenham Road site yielded the skeleton of a young man; this has not yet been analysed, and is probably only a few centuries old, but the Luangwa pottery there was clearly associated with iron slag and iron artefacts. Numerous grindstones at the same level suggest that cereal agriculture was important; a few cattle teeth were found; while two cowrie shells and a glass bead imply some contact, however indirect, with trade from the east coast. And the striking uniformity of the Luangwa pottery over so much of Zambia is in itself some indication that its makers were relatively mobile, travelling far and fairly fast in the course of migration and trade.

If we can assume a basic continuity between these immigrants and later inhabitants of north-eastern Zambia, we can also presume that at some stage the Luangwa-group peoples introduced new forms of government and new techniques of iron-working. This will be discussed in chapters 5 and 6; here it is enough to suggest that from the beginning of the second millennium much of northern and eastern Zambia was settled by people whose social organisation and technology may have enabled them to exploit these woodlands more effectively than their Early Iron Age predecessors. This would have increased the pressure on the surviving Late Stone Age inhabitants, either to allow themselves to be assimilated into Iron Age farming communities, or at least to adopt some Iron Age techniques. At Nsalu cave, for example, the upper layers of stone tools included an iron arrowhead, some coiled copper wire, and even a few glass beads which could only have been imported from overseas. At Nachikufu there is even evidence of iron-smelting among the latest stone tools, dated to between the fifteenth and nineteenth centuries, but this is probably the result of Iron Age people digging into Stone Age layers.

Western Zambia

Little is known as yet about the Early Iron Age in western Zambia, between the Copperbelt and the Angola border. This is partly due to the lack of excavation, whether by archaeologists or by modern commercial enterprises, but it is also due to the nature of the terrain. Much of the region is covered by Kalahari sands, which would have hindered the preservation of human artefacts. Bone does not survive in such soil, and huts in these parts were made from thatch rather than mud, so that a deserted village would leave few or no permanent traces of its structures. Moreover, pot-clay is scarce, confined mainly to a few areas on the upper tributaries of the Zambezi. Pot-making was therefore localised, and vessels were most commonly made of impermanent vegetable materials, such as wood or basketwork, while calabashes were also widely used.

Most of the Early Iron Age pottery found in western Zambia has come from sites along the upper Zambezi valley. Below the Lusu rapids the pottery seems to belong to the same general tradition as Early Iron Age pottery from the Victoria Falls area: it can thus be taken to represent the westernmost extension of a process of immigration from Rhodesia. Further north, there seem to have been a variety of local Early Iron Age styles, but they can probably all be attributed to the western stream of Early Iron Age immigration into central Africa, along with the early pottery traditions of the Batoka plateau, central and north-eastern Zambia. The earliest pottery of this kind in western Zambia comes from Sioma, on the upper Zambezi; this has been dated to the fifth to seventh centuries AD. Pottery from Lubusi, west of Kaoma, has been dated to the ninth century. Further east, at the Kamusongolwa rock-shelter, near Kasempa, pottery of a quite distinct type was found at a level dated to between the eleventh and thirteenth centuries AD. No Stone Age material was found at this level, but at Kandanda, on the Zambezi, some undiagnostic potsherds were found among stone tools dated to between the thirteenth and fifteenth centuries. This is the only evidence from western Zambia for the persistence of a Late Stone Age culture into the second millennium, but it is not surprising as this is an area where Kalahari 'Bushmen' from Namibia have maintained contact with agricultural peoples into the present century.

The most notable fact about pottery from the upper Zambezi is that it shows far more continuity between the styles of the Early Iron Age and those of the present day than is to be found elsewhere in the country. Most of the modern pottery of western Zambia, and adjoining parts of Angola and Zaïre, has been classified as belonging to a common 'Lungwebungu tradition' (named after the river) which is quite distinct from the later Iron Age pottery of eastern and southern Zambia. And there are clear affinities between the Lungwebungu pottery and the Early Iron Age pottery from Lubusi. It thus seems that there has been

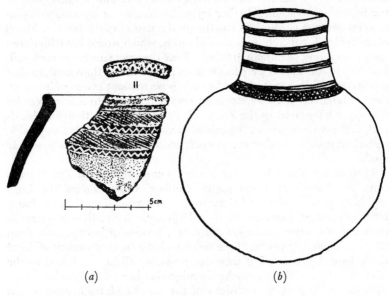

(a)   (b)

Fig. 9. Western Zambia
(a) Part of a bag-shaped Early Iron Age pot from Lubusi. The use of a false-relief chevron border (cut rather than stamped) is also illustrated on the modern pot shown in (b); this also comes from north-western Zambia and clearly differs in both shape and decoration from the modern Luangwa tradition pot shown on p. 37: comb-stamping does not occur in the Lungwebungu Tradition.

a basic continuity in pot-making traditions in western Zambia from the Early Iron Age to the present day. And this point helps to throw light on developments elsewhere. For among the modern peoples who practise the Lungwebungu tradition, pots are made exclusively by men. It thus seems reasonable to infer that this was also the case among the Early Iron Age peoples of western Zambia; and if it was true of them, it may well have been true of Early Iron Age peoples elsewhere. This possibility must be borne in mind when we consider the means by which new pottery styles may have been introduced during the later Iron Age in north-eastern and southern Zambia.

NOTES

1. The terms 'Stone Age' and 'Iron Age' are used primarily to distinguish different types of technology; they do not necessarily refer to different periods of time, since some groups of people continued to practise a 'Stone Age' technology long after other people in the same region had introduced or adopted an 'Iron Age' technology.

2. There is no archaeological evidence from Zambia for the cultivation of root crops, pulses or cucurbits, but it is likely that certain varieties have been grown there since the early Iron Age and incorporated in local crop-sequences. 'Indigenous' crops include cowpeas, pumpkins, watermelons and the 'Livingstone potato', while yams and taro may have been adopted well before the introduction of American crops such as cassava and sweet potatoes.

IV

The Iron Age in the South

The Iron Age sequence in southern Zambia is better known than that in any other comparable region in sub-Saharan Africa. Intensive excavations since the late 1950s have thrown much light on economic life, settlement patterns and cultural traditions in this region from the middle of the first millennium AD to the middle of the second millennium. This is due to a number of factors. The sites themselves are mainly concentrated in three areas, each of which formed a favourable environment for mixed farming peoples of the earlier Iron Age: the country immediately north and west of Livingstone, the Batoka plateau to the north-east and the Kafue flood plain. In all these areas certain sites attracted settlement at different periods, so that stratified deposits accumulated. In this way a valuable archaeological record took shape and the circumstances of more recent history have combined to bring this record to light. The country between Livingstone and the lower Kafue is traversed by the modern road and railway from the Victoria Falls to the Copperbelt; moreover, it includes much good farming country and has attracted European settlement. Thus there has been much modern building and farming which has cut deep into the soil and has occasionally revealed archaeological deposits. And the establishment of the Museum at Livingstone has meant that since 1938 there have always been one or more professional archaeologists resident in Livingstone; this has naturally stimulated excavation and survey work in areas within easy reach.

The main points to emerge so far from the archaeology of southern Zambia can be briefly summarised. During the fifth century AD the Batoka plateau, between the lower Kafue and the Zambezi, was settled by Iron Age farmers with a pottery tradition broadly comparable to those introduced at about the same time in central and north-eastern Zambia. About a century later the low-lying country north-west of the Victoria Falls was settled by immigrants from the south who developed a quite different pottery tradition. During the latter part of the first millennium AD this tradition spread on to the Batoka plateau. Early in the second millennium this tradition began to be replaced by another, quite separate, tradition, which is ancestral to the modern pottery styles of southern Zambia. Thus, as in north-eastern and central Zambia, the pottery record suggests that the present cultures, and the present inhabitants, are at least partly descended from people who established themselves in the same region nearly a thousand years ago. Finally, the other material remains from these southern sites have made possible some reconstruction of earlier Iron Age economies. These evidently supported relatively dense populations, who rapidly replaced or absorbed Late Stone Age communities: only in the Gwembe valley of the middle Zambezi did the latter leave traces of their survival into the Iron Age. And while the Iron Age communities flourished on the basis of subsistence farming they also traded among themselves. By the middle of the second millennium AD, one corner of southern Zambia had even been caught up in the gold trade between Rhodesia and the east coast.

The Shongwe Tradition

The earliest known Iron Age people in the Victoria Falls region seem to have come from Rhodesia in about the sixth century AD. These settlers established a pottery tradition which lasted throughout the first millennium; it has been called the 'Shongwe' tradition after a local name for the country around the Falls. Pottery belonging to the Shongwe tradition has been found at several sites not far to the north-west of Livingstone, none of which seem older than the sixth century. It is, however, possible that an earlier phase in this tradition can be detected in pottery from Situmpa Forest, on the upper reaches of the Machili river, about 145 kilometres north-west of Livingstone. This has in fact been dated to between the first century BC and the third century AD; the dating evidence is not very satisfactory and should probably be ignored, but it is convenient and probably logical to consider Situmpa before discussing the principal sites of the Shongwe tradition.

The Situmpa pottery is a small collection from a buried land surface on the edge of a dambo near the Machili Forest station, a few kilometres west of Mulobezi. This land surface was overlain by a thick deposit of Kalahari sand, which probably accumulated as a result of biological action some time after the site was abandoned. Despite the infertile sands of this area it would have had certain attractions for Early Iron Age people. The main tree-cover is teak forest, but a thick *mutemwa* undergrowth flourishes beneath this, and tends to predominate wherever the teak canopy is broken, as along the margins of dambos. Thus although the teak forest would have been difficult to clear with primitive iron tools, there was plenty of thicket which could easily be cleared by slash-and-burn methods, to make gardens for bulrush millet or sorghum. Furthermore, a dambo such as that near the Situmpa site would have provided grazing for domestic stock or wild animals and a supply of water on or near the surface. Iron ore sometimes occurs on the edges of dambos in the Kalahari sands, in the form of bog-iron or ferricrete. A piece of ferricrete was found at the Situmpa site; there is in fact no iron in the immediate neighbourhood, but we may suppose that it had been brought to the site from elsewhere for the purpose of smelting.

Pottery bearing a certain resemblance to the few diagnostic sherds from Situmpa has been found near Sesheke, on the Zambezi; at two places on the Rhodesian bank, just below the Victoria Falls; and at Siachelaba's Kraal, now submerged under Lake Kariba. These finds are undated, and we can do no more than guess that people closely related to the makers of the Situmpa pottery may have inhabited the middle Zambezi valley as far west as the Lusu rapids, at much the same period. It also looks as if they were fairly closely related to the makers of the earliest pottery further south and east in Rhodesia.

The main centre of pottery in the Shongwe tradition is in the Bovu Forest Reserve, about fifty kilometres north-west of Livingstone. Here the Kalahari sand is covered by *brachystegia* woodland, which is intersected by several dambos. We may suppose that in the early Iron Age, as in more recent times, water was obtained by wells sunk into the dambos, which were also used for dry-season grazing. Cultivation was probably concentrated in the upper reaches of dambos, where they were least liable to inundation; the soil could have been fertilised, as in recent times, with wood ash obtained from the surrounding *brachystegia* woodland. But the most interesting feature of the area is a massive outcrop of ferricrete at the head of the Kamangoza dambo. There is every sign that this was mined intensively at various times over a long period. Remains of about two hundred smelting furnaces are visible along the dambo margin. These were probably used some time between the sixteenth and early nineteenth centuries, but there are also traces of two large surface mines which have mostly been filled in, suggesting that they were exploited at a more distant period. This is confirmed by the archaeological record. Not only have the sites yielded remains of iron artefacts and smelters; they include stratified deposits which clearly show that the iron ore attracted human settlement at different times during the latter part of the first millennium and the early part of the second millennium AD.

The most varied collection of ironwork was recovered from Kumadzulo, a site immediately next to the iron mines. This is the earliest known settlement in the area; the single village surface at Kumadzulo has been dated to between the sixth and seventh centuries. The charred remains of sixteen pole-and-mud huts were found; they had clearly collapsed in a fire. The village was certainly abandoned in a hurry, for the inhabitants, who may altogether have numbered about 200, left behind many of their smaller tools and ornaments. These included spearheads, arrowheads, hooks, knives, chisels, needles, bodkins, a razor and a small hoe; there were also two iron bangles and straps, beads, thumb-piano keys and a few small iron sheets. Such objects were evidently hammered out from iron wire, as this was also found in some quantity: thus the art of wire-drawing in this part of Zambia may be almost as old as iron-working in general. Much iron slag was found, a fragment of a smelting draught-pipe, and a stone anvil. Several small stone flakes were also present, suggesting that even this thoroughly Iron Age community made some use of stone in tools such as hammers, though there is no sign of any Late Stone Age occupation in this area at this period. No human bones were found, but mandibles and teeth from an ox, and a small clay figurine shaped like an ox-head, suggest that the villagers may have kept short-horn cattle of the same 'Sanga' breed as was kept in later times in southern Zambia. There are a few remains of small game animals, which would have been hunted in the nearby dambos. Several copper objects – beads, bangles, coils of wire and two flat bars – testify to trade over a considerable distance, for the nearest sources of copper are in the Wankie area, in Rhodesia. The bars probably represent the form in which the copper was imported to Kumadzulo before being re-worked locally into ornaments. Perhaps it was bought in exchange for ironwork.

Since Kumadzulo is probably the earliest known Iron Age village site in the country north-west of Livingstone, the pottery found there is of special importance as evidence for changes within a continuous Shongwe tradition of pot-decoration. In the first place, some of the Kumadzulo pottery is decorated with parallel grooves: this is a motif which is unknown in any later pottery within this tradition, but which is characteristic of the Situmpa-type pottery. We may thus reasonably suppose that the Kumadzulo pottery is the outcome of a gradual process of cultural change in this region, in the course of which new decorative patterns gradually supplanted those of the Situmpa pots, and only one or two potters continued to apply the increasingly archaic pattern of parallel grooves. If this argument is accepted, the Kumadzulo pottery allows us to see the Situmpa pottery as the first phase in the Shongwe tradition.

The subsequent phases of this tradition are much more easily distinguished, since the Kumadzulo pottery can be compared with slightly later pottery from other sites in the Bovu Forest, and from sites nearer to Livingstone. The greater part of the Kumadzulo pottery is sufficiently distinctive to be regarded as evidence of a 'Kumadzulo

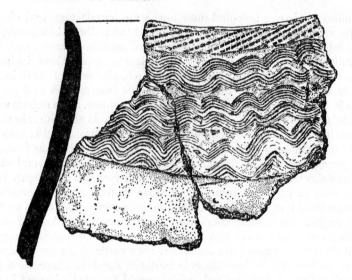

Fig. 10. Shongwe Tradition pottery
Part of a pot from Kumadzulo. The 'Kumadzulo Phase' in the Shongwe
Tradition frequently displays such comb-stamped rims, and lines, made by
dragging a comb or bunch of grass across the pot before firing. At Dambwa,
the same technique was used to produce somewhat different patterns.

phase', and the same sort of pottery has been found at the foot of two
stratified deposits a few kilometres from Kumadzulo: at Simbusenga
(where it is dated to around the eighth century), and at Tanzala. The
rest of the Kumadzulo pottery resembles that from the foot of the stratified deposit at Kamangoza, only a few hundred metres away from
Kumadzulo; this can probably be dated to about the ninth century,
and has been classified as a 'Yellow Sands' phase.[1] This type has also
been found at Dambwa, a seventh to ninth-century site just outside
Livingstone, but most of the Dambwa pottery constitutes a 'phase' of its
own which includes pottery from several other sites. Two of these –
Chundu (also seventh to ninth-century) and Zambezi Farm – are only
twenty to twenty-five kilometres west of Dambwa, but similar pottery
has been collected from the surface at Katombora, further west, and
from a few sites in north-western Rhodesia.

The typical settlement of peoples belonging to the Shongwe tradition
was a semi-permanent small village of pole-and-mud huts, beside a
dambo, as at Kumadzulo. At the nearby Kamangoza site a profusion
of animal bones and fish bones indicates the importance of hunting and
fishing. A few carbonised nuts and seeds suggest that some food-gather-

ing was practised. As usual there is no direct evidence of agriculture, beyond a few hoes, but we may assume that there was some cultivation of grain crops in ash-fertilised clearings. No trace of clothing survives, but needles and bodkins are sufficient proof of sewing: probably grass fibres were used in making garments from animal skins as there is no certain sign of cotton-spinning.

Both ironsmithing and smelting were fairly widely practised. The sites at Kamangoza, Chundu and Zambezi Farm yielded a variety of iron implements, while remains of iron smelting were found not only in the Kamangoza dambo but at Kabondo, which was likewise close to a large mine, and also at Dambwa and Tanzala. (The fact that smelting was practised in or beside villages in the Early Iron Age is of special interest, as in more recent times there has been a more or less universal taboo on smelting anywhere near a village; this was rooted in a belief that smelting has a symbolic sexual significance – a belief which was probably not characteristic of the Early Iron Age.) Copper wire and ornaments at several sites indicate that a trade in copper, probably across the Zambezi, continued to flourish. It is possible that there was some trade with people far to the north-east, for a little of the pottery from Kumadzulo and Zambezi Farm has much in common with Early Iron Age pottery from the Lusaka area. But there was virtually no contact, direct or indirect, with any trade routes linking the central African interior with the coast: the two cowrie shells found at Chundu must have arrived by some quite haphazard process of village-to-village barter.

As for the people themselves, some clue as to their physical appearance may in due course be provided by analysis of human skeletons found at both Dambwa and Chundu (where the dead were supplied with burial hoards of tools and ornaments). They probably displayed both negroid and 'bush' type features, as a result of intermarriage over the years between immigrant farmers and indigenous Stone Age people. Actual Stone Age economies, however, seem to have survived only in parts of the middle Zambezi valley, where Early Iron Age pottery has occasionally been found mixed with small stone tools: perhaps the valley served as a refuge area for Late Stone Age communities in retreat.

The country inhabited by the people of the Shongwe tradition was clearly well suited to Early Iron Age technology and economy. Iron ore was readily accessible, yet heavy iron tools were by no means essential: dambo margins could be cultivated and forest clearance kept to a minimum. These factors clearly outweighed the relative poverty of the soils, and in any case there was plenty of game and fish within easy reach. Hunting and gathering, in fact, were of key importance. Agriculture and iron-working were no less essential, but the techniques of both were still relatively undeveloped and people were less completely dependent on these skills than Zambian societies of the more recent past.

The Kalundu Group

The same would seem to be true of other Early Iron Age communities in southern Zambia, and their settlement patterns were governed by similar considerations. Away from the Zambezi valley, Early Iron Age settlement in southern Zambia seems to have clustered around areas where woodland and grassland converge, thus supporting a combination of hunting, gathering, cattle-keeping and slash-and-burn cultivation. And, as in the Victoria Falls area, repeated occupation of certain favourable sites created stratified deposits which help to clarify the archaeological record. One area especially congenial to Early Iron Age farmers was the watershed grassland which occurs in patches on the Batoka plateau, between the Zambezi and Kafue: this provided fine grazing for antelope, while little bush-clearance was needed to cultivate clumps of thicket, or the small stands of *miombo* woodland along the ridges. Seasonally waterlogged pans within the grasslands would have supplied water for both men and animals.

The earliest known settlement in such country is the Kalundu mound, a few kilometres south-east of Kalomo, where the lowest levels of occupation have been dated to about the fifth century AD. Further east, beyond Choma, the Kafue–Zambezi watershed is dominated by *munga* woodland, in which unusually fertile soils support a light canopy of trees standing in rich grassland. At Gundu mound, on the edge of this area, the beginning of a long Iron Age sequence has been dated to about the fifth century, and to the north, in the Kafue valley above Namwala, two more long sequences have been preserved in large mounds at Basanga and nearby Mwanamaimpa; these also appear to have been first occupied in about the fifth or sixth century. Here the Kafue flood plain, which is a vast expanse of grassland in the dry season, would have provided fine grazing for both game and cattle; this would have attracted Iron Age settlers just as strongly as the Late Stone Age hunters of Gwisho, further down the valley. It is also likely that the salt deposits near Basanga were from the first a powerful inducement to settlement. Salt was generally scarce in pre-colonial Africa, and to judge from later history Basanga was one of the few places in southern Zambia which yielded enough salt to supply the needs of more than one or two villages.

The earliest pottery from all these sites seems sufficiently alike to be regarded as belonging to a distinct Early Iron Age tradition: this has been provisionally called the 'Kalundu group' after the earlier pottery from the Kalundu mound. This tradition would seem to have developed quite independently of the Shongwe tradition. The Kalundu pottery has much more in common with Early Iron Age pottery, also of the fifth century, from central and northeastern Zambia, and it probably shares a common origin in Shaba. Kalundu-type pottery occurs in approximately sixth- and eighth-century levels at Basanga and Mwanamaimpa, and in levels dated to between the fifth and ninth centuries at Gundu.

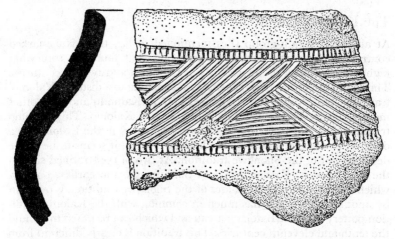

Fig. 11. Kalundu Group pottery
Part of a pot from the lowest level at Kalundu Mound. The ladder-like bands and grooves are typical of the Kalundu Group; the latter feature somewhat resembles the channelling in Kalambo Group pottery.

There are other ways in which the Kalundu-group people seem to have differed from those of the Shongwe tradition. The former may have kept rather more domestic stock, even if this was still less important as a meat source than wild game. They certainly made less use of iron tools: indeed, no hoes or axes at all were found in the earlier levels at Kalundu itself. Some smelting was evidently practised there and at Gundu, but iron ore is scarce on the plateau and it was probably obtained mainly from deposits near the Kalomo river. Trade was probably confined to very localised barter: a few cowries reached the Batoka plateau during this period but little or no copper, for none has been found in association with Kalundu-group pottery. The fact that these Kalundu-group sites are all mounds raises the question whether they might have been deliberate constructions. There seems to be no good reason for assuming this, and they are most probably no more than the result of the prolonged accumulation of debris. But the occurrence of Kalundu-group pottery at more than one level in certain mounds does suggest that the inhabitants may have moved more or less systematically from one mound-site to another, perhaps in a cyclical pattern that would eventually bring them back to their starting-point. The only evidence for the physical type of these people is the skeletons of two children, from the base of the Kalundu mound: these have not yet been classified.

The Kalomo Tradition

At all the Kalundu-group sites mentioned so far, there is a marked contrast between the earliest pottery and that found at somewhat higher levels, dated to between about the ninth and twelfth centuries. This later pottery has been classified as belonging to a distinct 'Kalomo' tradition, since it was first recognised both at Kalundu and at another mound, Isamu Pati, a few kilometres west of Kalomo. This Kalomo tradition does not in fact seem to have originated in the Kalomo area or anywhere else on the Batoka plateau; instead, it seems to be a late development of the Shongwe tradition. At two of the stratified sites in the Bovu Forest, Kamangoza and Simbusenga, the earliest pottery, which belongs to different phases of the Shongwe tradition, is overlain by another type which has much in common with the Kalomo tradition pottery from the Batoka plateau and which can be dated to around the tenth and eleventh centuries. This tradition is clearly different from the mainstream of the Shongwe tradition, but the differences can probably be explained as the result of gradual and piecemeal changes in local pottery styles, such as had earlier produced different 'phases' in this tradition. The conclusion to be drawn, then, is that towards the end of the first millennium the pottery style most commonly in use in the Victoria Falls area was adopted in areas well to the north-east which had previously maintained their own distinct style.

The reason for such a north-eastward diffusion of pottery decoration is not at all clear. At present it seems simplest to explain it as the result of a gradual drift of population away from the Victoria Falls area up on to the Batoka plateau and beyond. This might have been caused by the decline in rainfall which is thought to have affected central Africa in the latter part of the first millennium. Such a decline would have involved long droughts, and these in turn would have severely reduced the capacity of Kalahari sand country to sustain animal grazing and human cultivation. In such conditions, there would have been strong incentives to move towards the more fertile areas of the plateau, and the valley of the Ngwezi river, which rises near Kalomo, would have been a natural migration route. In support of this hypothesis of dispersal in adversity, it has been argued that there was an actual decline in population during this period: for in general the villages of Kalomo-tradition people seem to have been considerably smaller than those of their predecessors in the Victoria Falls area, even though the actual density of huts in a given space was much the same.

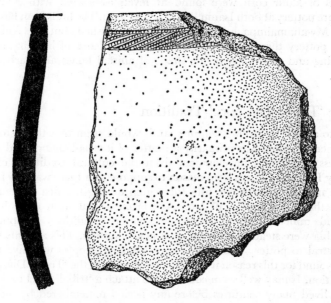

Fig. 12. Kalomo Tradition pottery
A typical Kalomo Tradition sherd from Isamu Pati, showing a single narrow band of fine comb-stamped hatching around the rim.

Whatever the reasons for this expansion of the Kalomo tradition, it appears to have established itself on the Batoka plateau fairly rapidly, for the earliest Kalomo pottery at Kalundu, Isamu Pati and Gundu, as well as at Kamangoza and Simbusenga, all belongs to about the ninth and tenth centuries. The tradition persisted on the plateau into the eleventh or twelfth century, and meanwhile its influence spread northwards, for Kalomo-related pottery appears above the Kalundu group levels at Basanga and Mwanamaimpa, and has been dated to between the eleventh and thirteenth centuries. Presumably this replacement of one dominant pottery tradition by another involved a major process of expulsion or cultural absorption, but the archaeological record can throw no light on this. In any case, there was clearly no marked change in economic practice: the material remains associated with Kalomo-type pottery are very much the same as those from earlier occupation levels. Ironwork and copper ornaments continued to be more common in the Victoria Falls area than on the Batoka plateau. Some iron smelting was practised near Isamu Pati, but the one hoe blade found there was quite worn out, suggesting that heavy iron tools were so rare as to be discarded only when they had lost all possible use. Seeds of kaffir corn were found at levels associated with Kalomo-culture pottery at both Isamu Pati and Kalundu. The finds from Basanga and Mwanamaimpa have not yet been published, but the Kalomo-type pottery there is associated with rich evidence of hunting, stock-keeping and gathering, in the shape of animal bones and carbonised nuts.

The 'Tonga Diaspora' Tradition

Up to about the twelfth century AD, it would seem that the history of southern Zambia was primarily a matter of internal change and more or less continuous development from the cultural traditions of the Early Iron Age. There is no reason to suppose that there was any large-scale migration of people into the region during the first millennium after the initial arrival of Iron Age farmers. But from early in the second millennium the indigenous pottery traditions of southern Zambia were steadily replaced by a new tradition. This appears to be ancestral to pottery made by Tonga-speaking peoples who live there today, and for this reason it has been referred to as the 'Tonga Diaspora' tradition. It may well seem confusing to attach a 'tribal' label to people who lived many centuries before any period remembered by modern Zambian peoples. It would certainly be unwise to assume any very close resemblance in terms of language or social institutions between the modern Tonga and the people of the Tonga Diaspora. Nevertheless, it seems likely that – as with the Luangwa tradition in central and north-eastern Zambia at about the same period – we are indeed dealing with evidence for a 'diaspora' or large-scale dispersal of peoples into what is now Zambia, and that such peoples were both culturally and physically the ancestors of some modern Zambians. At the same time, the intro-duction of the Tonga Diaspora tradition is as yet no easier to describe in any detail, far less explain, than the introduction of the Luangwa tradition. The two phenomena may well be related in some way, but at present we can do no more than review the evidence.

Pottery in this Tonga Diaspora tradition has been found at a number of sites (including several stratified deposits), not only on the Batoka plateau but also in the Victoria Falls area, where several phases in the tradition have been provisionally distinguished. The first occurs at Sinde, which has been dated to between the eleventh and thirteenth centuries; the next at Simonga and Simbusenga (twelfth to fifteenth centuries), and the third at Mukuni, east of Livingstone (twelfth to

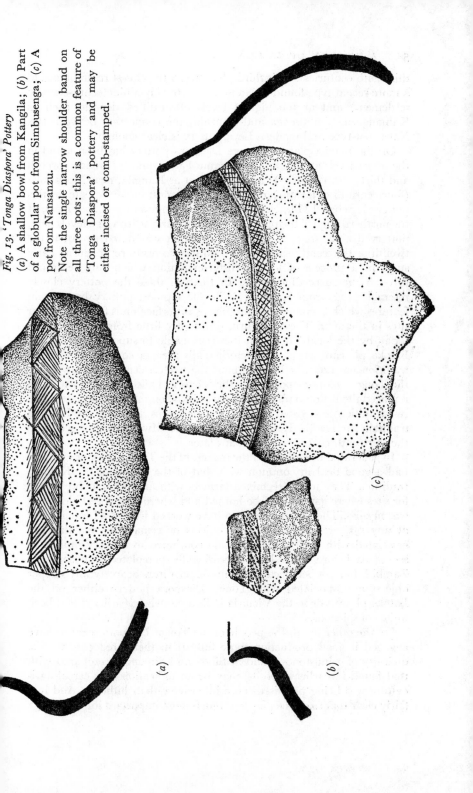

Fig. 13. 'Tonga Diaspora' Pottery
(*a*) A shallow bowl from Kangila; (*b*) Part of a globular pot from Simbusenga; (*c*) A pot from Nansanzu.
Note the single narrow shoulder band on all three pots: this is a common feature of 'Tonga Diaspora' pottery and may be either incised or comb-stamped.

thirteenth centuries). This third phase bears the closest resemblance to a more recent type found at Nansanzu (probably a nineteenth-century settlement) and at the highest levels of stratified deposits such as Kamangoza, Simbusenga and Tanzala; the connection between this Nansanzu-type and modern Leya pottery is clear enough.

On the Batoka plateau, Tonga Diaspora pottery has been found in the upper levels at Kalundu and Isamu Pati; Gundu; Ndonde (twelfth and thirteenth centuries); and as far east as Kangila, near Mazabuka (fourteenth to sixteenth centuries). But the most important site for this pottery is Sebanzi Hill, close to Gwisho Springs on the Kafue Flats, at the northern edge of the plateau. At the two lowest Iron Age levels here, pottery distinct from the Kalomo tradition was dated to about the twelfth or thirteenth century. This pottery seems to represent an early stage in a process of local stylistic evolution which can be traced through the succeeding levels. In three of these the pottery closely resembles that from Kangila, while the topmost pottery has certain features which become more prominent in surface finds from two other sites in the area. These, in turn, differ very little from pottery made today by the local Tonga, so it is reasonable to suppose that on the Batoka plateau, as in the Victoria Falls area, a continuous cultural tradition has flourished since about the twelfth century. But whereas the Tonga Diaspora pottery in the Victoria Falls area seems to have replaced the Kalomo tradition fairly quickly, on the Batoka plateau the two traditions co-existed for several generations, for there the Kalomo tradition survived at Kalundu, Basanga and Mwanamaimpa well into the thirteenth century and perhaps later.

In general, the economy of the makers of the Tonga Diaspora pottery had a good deal in common with that of the people of the Kalomo tradition. They too were mixed farmers with an apparent preference for sites where game could be hunted and where little forest clearance was needed. They do not seem to have worked iron at all intensively; at any rate, relatively few iron objects or remains of smelting are associated with their pottery. Trade continued to be very limited in scope; as before, glass beads occasionally percolated into southern Zambia, but copper became, if anything, rarer. Scarcely any copper objects are associated with Tonga Diaspora pottery either on the Batoka plateau or in the Victoria Falls area, where earlier it had been quite conspicuous.

On the other hand, the people of the Tonga Diaspora seem to have engaged in food production more fully than their predecessors. The quantity of grindstones found at Sinde and Simonga, compared with that found in earlier deposits, may be an indication that cereal agriculture was being practised more intensively than hitherto. And it is fairly clear that stock-keeping was much more important for the Tonga

Diaspora people than for those of the Kalomo tradition. This is shown by the marked increase in bones of domestic stock, in relation to bones of wild game, during the Tonga Diaspora occupations of Isamu Pati: the proportion rose from rather less than half to over four-fifths. This impression is borne out by the high proportions of domestic animal bones, especially cattle, at Sebanzi (perhaps three-quarters) and Kangila (perhaps two-thirds). Kangila, indeed, may have been a cattle-herding camp rather than a proper village, for there were hardly any remains of mud huts at the site. This expansion of stock-keeping at the expense of hunting may simply have been due to a natural growth of herds: besides, it is probable that the relatively arid climate of the later first millennium was succeeded by a somewhat wetter phase which would have improved conditions for grazing. It may also be that the milking of cattle was introduced from eastern into central and southern Africa early in the second millennium; if so, this could help to account for the importance attached to stock-keeping by the Tonga Diaspora people.

There were in any case some interesting cultural differences between the Tonga Diaspora people and their predecessors. They appear to have introduced the spinning of cotton, and perhaps its cultivation, for the second earliest level at Sebanzi yielded two spindle whorls. This is probably the earliest evidence for cotton-spinning in central Africa: spindle whorls have been found in the ruins at Zimbabwe, in Rhodesia, but these are not older than the fourteenth century. (It has been conjectured that the craft of cotton weaving was introduced to the region by Arabs: it is at any rate worth noting that spindle whorls were rare at Kilwa, a port on the East African coast, before the second millennium.) We have more definite evidence that pipe-smoking was introduced to southern Zambia by the Tonga Diaspora: smoking-pipes are unknown in Early Iron Age sites and first occur at Sebanzi. They were probably filled with hemp, which grows locally, for tobacco did not reach Africa from America until some centuries later. Another remarkable feature is the great number of clay figurines, usually of cattle, associated with Tonga Diaspora pottery at Simbusenga and Ndonde, as well as in the upper four levels at Sebanzi. Such figurines were made by earlier peoples in the region, but the increase in quantity may perhaps be due to some change in ritual practices.

Finally, the Tonga Diaspora levels at Isamu Pati seem to hint at some social differentiation based on wealth and status. There were several human burials at this site, nearly all associated with the latest phase of occupation, but all the skeletons were very simply adorned, except for that of a girl aged about fifteen. She was wearing twelve rows of snail-shell beads, ten large green glass beads, six ivory bracelets, and iron bangles on her ankles. Most interesting of all, two conus shells were suspended from her neck; these would ultimately have come from the Indian Ocean, and in later centuries discs cut from such shells were adopted as symbols of chieftainship throughout much of central and eastern Africa.

Ingombe Ilede

The most spectacular evidence from southern Zambia for the emergence of groups distinguished by wealth and social status comes from Ingombe Ilede, close to the confluence of the Lusitu and Zambezi rivers. At this site, richly furnished burials have been dated to about the fourteenth or fifteenth century AD. And the grave goods – which include objects in gold as well as copper, iron and ivory – provide the first clear sign of long-distance trade between Zambia and the east coast. They also bear witness to the introduction of metalwork more advanced than any previously known in Zambia. Thus Ingombe Ilede is one of the most important archaeological sites in the country. It is particularly interesting that these 'gold burials' should belong to a period on the borderline between 'prehistory' and 'history'; we can relate them to the evidence from early Portuguese writers that by this time Muslim traders were venturing far into central Africa. It would, however, be a mistake to regard Ingombe Ilede as important primarily for the history of southern Zambia. Its prosperity and sophistication arose when it became an outpost of the gold-trading regions of Rhodesia. As such, its main links were to the south and east, while its connections with other communities north of the Zambezi may well have been very limited.

Ingombe Ilede was in fact first occupied long before the 'gold burials' were deposited. In the course of the ninth and tenth centuries the site was inhabited by people whose way of life was very like that of Early Iron Age people elsewhere in southern Zambia. Their remains include carbonised seeds of kaffir corn, pottery, some fragments of copper, some iron slag, a few glass beads and a cowrie shell. It is possible, though by no means certain, that the thirty-one burials on the south edge of the site belong to this early period of occupation, but they are mostly of very young children and include no grave goods beyond small ornaments of copper, and beads of glass and shell. The pottery is somewhat puzzling, for it has no very close affinities with other pottery traditions in this part of central Africa. It is certainly quite distinct from the Kalomo tradition, which by this time was well established further west, on the Batoka plateau. There are important points of resemblance to the Tonga Diaspora pottery from Kangila, but that is certainly some centuries later.

It is, however, clear enough that these earlier inhabitants of Ingombe Ilede were a self-sufficient community whose trade, so far as they had any, must have been limited to the simplest exchanges with their neighbours. Their daily needs could well have been satisfied by the immediate environment. The Zambezi valley at this point is broad and shallow, and during the dry season the river subsides to reveal fertile plots of alluvial soil which can be cultivated year after year, and also stretches of rich grassland. Both these and the lower reaches of the Lusitu valley were frequented by large herds of game a hundred years ago, and we may suppose that the same was true in much earlier times. The early inhabitants of Ingombe Ilede certainly depended much on hunting: about three-quarters of their meat supply came from wild animals, and elephant bones were found at the lowest levels of the site. Fishing must have been an important activity, and a further inducement to settlement may have been the salt deposits near the Lusitu river, which we know were exploited in the last century. These various advantages would have outweighed the obvious drawbacks of life at Ingombe Ilede: the great heat, due to its low-lying position (about 400 metres), and the low rainfall. There are no iron deposits in the neighbourhood, but this would not have mattered very much, for iron hoes and axes were not needed to cultivate riverside gardens and such iron as was needed for knives, adzes, fish-hooks or arrowheads could well have been obtained from the Lusaka area, some eighty kilometres away.

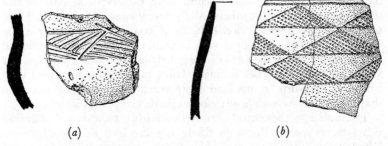

(a)   (b)

Fig. 14. Ingombe Ilede pottery
(a) A sherd from the earlier occupation; the band of alternating incised triangles is only one of several motifs found in the earlier Ingombe Ilede pottery, but it is common at Kangila.
(b) Sherds from one of the thin-walled, graphite-burnished beakers from the later occupation of Ingombe Ilede: the triangular blocks of comb-stamping are characteristic of the Luangwa Tradition.

From about the eleventh to the fourteenth century, Ingombe Ilede seems to have been uninhabited. It was then reoccupied by a group of people whose subsistence economy was similar to that of the earlier inhabitants, though they also traded in luxury goods of great value and prestige. Iron tools continued to be both simple and scarce, and wild game continued to provide the greater part of the meat supply, except in the very last phase of this later occupation. One useful advance had been made since the earlier occupation: cotton was grown and spun locally. Spindle whorls occur only in the upper levels at Ingombe Ilede, which confirms the evidence from Sebanzi Hill that the manufacture of cotton cloth was introduced to Zambia early in the second millennium. But for archaeological purposes the most important household goods from the later occupation are pottery of quite a new type, consisting of fine, thin-walled bowls and beakers burnished with graphite. These occur in the main deposit of the village, where they have been carbondated to the fourteenth or fifteenth century, but they were also found in the rich burials in the centre of the site, thus enabling us to apply this date to these burials.

There were eleven of these central burials, and most of them displayed more or less ostentatious personal ornaments. But in four burials the corpses were exceptionally richly adorned, while they were also furnished with a variety of grave goods. Strings of gold beads hung round their necks, and strings of coloured glass beads round both neck and waist. All four wore copper bangles on their arms, and one – a young man – wore ten gold bracelets at his elbows; he also carried a necklace of nine conus shells, one of which was mounted in a gold backing-cup. Pieces of cotton cloth were preserved on part of this skeleton, as on two of the others. All four were equipped with small iron tools for drawing metal wire. Lengths of iron wire were found in one burial, and lengths of copper wire in another. Three burials included copper ingots cast in the form of elongated, flanged crosses (another was found in one of the lesser burials). Three burials were furnished with iron hoes, unworn by use and more ceremonial than functional in shape; and in two burials were found single clapperless iron bells.

The finds from the central burials show fairly conclusively that during this late occupation Ingombe Ilede was involved in trade between Rhodesia and the east coast. Gold had been mined in Rhodesia at least since the latter part of the first millennium, and there are a few Arab reports of the export of gold from around the mouth of the Zambezi during the next few centuries. It is possible that the Rhodesian gold trade reached its height by the thirteenth century. Zimbabwe probably owed its prosperity in large part to the export of gold through the south-eastern regions of Rhodesia, and the most elaborate stone buildings there may be dated to around the end of the fourteenth century. And it would seem that at about the same time, or not much later, Ingombe Ilede obtained gold and copper from part of north-eastern Rhodesia. There were certainly very close links between the later inhabitants of Ingombe Ilede and people about a hundred kilometres to the south-east, on the Rhodesian plateau. Several sites in this area (now in Urungwe district) have yielded the fine pottery typical of the later occupation at Ingombe Ilede. One of these, Chedzurgwe, has been excavated and dated to about the fifteenth or sixteenth century, so it may have been inhabited at much the same time as Ingombe Ilede. The distinctive copper crosses found there have also been found at Chedzurgwe and other sites in the area, and the copper for these would have come from the numerous old workings not far to the east, near the Angwa river. No gold objects were found at Chedzurgwe, but it is likely that gold was handled in the neighbourhood, for there are several old gold mines, known to have been worked by Africans, to the south and east.

If Ingombe Ilede was receiving copper ingots and gold from Urungwe, it is probable that at least some was being re-exported eastwards, down the Zambezi. The numerous exotic imports, mainly glass beads but including seashells and pieces of possibly Indian cloth, would have come from the east coast, and the Zambezi seems the most obvious line of access. The river is navigable for much of its length, and it is very likely that by the twelfth or thirteenth century Arab traders in search of gold travelled up the lower reaches at least as far as Tete. Traders who penetrated beyond the Caborabassa rapids to the middle Zambezi would soon have appreciated the value of a place such as Ingombe Ilede: it was close to fords across the river, it could support a fairly settled local population, and it was within reach of the gold and copper mines of Urungwe and beyond. A further inducement may well have been the ivory available at Ingombe Ilede, for the deposits are littered with ivory fragments, presumably from herds grazing in the nearby valleys. The likelihood that Muslim traders, whether Arab or African, visited Ingombe Ilede is strengthened by the fact that two Muslim-style amulet holders were found beside one of the richest burials there.

The probability that Ingombe Ilede was a staging post between the northern part of Rhodesia and the east coast raises the question whether its history is in any way linked to that of the famous Mwenemutapa kingdom. Some time in the first half of the fifteenth century the first Mwenemutapa moved his capital from the southern part of Rhodesia to a site near the southern escarpment of the Zambezi, about three hundred and twenty kilometres east of Ingombe Ilede. The Mwene-mutapas then proceeded to carve out for themselves a new kingdom in the area, which became the centre of their loose-knit empire. By the end of the century, this kingdom was frequented by a great many Muslim traders, and it soon attracted the attention of the Portuguese. In about 1511 an adventurer called Antonio Fernandez visited Mwene-mutapa's kingdom and heard that both Muslims and local Africans bought copper from people who came from the king of 'Mobara' across a great river. This was probably the Hunyani, for 'Mobara' was clearly in Urungwe; local traditions there still remember the Mbara as early inhabitants who had originally come from north of the Zambezi. It therefore seems quite conceivable that the growth of Mwenemutapa's power near the Zambezi had the effect of drawing both long-distance traders and local metal-producers towards the royal capital and away from the middle Zambezi. In that case, the rise of Mwenemutapa could have brought about the decline of trade at Ingombe Ilede. On the other hand, it is also possible that it was precisely the growth of Mwenemutapa's new kingdom which encouraged long-distance traders to push as far west as Ingombe Ilede. If this was so, and if trade flourished there during the later fifteenth century, its decline may instead have been caused by Mwenemutapa's conquest of its trading partners, the Mbara of Urungwe, which probably took place early in the sixteenth century, soon after Fernandez's visit.

Fascinating as these glimpses are of communications between southern Zambia and a wider world beyond, the central burials at Ingombe Ilede are no less important for what they tell us about changes in technology and trading practices within central Africa. With regard to the latter, the eight copper crosses are especially interesting. They are almost identical in shape, and six are almost identical in size (about 30 cm long). Six weigh between 4,000 and 5,000 grams and of these, two pairs are each identical in weight. (Two crosses from Chedzurgwe were roughly the same shape and size as these, but rather lighter.) This implies that the crosses were at least intended to be of the same value, in which case they could have served, not simply as a convenient form in which to carry raw copper, but as standardised units of exchange. If, then, the crosses can be seen as a sort of primitive currency, this indicates that trade at Ingombe Ilede was of considerable scope and intensity. There was almost certainly some overlapping between the long-distance trade in luxuries, such as gold, copper, ivory, beads and cloth, and local exchanges of subsistence products. Copper was in demand among local people as well as among foreign traders. The former would have tended to pay for it with local products – ivory, livestock, salt, grain or possibly slaves. Foreign traders would rather have paid with beads, shells or cloth. Thus copper clearly provided a convenient medium for measuring the value of both local and exotic goods on a commonly agreed scale.[2] Furthermore, copper would have been an excellent medium for the storage of wealth over long periods, a most important consideration in societies where material goods so largely consisted of animal or vegetable products liable to rapid decay in tropical conditions.

The metalwork at Ingombe Ilede represents certain notable advances on the simple techniques characteristic of the Early Iron Age. One of the most important activities at the site was evidently the drawing of copper wire, for making bangles. Wire-drawing tools, such as were found in certain burials, would have been used to transform the imported trade wire (about 2·5 mm thick) into a very fine wire which was then wound round a fibre core before being shaped into bangles. (The same skill was practised at Chedzurgwe, where the bangle wire was between 0·3 mm and 0·5 mm thick: the earliest bangle wire at Sanga, in Shaba, is as fine as 0·2 mm.) Wire-drawing had of course been practised many centuries earlier in parts of southern Zambia, but the finest wire from Kumadzulo or Kamangoza is not less than 1 mm thick. Alloying was practised at Ingombe Ilede, probably to make copper easier to work; two bangles were alloys of copper and tin, while a fragment of lead was found in one burial.

However, it is the three iron bells from Ingombe Ilede which are of most technological interest. For these each consist of one sheet of iron, cut in an hour-glass shape and then folded over, so that the edges could be welded into a narrow flange. This attests a much higher order of skill than is found in any earlier ironwork in Zambia. South of the Zambezi, the earliest evidence for such skilled work is a double iron bell from Zimbabwe, which probably belongs to the late fourteenth century. North of the Zambezi, fragments of single iron bells may be dated to about the twelfth century at Sanga, where they were associated with the highly skilled copperwork. It might therefore seem as though the techniques of flange-welding spread south from the Zaïre region some time in the first half of the second millennium. But there is no sign that this technique was actually practised at Ingombe Ilede. There is very little evidence of any iron-working there, and it is most probable that the iron bells, together with the large ceremonial hoes and the wire-drawing equipment, were imported from some other community more adept at iron-working.

The main significance of these iron bells is rather as possible evidence for the range and direction of economic and political influences among central African peoples. For such bells have long been widely known in the Zaïre basin as symbols of chieftainship. Their occurrence at Ingombe Ilede and Zimbabwe may be evidence that by the fourteenth or fifteenth century, whether through trade or migrations, these communities had made contact with traditions of territorial chieftainship which had developed further north. It is certainly clear that at both places there was some degree of social stratification. In the case of Zimbabwe, the massive stone buildings testify to large-scale economic and social organisation. In the case of Ingombe Ilede, we have no such evidence. Its character as a trading entrepôt might well have enabled a small group of people to acquire considerable wealth without necessarily exercising any very extensive political authority. In this respect, indeed, the richest burials there may not be more significant than that of the solitary rich girl at Isamu Pati. Nevertheless, there is a striking resemblance between the iron bells and long-bladed hoes at Ingombe Ilede and similar objects from the grave of a nineteenth-century Soli chief near Lusaka. It is thus very tempting to suppose that the skilled ironwork at Ingombe Ilede came from the Lusaka area, and that the same iron-working tradition persisted there until very recent times. This would certainly reinforce the hypothesis that the ruling group at Ingombe Ilede may in some way be associated with the movements from the Shaba region which are thought to have introduced chieftainships to Zambia in more recent centuries.

At the same time, it should be noted that, except for these hoes and bells, there is as yet no evidence that the trade of Ingombe Ilede extended in any direction into Zambia. Thus the importance of Ingombe Ilede for Zambia's economic and political history remains something of an enigma. To answer the sort of questions which it raises about the development of trade routes and the growth of chieftainship in Zambia, it is necessary to turn to more recent periods and abandon the evidence of archaeology for the first written records, and the oral traditions of Zambia's present societies.

NOTES

1. Like 'Stone Age' and 'Iron Age', these archaeological 'phases' do not necessarily refer to distinct chronological periods. They indicate different styles, which may co-exist within any given period, although one style may tend to predominate at any one site or time. Thus these phases may follow each other in a broad chronological sequence, but with a good deal of overlapping.

2. It is worth noting that the emergence of a copper currency in this manner did not necessarily depend on the stimulus of trade from the coast: standardised copper crosses, of a rather different type, were in use at Sanga, near Lake Kisale in Shaba, perhaps by the twelfth century. Flanged copper crosses somewhat similar to those from Ingombe Ilede have also been found at Sanga, and may be dated to the fourteenth century or later. (I am indebted to M. Pierre de Maret for advice on the chronology of Sanga, based on new radio-carbon dates.) Moulds for flanged crosses similar to those at Ingombe Ilede have been found at Kipushi, just inside Shaba, and dated to about the fourteenth century.

V

The Peoples of Zambia
c. 1500 − c. 1700

In the last three chapters, the history of Zambia has been discussed, not so much in terms of people, as in terms of what they made and left behind them. It is only when we turn to the last few centuries that we can begin to form some picture of particular groups whose identities can be defined in terms of language or social organisation. There is rather little archaeological evidence which can be dated later than 1500 or so, but it is just this later period for which we can begin to make some use of the evidence preserved by Zambia's present inhabitants – mainly their own stories about the past, but also their other cultural traditions: their languages and their social and political institutions.

Traditions and 'Tribes'

At this point a word of caution may be in order. When we consider the pre-colonial history of a country such as Zambia, there is a strong temptation to think of it in two main parts: a remote period which we know about only from archaeology, and a more recent period which begins with the earliest remembered history of the present inhabitants. Historians, after all, are interested in events involving named individuals, and very often in Africa the earliest evidence of such events seems to come from oral traditions explaining how groups now known as 'tribes' came to be where they are. There are many such 'tribal histories' in Zambia. Most of them describe, in more or less picturesque detail, how a 'tribe' was founded by a band of adventurers arriving from Luba or Lunda country, in southern Zaïre. In general these stories contain a large kernel of truth, but it is important to realise that they do not necessarily give us the literal truth. Such stories of 'tribal' origins are usually myths. Their main purpose is not to record what really happened, but rather to explain and justify the customs and institutions of the present day. They may well be based on actual historical experience, but the original memory of that experience has been compressed and transformed into moral lessons for the latter-day listener. This is why such myths, all over the world, are full of fanciful and miraculous events: one of their main purposes is to relate the natural, everyday world to a supernatural world of gods and spirits and it is a common feature of myths that they include standardised episodes and characters which are mentioned again and again in the traditions of widely separated peoples. This is clearly due to borrowing rather than to the recollection of actual events which happened in the way they are told. Many Zambian myths of origin include, for example, stories of a Babel-like tower, and of royal incest, which are told all over central Africa.

We must be careful, then, not to take traditions of tribal origin at face value. We must consider what sort of purpose they serve for the people who tell them. And in every case we can see that they help to provide a sense of community and political identity. They establish why, for example, a group of people have certain customs in common and acknowledge the rule of certain chiefs. Like so much history, in literate as well as illiterate societies, these traditions of origin often support the position of a ruling class. Such rulers might in fact be descended from quite small groups of intruders, who gained power over long-established communities. But where there was no sharp economic or social division between such intruders and their subjects, the latter would not long retain an awareness of their own separate histories. In any society, after all, it tends to be the political institutions and the ruling groups which preserve the longest histories and have most interest in maintaining the ideas and beliefs underlying the social order. Thus in the course of time a story about the ancestors of kings or chiefs would come to be regarded as a story about their subjects' ancestors as well: in this sense, royal history would become tribal history.

We can now see that the average story of a 'tribal' migration is most unlikely to reveal the actual origins of the peoples who tell it. In so far as it is based on historical events, it is most likely to refer to movements by small, if important, groups of people – the founders of chiefly dynasties and their followers. However long the history of such a group, it is likely to overlay the much longer, if forgotten, history of other and earlier inhabitants. And this conclusion fits in with all the other evidence. We have already taken note of the archaeological arguments for supposing that a significant proportion of the ancestors of Zambia's present population may have settled in the country nearly a thousand years ago. In this chapter we shall see that other approaches – the study of languages and comparative ethnography – can also help us to form a picture of Zambian societies at a time before the establishment of the chiefdoms known today, and thus largely beyond the reach of oral narratives. As we shall see in the next chapter, the histories of these chiefdoms cannot, in general, be traced back earlier than the seventeenth century. So the task of this chapter is to summarise what we know, or can reasonably guess, about Zambia's peoples during the preceding two or three centuries. It will scarcely be possible to refer to distinct historical events, but it will be possible to form some idea of the social patterns which had taken shape in Zambia by 1500 or so, and the kind of changes which took place before the rise of the various kingdoms and chiefdoms which dominate the more recent past.

One final point should be made. In discussing this phase of history, as also the earlier 'archaeological' past, it is best to avoid, as far as possible, any reference to the names of individual tribes. 'Tribe', like 'nation', is a confusing and emotive word which the historian must use with great care. A tribal name, after all, can mean a variety of things. Occasionally, it may refer to a clearly defined group of people: for example, all the subjects of a certain king, or of chiefs belonging to a certain clan. But frequently a tribal name has no such precise meaning. Sometimes it may simply be used of people speaking the same language; or it may be no more than a word used by one set of people to refer to another set of people – 'the valley folk', 'the plains folk', 'the people of the west'. In such cases, the people thus named may not themselves be aware of any special unity: they may well have their own names for different groups among themselves.

The extent to which a particular tribal name acquires a distinct meaning, accepted both by outsiders and by the people themselves, clearly depends on the way in which social and political changes affect a people's sense of identity as against everyone else. Tribes, in short, are not actual social organisations: rather, they are states of mind. The awareness of belonging to a 'tribe' simply reflects social and cultural conditions at a certain point in time. Indeed, some of the tribes recognised today, such as the Soli, were not regarded as distinct peoples until British colonial officials grouped them together for purposes of administrative convenience. It is thus not very useful to assert, for example, that there are seventy-two (or -three, or -four) tribes in Zambia. We do not know what meaning is being given to the word 'tribe': it might be used to refer to differences in language, or political organisation, or a mixture of both. And it is with observable differences such as these that the historian must be mainly concerned. What people call each other at different times is of no great account. The groupings which most affected people's relations with each other were formed by the more durable ties of language, religion, kinship, clan and chieftainship.

These ties might well, in time, give rise to a sense of 'tribal' identity. As we have seen, this is often an aim of royal or chiefly traditions, and it is in this sense that such traditions may indeed relate the origin of 'tribes': they may illustrate the growth of 'tribal feeling' as a result of subordination to a common political authority. But it is precisely this fact which should warn us against assuming that the tribes acknowledged, say, a hundred years ago, necessarily existed in the same sense two or three hundred years ago. By and large, it is best to think of 'tribes' as simply the by-products of social and cultural change. Rather than try to trace the history of Zambian tribes, the historian should look for the various lines of social cohesion and division which underlie the shifting kaleidoscope of tribal names.

Admittedly it is impossible to avoid all reference to tribal names. They are, after all, the only names we can use – apart from the archaeologists' categories – to refer to different groups of Zambian peoples. But in this chapter, at least, tribal names are used only to indicate broad cultural patterns, especially in terms of language. They are not meant to denote political units of any kind, nor indeed is it to be assumed that they were actually in current use during this period. Further research may well enable us to devise a more suitable terminology for this all-too-obscure phase of Zambian history: meanwhile, it seems best to strive for accuracy rather than elegance of expression.

Economic Foundations

We may now begin to summarise what we know of Zambia around 1500. By this time, there were probably few people still practising a Stone Age economy of hunting and gathering. To judge from the archaeological record, and from the situation today, such people survived mainly in swamps and deserts which held no appeal for farmers. They would seem to have descendants among the small-statured men who still inhabit the Kafue Flats, the Lukanga Swamp, and the marshes south and east of Lake Mweru and east of Lake Bangweulu; while in the arid country west of the upper Zambezi there are 'Bushmen' similar to those of the Kalahari. Late Stone Age groups may have persisted until fairly recently in the more densely wooded parts of northeastern Zambia, but for the most part they had been absorbed or killed off by more numerous groups of Iron Age cultivators.

By 1500 much of Zambia was occupied by farming people who were more or less ancestral, in both a cultural and physical sense, to many of the present inhabitants. Central and north-eastern Zambia was dominated by people whose pottery belonged to a common 'Luangwa' tradition, which had probably spread eastwards and southwards as a result of migration from the Shaba region since the eleventh or twelfth century. Southern Zambia was dominated by people whose pottery belonged to the so-called Tonga Diaspora tradition, which also developed early in the second millennium. In western Zambia there seems to have been no comparable change in pottery style or population. It seems likely that many of the peoples of western Zambia had ancestors in the region well before AD 1000, and that their pottery traditions have changed relatively slowly over the past thousand years.

The migrations reflected in the Luangwa and Tonga Diaspora traditions not only resulted in new styles of pottery; they also brought about changes in economy and technology. Compared with their predecessors in southern Zambia, the Tonga Diaspora people were herdsmen rather than hunters, and they probably grew cereal crops more intensively. They grew and spun cotton, and smoked hemp. Contacts with trade from the east coast continued to be very limited, but the site at Isamu Pati indicates that a few families may have become a good deal richer than their neighbours; this may reflect some sort of political leadership.

Much less is known about the peoples who introduced the Luangwa tradition in the north-east. But it does appear that they were able to occupy the woodland more effectively than their predecessors. It was only during the second millennium AD that Late Stone Age hunters in this region were gradually absorbed by Iron Age communities. The growth and expansion of the latter must have depended directly on their ability to raise cereal as well as root crops in the woodlands. This meant some sort of slash-and-burn cultivation. At first this may well have been rather simple: a matter of clearing space in which to turn over the soil with hoes in order to plant kaffir corn, which seems to be the oldest cereal crop in the region. But a major step forward would have been taken with the introduction of millet cultivation by the *citemene* system, described in Chapter 1.

The origins of this system are obscure. It is not characteristic of the Luba region of the southern Zaïre basin, and it may well have been developed on the northern edges of the plateau between the Luapula and Luangwa. But it would certainly have benefited from any improvement in iron technology. Although *citemene* cultivation calls for little or no hoeing – since the seed is sown in a bed of wood ash – it does depend heavily on the use of axes, for lopping the branches of trees. It would not seem unreasonable to connect both the expansion of Luangwa-tradition peoples and the spread of *citemene* cultivation with the gradual spread of advanced methods of iron-working which for the first time made possible the clearance of woodland on a large scale. As yet, however, this is mere speculation. We do have evidence that the technique of flange-welding, and the making of sheet-iron, may have spread southwards from the Shaba region during the first half of the second millennium. But these techniques were applied to the making of ornaments and ceremonial objects; there is no clear evidence of any significant improvements in the manufacture of iron tools.

Languages

Such, then, were the economic foundations of Zambia's population about five hundred years ago. We must now consider what can be said about its social and cultural patterns. It is perhaps most convenient to begin by assessing the language situation. We have already seen that over most of Zambia there has been a broad measure of cultural continuity, as witnessed by pottery styles, over the past millennium. It is thus highly probable that the languages spoken in Zambia around 1500 or so were broadly similar to most of those spoken today. But language changes over the course of time; dialects develop; and invaders may impose their own language at the expense of others. It is thus no easy matter to guess at the language situation in Zambia in earlier times. It is very probable that Bantu languages have been spoken in the region since the beginning of the Iron Age. But as yet we cannot trace in any detail how these early languages were gradually transformed into the various languages and dialects we know today. All we can do here is make some very rough classifications among these modern languages, based on the extent to which they resemble each other, and consider how far their resemblances and differences may reflect patterns of regional differentiation over the centuries.

The African languages spoken today in Zambia can be classified in nine main groups, if we exclude one language, Silozi, known to have been introduced during the last century. These nine groups are shown on the table opposite.

Local changes within each of these groups have produced the languages and dialects spoken today. It is probable that in the distant past – say a thousand years ago or so – there were far fewer such differences within each one of these groups; it is also possible that each group may correspond more or less to a single language which has since been modified into several different forms. We cannot as yet say *when* any one such language, such as 'Luyana', existed, if it ever did, nor can we be sure that it would have been spoken in the area covered by the equivalent language group today. But if we also take into account the archaeological evidence, we can begin to perceive some possible patterns of linguistic change and continuity.

Until quite recently, it was widely supposed that the main centre for the first dispersal of Bantu-speakers throughout Africa south of the Equator was somewhere in the region of south-eastern Zaïre and north-eastern Zambia. It was argued on linguistic grounds that the Luba and Bemba languages were older than any other Bantu languages in eastern, central and southern Africa, and that therefore the main phase of the Bantu dispersal must have originated where Luba and Bemba are

Region	Language group	Principal modern languages	Other related languages
North-West	N.W. LUNDA	Lunda	
	WIKO	Luvale Luchazi Mbunda Chokwe	
	NKOYA	Nkoya	Lukolwe, Mbwela
	LUYANA	Kwangwa Kwandi Makoma Mashi	
	KAONDE	Kaonde	
East	CHEWA	Nyanja	
South	CENTRAL	Tonga	Toka, Leya, Subiya, Totela Ila, Sala, Lenje, Soli
North-East		Bemba	Lamba, Swaka, Lala, Bisa Aushi, Chishinga, Shila, Tabwa Unga, Twa Ambo
East			Kunda, Nsenga
East	TUMBUKA	Tumbuka	Senga
North-East	CORRIDOR	Mambwe Inamwanga Lambya Nyika	Lungu Iwa Tambo

NOTE:
This table is based on a study by M. Kashoki (University of Zambia) and W. M. Mann (School of Oriental and African Studies, London). Twenty-five Zambians, each with a different mother tongue, were asked to translate the same set of one hundred words into their own languages. Their answers were analysed by a computer, which produced diagrams showing the relative distances between the twenty-five languages, i.e. the degree of similarity or difference between them. This table is therefore only a very rough outline of the present language situation; it would certainly have to be modified if more thorough comparisons were made.

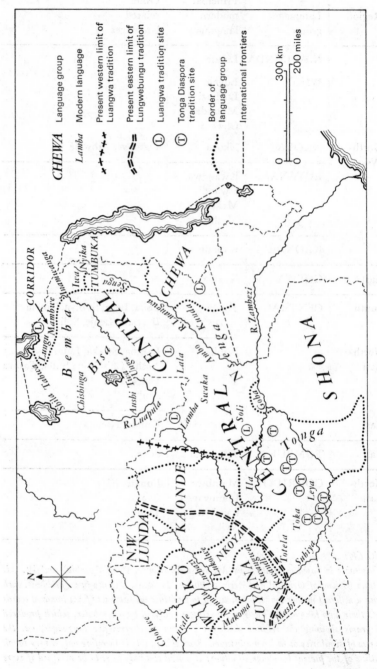

spoken today. This theory, however, has been challenged by recent research. On both linguistic and archaeological grounds it now seems clear that this Bantu dispersal originated north of the equatorial forest, as was noted in Chapter 3. Nevertheless, it remains possible that there was indeed a major dispersal of Bantu-speakers from south-eastern Zaïre which gave rise to many of the Bantu languages spoken today in central and southern Africa. What now seems clear is that such a dispersal would have taken place long after the original Bantu settlement of the region; so far from occurring around the beginning of the Iron Age in central Africa, it would have happened no more than a thousand years ago.

As we have seen, there is clear archaeological evidence for the introduction of new pottery traditions over much of Zambia in about the eleventh or twelfth century AD, and we know that at the same period comparable Later Iron Age pottery was introduced elsewhere in central and southern Africa. We have also seen that, in Zambia at least, there is good reason to suppose that at least one of these new traditions, the Luangwa tradition, was introduced as a result of large-scale migration, and it seems very likely that this is true of Later Iron Age pottery elsewhere. Since such Later Iron Age immigrants imposed their own pottery styles quite quickly, it is probable that they also imposed their own languages. Thus, just as much modern pottery in central and southern Africa is directly 'descended' from styles introduced in about the eleventh century, the same may also be true of most modern Bantu languages in these regions.

As yet, it would appear impossible to confirm or reject this theory on strictly linguistic grounds. But it is worth noting a few points of comparison between the archaeological and linguistic evidence available for Zambia. First, we may recall that part of western Zambia seems to have remained largely unaffected by the migrations which evidently introduced the Later Iron Age. On the upper Zambezi, the extent of the Luyana and Wiko[1] language groups roughly corresponds to that of the Lungwebungu pottery tradition. The fact that two language groups can be distinguished in this relatively limited sector of the Zambezi valley may well indicate that they have been spoken there for a long time, and this would agree with the archaeological evidence for continuity in this area since the early Iron Age. It is also noteworthy that the language of the Kaonde people seems to constitute a distinctive group of its own, for the present extent of the Kaonde language today largely corresponds to a gap between the present easternmost limit of the Lungwebungu pottery tradition and the present westernmost limit of the Luangwa tradition. These facts suggest that the culture of this area has long developed relatively independently from those of the surrounding regions in Zambia.

Elsewhere in Zambia, it is probable that all the various language groups which exist today reflect the impact of the migrations which evidently introduced the Later Iron Age. The very large 'central' group of languages overlaps much of the region within which new pottery traditions were introduced early in the second millennium. At the southern end of this central group, the present extent of Tonga and other languages of the 'Bantu Botatwe'[2] roughly corresponds to the extent of the Tonga Diaspora culture as defined by archaeologists. Further to the north and east there is a considerable overlap between the present extent of Bemba and closely related languages and the region of the Luangwa pottery tradition. Still further east, the Chewa language group may also be assumed to have developed among peoples of the Luangwa tradition, but the natural frontier of the Luangwa valley tended to separate it from the central group and the Chewa group probably reflects developments within the eastern Bantu region that extends over central and southern Malawi and eastern Mozambique. The same may be true of the Tumbuka group, while in the extreme north, between Lakes Malawi and Tanganyika, the Corridor group seems to be a southern extension of languages now spoken in East Africa.

Social Organisation and Religion

We must now consider what we know, or can reasonably conjecture, about the social institutions of Zambian peoples in the sixteenth century. Our evidence for this is mainly the result of comparing their present institutions. This kind of approach leans heavily on the argument that those institutions which are most widespread are also likely to be relatively old, though of course other lines of reasoning must also be employed, and all such inferences must be seen in the light of what we know from other sources about change in the more recent past.

Two points about Zambia in the sixteenth century can be made with some confidence. First, everyone belonged to clans. Each clan was named after some kind of natural phenomenon, usually an animal. Members of a clan were all kinsmen: they believed they were descended from a common ancestor, even if his name and relationship to living people was no longer remembered. The functions of clans varied a good deal. Their most widespread purpose was to help define whom one could marry. To avoid any possibility of incest, people were usually expected to marry outside their clan: such clans may be called 'exogamous'. The second point we may assert is that descent was usually matrilineal: it was reckoned in the female line. Inheritance to clan membership and other social positions, and also to property, commonly passed from a man to his sister's son. This custom still prevails among many Zambian communities, and it is also typical of many other peoples in the central African woodland: there is in fact a 'matrilineal belt' stretching across Africa south of the equatorial forest, from the Atlantic to the Indian Ocean. The main exception to this general rule in Zambia, during the sixteenth century, would have been the peoples of the Corridor language group, between Lakes Malawi and Tanganyika: in their custom of patrilineal descent, as in their languages, they represent a southward extension of East African cultural traditions. Another possible exception would be the Luyana-speaking peoples of the upper Zambezi: in recent times their descent pattern has mostly been bilateral – they have traced descent in both male and female lines; but it is possible that this is the result of patrilineal influences upon a system that was originally matrilineal.

It is likely that there was also a broad uniformity in the religious beliefs of Zambian peoples four or five hundred years ago. There was a general belief in a High God. In most of the far west, he was called Nyambe or Nzambi; elsewhere, he was usually called Lesa. This High God was venerated as the creator of all things. He was not usually believed to take an active part in human affairs, but ultimately he controlled the condition of the whole natural world – human, animal and vegetable. The High God might sometimes be influenced by approaching him through other spirits, and in some areas spirits were identified with the various forces of earth and sky. In the north-east, for example, prayers were made to spirits who controlled wind and rain, lightning, thunder and earth tremors; who sent locusts and other pestilences; and who determined success in searching for game and wild food. Besides such beliefs in gods and nature spirits, there was a widespread belief in the power of ancestral spirits. As elsewhere in Africa, the line between life and death was not drawn nearly so sharply as in modern industrial societies. The dead lived on, more or less strongly, as spirits, and it was believed that, in contrast to the High God, they often took a keen interest in the affairs of the living. If, for example, a family was stricken by disease or death, this might well be attributed to the displeasure of some ancestral spirit. In that case, the spirit would have to be appeased, not only by a change in behaviour but also by offerings and perhaps the performances of special rituals.

There was also another kind of explanation for misfortune: witchcraft. This was simply one aspect of the general use of magical charms for self-protection. Everyone was accustomed to use charms to ensure success in housekeeping, farming, fishing, hunting, war and love. But if someone seemed to be rather too successful, he might be suspected of practising magic, not just for his own good but to harm other people. So, too, if a man had a run of 'bad luck', or if a community was disturbed by feelings of jealousy or actual physical disease, it might well be suspected that someone had been practising black magic witchcraft. The detection of supposed witches was usually undertaken by special diviners ('witch-doctors') who might also know much about herbal medicines. The suspect was then tried by ordeal: this most commonly took the form of tasting poison, which only the innocent vomited.

Within this common pattern of custom and belief, we can discern certain regional variations which had probably developed by the sixteenth century. There are, for instance, important respects in which the peoples of the Wiko, Kaonde, Bemba, Chewa and Tumbuka language groups can be distinguished from the rest. Among these peoples, the main unit of social organisation was probably the corporate descent group – that is to say, a group of matrikin tracing a common ancestry over perhaps five or six generations, and claiming certain rights as a group over or against the claims of similar groups. These rights included the collective ownership of 'pawns' – marriageable women who were transferred from one descent group to another in payment for offences and in settlement of debts.

Such pawnship was not in the least a form of slavery: it was simply a way of setting limits to the operation of kinship rules, in order to strengthen the solidarity of descent groups. For in a matrilineal society, a kinship group clusters round the women within it. A headman wants to keep his female relations at home, and to bring young men in from outside to marry them and enlarge the kinship group within the village. This clearly undermines the authority of other headmen over their junior male kinsmen, as these leave their own villages for their wives' villages. One way of counteracting this tendency was to recognise that wrongs could be compensated by suspending the normal rules of kinship. A woman paid over as a pawn ceased to belong to her own clan and instead belonged to her owner's clan. Thus her children would increase the numbers of the owner's local clan-section. At the same time – in contrast to the normal rule of clan exogamy – a pawn woman could marry within the clan of her adoption. Her owner could marry her off to a junior kinsman, who would thus be encouraged to stay in his village instead of going elsewhere for a wife. Moreover, both the status of pawn, and rights over pawns, were transmitted from one generation to another. In societies where there was little durable material wealth, this provided a strong inducement for men to become leaders of their descent group, in whom the rights to pawns were vested. This in turn served to hold the descent group together as an organisation of people pursuing common interests and centred on a particular village or neighbourhood.

There is another important point of resemblance between the Wiko–Kaonde–Bemba–Chewa–Tumbuka group of peoples. This is the way in which they perform the girls' initiation ceremony, usually called *cisungu* in central and north-eastern Zambia; *cinamwali* in the east; and *nkanga* in the far west. This ceremony prepares young girls for marriage and combines various rituals with practical education. There are several common features of the ceremony, as practised by the peoples named above: the rites are performed for individual girls, who are kept for a time in seclusion, and mimes and dances serve to express different stages of the ceremony.

To some extent, then, we may think of this large group of Zambian peoples as sharing important elements of social and cultural organisation which may perhaps reflect a common inheritance from a long-established matrilineal tradition. But within this large group we can distinguish major differences. In the far west, among the Wiko peoples, there is also an initiation ceremony for boys. In some respects this resembles the ceremony for girls, but the boys' ceremony includes circumcision, and masked dancers (representing different kinds of spirits) play an important part in the process of instruction. These rites for boys are a major point of resemblance between the peoples of north-western Zambia and their neighbours to the north and west, in Zaïre and Angola. We must also note that these Wiko people (represented today by the Luvale, Luchazi and Chokwe) belonged to a common system of clans. Among peoples of the Bemba group further east, there is a quite different set of clan names. Many of these peoples belong to clans which are widely dispersed between the Lualaba, in the west, and the Luangwa, in the east. These different patterns of clan-distribution may well be the outcome of prolonged but distinct processes of migration by clan-sections within these two regions

Within the Bemba group of peoples there were further local differences. One institution which may have been of some antiquity around Lake Bangweulu and the Luapula river was the Butwa secret society. It is not clear whether the name Butwa is derived from the short-statured fishermen, called Twa, who still inhabit the swamps near the lake. In the nineteenth century Butwa was certainly widespread among the Twa, but it also had members among the Unga, Bisa, Lamba, Aushi, Shila and Tabwa. And the various functions of Butwa were similar to those of other secret societies. It provided social insurance: members helped each other in time of sickness and arranged respectable funerals. It honoured the spirits of natural forces, to ensure good hunting or harvests. Young initiates were instructed in sexual behaviour, more senior members learned the secrets of special poisons and medicine, and the society had its own esoteric language. It also provided much entertainment. Women members formed travelling bands of singers and dancers to attract new recruits, and Butwa ceremonies were the occasion for night-long dancing, drinking and dressing-up. Like other similar societies, Butwa was said by outsiders to indulge in shocking orgies. But much of its enduring appeal lay in the network of links it provided between scattered communities, regardless of clan or kinship ties, or political borders. Butwa claimed supreme authority over its own affairs, and it came to be regarded as a subversive influence by chiefs who either would not, or could not, join it.

North of Lake Bangweulu, and mostly in what is now Bemba country, beliefs in a High God, in spirits of natural forces, and in ancestral spirits were supplemented by beliefs in spirits called *ngulu*. These were not forces of nature: rather they represented the land in which they had their abodes. *Ngulu* inhabited strange natural features, such as rocks or waterfalls, where they received offerings from hereditary priests. They were not believed to be spirits of dead people, but they had names which were also given to people, and they were sometimes thought of as early inhabitants of their various countries.

East of the Luangwa, a somewhat different religious system took shape among the Chewa- and Tumbuka-speaking peoples. At an early stage in their history they seem to have shared much the same cult of a High God. He was believed to act upon men through a snake-spirit, who roamed far and wide. This spirit could possess people, in the sense that they might go into a trance and become its mouthpiece. This might happen to anyone, but it happened most regularly to the snake-spirit's own 'wives', each of whom was associated with a shrine on a hill. Among the northern Chewa (i.e. those in eastern Zambia and central Malawi), such spirit-wives came to be organised in a hierarchy subordinated to a central shrine at Kaphirintwa, under the senior spirit-wife, Makewana. They all belonged to the Banda clan, though the priestly functions of making prayers and offerings were exercised by men of the Mbewe clan. There was one religious institution which was typical of the Chewa-speaking peoples in general, as distinct from the Tumbuka. This was the *nyau* secret society. Its main purpose was to revere ancestral spirits, who were represented by special masks (which only men could wear). The main occasions for *nyau* ceremonies were funerals and the initiation of girls.

In terms of social and cultural organisation, the Tonga-speaking peoples of southern Zambia stand somewhat apart from the broad range of peoples we have so far discussed. In terms of language, they are not at all remote from the peoples of the Bemba group and clearly belong with them to the larger 'central' group. But southern Zambia provided a rather different environment from the woodlands occupied by the Bemba-speakers, and this could well account for distinctive features in the institutions and customs of the Tonga-speaking peoples. Admittedly, there is very little evidence indeed on which to base even guesses about their social life four or five hundred years ago. There was, however, one obvious respect in which most Tonga-speakers differed from most other Zambian peoples. This was their possession of cattle. Among the Ila this eventually gave rise to some emphasis on patrilineal descent: in this way a great variety of kinsmen might have claims to the use of cattle in any one man's herd. The early Tonga-speakers may be presumed to have had some form of initiation ceremony for girls, but this would have been rather different in form from than found further north. They were probably organised in rather small corporate kinship groups; they do not seem to have practised pawnship in the full sense of inheritable rights over people.

On the Batoka plateau, and in the Gwembe valley, the most far-reaching bond between villages was provided by 'rain shrines'. Rainfall in this region is relatively low and varies greatly from year to year, so attempts to control rain were of critical importance. Rain shrines were built at the graves of prominent men, such as those who had led the way in opening up new country for cultivation. Shrines were also founded by men who had themselves been 'rain-makers', and the care of their shrines might be entrusted to their descendants. But it would not appear that rain-cults on the plateau lasted more than a few generations, for villages there seem always to have been rather unstable communities, with constant movement of people from one small group to another. In this respect, the plateau Tonga are somewhat different from their Ila-speaking neighbours to the north. These had several localised cults for communal divinities, and while some were short-lived, as among the Tonga, a few seem to have lasted for long periods and prevailed over large areas. Throughout Ila country prayers were made to a spirit called Bulongo. The Ila may also be contrasted with the Tonga in terms of their clan system, which is largely distinct.

Political Organisation

Up to this point, little or nothing has been said about political organisa-tion – the way in which power was controlled and distributed. This is partly because it is even more difficult to make intelligent guesses about early forms of political structure than about other aspects of society. Patterns of marriage, kinship and village organisation, or religious belief, tend to change relatively slowly, and in the absence of clear evidence for great convulsions it is reasonable to take the evidence of recent times as a guide to conditions in the remoter past. Political organisation, however, is much more liable to change. Part of the busi-ness of politics, after all, is to regulate the relations between people within one system and people outside it. So changes in the outside world – whether migrations, invasions, or the spread of new ideas – are more likely to cause changes in political relations than in other kinds of social relations. It is thus difficult to make reliable conjectures about early political organisation in Zambia simply on the basis of what we know about more recent times.

We can at least be reasonably sure that in most parts of Zambia, in the sixteenth century, the lineage was still the main unit in political relations. We have already noted the likelihood that over much of the country people belonged to descent groups which exercised corporate rights. It seems very probable that these rights were claimed in what we would call both civil and criminal cases. It was, in short, the lineage group which regulated disputes and if two given lineage groups failed to settle a quarrel, it could always be referred to the elders of a more senior branch of the lineage; beyond this, the senior representatives of the clan might intervene. Indeed, we have some direct evidence that this kind of lineage organisation may be of considerable antiquity. Among the Luvale people, in the far north-west, matrilineages are still traced back over many generations, far deeper than anywhere else in Zambia. This is because until quite recent times their political relations continued to be largely determined by lineage structure; for judicial and political purposes a man belonged to a specific group of kinsmen, whose relationship to other kin groups could be precisely defined in terms of their respective position on a long family tree. Such a family tree consisted partly of a genealogy recording a person's immediate ancestors; this usually reached four or five generations into the past. These relatively shallow genealogies were then connected by means of a much longer genealogy listing the women from whom all the various lineages were descended. At the top of the family tree came the clan founder. Some of these Luvale genealogies cover as many as seventeen generations, and even then it is likely that they have been 'telescoped'. It is thus probable that several Luvale lineages had taken shape by the sixteenth century, while the Luvale clans are presumably older still.

This evidence for the early importance of clan and lineage in political organisation receives some support elsewhere in Zambia. For example, the earliest people remembered in the lower Luapula valley (apart from a few pygmies who have disappeared) were the Bwilile, whose leaders were heads of clans and lineages. But we must also note that in some areas political functions would also have been exercised by the leaders of local cults. In recent times, priests in charge of shrines among the Ila and Tonga have played a part in resolving disputes and even in forming military alliances. It is very likely that such political roles for religious leaders were common in many other areas as well, before chieftainship became the main form of political authority. As yet, however, we can only speculate on such a possibility. The pre-colonial political history of Zambia – as opposed to its social or religious history – really depends very largely on oral traditions which relate political events. And these traditions, as we have seen, are primarily concerned with chiefs. We must therefore turn to examine the origins and growth of chieftainship in Zambia.

NOTES

1. 'Wiko' is the name given by the Lozi people to various peoples further to the north-west.
2. 'Bantu Botatwe' means 'three peoples' and is sometimes used to refer to the Tonga, Ila and Lenje, whose languages are broadly similar.

VI

The Growth of Chieftainship
c. 1700 – c. 1840

Chieftainship has long been the characteristic political institution of most peoples in Zambia. By the end of the nineteenth century, nearly everyone was governed by chiefs: individual men (and occasionally women) who controlled the use of force either among specific groups of people or else, more often, over everyone who happened to live in a specific territory. In this chapter an attempt will be made to trace how this form of government first developed in Zambia, and how it gradually spread and took different forms in varying circumstances. And before we look into the difficult question of how and when chieftainship began, it may be helpful to define what chieftainship has most commonly meant in Zambia, and to indicate how it has shaped our knowledge of the past.

The Nature of Chieftainship

Zambian chiefs varied a great deal in the nature and extent of their authority. Some were not much more than village headmen; at the other extreme there were rulers who should really be called kings, since they were each acknowledged to be the senior ruler in a hierarchy of chiefs, great and small. Some chiefs owed their position to the prevailing rules of succession and inheritance; others might be chosen according to other rules, or simply on the basis of personal merit. But in one form or another, chieftainship was the most important political institution. It was the chief – assisted by his more senior subjects – who was responsible for seeing that law and custom were upheld; that the guilty were punished; and that his people were protected from their enemies. The more important chiefs controlled the administration of the poison ordeal for discovering witches, and all chiefs levied tribute, in labour, game, food crops, beer and local craft-work. This usually enabled them to live in a little more comfort and style than their subjects, but much hospitality was expected of them. Ideally, they met the needs of important visitors, and also those of their subjects who were unable to provide for themselves; they maintained food reserves to meet the threat of famine, and in receiving tribute a chief commonly made some payment in return: such 'reciprocal' exchange was one of the most important means of circulating scarce commodities such as salt, iron-work or foreign cloth.

There was also a religious dimension to chieftainship. Not only did a chief control the use of land by determining rights to cultivate or fish; he was also expected to care for the health of the land. If the rains were too short or too late, or if crops and animals were assailed by pests, it was the duty of a chief to intercede on behalf of his people by arranging prayers and offerings to the spirits of his ancestors or whatever other spirits were thought to exert power over the land. And occasionally this religious function of chieftainship went further. Some chiefs were regarded as 'divine kings', whose own bodies were thought to epitomise the condition of the whole country. If they fell ill, or failed to observe certain rituals and taboos (especially concerning sex and fire), the land itself would suffer, and the people with it. It might even happen that a dying king would be strangled, in order to prevent the disasters which would follow if his disease was allowed to run its natural course.

Even so, the death of an important chief meant that his country fell apart. There might be some form of regency, but succession wars were frequent, and sometimes prolonged. Meanwhile, many of the dead chief's wives and servants would be killed and buried with him. Death also awaited those who were accused by diviners of having killed the king by witchcraft. In any case, there was a period of licensed anarchy at the capital: law and order were temporarily in abeyance, and this served to underline the vital necessity of having a chief.

The prevalence of chieftainship in pre-colonial Zambia has had a great influence on oral traditions. It is chiefs, more than anyone else, who have had an interest in maintaining and controlling a collective record of past events, whether real or imaginary. Like other rulers, they needed such a record both to provide precedents for present practice and to justify the political system which they dominated. So the stuff of most oral traditions in Zambia is the activities of chiefs: the rise of dynasties, the foundation of chiefdoms, wars of conquest or quarrels over succession. And it is mainly in and around the courts of chiefs that such traditions have been preserved, whether by special officials or – perhaps more commonly – by men who have acquired their knowledge simply as part of the business of getting ahead in the service of their chief.

Moreover, it is primarily these traditions of chieftainship which provide clues to the chronology of Zambian history during the last few centuries before colonial rule. Genealogies of chiefly families are often remembered in some depth, in order to show the relationships between living members of a dynasty. Thus it is often possible to make a rough estimate of the duration of time by reckoning in generations. And where genealogies are lacking it may still be possible to form some idea of time-depth from the number of chiefs who are said to have succeeded each other. At the same time, we must remember that most chiefly traditions are only likely to throw much light on the dynasties who maintain them. Traditions about earlier dynasties who have long since been defeated and dispersed are unlikely to survive. Thus what we can learn about particular chieftainship and dynasties in Zambia may not necessarily tell us much about the origin of chieftainship as an institution.

The Roots of Chieftainship

This point must be borne in mind as we turn to consider what in fact the traditions appear to tell us about early chiefs in Zambia. Among nearly all the peoples of central and north-eastern Zambia there is general agreement that the first chiefs came from the country of the Luba, in south-eastern Zaïre. In north-western Zambia traditions of chiefly origin point rather to the Lunda, in south-western Zaïre. These traditions are supported by the close resemblance in certain respects between Zambian chieftainships and those of the Luba and Lunda. There are, as we shall see, similarities in political ideas; there are also similarities in the vocabulary of political institutions, and in the insignia of chieftainship, such as iron bells and bowstands, and wooden slit signal, or 'talking', drums.

To judge from the genealogies and chief-lists of the dynasties which have survived in Zambia, it would seem that most of them were founded in the seventeenth or early eighteenth century. But we should not conclude from this evidence alone that hitherto chieftainship was more or less unknown in what is now Zambia. In the first place, knowledge of older chieftainships which have disappeared may have been suppressed or otherwise forgotten. In the second place, as we noted in the last chapter, stories of origin and migration are often to be interpreted as myths rather than as narratives about historical events and characters. A story of founding chiefs migrating from Zaïre may well be true in so far as it reflects the spread of peoples and ideas from that region, but it may well telescope into a single dramatic episode a series of events and processes which spanned a period of decades or even centuries. Finally, there are various positive indications that chieftainship existed in and around Zambia well before most of the present dynasties seem to have been established. It is worth considering this evidence before looking at the nature of Luba and Lunda influences, and the impact which these had in different parts of Zambia.

We have already seen, in Chapter 4, that there are a few archaeological sites which provide evidence for early chieftainship in central Africa. The oldest of these sites is in fact in Luba country: the cemetery at Sanga, near Lake Kisale in the Shaba province of Zaïre. Excavations there revealed fragments of single iron bells of a type which has long been known in the Zaïre basin as a symbol of chieftainship. These bells may be dated to about the twelfth century. The associated remains, including highly skilled copperwork, strongly suggest that by this time the area was indeed dominated by some sort of wealthy ruling group. Much the same conclusion may be drawn from two other sites, further south, where similar bells have been found and dated to a somewhat later period, around the fourteenth or fifteenth centuries: Ingombe Ilede and Great Zimbabwe. These may well be evidence for the southward expansion of an improved iron technology; they are certainly evidence for a southward expansion of trading contacts and political symbolism. For it is clear enough that these bells were adopted as symbols of power and wealth, and not simply as ingenious ornaments. This is sufficiently proved by the scale of stone-building at Great Zimbabwe, and the rich variety of goods, including exotic imports, found both there and at Ingombe Ilede.

As yet, we know too little about the relationship of these sites to each other, and to centres of trade and political power further north. But it is worth noting that oral traditions in Zaïre and Angola provide some evidence for the growth and expansion of large-scale chieftainship in Lunda country in or before the fifteenth century. This theory contradicts the long-held view that Lunda chieftainship was of little significance before the seventeenth century. Lunda traditions trace the origins of Lunda kingship to the marriage between a Lunda princess and a Luba hunter. This is said to have caused a dispersal of Lunda chiefs, both to the north-west and to the south, into what is now western Zambia, and it was long supposed that this dispersal could be dated to the sixteenth century. But recent analysis of Lunda traditions suggests that this 'Lunda love-story' refers, not to individual chiefs but rather to the movements of titled chieftainships – a process which may well have spanned two or three centuries. It thus seems very likely that some sort of kingdom, including a number of titled chiefs centred on a court, had emerged in Lunda country well before the fifteenth century, and that it was in this century, if not earlier, that Luba intervention stimulated the first major thrust of Lunda expansion.

There is, then, good reason to believe that kingdoms or chiefdoms had been established in areas close to what is now Zambia by the fifteenth century. And even though oral traditions within Zambia do seem for the most part to refer to a rather later period, they none the less provide a few clues to the existence of chiefs before the rise of the dynasties known today. In the north-east, in Bemba country, there is a dim memory of an early chief called Mulopwe, which is simply the usual Luba word for chief. There may well have been other chiefs in the region, now remembered only as names of *ngulu* spirits. In the lower Luapula valley it is believed that chiefs – in the sense of rulers who received tribute – were introduced by some of the first clans to settle in the valley after the Bwilile, and one of these chiefs, Lubunda, may have come from Lunda country. Finally, on the upper Zambezi, there are hints of some kind of chieftainship preceding the emergence of the main Luyana (Lozi) dynasty.

All in all, then, it seems quite possible that chieftainship may have been implanted in at least a few parts of Zambia by the sixteenth century, and that this owed something to influences emanating from the Luba and Lunda. But it is misleading to think of the origins of chieftainship, or any other custom or institution, simply in terms of diffusion from somewhere else. However important outside influences may be, they are unlikely to take root unless local conditions are favourable. To judge from what is known from other parts of Africa, we should think in terms, not so much of invasion and conquest, but rather of newcomers acquiring authority by virtue of techniques and ideas which were found to be both attractive and adaptable. We may suppose that here and there the resources of lineage and clan organisa- tion proved unequal to the resolution of long-standing feuds, or to the efficient exploitation of the natural environment. And to an ambitious leader seeking to entrench his power there was considerable appeal in certain features of chieftainship as it developed among the Luba and Lunda. A brief account of these may go some way towards explaining why from the seventeenth century, if not earlier, chieftainship spread so widely across Zambia.

The most important political idea of the Luba was their belief that the ability to rule was essentially an inborn quality, which could only be transmitted through a single line of descent, whether male or female. In practice, of course, there were several such royal lineages or clans: the important point is that within any one kingdom all the chiefs should ideally belong to the same lineage as the king. The problem facing early Luba kings was to establish the idea of kingship: to create a central focus for large-scale government where none had previously existed. Among peoples whose social organisation was regulated on lines of kinship, one obvious way to create a central focus was to make one particular family the source of political authority, so that the bonds of family relationship served to link all parts of the kingdom together. And if this idea suited the king, it also lent prestige to chiefs: in so far

as chieftainship was confined to a single royal line, it was more exclusive; it also meant that chiefs might have opportunities to inherit senior
positions within the kingdom, including the kingship itself.

This conception of political authority undoubtedly played an
important part in the growth and spread of kingship and chieftainship
among the Luba and their neighbours. But it is easy to see the drawbacks of relying so heavily on a theory of divine right. Within a royal
lineage all the men had inherited the ability to rule; they were thus
likely to suppose that they had also inherited the right to rule, and over
the course of time such royal kinsmen naturally increased in number.
There would thus be competition for succession both to the kingship
and to the subordinate chieftainships. So Luba kingdoms were often
split by internal dynastic conflicts and unsuccessful claimants might
well secede to set up their own kingdoms.

Here, then, was a problem of political integration: how to retain the
allegiance of chiefs and headmen in the relatively sparsely populated
woodland of the upper Zaïre basin. A somewhat different approach was
adopted by the Lunda. They placed much less emphasis than the Luba
on royal blood as a qualification for political office. Instead, they found
ways of associating non-royal officials with the royal family and giving
non-Lunda subjects key positions in the Lunda kingdom.

The most important Lunda idea was the notion of 'perpetual kinship' and the related custom of 'positional succession'. When a chief or
headman succeeded to a title, he regarded certain other title-holders
as 'father' or 'brother' or 'son', regardless of their actual relationship to
him. If, for example, the original holders of two Lunda titles had been
father and son, their respective successors would continue to regard
each other as father and son even if they were really quite distant
cousins. In other words, perpetual kinship linked titled positions rather
than individual people. In taking over such a position, a Lunda ruler
assumed the same ties of perpetual kinship as had bound his pre-
decessor. This held good even if the two men were not in fact kin at all,
which might be the case if the new title-holder was appointed to his
position instead of inheriting it. This custom is called 'positional
succession': an office-holder succeeds, not only to certain rights and
duties, but also to certain fixed social relationships. The succession is so
complete that the office-holder is actually identified with his predecessors: in a sense, he becomes them. Thus a Lunda kingdom ideally
consisted of a web of titled positions, linked in a hierarchy of perpetual
kinship, and occupied by men of quite diverse background and kinship
affiliation. In this way the familiar language of kinship was extended
far beyond the family or lineage. Strange and distant groups could be
assimilated into the circle of a more or less fictitious family, centred
on the king. Among peoples for whom kinship was a fundamental

principle, this was a most effective device for extending the range of social intercourse and enlarging the field of behaviour according to familiar rules.

The other major contribution of the Lunda was the importance they attached to 'owners of the land'. This was in fact a Luba idea, but the Lunda exploited it as a technique of imperial expansion. When a Lunda kingdom took over territory which had previously been ruled by an independent chief, he might be left in control of his own chiefdom but he would have to submit to the king's higher authority. The king, however, accorded him special respect, for it was believed that the spirits of the chief's ancestors continued to exert a supernatural power over his country. For this reason such a chief was called an 'Owner of the Land', and his position would normally be inherited by members of his own lineage. Some 'owners of the land' might be further attached to the kingdom by being given positions of perpetual kinship to the king, and by being assigned special functions in royal rituals. Together with other chiefs or headmen, they might form a group of councillors with an important part to play in the selection and appointment of kings and chiefs. Such councillors could act as an important check on the king, in so far as they were more concerned to uphold the dignity of kingship than to support individual kings, with all their human frailties.

The East and North-East

We have now reviewed what we know about the earlier history of kingship and chieftainship in and around Zambia. We have formed some idea as to how and when this hierarchical type of organisation may have begun to take root among the clans and lineage groups which at one time constituted the political structures of most Zambian societies. We may now begin to look at the outlines of political history as they can be traced through the traditions of kingdoms and chiefdoms which have lasted into the present century.

Perhaps the oldest of the surviving chiefly dynasties in Zambia is that of Undi, in the south-east. The Undi dynasty belongs to the matrilineal Phiri[1] clan, which may have reached what is now southern Malawi by the fourteenth century. The Phiri claim to be of Luba origin and to have come from the north. One of their leaders, Kalonga, established a kingdom at the south-western corner of Lake Malawi. This gradually expanded, and new chiefdoms were created as a result of marriages between Phiri women and local clan leaders. Some time in the sixteenth century, the first Undi, who was a brother of the ruling Kalonga, split off as a result of a succession dispute. Undi went west, and in due course set up his own capital at Mano. A Portuguese source indicates that an Undi was living there by 1614. In the course of time various subordinate chiefdoms were created for other members of the Phiri clan. Undi also came to levy tribute from a few non-Phiri kings, such as Mkanda, and he created a chieftainship for one of the Nsenga clans near the lower Luangwa. The important task of praying for rain was mostly reserved for special priests under the supreme authority of the priestess Makewana, who had probably been established well before Undi's arrival.

These political developments led to changes in 'tribal' identity. It would seem that the peoples of the Chewa language group, in eastern Zambia, Malawi and Mozambique, were once generally known as 'Bororo'. But those who came under the rule of Undi and Mkanda mostly became known as Chewa, in contrast to the Nyanja near Lake Malawi and the Mang'anja athwart the Shire valley. At the same time, the rulers of the Phiri clan were commonly called Maravi, and this name was often applied to their subjects as well. (It was for this reason that the name Malawi was eventually adopted for the modern nation.)

West of the Luangwa valley, as far as the upper Kafue basin, there are a great number of matrilineal chieftainships which trace their origins directly to Luba country. On the north-eastern plateau, between the Luangwa and the Luapula, two chiefly clans became especially prominent: these were the *ng'andu* (Crocodile) and *ng'ona* (Mushroom) clans. By the end of the seventeenth century, members of the Crocodile clan, under their leader Chitimukulu, established a kingdom among people who were probably already known as Bemba and were already ruled by small chiefs of Luba origin. Henceforward, the name Bemba was used of all the subjects of Chitimukulu.

At first the Bemba were of no great significance. They occupied woodland which was best cultivated by the *citemene* system: this meant that the population remained very scattered and produced little beyond their own needs. But it seems that the very poverty of Bemba country early provoked them to prey on their neighbours. They raided the Iwa and Mambwe for cattle, and by the early nineteenth century they were well known for their warlike behaviour. Furthermore, the Bemba kingdom retained an important degree of cohesion. It was based on ties of kinship, but these were manipulated in such a way as to counteract the pressures for secession. During the eighteenth century the king exercised very little authority over the other royal chiefs, but these retained a stake in the kingdom, for the kingship was circulated between the various royal lineages which held the main chieftainships. Succession wars were frequent, but they emphasised the underlying unity of the kingdom.

In the first half of the nineteenth century this pattern was modified: one of these royal lineages gained a monopoly of succession to the

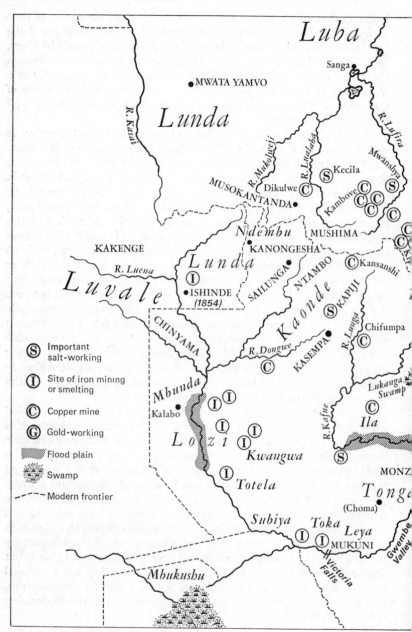

Luba

Sanga

• MWATA YAMVO

Lunda

R. Kasai

R. Mukulweji

R. Lualaba

R. Lufira

Mwanshya

Kecila ⑤

Kambove ⓒ ⓒ ⓒ

MUSOKANTANDA Dikulwe ⓒ

ⓒ ⓒ ⓒ

MUSHIMA

Ndembu

KANONGESHA

ⓒ Kansanshi

KAKENGE

Lunda

SAILUNGA

NTAMBO

ⓒ

Luvale

R. Luena

ⓘ

•ISHINDE
(1854)

CHINYAMA

Kaonde

⑤ KAPIJI

R. Lunga

Chifumpa

ⓒ

R. Dongwe

ⓒ

KASEMPA

**Important
salt-working** ⑤

**Site of iron mining
or smelting** ⓘ

Copper mine ⓒ

Gold-working ⓖ

Flood plain

Swamp

Modern frontier - - -

Lukanga
Swamp

ⓒ

Ila

R. Kafue

Mbunda

Kalabo •

ⓘ ⓘ

ⓘ

ⓘ ⓘ

Lozi

ⓘ

Kwangwa

⑤

MONZ

ⓘ

Totela

Tonga

(Choma)

Subiya   *Toka* *Leya*

ⓘ ⓘ MUKUNI

Gwembe Valley

Victoria Falls

Mbukushu

kingship. At the same time new conquests were made, and these provided other posts for the king's relations: one new chieftainship went to his brother, while another went to his son (who could not be feared as a rival). Thus power was increasingly concentrated within a small circle of the king's close relations, while the other lineages were no longer strong enough to pose an effective challenge. One other factor in the continued unity of the Bemba kingdom was the group of hereditary councillors (*bakabilo*) who lived around the capital. It was they who organised the rituals of kingship and determined the succession both to the kingship and to the senior chieftainships. They were all commoners, and thus they represented the people in upholding the ideal value of kingship as against individual kings.

It is clear that the growth of Bemba kingship made a considerable impact on older institutions. If there had previously been corporate lineages practising pawnship, these were reduced to insignificance as political and judicial business was taken over by lineages within the royal clan. The cult of royal ancestors either incorporated or supplanted the cult of *ngulu* spirits. These became to some extent a rival religious system; the *ngulu* spirits became increasingly mobile, inasmuch as they could possess ordinary people far from their own shrines. The growth of Bemba kingship also led to an unusual elaboration of the girls' puberty rites (*cisungu*): in this matrilineal society, such rites underlay the whole structure of rituals whereby the supernatural powers of Bemba rulers were maintained.

South of the Bemba the plateau was dominated by chiefs of the Mushroom clan. Their subjects all came to be known as Bisa. There was never any one Bisa kingdom, but three Bisa chiefs were especially important by the later eighteenth century: Mukungule, above the Muchinga escarpment; Mwansabamba, near the salt marshes of Chibwa; and the chief of Lubumbu, north of Lake Bangweulu, whose territory at this period was probably rather larger than that of the Bemba. Each of these chiefs had a few subordinate chiefs. Elsewhere in the region there were no comparable hierarchies. Around Lake Bangweulu there are a number of peoples – the Bena Mukulu, Bena Chishinga, Bena Ng'umbo – whose chiefs all belong to the Drum (*ng'oma*) clan, but they do not seem to have formed any binding alliances.

The growth of chieftainship among the Bisa and Bemba seems to have stimulated a further expansion of chiefs to the north-east and north-west. Nkuba, the senior chief of the Shila people at the south end of Lake Mweru, claims that his ancestor belonged to the Bemba royal family. The chiefs of the Senga people, on the upper Luangwa, trace their origins to the Bisa, and it was evidently this intrusion which gave the Senga a distinct identity, for in other respects they are clearly related to the Tumbuka people further east. There is a somewhat similar contrast between chiefs and commoners among the patrilineal peoples of the Malawi–Tanganyika Corridor, whose main affinities are with peoples further north, in what is now Tanzania. The Namwanga chiefly dynasty claims Bisa origin; the Iwa dynasty is an offshoot from the Namwanga; and the Mambwe dynasty of Nsokolo may have been founded by a fugitive Bemba. All three dynasties adopted the patrilineal descent observed by their subjects. South and west of Lake Tanganyika, chieftainships were founded as a result of a quite separate process of migration, mainly by Leopard clan chiefs from west of the lake. They established matrilineal chiefdoms among the Tabwa and western Lungu, who closely resemble the Bemba; they also founded a chiefdom among the eastern Lungu, who belong to the Corridor group.

In central Zambia, there are also many chieftainships which trace their origins to Luba immigrants. The chiefdoms of the Kaonde, in the basin of the east Lunga river, were established in the course of the eighteenth century by intruders from the north who belonged to several different clans. Among the Lamba, Aushi and Lala, the rise of chiefly dynasties seems to have been due to a common process of settlement by 'Luba' immigrants. Some Lala chiefs were probably established by the early seventeenth century, for Portuguese on the lower Zambezi heard at this period of 'Kankomba', which is a praise-name used by several Lala chiefs. But in much of this region chieftainship may have been little known before the late eighteenth century. It was mainly diffused by the *nyendwa* clan, which founded all the chiefdoms of the Ambo, Swaka and Lima, and all but one of the Soli chiefdoms. Even so, it was not until the later nineteenth century that the *nyendwa* gained control of all the Lala chieftainships, and they still remained more or less independent of each other. In general, the political history of central Zambia is characterised not by centralisation but by fission and migration. Around the end of the eighteenth century there was a considerable eastward movement across the middle Luangwa, and this seems to account for certain chiefs and commoner families among the Nsenga and Kunda.

The South

The southward spread of Luba-derived chieftainship across central Zambia stopped short of the lower Kafue river. It would seem to have taken root mainly among peoples whose languages and institutions were already more or less closely associated with those of the Luba. It made very little impact among the Bantu Botatwe, or Tonga-speaking peoples, of southern Zambia. There were a few exceptions. The Soli, as we have just seen, mostly came under the rule of *nyendwa* chiefs. The Lenje, east of the Lukanga swamp, have a chief, Mukuni, who claims

Luba origin. It is also said that the first Mukuni went west to found a chieftainship among the Leya, near the Victoria Falls. By and large, however, the peoples of southern Zambia were unaffected by traditions of Luba chieftainship. If these peoples did come under much pressure from Luba-style chiefs, they may well have been able to offer resistance. Not only were they culturally more remote from them than were peoples further north; many of the southern peoples occupied relatively favourable land for farming and grazing, and may have formed denser settlements than were common elsewhere.[2] It is also likely that the various local cults provided at least as efficient a means of resolving disputes as small-scale Luba chieftainship could provide.

Whatever the truth in this speculation, chieftainship of any kind seems to have been uncommon among the Ila and Tonga until well into the nineteenth century. This is one reason why little is known of their pre-colonial history. Lacking dynasties or other deep lineages, their perspectives of the past have probably always been extremely fore-shortened. What we do know suggests that this southernmost part of Zambia, in contrast to the rest of the country, has been much affected by migration from the south. It is likely that the name Tonga, which was adopted by, or applied to, the inhabitants of the plateau and middle Zambezi valley, was originally used only of peoples south of the Zambezi; some of these then fled northwards across the river, to escape Shona chiefs, and the name came with them. Some of these refugees would at first have settled among Bantu Botatwe people in the Gwembe valley, but these have long been subject to recurrent famines which have prompted migration onto the plateau. This in turn provoked a gradual drift westwards on the plateau. Such conditions of continued migration and dispersal could well have favoured the gradual absorption of outsiders. The Goba (valley) people near the Zambezi–Kafue confluence are southern immigrants who retain their Shona dialect and have not been fully assimilated by the indigenous peoples on the north bank.

The North-West

In contrast to the great number of Zambian chieftainships claiming Luba origin, there are few which are derived, in one way or another, from the Lunda. Among these few, however, are two of the most important Zambian kingdoms: that of the eastern Lunda, on the Luapula, and that of the Lozi, on the upper Zambezi. And in most cases the links with the Lunda are much clearer than those with the Luba. The traditions of Luba origin speak of Luba country only in the vaguest terms, and it is virtually impossible to relate them to particular Luba kingdoms and chiefdoms. This is at least partly because Zambian chiefdoms maintained no links, whether in the form of travel, trade or tribute, with Luba country. Almost all the Lunda-derived dynasties, on the other hand, trace their origin to a place well known to history: the capital of the Lunda king Mwata Yamvo. And some Lunda-derived dynasties kept up the connection by maintaining contacts with Mwata Yamvo.

The traditions of Lunda origin should not, of course, be uncritically accepted, any more than those of Luba origin. This point is especially important in the case of Luvale chieftainship, on the borders of Zambia and Angola. Luvale and Lunda traditions suggest that this was a direct offshoot of the Lunda kingdom. It now seems most likely that the relationship was in fact rather distant. As we saw earlier, there was probably some Luba intervention in the Lunda kingdom in or before the fifteenth century. This caused two chiefs, with the titles Kinguri and Kinyama, to move to the south-west. This may be how chieftain-ship of a kind first took root among the ancestors of the Chokwe and Luvale people. But it was evidently slow to establish itself. It is fairly clear that the first holder of what is now the senior Luvale title, Kakenge, lived no earlier than the early eighteenth century. The very fact that the Kakenge dynasty is matrilineal implies that it was founded by Luvale, for Lunda dynasties are patrilineal.

Indeed, the whole character of Luvale chieftainship was rather different from that of the Lunda. No kingdom was established. The Kakenge dynasty monopolised chieftainship (and both men and women could succeed), but as so often among the Luba chiefdoms, junior members of the dynasty split off and became more or less independent. By the end of the eighteenth century, a new chieftainship, Chinyama, was rather more important than Kakenge, and other rival chieftainships emerged during the nineteenth century. Even so, many Luvale remained outside the jurisdiction of their chiefs. Commoner lineage groups continued to play an important role in politics, and clan membership counted for more than attachment to a particular territory. The growth of 'tribal identity' among the Luvale (or Luena, as the northern Luvale are called) certainly owed something to the growth of the Kakenge dynasty, but it probably owed no less to their distinctive, and unusually mobile, way of life, based on hunting and fishing rather than semi-permanent agricultural settlements.

East of the Luvale, along the Zaïre–Zambezi watershed, the Lunda kingdom made a rather greater impact. During the first half of the eighteenth century there was a great movement of Lunda colonisation and conquest through the country south-east of Mwata Yamvo's capital. Here there were a number of small chiefdoms akin to those of the Luba. The Lunda recruited support by granting honorary Lundahood to some of the more prominent leaders, and a few even became 'perpetual sons' of Mwata Yamvo. Two such leaders, Ishinde and Kanongesha, moved south from the Mukolweji river and founded chieftainships on the headwaters of the Zambezi, among the Lukolwe peoples, whom they called Mbwela. These 'Lunda-ised' intruders, together with their followers, called themselves Ndembu, and this name was adopted by their subjects. However, the unity imposed by the Ndembu chiefs was primarily ritual in character; they made few demands on the Mbwela. And the Ndembu chiefs retained a strong sense of being Lunda. They observed the Lunda custom of patrilineal descent, even though the Mbwela were matrilineal; and they continued to regard their 'father' Mwata Yamvo as their overlord: there is a record of Kanongesha sending tribute to him in 1802.

Around the headwaters of the Lualaba, Lunda adventurers encountered some of the first chiefs of what are now the Kaonde people. So great, indeed, was the prestige of Mwata Yamvo by the early eighteenth century that one Kaonde chief, Mushima, had at his own request been invested with a Lunda title by the Lunda king. This did not, however, help him very much, for Musokantanda, a 'perpetual son' of Mwata Yamvo, attacked and defeated Mushima. Musokantanda made himself overlord of the northern Kaonde and in due course appointed another Lunda chief, Sailunga, to collect tribute from Kapiji and Ntambo, two Kaonde chiefs. Further south, Musokantanda's authority was seldom acknowledged, and he never subdued Kasempa, who became the leading Kaonde chief.

The Kingdom of Kazembe

It was in the Luapula valley, about 800 kilometres east of Mwata Yamvo's capital, that the Lunda empire made its greatest impact on what is now Zambia. This eastward thrust seems to have owed its first impetus to a search for salt – a rare commodity in west-central Africa. Early in the eighteenth century the Lunda seized the salt pans at Kecila, on the upper Lualaba. They were helped by a man called Nganda Bilonda, and Mwata Yamvo rewarded him with the honorific title of Kazembe. Kazembe pushed on eastwards to the Lufira river. He would thus have gained control of the copper mines around Kambove and the salt pans at Mwanshya. His successor as Kazembe was given charge by Mwata Yamvo of the whole region of Lunda conquest east of the Lualaba. Around 1740 Kazembe II invaded the lower Luapula valley; he defeated the Bwilile and the chiefs of Shila and he made a capital for his new kingdom near the south end of Lake Mweru. Here he was well beyond the reach of his overlord, Mwata Yamvo, but he continued to send tribute to him, in salt and copper, for by now Mwata Yamvo had access to European goods from the west coast and

Kazembe was anxious to maintain a share in this trade. The Lunda claim that they brought guns to the Luapula; they had no bullets, but the mere sound of firing was enough to terrify the local people. More important, an American root crop, cassava, reached the Luapula from the west, and by the end of the eighteenth century it had become the staple crop around Kazembe's capital.

The economy of the lower Luapula was a major factor in the continued power of Kazembe's kingdom. For 150 kilometres south of Lake Mweru, the river meanders through a broad valley. Much of this is permanently under water, but there are patches of fertile alluvial soil between the valley and the wooded plateaux beyond it. The river itself abounds in fish, while there was once plenty of game along the valley margins. Thus the lower Luapula has long attracted human settlement. Immigration was further encouraged when cassava was introduced, since this is a highly convenient crop for fishermen with little time to spend in their fields. The security offered by Kazembe's government also proved an attraction, and in time the heartland of this eastern Lunda kingdom became quite thickly populated. The river simplified communications; both land and water yielded a modest food surplus; and it was relatively easy to establish a fairly centralised form of government.

The structure of Kazembe's kingdom resembled that of Mwata Yamvo's. Succession to the kingship was restricted to one dynastic line and usually went from father to son. Other members of the dynasty might be given appointments at court or on the battlefield, but they were excluded from any important hereditary posts in territorial administration. The central part of the kingdom, in and around the lower Luapula valley, was divided into districts, each under a titled governor. The governors' titles were usually hereditary and remained within non-royal Lunda lineages. The governors held judicial courts, but their main task was the collection of tribute. This was forwarded to the capital, where Kazembe redistributed much of it among the governors: the court was a clearing-house where the products of the river were exchanged for those of the surrounding woodland. Kazembe's governors liked to say that their work, when visiting the royal capital, was 'to drink beer': they discussed high politics over long beer-drinks with the king, but they also shared in the royal tribute. It was the governors who played the leading part in choosing and installing a new king. Beneath them came hereditary village headmen, most of whom belonged to the various matrilineal peoples who had long inhabited the region. The senior headmen were respected as 'owners of the land' and were often invested with Lunda insignia: a skirt and cowhide belt. Further afield, chiefs who submitted to Kazembe were allowed to retain their authority so long as they paid tribute: some of them also became honorary Lunda. At all levels both Lunda and non-Lunda title-holders were linked by ties of perpetual kinship. There was no standing army, but in time of war both the governors and Kazembe himself raised sizeable conscript armies.

Thus despite its great extent, Kazembe's kingdom achieved a remarkable cohesion. Yet one of its most striking features was the way in which this unity co-existed with, and indeed contributed to, the continuing diversity among Kazembe's people. The kingdom was essentially a conquest state. The intruding Lunda adopted the Bemba speech of their subjects, but Lunda survived as a court language, and the Lunda themselves remained a small and distinct group, jealous of their special privileges. The judicious grant of Lundahood to important subjects only served to emphasise that the Lunda were rulers, and rulers, Lunda. Besides, the Lunda governed a variety of peoples with different cultural and political traditions – not only Bwilile and Shila, but groups of Aushi, Chishinga, Mukulu and even Bemba. The kingship of Kazembe united them in a common obedience, but it also gave a special importance to their differences. In the heartland, there was keen competition for space to fish and hunt in the enclosed valley floor. The various clan-sections had a strong interest in maintaining claims to particular areas of land, and they sought to uphold these by gaining honour and influence at the king's court. At the same time, these subject groups could never, as groups, become Lunda, and those who had arrived from the plateaux retained a sense of belonging to their original tribes: indeed, this was especially true of the Lunda themselves. It is this remarkable diversity in unity which largely accounts for the keen interest in history which foreigners have long observed in Kazembe's kingdom: history helps to emphasise both the common bonds provided by the kingship and the separate identities and interests of the component groups.

The Lozi Kingdom

The Lozi kingdom, on the upper Zambezi, makes an interesting contrast with that of Kazembe. Both kingdoms developed an imperial structure, and both were favoured by a relatively prosperous valley environment which encouraged dense settlement. But whereas Kazembe's kingdom also owed much to its Lunda origins, that of the Lozi owed little to the Lunda. There are hints in Lozi tradition of an early link with Mwata Yamvo, but Lozi kingship, like Luvale chieftainship, was probably the result of a quite gradual process of migration from the north. Some time in the later seventeenth century the first remembered king settled near Kalabo, where the indigenous Luyana-speaking people had a shrine for their cult of the High God, Nyambe. This cult was incorporated in a new cult of kingship: in time the first Lozi king was widely believed to have been descended from Nyambe.[3]

This Lozi myth expressed an important truth: where the dynasty came from mattered much less than the character of the land they colonised. The great formative influence on the Lozi kingdom was the flood plain of the upper Zambezi. This is a sharply enclosed area of fertile land surrounded by the poor soils typical of western Zambia. During the dry season, when the river is low, the plain affords good grazing for cattle, and comparatively rich alluvial soil for cultivation; there are also patches of very favourable land along the plain margins. Thus parts of the plain have long supported unusually dense and stable settlements, in marked contrast to the scattered population of the surrounding woodland. Within the plain, people could cultivate the same plot year after year: when they moved, it was only as part of an annual migration between permanent settlements on the margins and on the plain itself. For as the flood-waters rise towards the end of the wet season, settlements on the plain become islands and must be abandoned. In the central part of the plain, this retreat (known as *kuomboka*) has long been led by the Lozi king himself, in an impressive procession of barges and boats across the plain to a winter capital on the eastern margin.

In the early days of the Lozi dynasty, the flood plain was mostly governed by relatives of the king, but in the eighteenth century they were replaced by a kind of royal bureaucracy. This development, unusual anywhere in Africa, was made possible by the plain itself. Specific plots of land there came to be valued as a means of supporting large groups of followers. There was competition for control over them, and they could be shared out, like cattle, as political spoils. The king, as guardian of the land, could build up a following of loyal officials by allotting them estates on the plain; furthermore, these estates were assigned, not to individuals, but rather to the offices they held: when they fell from favour, they lost both job and land. In this way, Lozi kings had an opportunity to make political appointments on the basis of personal merit rather than birth. This was a source of great strength in facing their rivals both within and outside the kingdom.

There were three main classes of Lozi officials, all of whom were commoners. First, there were the officials of the royal household. Some of these performed ritual duties similar to those of courtiers at other African capitals, but there were others with specific practical tasks, such as the storage of tribute goods, or the building of royal barges and canoes. Second, there were territorial governors. These acted mainly as judges, for there was a third class, the *makolo* chiefs, each of whom controlled a group of people for purposes of raising an army, collecting tribute and recruiting labour. Economic organisation loomed very large in Lozi government. Lozi kings sought to tap the resources both of the plain and of the surrounding woodland. The plain could yield sorghum, root crops, fish, cattle, otter skins and basketwork; but the woodland provided iron, woodwork, bark-cloth, bark-rope, fishnets, wild fruits, honey, salt and game. It was thus important to levy tribute as widely as possible. Besides, the efficient exploitation of the flood plain called for communal labour on public works: to dig channels, build fish-weirs and dams, and amass mounds that would raise villages above the annual flood-waters.

The various officials all belonged to a great central council which met from time to time at the capital. This was too large a body to meet very often, but most matters of importance were discussed by the more senior officials, meeting in two inner councils. The most senior council members, led by the *ngambela* (prime minister), also had regular meetings with the king. Thus major political decisions usually reflected a compromise between the king himself and the various ranks of appointed officials. The royal family – apart from the king – had very little power. Princes and princesses might intrigue at court, but they were excluded from political office. There was one major exception. As a concession to the great length of the kingdom, the sixth king created a southern capital which was usually occupied by a son or daughter of the king. To some extent this became a focus for rivalry and opposition, but a variety of checks and balances helped to keep it firmly linked to the senior northern court.

Lozi government, then, was centralised to a remarkable degree. The inhabitants of the flood plain were involved in a complex web of economic and political ties which linked them all to the councils at the king's capital. This gave them a strong sense of being a single people, the Lozi. But the Lozi kingdom was not confined for long to the flood plain and its margins. In the mid-eighteenth century, under their sixth king, Ngombala, the Lozi made extensive conquests among their more scattered and less organised neighbours, such as the Mbukushu in the west, and the Subiya and Toka in the south-east. The main purpose of these conquests was to enforce the regular collection of tribute in the woodland areas beyond the plain. This task was supervised by Lozi officials posted to the courts of subject chiefs, who were otherwise left more or less independent. In this way the Lozi kingdom took on an imperial aspect: it consisted of a highly centralised heartland, inhabited by the Lozi themselves, surrounded by a larger but more loosely controlled region inhabited by subject peoples such as the Mbunda, the Kwangwa and the Totela.

At first this imperial expansion proved very profitable to the Lozi monarchy. The seventh king, Yubya, was notoriously extravagant: his wife used to bathe in milk and once asked, 'What is it to lack?' But the growing body of Lozi officials felt they knew this all too well. Many, of course, had estates in the plain, but they also wanted a share of royal tribute, and they were not content to depend on the king's whim for occasional gifts. Yubya was obliged to allow his officials to retain a share of the tribute they collected. Around the end of the eighteenth century further concessions were made by the tenth king, Mulambwa, who granted certain legal as well as economic privileges to his senior chiefs. Already, the bureaucracy created to execute the king's will was showing a will of its own. To counteract this, Mulambwa sought to cultivate the support of certain subject peoples, especially the Mbunda. Inevitably, this created new tensions and rivalries within the kingdom, between the Lozi themselves and the non-Lozi. Such tensions played an important part in the internal upheavals of the Lozi kingdom in the nineteenth century.

NOTES

1. Pronounced 'Piri'.
2. See pp. 135–8.
3. For the sake of simplicity, I refer to this kingdom as 'Lozi' from its foundation, though 'Lozi' is in fact the word applied to the Luyana (or Lui) people by their Kololo conquerors in the nineteenth century.

VII

The Expansion of Trade
c. 1700 – c. 1840

Up to the eighteenth century the principal forces for change in what is now Zambia were African in origin. Social and economic patterns had been shaped by a continuing flow of peoples and ideas across the central African woodland. Zambia itself was remote from either coast and long remained unaffected by either Arab or European activities. The outside world valued tropical Africa mainly for its gold, ivory and slaves, and it was not until the eighteenth century that the search for these commodities was carried into the unknown country north of the middle Zambezi.

The immediate stimulus to this expansion of overseas trade came from settlements on the east and west coasts. Arabs and Swahili on the east coast had long sought ivory and gold for export to India. By the seventeenth century the gold trade of Rhodesia had been taken over by traders based on the Portuguese colony of Mozambique; during the eighteenth century they also gained a major share in the ivory trade with India and began exporting slaves to islands in the Indian ocean. On the west coast the Portuguese in Angola sold slaves to sugar planters in Brazil, and in the course of the eighteenth century they extended their supplies by buying slaves from Africans in the interior. But in meeting the demand for such export commodities, African initiatives were also important. To understand how Zambian peoples formed links with traders in touch with markets overseas, we must first consider the trade which they had already developed among themselves. This chapter, then, begins with a discussion of local trade within what is now Zambia before moving on to examine the growth of overseas trade, mainly but not entirely through the Portuguese, during the eighteenth and early nineteenth centuries.

Local Trade

It has too often been supposed that trade in Africa only began with the export of gold, ivory and slaves. These were only the most glamorous and horrific results of a long process of economic interaction between African societies, as well as between Africa and the outside world. For most people in Zambia, as elsewhere, the important items of trade were local products which met everyday needs: foodstuffs, metalwork, pottery, clothing, cosmetics. There was no money, but some goods, such as wire, copper crosses, beads and cloth, were occasionally used as currency, since they were in general demand and could be exchanged for the goods which a buyer really wanted. There were no regular markets, but the courts of chiefs could serve as centres for redistributing the varied tribute levied from their subjects. As we have seen, such redistribution was a prominent feature of the Lozi kingdom and Kazembe's. Even in less favourable environments, as in Bemba country, chiefs were able to increase their power by promoting the exchange of local products, as well as by outright raiding.

Whatever form it took, such local trade largely determined the capacity of Zambian societies to take part in long-distance trade. Patterns of local exchange and industry shaped and sustained the trade routes between the African interior and the coast. Conversely, the growth of coastal trade could stimulate the production of goods for consumption within African societies as well as goods for export overseas. Indeed, this point must be borne in mind as we turn to survey the main outlines of trade within Zambia. Much of our evidence comes from European visitors, such as David Livingstone, in the second half of the nineteenth century. During this period economic life was increasingly affected by the trade in ivory and slaves. Nevertheless, the location of the most important resources, especially iron and salt, give us some clue to likely patterns of trade in earlier times, for such basic materials would long have been in great demand.

In north-eastern Zambia the growth of the Bemba kingdom, as well as Kazembe's, seems to have stimulated extensive exchanges across the plateau between the Luapula and Luangwa. In this thickly wooded country iron was particularly important. There was little workable iron ore within Bemba country itself, but there were several sources on its borders. To the north both the Lungu and Mambwe were well known as iron-workers. Lungu smiths came to settle under Bemba chiefs, to whom they paid tribute in hoes and axes. In Mambwe country, in 1879, there were eight furnaces on one hillside, each capable of smelting nearly half a tonne of iron ore. To the east, iron was smelted by the Iwa of Kafwimbi, and by a small group known as Sukuma. There were a few smelters in Bisa country, but the southern Bisa obtained their iron from the Lala, whose output was famous for its quality and quantity: there was a particularly large open mine in the country of chief Mailo. The Bemba probably gained access to Lala ironwork only in the 1880s: more important for them were the industries west of Lake Bangweulu.

Those of the Chishinga chief, Chama, were especially productive, though smelting was also practised close to Kazembe's capital. Further south there were two centres of iron production in Aushi country, but the supply was sufficient only to meet the demands of the Aushi themselves.

Salt was scarcer than iron. Many dambos furnished a saline grass which was burnt to yield a salty ash for immediate and local use, but there were only two places in the north-east where salt was produced in any quantity. One was Chibwa marsh, near Mpika. Here there is a great abundance of rich saline grass, which yields a remarkably pure salt. This was noted by a Portuguese explorer in 1832; both Bemba and Bisa were making salt, and it commanded a high price. For the last two months in the dry season, people from the surrounding country would come to make salt at Chibwa. Each worker had to pay a ball of salt to the local chief, and when the Bemba took over the area he in turn had to send a hundred cakes every year to the Bemba king and to another senior chief. Intensive salt production also took place near the north end of Lake Mweru: there are several outcrops of saline soil near chiefs Puta and Kaputa. These were mostly worked by the local Bwile and Tabwa people, who sold the salt in standard loads of about eleven kilos.

The exchange of iron and salt promoted the exchange of other commodities. Both Bemba and Bisa sold salt and iron to the Senga, on the upper Luangwa, who in return supplied tobacco, mats and baskets, and also grain and cotton. The Senga and Tambo wove cloth from their own cotton, and so did the Lungu, who sometimes paid tribute in cotton to the Bemba. The Bemba themselves were well known for their skill in making bark cloth; this was the usual material component of marriage payments, and some may well have been traded to neighbours in less densely wooded areas lacking in the necessary trees. The Unga, in the swamps of Lake Bangweulu, and the Bisa in Lubumbu exported dried fish, nets, mats and baskets; otter skins were traded all round the north and east of the lake, and the Unga exchanged fish and antelope meat for ironwork from the Bena Mukulu. Cattle and other livestock were unimportant in plateau trade since they could be bred only in tsetse-free areas. The Bisa chief Mungulube had some cattle at one time, but the only people who kept herds of any size were the Lungu, Mambwe and Iwa. The Bemba, however, frequently raided these peoples for cattle, and they sometimes levied tribute from them in cattle, sheep and goats. Such levies increased the ability of Bemba chiefs to attract a following and thus, indirectly, to draw tribute from their own people.

In central Zambia, trade tended to gravitate towards the middle Zambezi, along the lower reaches of the Luangwa and Kafue rivers.

Since the early Iron Age, the main centre of iron production in this region had been east of Lusaka. In the nineteenth century the Soli were well known for their skill as smelters and smiths, and many iron-smelting furnaces can still be seen along the upper Chongwe valley. On the lower Luangwa, much iron was imported from the Nsenga, around Petauke: we have records of this trade for the years around 1760 and again in 1860–1. At the latter date iron also reached the lower Luangwa from the Lala and the north-western Chewa. Further west, iron was always scarce. Despite the Soli industry, wooden hoes were still being used in the mid-nineteenth century on the lower Kafue and over the Batoka plateau.

Salt was produced on the Lusitu river, near the mouth of the Kafue: Livingstone noted that it was 'sold in large quantities and very cheap',[1] and some may have been bought by the Nsenga in exchange for their iron. There were several salt deposits along the north bank of the Zambezi, between the Kafue and the Luangwa, but there was very little salt in eastern Zambia. Late in the nineteenth century salt was produced for sale in Ila country, to the south of Mumbwa. Cotton was grown and woven by the Nsenga; in 1860 it was also grown by Zezuru immigrants on the Chongwe river and by the We, below the Kariba gorge, though they themselves had little use for clothes. Further up the Zambezi the valley Tonga supplied red ochre and bamboo to the plateau Tonga in return for tools and weapons which the latter made from imported iron.

Trade in western Zambia was dominated from the later eighteenth century by the Lozi kingdom, on the upper Zambezi. As we have seen, the Lozi capital was the focus for the exchange of a wide variety of products from the flood plain and the surrounding woodland. Two items were specially important. The Totela supplied a redwood suitable for boat-building; and both they and the Kwangwa smelted and forged iron obtained from mines in the dambos east of the plain. The work of these smiths was highly praised by an English trader in 1853: he reported that they smelted an abundance of iron:

of a very superior quality, and manufacture it into implements, which considering their rude materials, would astonish any Europeans. Hoes, spears, lances, battle-axes, bows and arrows, are abundant and cheap, of excellent workmanship, and are even chased and ornamented.[2]

A Czech traveller later remarked of the Totela that 'After the Zulus they are probably the best native iron-workers in Southern Africa.'[3] The Totela also supplied ironwork far to the west, to the Mbukushu on the Okavango river; in the east, they sold it to the Tonga and the Ila. North of the Victoria Falls iron had been smelted in the early Iron Age at Kumadzulo and Dambwa. There are many remains of smelters in this area at sites which were occupied in the last few centuries. Those around Kumadzulo may well have been used by Toka in the mid-nineteenth century, but the smelters further east seem by that time to have been abandoned. In the far north-west the Ndembu obtained iron from mines in chief Ishinde's country, while there were iron mines in Luvale country between Balovale and Kabompo.

There were two main sources of salt in western Zambia. One was at Basanga, at the western end of the Kafue Flats; when the flood-waters recede a saline soil can be scooped up from the edge of the plain. The local Ila traded this salt to the Totela in exchange for ironwork. Over three hundred kilometres to the north, at Kaimbwe near Kasempa, plenty of good salt was obtained from a hot spring; some of this was exported eastwards to the Lamba. Salt reached the Lozi flood plain from the Nkoya and pans to the west. The Luvale extracted salt from grass in several places, but produced only enough for their own needs. The Luvale did export pottery; this was a rare commodity on the upper Zambezi and some Luvale pots were taken as far south as the Victoria Falls.

The Copper Trade

In some parts of Zambia, copper was also an item in local trade, though as it is softer than iron it was much less useful. The Kaonde sometimes made hoe blades and spearheads from copper, but such practical uses were exceptional for iron served these purposes far better. Copper was seldom used to make anything but ornaments, especially bracelets and anklets. Nonetheless, the demand for these can be traced back to the early Iron Age. Copper was imported to the Victoria Falls area in about the sixth century, while copper ornaments found at Chondwe, near Ndola, may belong to much the same period.[4] Copper bangles were worn by people at the mouth of the Kafue in the 1690s, and copper bars and bracelets served as a form of currency in Kazembe's kingdom around 1800.

In most of these cases the copper would have come from outside Zambia: people along the north bank of the Zambezi imported it from across the river, while Kazembe levied tribute from mines in Shaba.[5] But as we saw in Chapter 3, copper has been produced as well as used in Zambia since the early Iron Age: at Kansanshi, copper was being mined by about the fifth century, and there are several other sites of African copper mining in north-western and central Zambia. At Bwana Mkubwa, near Ndola, one African working was nearly one kilometre long and up to forty-eight and a half metres deep. There were also a great many workings between Mumbwa and the Hook of the Kafue, some of them up to twelve metres deep and fifteen metres wide. Elsewhere in the north-west there were smaller copper mines at Chifumpa, near Kasempa, and on the lower reaches of the Mwom-bezhi and Dongwe rivers. In central Zambia there were small workings at Kachyoba, near Lusaka; Kalulu near Rufunsa; and near the river Lukasashi.

These old workings – some of which are still visible – testify to the importance of copper in pre-colonial trade. African miners seem to have pushed their quest for copper to the limits imposed by their simple techniques.[6] They located copper ores by searching for outcrops of malachite (copper carbonate), and their diligence greatly impressed J. A. Bancroft, the geologist chiefly responsible for the discovery of the ore-bodies now worked on the Copperbelt:

> I can testify to their thoroughness; there are very few outcrops containing copper minerals that they did not find and test for the possible production of malachite.[7]

Clearly, then, there was a considerable demand for copper from Zambian mines as well as from Shaba and the mines south of the Zambezi. It is not, however, clear just where this demand was coming from. We know that Kansanshi was exploited most intensively some time between about the fifteenth and eighteenth centuries: this is proved by radio-carbon samples from the longest trench and from a thick layer of smelting debris. But it is not yet known where the copper went; perhaps Kansanshi supplied Lunda trading networks to the north. In the later eighteenth century, as we shall see, copper was sold to Portuguese agents at Zumbo, by the Luangwa–Zambezi confluence. This copper was brought from the north-west: it may have come from Bwana Mkubwa, and perhaps also from some of the smaller mines closer to the Zambezi and Luangwa. It is indeed possible that before the nineteenth century long-distance trade provided the main stimulus to copper production within Zambia. Local demands for Zambian copper may have been quite restricted until the late nineteenth century, when the rapid growth of trade expanded the market for all kinds of local products, including copper ornaments.[8]

The Portuguese at Zumbo

It was not copper, however, but the search for gold which brought about the first substantial contacts between what is now Zambia and the world overseas. For until the later eighteenth century it was mainly gold which attracted traders from overseas to east-central Africa. Slaves in this region were wanted for use within Africa rather than for export abroad. Copper and ivory were in some demand, but this was not yet keen enough to sustain trade without the further stimulus of gold. And the main sources of gold lay along the great granite ridge which runs across what is now Rhodesia. This gold, produced by African miners, was being exported to Arabs on the coast by the tenth century. It played an important part in the trade of the western Indian Ocean, in the rise of towns on the East African coast, and in the growth of a kingdom centred on the stone buildings at Great Zimbabwe. The main route to the coast lay south of the goldfields, probably along the Limpopo river. It is very likely that by the fifteenth century, if not earlier, gold was also being exported down the Zambezi valley: this is strongly suggested by the remains at Ingombe Ilede, which may well have been visited by Arab or Swahili traders. But Ingombe Ilede was essentially a western outpost of the gold regions. By 1500 the numerous Muslims who ventured inland were concentrated around the capital of Mwenemutapa, which was situated some distance to the east, lower down the Zambezi.

It was the Portuguese in Mozambique who first began to involve parts of Zambia in regular trade with the outside world.[9] In the course of the sixteenth and early seventeenth centuries, the Portuguese ousted the Muslims from the gold trade of central Africa. At first, like the Muslims, they ignored the country north of the middle Zambezi, since it seemed to have no gold. But in about 1684 the Rozwi king drove the Portuguese right off the Rhodesian plateau and back to their bases at Tete and Sena on the lower Zambezi. Thereafter the Rozwi dominated the gold trade south of the Zambezi, and the Portuguese began to take a new interest in the country on the north bank. By 1696 traders from Tete seem to have reached the lower Lunsemfwa valley, west of the Luangwa, and the mouth of the Kafue: they brought back ivory, gold and copper. A few years later a trading post was founded at Zumbo, to the east of the Luangwa–Zambezi confluence, by traders from the Portuguese colony of Goa, in western India. In 1732 another post was opened at Feira, across the Luangwa. Through their agents at Zumbo and Feira, the Portuguese succeeded in re-opening the gold trade with the Rozwi, but they also looked further afield.

The leading personality at Zumbo was a Dominican priest, Father Pedro de Trinidade, who lived there for twenty-five years until his death in 1751. For much of this time he supervised the trade with the Rozwi across the river, but he also discovered gold about thirty-two kilometres east of Zumbo and set his slaves to work it. Fr Pedro became so rich and powerful that long after his death his spirit continued to speak through mediums to the local people. Quite possibly it was also in Fr Pedro's time that the old gold workings at Moiya, west of Zumbo, were first exploited. In any case, we know that by the middle of the century Zumbo was trading in Zambian copper. In 1762 it was reported that people from Lenje country

come every year to Zumbo to trade in ivory and in copper, which
they bring ready smelted in great bars, and of which there is great
abundance. For its quality it is preferred in India to that which
comes from Europe.[10]

During the height of this trade at Zumbo, perhaps as much as three
tonnes of copper and 500 ivory tusks were sold there in a year. They
were exchanged mainly for cloth, from Goa, though later in the century
this was supplemented by cloth made from cotton grown on Portuguese
estates on the lower Zambezi. Sometimes the 'Portuguese' traders (many
of whom were Indians from Goa) kept all their trade goods for buying
gold from the south, so that the Lenje had to go back with their ivory
and copper unsold. But in 1783 the Portuguese were sufficiently interested to send agents with Indian beads and cloth to buy ivory and
copper from the Lenje, and ivory from the Nsenga. By the 1790s
groups of Lamba, Ambo and possibly Lala were also trading with
Zumbo, while a good deal of ivory was reaching Zumbo from Simamba's,
in Tonga country west of the Kariba gorge. People as far west as the
Toka, near the Victoria Falls, were travelling to Zumbo by 1800; some
were said to have liked it so much that they never returned.

Nonetheless, conditions for trade at Zumbo were far from ideal.
There was no African ruler strong enough to keep the foreign traders in
order, and after Fr Pedro's death there were frequent conflicts between
Portuguese, Indians and the local people. Besides, Zumbo was a long
way from the coast, and transport costs often outweighed the profits to
be had from trade. Indeed, the very remoteness of Zumbo encouraged
the Portuguese to use it as a convict settlement, which did not make for
greater peace or prosperity. Then, in the late eighteenth century, the
Rozwi kingdom was troubled by droughts and internal disputes; these
interfered with the production and export of gold and Portuguese pur-
chases were drastically reduced. Meanwhile, the Portuguese at Zumbo
came under increasing pressure from their neighbours on the north
bank of the Zambezi. In 1804 Zumbo was destroyed by an Ambo or
Nsenga chief; two years later the Portuguese built a new fort, across the
Luangwa at Feira, but there were recurrent clashes with the Nsenga
chief Mburuma, and in 1836 both Feira and Zumbo were abandoned.
The Portuguese never reoccupied Feira, and the ruined walls which
can be seen there today testify to their last attempts to defend it in the
early nineteenth century.

Gold and the Chewa

It was not from Zumbo but from the southern Chewa kingdom of Undi
that the Portuguese first began to penetrate far into what is now Zambia.
Undi probably sold ivory to the Portuguese during the seventeenth

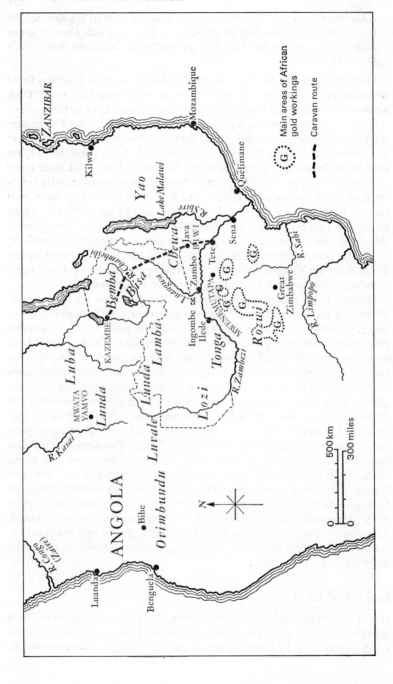

century, and such trade would help to account for the early expansion of his dominions. But in the first decades of the eighteenth century gold was discovered in the country around Tete, on the lower Zambezi, and this encouraged further exploration northwards. By about 1760, gold was found in Mano, Undi's own kingdom. There were also gold mines in the country of his subordinate Biwi, and in about 1790 gold was found at Java, in another tributary chiefdom. Around the same time, yet another gold mine was opened at Missale, in the country of Mkanda.

These discoveries proved disastrous for the southern Chewa. They do not seem ever to have mined the gold themselves and their chiefs allowed Portuguese, Indians and African slaves to settle round the mines and work them, in return for annual tribute. Such arrangements undermined Chewa political organisation. Undi lost any monopoly he may once have enjoyed over trade with the Portuguese, for they now dealt direct with the subordinate kings and chiefs closest to their mines. And even these rulers often failed to prevent Portuguese settlers from sending in their own hunters, armed with guns, to collect ivory regardless of the traditional rights of chiefs over big game. Nor was there any central control on the Portuguese side: the colonial government at Mozambique was quite unable to direct or restrain the activities of settlers in and around Tete. As a result, there was constant fighting between the Chewa and the Portuguese forces. By the end of the eighteenth century, the rush for gold and ivory left Undi with very little authority outside his own kingdom of Mano. Real power among the southern Chewa now lay largely with a family of Goan adventurers, the Pereiras. It was they who, in 1796, organised the first Portuguese expedition into north-eastern Zambia. But the initiative for this venture was African in origin.

Kazembe, the Yao and the Bisa

The growth of overseas trade in north-eastern Zambia was primarily a response to demands for ivory and copper, and it was the result of collaboration between the Lunda kingdom of Kazembe, its Bisa neighbours and the Yao people east of Lake Malawi. Kazembe's kingdom had been involved in long-distance trade ever since its foundation in the earlier eighteenth century. It was during this same period that Kazembe's suzerain, Mwata Yamvo, first obtained regular access to European goods from the west coast. Some of these were carried eastwards to Kazembe's capital on the Luapula, in exchange for salt and copper. By the later eighteenth century, Kazembe was also sending slaves to Mwata Yamvo, who exported them northwards to the lower Zaïre. But Kazembe's Lunda maintained the eastward impetus of their original migration. Indeed, it is possible that one of the motives for this migration had been a desire to trade directly with the Portuguese in the east, of whom rumours had reached the interior from the west coast. At all events, Kazembe III (reigned *c.* 1760–1804/5) subdued several chiefdoms east of the Luapula, among the Chishinga, Tabwa, Lungu and Bisa. By the end of the century, Kazembe's overrule was acknowledged as far east as the Chambeshi river. And in conjunction with Bisa traders Kazembe rapidly opened up trade routes leading to the east coast.

The details of this momentous development are still obscure, but two points are worth noting. In the first place, it is likely that the western Bisa had been active for some years in local trade. They occupied an ecological borderland, between the great swamps around Lake Bangweulu and the woodland of the Bemba plateau; in the nineteenth century, as we have seen, they traded extensively in the products of these regions. If they had thus acquired some experience of trade and travel, it would not be surprising that when they came under Kazembe's rule they should have become willing partners in his ivory and copper trade, especially since the Lunda regarded themselves as natural rulers rather than traders.

In the second place, it was clearly the Bisa who linked up Kazembe's trade with that of the Yao. By the middle of the eighteenth century, the Yao were well established as the leading African traders in east central Africa. They had long sold ivory to the Portuguese at Mozambique, though for various reasons they were increasingly taking their ivory to the Swahili port of Kilwa. Ivory from both these ports was mainly exported to India. Here there had long been a market for African ivory, which is softer than Indian ivory and thus more suitable for carving. Shipping ivory across the Indian Ocean was an expensive and hazardous enterprise, demanding sizeable capital investment, but by the eighteenth century there were a number of Indian financiers in the Mughal empire who were able and willing to supply this.

There was thus a greater demand than ever before for ivory along the East African coast. The Yao responded to this demand with great energy. The search for cheap ivory carried them far beyond their own country. They pushed westwards around the south end of Lake Malawi, and by 1753 Yao traders had reached the Chewa chief, Biwi. Here they could well have heard about the elephant herds in the lower Luangwa valley. By 1766 some Yao traders had actually reached Zumbo, where they sold cloth more cheaply than the Portuguese. They even crossed the Zambezi into Rozwi country and briefly challenged the Portuguese as the Rozwi's principal trading partners. This threat, however, was not maintained; instead, the Yao gained access to the products of Kazembe's dominions by making contact with the Bisa.

The Bisa are said to have known about the white men on the east coast when Kazembe's Lunda first conquered them. The southern Bisa could well have learned about both the Portuguese and the Yao from other Zambian peoples, such as the Lala, who could already have known something of the trade at Zumbo; it may even be that trade in Lala ironwork played a part in spreading such information. Whatever the process, by the 1780s, if not earlier, the Bisa were carrying both ivory and copper from Kazembe's across the Luangwa valley and on to the south end of Lake Malawi, where they exchanged them with the Yao for foreign beads and cloth. The Yao by this time were taking most of their ivory to Kilwa or Zanzibar, though some still went to Mozambique, and occasionally the Bisa themselves took Kazembe's ivory to the Portuguese at Quelimane, which lay well south of the Yao sphere of operations.

Kazembe and the Portuguese

In this way, then, a trade route from the east coast was created which linked up at Kazembe's with other routes leading right across the continent to the west coast. It might be supposed that Kazembe would have been well content with this achievement. Certainly the east coast route was more to his advantage than the western routes, which were much longer and ran through the country of his nominal overlord, Mwata Yamvo. Yet the very importance of this eastern route meant that Kazembe was anxious not to become too dependent on any one group of middlemen. He thus sought to make direct contact with the Portuguese on the lower Zambezi. Bisa traders, in the course of their travels to meet the Yao, passed close to the Chewa goldfields, and when Gonçalo Pereira began mining at Java around 1790 the news soon reached Kazembe. In 1793 a party of Bisa visited Pereira with ivory for sale, and told him that Kazembe wished his friendship. Pereira sold the Bisa some cloth and sent two of his own slaves to Kazembe. In 1796 his son Manuel set out for Kazembe's in the company of several Bisa. The expedition was a great success, and early in 1798 Manuel arrived back in Tete with three hundred Bisa and two ambassadors from Kazembe's. They announced that Kazembe wished to open a trade in ivory with the Portuguese at Tete and invited them to establish a trading post on the Luangwa, near his eastern borders.

This news arrived at a remarkably apposite moment. For the Portuguese government had just decided to launch a major expedition to make the first journey between its colonies in Mozambique and Angola. The purpose of this expedition was strategic. In 1795 Britain had captured the Cape from the Dutch, and it was feared in Lisbon that the British might soon seek to drive a wedge northwards between the Portuguese colonies. To forestall this, Francesco Lacerda, a distinguished Brazilian scholar, was instructed to open a route from the lower Zambezi to the west coast. Lacerda arrived in Tete shortly before Manuel Pereira's return. When he heard of Kazembe's invitation to trade, he at once decided to take it up himself. Not only did the Lunda trade route seem to offer a path across the continent; there seemed every chance that the Portuguese could now supplant the Yao and the Arabs as Kazembe's main suppliers of beads and cloth.

These ambitions came to nothing. Accompanied by both Pereiras, Lacerda's expedition reached the Lunda capital, but Lacerda himself died on arrival. His colleagues failed to reach any sort of agreement with Kazembe, who was reluctant to allow the Portuguese to continue further west and so threaten his trade with Mwata Yamvo. The expedition was obliged to turn back, and it now ran into trouble among Bisa chiefs who also feared the Portuguese as trade rivals. Fighting broke out; the Portuguese burnt a village, and they were only restrained from burning more by the elder Pereira: it was thanks to his bushcraft that the travellers escaped and eventually reached Tete.

For a short while Kazembe maintained contacts with the Portuguese. He was visited by a few private traders from Sena and Tete and it is possible that some Bisa traders continued to visit Tete. Meanwhile, in 1802, the governor of Angola took the initiative: he dispatched two half-caste traders from Kasanje to cross Africa by way of Mwata Yamvo's and Kazembe's. These *pombeiros* were held up for years at a time on the way, but they finally reached Tete in 1811. They reported that Kazembe IV (who had succeeded his father in 1805) was well accustomed to white traders; he had been much concerned to keep open a route for traders from Tete, and indeed he had exchanged embassies with the governor there in 1810–11. In 1814 Kazembe sent another embassy to Tete and a Portuguese trader from thereabouts visited him in the same year. Thereafter, however, Kazembe's trade with the Portuguese virtually ceased.

The main reason for this was that the Portuguese colonists on the lower Zambezi were no longer much interested in Kazembe's ivory. They had found a new source of wealth: the slave trade. In the later eighteenth century the Portuguese at Mozambique had begun to supply slaves to the French sugar plantations on Réunion and Mauritius. In the early nineteenth century eastern Africa faced a new demand for slaves, from Brazil, which hitherto had relied mainly on Angola. By 1820, slaves had largely replaced gold and ivory as the principal exports from the lower Zambezi region, and many of these slaves came from Chewa country, by way of Tete. As yet, the Bisa saw no profit in the slave trade; they gave up whatever trade they had had with Tete, and took all their ivory to the upper Shire valley, where the Yao continued to offer favourable prices, while those few Portuguese who wanted Bisa ivory obtained it with great difficulty.

Around 1820, the Portuguese governor on the lower Zambezi sought to reopen trade with the lands of Kazembe. The latter sent envoys to Tete in about 1822, and this encouraged the governor to revive the project of a trading post in the Luangwa valley. He bought some land from a minor Chewa chief near the trade route crossing, and in 1827 this was occupied by a military force. No trade goods were supplied to this outpost, and in 1829 the garrison was withdrawn. But it may have been news of this venture which prompted Kazembe to send an ivory caravan to Tete in 1830. This in turn encouraged the Portuguese governor to send an expedition to Kazembe in order to obtain a commercial treaty. This mission was entrusted to two army officers, José Monteiro and Antonio Gamitto. The latter was a highly intelligent and observant young man, who from the first had doubts about the expedition. It was badly equipped and worse conceived: Gamitto considered that it had simply been organised for the glory of the governors in Mozambique and the lower Zambezi. The party reached Kazembe, but was much depleted by sickness and death. They soon formed the impression that Kazembe now had no serious interest in regular commercial relations. Besides, his monopoly of long-distance trade, and his arbitrary price-fixing, seemed to preclude any hope of profitable business. Kazembe, for his part, was understandably suspicious of visitors who were, after all, soldiers and not *bona fide* traders. After further hardships, the Portuguese returned to Tete and composed a depressing report which effectively discouraged any further such ventures. The one solid gain from this expedition was Gamitto's journal, which is a major pioneering contribution to the ethnography and history of central Africa.

Gamitto has left us a remarkably clear, if partisan, picture of Kazembe's kingdom and its external relations in the earlier nineteenth century. The capital, near Lake Mofwe, was very large – about three kilometres across; and the streets were 'wide, straight, and very clean'. One of Kazembe's most senior officials was partly responsible for urban administration: he supervised an inspector of public works, and also the judges who heard minor cases in each street. Stringent fire precautions were observed: all buildings were of wood and thatch, so household fires were put out every night. In the middle of the town was a great square, quite bare of grass, and at one side was Kazembe's palace, standing in a rectangular enclosure of trees. Here Kazembe IV received his Portuguese visitors and made a great display of Lunda pomp. Around the king were gathered his principal kinsmen and ministers, his four chief wives and four hundred concubines, and several bands of musicians; beyond them, thousands of armed men crowded out the square. Kazembe himself sat on a cloth-covered stool placed on a lion-skin spread out over a carpet of leopard-skins:

His head was ornamented with a kind of mitre, pyramidal in shape and two spans high, made of brilliant scarlet feathers; round his forehead was a dazzling diadem of beads of various kinds and colours. Neck and shoulders were covered with . . . a string of alternately placed little round and square mirrors, in symmetry. This fell round his shoulders and over his chest, and when struck by the sun's rays it was too bright to look upon.[11]

This outward show of magnificence was somewhat deceptive. The kingdom had lost much of the power and prosperity it had enjoyed in Lacerda's day, and Kazembe IV Keleka was by no means the equal of his father. Kazembe III Lukwesa had been feared, but also respected, and his memory was still cherished in Gamitto's day. The Lunda told Gamitto how once, when Lukwesa was drunk,

he made an unjust order to have a negro killed, and this was promptly executed as usual. But afterwards, recognising the injustice he had done, he commanded that none of his orders should be carried out if he was drunk when he gave it, or even if he had been drinking but no longer appeared drunk. Any person who obeyed such orders would be held responsible for the consequences. After this he established the custom of drinking Pombe [beer] only at night, thus instituting the parties which we have mentioned. These were continued as a matter of custom although he himself did not drink; for as he said, the Mambo [king] must always be ready to hear and deliberate unaided.[12]

But Kazembe IV was a brutal and bloodthirsty despot, who provided plenty of work for his spies, his thirty policemen and his chief executioner. People only lived near the court if they had to: the capital was 'a desert today compared with what it was in the past'.[13] Kazembe IV's neglect of custom, and his ill-treatment of the Portuguese, were blamed by the Lunda for an outbreak of smallpox: his diviners boldly declared that this was a punishment sent by the angry spirit of Lukwesa. Besides, Kazembe's violence injured trade and industry: repressive campaigns had interfered with production, and little ivory or copper reached his court. It is also clear that Kazembe IV's control of his outlying dominions was undermined by powerful neighbours. In the northwest, the expanding Luba kingdom began to challenge Kazembe's access to copper and ivory: a Luba embassy visited Kazembe's while Gamitto was there and it was probably soon after this that a Luba army attacked Kazembe's capital, though it was forced to withdraw. Meanwhile, in 1829–31 the Bemba advanced south in search of beads and cloth, and conquered several Bisa chiefdoms subject to Kazembe.

Bisa trade survived this invasion, but Kazembe lost much tribute, and the fear of Bemba raiders still further deterred the Portuguese from using this route into the interior.

The West and Angola

In north-western Zambia access to goods from the coast was first brought about by the expansion of trade further west, in what is now central Angola. This was a rather late development. In 1696 it was said that Africans reached Angola from the middle Zambezi, but this was probably an exceptional event. Trade between the Zambezi and the west coast was primarily a result of the growth of trade among the Ovimbundu, on the Benguela Highland. These people became as famous for long-distance trade as the Bisa, and it seems likely that their commercial enterprise also owed much to a lively local trade, solidly based on iron production. The Ovimbundu were probably selling slaves and ivory to Portuguese traders up country by the earlier eighteenth century, but such trade increased considerably in the 1770s, when the Ovimbundu established direct relations with the Portuguese on the coast. This evidently prompted both the Ovimbundu and Portuguese or half-caste traders to penetrate eastwards into the interior. By the 1790s the Luvale, on the western headwaters of the Zambezi, were accustomed to obtain cloth and beads from 'white men' from the west, and some Luvale went westwards themselves. As a result of information supplied by a Luvale, a Brazilian and a Portuguese led expeditions in 1794–5 from Benguela through Ovimbundu country and as far as the Luvale chiefs Kakenge and Chinyama (then living in what is now eastern Angola).

It would seem that as yet the traders from the west had not reached the Lozi kingdom, but they knew of its existence: indeed, the reports of the 1794–5 expeditions indicate that by this time the Lozi had made their villages on mounds in the Zambezi flood plain, the building of which was organised by King Mulambwa. In any case, the Lozi soon sought to take part in this new trade among their northern neighbours. Mulambwa sent men to the Luvale to buy European cloth, beads and crockery, and the southern Lunda brought cloth to Mulambwa in exchange for cattle. In due course some Mambari (a term loosely applied to Ovimbundu or coloured traders from the west) came south to buy slaves from Mulambwa, but they had no success, for Mulambwa needed all the labour he could get for the work of building mounds and fish weirs on the flood plain.

Throughout the first half of the nineteenth century the Mambari appear to have concentrated their energies to the north and east of the Lozi kingdom. From early in the century they bought slaves from the

Lunda chief, Ishinde, and from the Lamba chief, Nkumine. By 1830 traders travelled between the Luvale chief Kakenge and Kazembe on the Luapula. The abolition, in 1834, of the Portuguese royal monopoly in ivory gave a new impetus to trade eastwards from Angola. In the early 1850s the Luvale were well known for having guns and cloth, and Kakenge was busy selling slaves to Mambari; the Lunda chief Ishinde had several guns. Traders in slaves and ivory, Mambari as well as Bisa and 'Portuguese' from the east, frequented the country around the Kafue Hook. Mambari, Luvale and Bisa traders all visited the Lamba, and the Lenje were said to have plenty of beads and cloth. Monze's village, among the plateau Tonga, was visited both by Mambari from the west and by Nsenga ivory traders from the east.

NOTES

1. D. and C. Livingstone, *Narrative of an Expedition to the Zambezi and its Tributaries* (1865), 225.
2. James Chapman, *Travels in the Interior of Southern Africa* (1868), I, 172.
3. E. Holub, (tr. C. Johns, ed. L. Holy), *Travels North of the Zambezi* (Manchester, 1975), p. 45.
4. See pp. 35 and 45.
5. See pp. 45, 58–9 and 94.
6. For a description of the pre-colonial copper industry in Central Africa, see Appendix I, p. 253.
7. J. A. Bancroft, *Mining in Northern Rhodesia* (1961), 39.
8. See pp. 144–5.
9. 'Portuguese' is used here in a cultural sense, to denote people who could speak some Portuguese and considered themselves subjects of the King of Portugal. Physically, such people might be very different: white Europeans, Indians from Goa, 'half breeds' of various kinds, and people largely or wholly of African stock.
10. Anon., 'Memorias da Costa d'Africa Oriental' in A. A. de Andrade (ed.), *Relações de Mozambique Setecentista* (Lisbon, 1955), 204. The European copper bought in India probably came from Cornwall, in England.
11. A. C. P. Gamitto (tr. Ian Cunnison), *King Kazembe* (Lisbon, 1960), II, 18.
12. ibid., II, 130.
13. ibid., II, 115.

VIII

African Intruders
c. 1840 – c. 1890

From the middle years of the nineteenth century, the peoples of Zambia were exposed to a variety of new external pressures. Hitherto, their main lines of contact with a wider world had run to the east, through Mozambique, and west, through Shaba and Angola. And in general this contact took the form of trade. Manufactured goods from overseas were imported – mostly by Africans – along routes which led inland from Portuguese colonies on the west coast and Portuguese and Arab colonies on the east coast. These patterns of trade continued during the later nineteenth century. But from about 1840 onwards there were important changes both in the direction and in the nature of Zambia's external contacts. The new lines of communication ran north and south. And from all directions Zambia attracted invaders and raiders as well as traders.

Most of these intruders were African. From the south came the Ngoni and Kololo, warrior herdsmen who had fled north from the upheavals caused by Shaka's Zulu empire. From both east and west traders linked to Portuguese colonies came to hunt for slaves as well as elephant. From the north came traders from East Africa, both brown and black, who likewise sought slaves as well as ivory. Finally, a few white ivory traders came from the south. All these intruders profoundly altered the political shape of Zambia. Some peoples were conquered by them, and most became involved in the export of ivory and slaves. These were exchanged for new goods and weapons which greatly increased both the means and the incentives for pursuing internal rivalries and wars of plunder and conquest.

Thus in the course of the nineteenth century the peoples of Zambia were harassed both by invading warriors and by traders seeking slaves and ivory on a larger scale than ever before. This expansion of trade was primarily a response to the demands of consumers in Western Europe and North America. Throughout the eighteenth century, Zambian ivory had mostly gone to India, while the slave trade made relatively little impact. But during the first part of the nineteenth century, Western Europe and North America were greatly enriched by the Industrial Revolution; their populations were growing fast; and they provided expanding markets both for luxury items made of ivory and for tropical crops – sugar, cotton, coffee, cocoa and cloves. In many places these continued to be grown by slave labour, even though most European countries officially opposed both slavery and the slave trade. So the search by African traders for slaves as well as elephant was pushed ever further into the interior, and by the middle of the nineteenth century Zambia was one of the few remaining areas which still offered ready supplies of both.

Our sources of information for this period are comparatively rich. For most areas oral traditions provide fairly detailed narratives which cover much of the nineteenth century. These can often be compared with written records. Livingstone reached the Zambezi in 1851, and thereafter there is a growing volume of evidence from European explorers, traders and missionaries. Taken together with the oral traditions, these eye-witness accounts enable us increasingly to reconstruct the history of Zambia in terms of individual men and women as well as material artefacts, institutions and patterns of social change.

The Ngoni

In the years between 1840 and 1880 or thereabouts, large parts of Zambia, Malawi and Tanzania were conquered and settled by various groups of Ngoni. Their original homeland was in what is now Zululand, but in about 1820 they fled north from Shaka to the high plateau beyond the Limpopo. In 1835 one Ngoni leader, Zwangendaba, led his band of warriors across the Zambezi, not far below Zumbo. Over the next ten years or so they moved gradually northwards through the country between the Luangwa river and Lake Malawi, swelling their ranks with captives as they went. They settled for a time among the Fipa in south-western Tanzania, but in about 1845 Zwangendaba died. There was a bitter struggle over the succession to his position as Ngoni paramount and as a result several groups split off and migrated in different directions. One group went north, another went east, while a third went south-east towards the southern end of Lake Malawi. Most of Zwangendaba's sons also went to the south-east; in about 1855 they invaded Tumbuka country and elected Mbelwa as paramount.

Meanwhile, two other sons of Zwangendaba, Mperembe and Mpezeni, had formed followings of their own and had moved south of Lake Tanganyika into Bemba country. In about 1850 these Ngoni defeated two Bemba chiefs in Chinsali district. Mpezeni went on south, but Mperembe's Ngoni advanced into the heart of Bemba country. They were repulsed by the Bemba king, but they settled near his southern borders and for a few years raided both Bemba and Bisa south of the Chambeshi river. They then moved north once again, to the Lungu near the south end of Lake Tanganyika, and then further east, to the Mambwe. Here they renewed their attacks on the Bemba, but in about 1870 the Bemba king Chitapankwa mounted a grand alliance of chiefs which severely defeated the Ngoni. Mperembe withdrew to the east, and finally settled near the Ngoni of Mbelwa in what is now Malawi.

It was Mpezeni who created the principal permanent Ngoni settlement in Zambia.[1] By 1860 he had crossed the Luangwa into Nsenga country. During the next twenty years he gradually encroached on the northern Chewa kingdom of Mkanda. At the beginning of the century this had been relatively prosperous and well populated, with numerous herds of cattle. It attracted Bisa immigrants, and Mkanda profited from the Bisa trade route to the Yao, which passed through his country. By 1830 Mkanda was virtually independent of Undi, the Chewa paramount; he was certainly more powerful in his own kingdom than Undi in his. By the mid-nineteenth century, if not before, the northern Chewa had largely replaced their staple crop, millet, with maize, which reached them from the Portuguese on the lower Zambezi. This greatly increased the agricultural productivity of Mkanda's kingdom. Yet Mkanda's maize fields and cattle were also his undoing, for they powerfully attracted the Ngoni. By 1880, Mpezeni had killed Mkanda and overrun his kingdom.

The victories of the Ngoni in Zambia, as elsewhere, were mainly due to the fact that, unlike their opponents, they were deliberately organised and trained for war. This is not to say that Mpezeni's warriors were full-time soldiers; they spent much time in agriculture and cattle-herding. But they also obtained grain and cattle by levying tribute from their Nsenga and Chewa neighbours, or simply raiding them; and Mpezeni attached little importance to long-distance trade. Like the Zulu, the Ngoni developed a system of age-regiments: every few years, all the boys of a certain age-group would be recruited to form a new regiment. They would train and go to war together, fighting hand-to-hand in Zulu style with a short stabbing spear. Each regiment formed an avenue for promotion on the basis of military skill rather than birth. This 'meritocracy' reflected the fact that the Ngoni were continually swelling their numbers by incorporating war-captives in their regiments. Such men obviously could gain no promotion among the Ngoni on a hereditary basis, but they were free to compete for positions of military leadership according to their ability. For most purposes such ex-captives became Ngoni, and they had good reason to stay in a successful Ngoni group rather than risk the hazards of life back among their own people. This recruitment of captives meant that Mpezeni's Ngoni quickly adopted the language of the Nsenga, among whom they lived, raided and married during the 1860s and 1870s. Ngoni political organisation continued to be dominated by kinship; as we have seen, rivalries within the royal family had caused a whole series of divisions after Zwangendaba's death. Even so, Mpezeni was able to exert considerable influence by distributing cattle among his subordinates. And the military organisation was a strong force for unity among the subjects of any one Ngoni chief. It was seldom that other peoples could organise a large enough force to defeat an Ngoni chief – as the Bemba finally did.

East African Traders in the North-East

In the course of the nineteenth century, much of north-eastern Zambia was drawn into the orbit of long-distance traders from Zanzibar and what is now the coast of Tanzania. This was not a wholly new development. As we saw in the last chapter, the growth of trade between Kilwa and India during the eighteenth century had stimulated the export of ivory from the Lunda king Kazembe. Bisa traders took it south-east, to the southern end of Lake Malawi, where the Yao carried it on to Kilwa. But during the nineteenth century there were major changes in the pattern of trade between north-eastern Zambia and the east coast.

In the first place there were changes in the patterns of Bisa trade. During the first half of the nineteenth century, the Bisa maintained and indeed increased their reputation as the principal ivory traders west of Lake Malawi. In the 1820s and 1830s the market for ivory at Zanzibar rapidly grew in response to new demands from Britain and the USA. Yet at just this period Bisa trade with Kazembe's ran into new difficulties. It apparently received little encouragement from Kazembe IV (1805–*c*.1845), and around 1830 the Bemba attacked his trade route to the south-east with virtual impunity. For the next twenty years or so, the Bisa chiefdom of Mwansabamba, in Mpika district, was under Bemba rule. Bisa traders reacted by extending their field of operations in various directions. Many Bisa moved east into Chewa country, from which, according to Gamitto, they

> go and buy ivory where they know it is to be had. They travel for a month or more to reach a place where they can buy it cheaply, and they do the same to sell it at a better price.[2]

The Bisa continued to sell much of their ivory to Yao traders, but increasingly they carried it themselves to Kilwa, and even all the way to Zanzibar. During the 1850s, traders from the northern Bisa were active to the north of Bemba country; they visited the Tabwa and travelled to Kilwa by way of Ufipa. The search for ivory also took Bisa traders far to the south and west. In the 1850s, they visited the Lamba and the country around the Kafue Hook. In 1856 an Ila chief below the Kafue gorge sent ivory to other chiefs on the Zambezi and received in return English cotton goods brought up from Mozambique by Bisa traders. One Bisa party was bold enough to seek trade among the fearsome Ndebele, south of the Zambezi, though they were robbed and barely escaped with their lives. In 1863 Livingstone met some Bisa beside Lake Malawi who were familiar with chiefs of the southern Lunda, on the headwaters of the Zambezi: as he observed,

> These Babisa are great travellers and traders, and, in fact, occupy somewhat the same position in this country as the Greeks do in the Levant.[3]

By this time, however, the great days of Bisa trade were over. The very fact that they travelled so widely was due not simply to the decline of their trade with Kazembe but to growing insecurity throughout the country between Kazembe's and Lake Malawi. This was largely due to Ngoni invasions. Around 1850 the Bisa near Mpika rose against their Bemba conqueror and killed him, but the Bemba king failed to retaliate, since he was now distracted by Mperembe's Ngoni. The latter soon supplanted the Bemba as the scourge of the southern Bisa, and meanwhile Mpezeni harassed the Bisa and Chewa east of the Luangwa. By 1861 Ngoni raids had caused one Bisa chief from Mpika to flee eastwards and settle near the south-western corner of Lake Malawi.

It was not only the Ngoni irruption which undermined Bisa trade on either side of the Luangwa. During the first half of the nineteenth century a new line of trade was opened up between north-eastern Zambia and the east coast. This drew Kazembe, and also the Bemba, into the commercial orbit of Arabs, Swahili and Nyamwezi in what is now Tanzania. In the first few decades of the century there was a rapid expansion of trade between the island of Zanzibar and the *mrima* coast opposite. This was mainly due to the growing demand for ivory in the western world, but it was also due to a new demand for slaves in Zanzibar to work on the clove plantations which were developed there from the 1820s onwards. As a result Arab and Swahili traders began to penetrate the hinterland of the *mrima* coast, whereas previously they had concentrated on the hinterland of Kilwa, further south. By about 1830, coastal traders were buying ivory in western Tanzania from the Nyamwezi people, who themselves sent their own caravans to the coast. Kazembe was soon drawn into this new trading network. There were Swahili at his court in 1831: we do not know what route they took, but in the 1840s Arabs came south down Lake Tanganyika to visit Kazembe and some continued west into Shaba (then known as Katanga). A few went on from there to the west coast, and one Arab, Said ibn Habib, visited the Lenje, Ila and Lozi on the way.

Such westward ventures by traders from the east coast seem to have been halted by the growth of a Nyamwezi colony in Katanga. Nyamwezi traders had bought copper in Katanga since the 1830s. From the 1850s onwards, one such trader, Msiri, remained in Katanga. He and his colleagues – now known as 'Yeke' – began to arm themselves with guns. Instead of trading with Kazembe or his governors, Msiri made alliances with local chiefs, extorted ivory from them and seized control of the copper mines. Msiri severed Kazembe's links with Mwata Yamvo and Angola, and by 1880 he had established a kingdom of his own. Its capital, the sprawling town of Bunkeya, attracted many immigrants and was visited by traders in slaves, copper and ivory from the west as well as from the east.

The reasons for Kazembe's inability to suppress Msiri's Yeke are not yet clear. Earlier in the century, Kazembe's control over the copper mines may have been disputed by the main Luba kingdom, but they were certainly under his rule by 1845. It may, however, be significant that the beginnings of Msiri's rise to power coincided with the closing of Kazembe's trade route to the south-east as a result of Ngoni raids. There was, of course, the new route to the north-east, but this proved to be a very doubtful advantage: like the Yeke, the Arabs and Swahili also became local potentates. At first, their expeditions were relatively weak: one was beaten up by the Tabwa chief Nsama around 1840. But a series of expeditions in the 1860s, led by the Arab trader Tippu Tip, proved that much profit could be had from trade with the Bemba. Bemba chiefs were able to organise the supply of large quantities of ivory; at the same time, they were sufficiently united to deter foreigners from settling among them. Instead, the Arabs and Swahili settled among the Lungu, to the north, and among the Bwile, near Lake Mweru. In 1867 Tippu Tip's guns crushed Nsama's Tabwa, and more traders settled in their country. These trading settlements were by no means united, but they had a great advantage over neighbouring chiefs in that their contacts in East Africa, especially the great entrepots up country, Tabora and Ujiji, gave them ready access to trade goods, firearms and even military reinforcements.

Thus Kazembe's kingdom, which in 1800 had been the most extensive and powerful in what is now Zambia, had by 1870 been greatly reduced by the encroachments of foreign traders. He might refuse to do business with them, but the loss was more his than theirs, for they could easily take their business to other chiefs in the region. Moreover, the Arabs and Swahili began to interfere in the internal politics of Kazembe's kingdom. In 1872 a Lunda prince, Lukwesa, gained Arab and Swahili support and killed Kazembe VII, and the new Kazembe now depended for his position on external alliance. It was not long before Lukwesa in his turn was deposed, which drove him this time into the arms of the Yeke, and this new alliance provoked Lukwesa's successor to seek Bemba aid.

The Bemba, by contrast, had done very well out of the East African trade. They hunted elephant, using heavy spears, both in their own country and in the upper Luangwa valley. East African traders came to buy their ivory, but mostly kept clear of Bemba politics. By about 1880 the Bemba also exported numerous slaves. Hitherto the East African traders in the region had tended to regard slaves as a poor second-best to ivory; slaves were bought mainly to carry ivory to the coast, since there were no free porters to be hired. In the late nineteenth century, however, ivory became scarcer, if also more valuable. Meanwhile, the demand for slave-labour rose in the interior, among both Arabs and Africans, since slaves were becoming cheaper. This was due to the fall in slave-prices at the coast, where their export was outlawed in 1873, so that they became harder to sell. The Bemba were ready enough to supply slaves, since they had no use for extra labour in their infertile homeland, and Bemba slave-raiders became the terror of the north-eastern plateau. In exchange for slaves and ivory, Bemba chiefs obtained beads and cloth. They did not buy firearms in any quantity until the 1890s, but they increased the supply of spears from local iron-workers by paying them in imported cloth. Cloth, indeed, became a kind of currency, and by distributing it to their followers Bemba chiefs won support for new raids and conquests. In the 1870s and early 1880s, relatives of the Bemba king Chitapankwa took over much new territory to the south and west from the Bisa, Lungu and Tabwa. The Bemba kingdom became at once much larger and more closely knit together by ties of royal kinship, while Kazembe's diminishing kingdom fell victim to internal strife.

Meanwhile, Msiri's Yeke exerted pressure not only on Kazembe's kingdom but on peoples living further south in what is now Zambia. Yeke raiders crossed the middle Luapula and harassed the Aushi, Unga and even the westernmost Bisa. Around 1880 the Kaonde chief Kapiji Chibanza also began paying tribute to Msiri. Kapiji controlled the copper mine at Kansanshi, but Msiri wanted his ivory and gave him cloth in return for it. In about 1885 the Lamba chief Nkana submitted to an expedition sent by Msiri, and even adopted his name, though a neighbouring Lima chief held his own and was allowed to retain a half-share of his ivory.

The Chikunda in the South-East

In the north-east, then, the main initiatives in long-distance trade came to be taken by intruders from East Africa. Bisa traders suffered in consequence, and in south-eastern and central Zambia Bisa traders lost the ground they had gained in the 1840s and 1850s to African traders from the lower Zambezi. From the 1860s such traders extended the search for ivory and slaves along the middle Zambezi and far up the Luangwa valley, at a heavy cost in human life.

The centre for these activities was Zumbo, at the confluence of the Zambezi and Luangwa. The Portuguese outposts there and at nearby Feira had been withdrawn in 1836, owing to the decline of the Rozwi gold trade and the advent of Ngoni and Ndebele marauders. For the next twenty years, few traders from the lower Zambezi went as far west as Zumbo, mainly because the trade of this region was largely controlled by the Pereiras, the Goanese overlords of the southern Chewa. An Italian trader, Simoens, once got as far as the Kariba gorge, where his guns secured him many tusks and slaves, but he was killed below Zumbo some time before 1853. Then, in the middle 1850s, a half-caste trader called Santanna, locally known as Chikwasha, was allowed to hunt in the country of Mburuma, the Nsenga chief west of Zumbo, provided he paid tribute. In 1860 Santanna used his guns to kill Mburuma and several of his men, and extracted a grant of land from Mburuma's successor. This encouraged the Portuguese authorities in Mozambique to reopen Zumbo as a trading post in 1862.

The official aim in reopening Zumbo was to expand the ivory trade and so increase revenues. But here, as elsewhere in Africa, the growth of an ivory trade encouraged the growth of a slave trade. Portuguese society on the lower Zambezi was based on slave-holding, and by the mid-nineteenth century its demand for slaves was greater than ever before. The overseas trade in slaves still flourished in Mozambique; it was officially abolished in 1842, but it nonetheless continued into the 1880s to supply Brazil as well as the French island of Réunion (where slaves were politely disguised by the term 'engagé labour'). There was also a constant need to replenish estates and households depleted by slave revolts, escapes and deaths from disease. Meanwhile, the demand for ivory on the Portuguese coast was rising as fast as at Zanzibar, and slaves were needed to obtain the ivory. Some were used to carry it, though for long stretches of the Zambezi large flat canoes could carry three tonnes at a time. But the chief use of slaves was as hunters and soldiers, for around the middle Zambezi both slaves and ivory were obtained mainly by force. There were in this region no powerful local rulers, as there were among the Lunda, Bemba or Lozi. Besides, traders from the lower Zambezi had the advantage of access to more or less efficient firearms from Europe. Rather than co-operate with the numerous small chiefs of central Zambia, the traders had every inducement to use brute force, not only to enslave African villages but to hunt for elephant regardless of local rights and customs.

Thus from the 1860s onwards the country around Zumbo attracted a number of more or less bloodthirsty adventurers – black, white and brown. The Portuguese government continued to exert little or no control west of Tete; instead, it granted official positions and titles of land to the new traders, and left them free to raise their own armies. Some of these traders, and many of their soldiers, had escaped from the black slave armies of Portuguese estates on the lower Zambezi. Such slave soldiers were known as Chikunda. Their ethnic origins were very diverse, but they had developed their own distinct cultural identity and spoke a language, Nyungwe, which was a mixture of both Nyanja and Shona dialects. In this way the expansion of long-distance trade in central Zambia in the later nineteenth century brought about the migration of a new African 'tribe', the Chikunda, which had been formed under European pressure but was thoroughly African in its customs and institutions.

Among the leaders of these Chikunda immigrants, two men were especially notorious. One of the first traders to visit Zumbo after it reopened was a Portuguese-speaking black man from Tete, José do Rosario Andrade, better known as Kanyemba. Kanyemba made his base on the south bank of the Zambezi, a little way upstream from Feira. In 1876 he led 600 men on a slave hunt among the Gwembe Tonga; two years later, he took 200 men into the country of the Lenje chief Chitanda (who himself acquired a reputation for frightfulness). In 1883, Kanyemba was appointed to an official Portuguese captaincy over the country west of the lower Kafue, based on Sialuselo ('Nhauçoe'). By 1890 Kanyemba was said to command 10,000 men; he had a vast harem; and he practised castration extensively.

Hardly less brutal, and still more powerful, was Kanyemba's black son-in-law, José d'Aranjo Lobo, called 'Matakenya' (jiggers) after the flea which burrows into the feet. In the 1860s and 1870s Matakenya raided the Nsenga east of the lower Luangwa. In 1878 he was appointed to the captaincy at Zumbo, though his headquarters remained at Panhame, further down the river. In 1882 Matakenya went far up the Luangwa into Bisa country, in search of slaves and ivory, and by 1890 he had agents posted as far north as the Luangwa crossing east of Mpika; the valley, once populous, was now deserted. Further north, the Luangwa was terrorised by Arab traders from the north end of Lake Malawi; they were good customers for Kanyemba's eunuchs. The plateau east of the Luangwa was largely dominated by the newly settled Ngoni chief Mpezeni, but in defeating Mkanda's Chewa he had been helped by Chikunda hunters armed with guns. West of the Luangwa, throughout the 1880s, Matakenya and his agents raided as far as the upper Luapula, while groups of Chikunda settled among the Lala, Lamba and Lenje. A Lala chief, probably Mboloma, ceded land to Matakenya in 1885, and in 1890 one of Matakenya's brothers was given a captaincy over the same chief's territory. In 1893 Matakenya was described as

> a colonel in the Portuguese Army, and a fairly well-educated man, but one of the most ruthless slavers and devastators on the Upper Zambezi. He is said to be very wealthy, and has £10,000 put by in a Lisbon Bank. . . . Matakenya himself has one thousand good guns, and can put as many as twelve thousand armed slaves into the field, mostly armed with muzzle loaders. At the fort at Zumbo there are stored from eight to nine thousand breech-loading guns . . . together with nearly one million rounds of ammunition for the same. These are at Matakenya's disposal if he likes to take them.[4]

Only in the far west was there an African ruler with forces on anything like this scale.

The Kololo in the West

As in eastern Zambia, so too in the west the middle and later nineteenth century was a time of violent upheaval, caused both by the growth of trade in slaves and ivory, and by invaders from South Africa. Like the Ngoni, the Kololo and Ndebele were warrior herdsmen who had been forced northwards by the Zulu. The Kololo were followers of Sebituane, chief of a Sotho tribe called the Fokeng in what is now the Orange Free State. In 1823 Sebituane led his people away to the north, through the countries of the Tswana-speaking peoples and across the swamps and deserts of the eastern Kalahari. Some time in the 1830s the Kololo crossed the upper Zambezi at Kazungula, above the Victoria Falls. They were attracted northwards by the cattle of the plateau Tonga and Ila, but they were also threatened from the south by the advance of Mzilikazi's Ndebele. In about 1840 Sebituane defeated an Ndebele army near Siachitema's, not far east of Kalomo, but he now took his Kololo back into the cattle-rich country of the Ila, along the Kafue flood plain. They went as far east as the Sala when Sebituane heard that the Ndebele were again approaching. Inspired by a prophet, he now turned west and made straight for the capital of the Lozi kingdom, on the upper Zambezi.

The Kololo found the Lozi torn by a dispute over the royal succession. Sebituane soon occupied the heart of the kingdom. For a time, the Lozi king, Mubukwanu, remained in the flood plain, but at this stage the main challenge to Kololo conquest came from other South African invaders. A band of warriors led by Nxaba advanced up the Zambezi from its confluence with the Chobe. They were massacred by Sebituane, who now took over the southern part of the flood plain, around

Senanga. Then Mzilikazi sent two expeditions against the Kololo; in resisting the second, in 1850, Sebituane was almost drowned, but as on the first occasion he contrived to starve most of the Ndebele to death.

In spite of these victories the Kololo continued to be much afraid of the Ndebele. This fear was an important factor in their dealings with long-distance traders for Sebituane knew that white men had weapons so powerful that they would surely dispose of the Ndebele once and for all: at the start of his great migration, in 1823, he had witnessed a crushing victory by some coloured Griqua musketeers. Thus Sebituane was anxious to make contact with the Mambari traders from the west who had visited the upper Zambezi since the beginning of the century.

At first the Mambari had most frequented the country north and east of the Lozi, who preferred to employ slaves themselves rather than to sell them. But the revival of the Portuguese ivory trade after 1834 encouraged the Mambari to renew attempts to trade with the Lozi. By 1848 the Lozi king Mubukwanu had abandoned the central flood plain to the Kololo and had established a new capital at Lukulu, at the north end of the plain. Here he continued to receive varied tribute, and by 1848 this included ivory, which suggests that he was doing business with the Mambari. At all events he received a visit in that year from Silva Porto, a white trader based on the Ovimbundu chiefdom of Bihé.

Shortly afterwards, Mubukwanu died and was succeeded by his son Imasiku. Sebituane now launched a successful attack on Lukulu, and Imasiku fled up the Kabompo river to Lukwakwa. It seems clear that Sebituane's aims were both to complete his conquest of the flood plain and to increase his share of the western trade. He had already received cloth on occasion from Lunda chiefs, in exchange for cattle, but he wished to obtain guns as well, for defence against the Ndebele. In 1850 Sebituane was at Naliele, near the former Lozi capital, when some Mambari came down the Zambezi. They met Sebituane at Libonta and he offered them cattle and ivory, but they wanted slaves, and with some reluctance Sebituane supplied a few in order to obtain guns. A party of Kololo then joined the Mambari in a raid on the Ila; the Mambari took away about 200 slaves, and in return supplied the Kololo with much English cloth.

Meanwhile, Sebituane had also been trying to make contact with white men to the south who wished to visit him. These men were David Livingstone, then working as a missionary at Kolobeng, among the southern Tswana, and his companion William Oswell. In 1851, together with Livingstone's wife and children, they reached the Chobe river. Sebituane had already come south to meet them and had made a camp at Linyanti. A few weeks after welcoming Livingstone's party, Sebituane died of pneumonia, but he was succeeded by his young son Sekeletu, who shared his fears and ambitions. Sekeletu, indeed, made

X Portuguese treaty

◑ Lozi official, 1899

V Lozi cattle post, 1899

••••• Border of Lozi reserved area, 1899

Ⓒ Copper mines

Ⓡ Wild rubber

- - - Modern frontiers

●MWATA YAMVO

Katanga

Yeke

●MSIRI Ⓒ

Ⓒ

Lunda

Ndembu

KAKENGE

●ISHINDE

Ⓒ Kansanshi

Luvale

Kaonde

Ⓡ

Mbunda

V V V

Lukulu●

Libonta

Kaunga●

Lealui

Naliele

●KASEMPA

R. Kabompo

R. Dongwe

Lukwakwa

Hook of Kafue

V Ⓡ

V

Mbwela   *Mashi*

◑

◑

◑

Lozi

Senanga●

R. Zambezi

R. Kwando

Totela

R. Njoko

SHEZONGO

R. Machili

Lukanga Swamp

KAINGU Kafue Flat

Sa

●Ila

◑

MAPANZA●

(Kalomo)●

(Zimba)●

●SHALOBA

MONZE●

(Choma)●

To

Batoka plateau

SINAMA

WANKIE●

Subiya

Sesheke

Linyanti

◑

R. Kwito

Caprivi Strip

R. Chobe

Kazungula

Pandamatenga

Toka

Victoria Falls

Tawana ✳✳✳✳ Lake Ngami

Ngwato

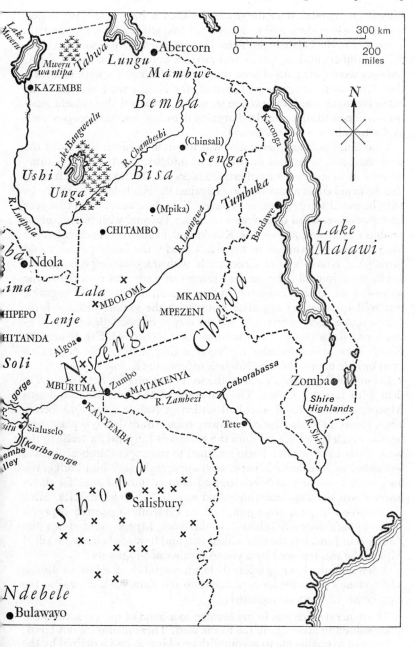

Linyanti his capital, since the swamps of the Chobe provided protection from Ndebele raiders, and he also hoped that white men would provide an answer to the Ndebele problem. He continued to buy guns and cloth from Mambari traders, but he was anxious to be independent of them; not only were their guns of poor quality, but their prices were unattractive. Even in their refuge at Linyanti, the Kololo were masters of an extensive system of local exchange, and so enriched they would have been inclined to strike harder bargains than less powerful peoples such as the Luvale or southern Lunda.

Thus Sekeletu's long-term aim was to establish direct links with the west coast and so cut out the Mambari middlemen. At the same time, he needed to secure his northern frontiers, on the Lozi flood plain, so that he could concentrate his forces against the Ndebele in the south. In 1853 he found an opportunity to pursue both these aims, for in that year Livingstone returned to Linyanti from the Tswana, with plans both to establish a mission among the Kololo and to find a convenient route from the upper Zambezi to the sea. Clearly, the latter project could further the Kololo aim of direct trade with the coast, especially since Livingstone himself believed that European trade was essential to the success of an African mission.[5] And as a neutral outsider, Livingstone was well qualified to negotiate peace with the various chiefs – Lozi, Lunda and others – who might bar the way to the west. Besides, Livingstone was the son-in-law of the missionary Robert Moffat, whom the Kololo knew to be a friend of the Ndebele king Mzilikazi; he might thus even be able to persuade the Ndebele to leave the Kololo in peace.

Before anything could come of the west coast project, Sekeletu had to deal with internal unrest. The governor of the Lozi heartland was Mpepe, a Kololo royal who had settled at Naliele some time before 1850. He seems to have levied extensive tribute from the flood plain, and he was much better placed than the Kololo at Linyanti for trade to the west. Early in 1853 Silva Porto returned to the upper Zambezi; he was welcomed at Naliele by Mpepe, who apparently gave him both cattle and ivory belonging to Sekeletu, and allowed him to hunt for slaves lower down the Zambezi valley and among the Toka and Ila. Silva Porto gave Mpepe a large gun, and he evidently supported Mpepe's plans to assassinate Sekeletu. To this end, Mpepe went down the Zambezi in June, but the plot leaked out, and it was Sekeletu who killed Mpepe; he was replaced by a young brother of Sebituane.

A few months later Sekeletu held an assembly of elders to discuss Livingstone's plans for an expedition up the Zambezi and over to the west coast. Livingstone reported:

> The general voice was in my favour; so a band of twenty-seven were appointed to accompany me to the west. These men were not hired, but sent to enable me to accomplish an object as much desired by the

chief and most of his people as by me. They were eager to obtain free
and profitable trade with white men.[6]

Thus Livingstone's great march to the west was as much an African as a
European venture, even though Europeans have almost always described it as simply another journey of discovery by an intrepid white
man with 'faithful' black followers. The expedition was largely managed
by two senior Kololo, Pitsane and Mohorisi, and it was equipped by
Sekeletu with cattle, as gifts for chiefs, and ivory for sale to the Portuguese. The party duly made peace with Imasiku, the Lozi prince in
exile at Lukwakwa, and with the Lunda chief Ishinde. In 1854 they
safely reached the port of Luanda, where the prospects for trade seemed
so good that after their return in 1855 Sekeletu sent two more ivory
caravans to Luanda, one of them led by Pitsane. In about 1859 a Kololo
party reached Benguela, thus making a more direct challenge to the
Mambari traders, though their attempt to bring horses back with them
was unsuccessful. The Kololo ventures may have prompted the Mambari to lower their prices; at all events, the latter were buying plenty of
ivory at the Kololo capital by 1860. This was despite the fact that Sekeletu had gone so far as to prohibit the export of slaves from his dominions. He backed this up by enforcing a royal monopoly of ivory; without
free access to ivory, the Mambari found the slave trade alone unpro-
fitable.

Despite their success in extending the trade of the Lozi kingdom, the
Kololo remained basically insecure. They lost the services of Livingstone as a mediator, for on his return from Luanda in 1855 he went on
down the Zambezi and then home to England. He revisited the Kololo
in 1860, but by then he had abandoned his plans for a mission among
them. The Kololo continued to be obsessed by fears of Ndebele invasion,
and for this reason they kept their capital in the south, either at Linyanti
or at nearby Sesheke, in order to prevent the local people allowing the
Ndebele into the upper Zambezi valley. This policy met with some
opposition: the younger Kololo, including Sekeletu himself, were eager in
1855 to move the capital north to the Lozi flood plain, where it would
be closer to traders coming from the west. But older Kololo who had
risen to prominence through cattle-raiding rather than trading dis-
trusted this scheme; their views prevailed; and most Kololo remained
in the south.

Thus fear of the Ndebele distracted the attention of the Kololo away
from the heartland of the Lozi kingdom. The Kololo, indeed, never
really came to terms with the peculiar nature of this kingdom. Whereas
they, in their wanderings, had become footloose herdsmen and raiders,
the Lozi had developed one of the most complex and intensive systems
of agriculture in pre-colonial Africa. There was evidently no violent

disruption of the Lozi system of tribute and exchange, and Kololo agents were posted to local chiefs and headmen throughout much of the kingdom. And by marrying their women to Lozi men, the Kololo began to impose their language with astonishing speed on the various dialect groups of the kingdom. The original Lozi language, Siluyana, eventually survived only as a special court language, whereas the Kololo language actually came to be called Silozi and was an important unifying influence. All the same, it seems fairly clear that the Kololo failed to integrate the peoples of the flood plain under a centralised government such as the Lozi kings had administered. There was certainly widespread discontent among the Lozi under Kololo rule, and meanwhile Lozi kingship had been maintained in exile by the rival princes to the north. Imasiku had been killed in 1860, but other princes continued to work for a restoration, and in 1864 a Lozi aristocrat, Njekwa, advanced south through the flood plain. It was now the Kololo who failed to mount any concerted defence. Sekeletu had died in the previous year, and once again there was conflict over the royal succession. Besides, many Kololo had died from malaria. This was rife in the Zambezi valley, and the Kololo, whose original home was in healthy highland country, had no immunity. When the Kololo army met the Lozi under Njekwa, they were killed almost to a man. The Lozi prince Sipopa now arrived from Lukwakwa and became king.

The Restored Lozi Kingdom

The restoration of the Lozi monarchy did not by any means bring peace or unity to the divided kingdom. Sipopa represented only one faction among the royal exiles. Those who remained in Lukwakwa had set up a rival dynasty, which posed a standing threat to the northern borders of the flood plain. Thus Lozi monarchy did not in itself provide a single focus for reuniting the kingdom. Instead, Sipopa sought to strengthen his position by gaining support from various non-Lozi groups.

In the first place, Sipopa relied heavily on Mbunda diviners. Lozi exiles in the north had been much influenced by Mbunda, and Sipopa himself had spent four years in Lukwakwa. The Mbunda lacked any centralised chieftainship; conflicts among them were often attributed to witchcraft, and it was the business of diviners to discover the supposed witches. This sort of justice now became common at the Lozi court. Sipopa's rule became increasingly secretive and despotic, and opposition spread along the valley. So in 1874 Sipopa sought a new power base: he moved his capital to Sesheke, in the far south. Here he had ruthlessly suppressed a revolt by Subiya and Toka in 1865–6, but he now sought support by giving some of them government posts and even estates in the flood plain.

Sipopa's most far-reaching alliance was with an English trader, George Westbeech, who arrived from the south in 1871. Several traders from the south – white men, Tswana and Griqua – had visited the Kololo king Sekeletu, but on the whole he had found the Mambari less demanding. Westbeech, however, was a special case: like Livingstone, he was welcomed as a possible means of protection against the Ndebele. Westbeech had traded with Mzilikazi for several years, and after Mzilikazi's death in 1868, Westbeech had gained the confidence of his successor Lobengula. Sipopa thus saw friendship with Westbeech as a guarantee against Ndebele attacks; besides, Westbeech was trading on a large scale and could afford to offer more reasonable terms than earlier southern traders. Sipopa let him build a house at Sesheke and allowed him to set up his own village at Pandamatenga, south of the Victoria Falls. This was a no-man's-land between the spheres of Lozi, Ndebele and Tswana influence; it was also the furthest point to which Westbeech could bring his wagon-teams of oxen without exposing them to tsetse. Westbeech exported several hundred tusks each year, and sold Sipopa guns, powder and cloth superior in quality to that which came from the west. Mambari trade suffered in consequence, though in about 1874 Sipopa was ready enough to sell ivory to a Portuguese trader who brought slaves from Msiri's in Katanga.

Despite his various new sources of support, Sipopa was no more successful than Sekeletu had been in using Sesheke as a base from which to control the heart of the kingdom in the flood plain. Sipopa's attempts to rule through terror provoked a general revolt in 1876, which brought about his death. His prime minister now sought supreme power by installing Mwanawina, a young nephew of Sipopa, on the throne, but in 1878 there was another revolt. Mwanawina fled to the southeast and he was replaced by Lubosi, a prince from another branch of the royal family. Lubosi now established the royal capital at Lealui, in the Lozi heartland. Royal rivalry persisted, however, and in 1884 Lubosi was himself expelled by an alliance of princes, senior chiefs, Mbunda diviners and groups of Subiya and Toka. The leader of this alliance, Mataa, became prime minister, and enthroned Akufuna Tatila, a young prince from Lukwakwa. This piece of king-making was no more successful than the last: in 1885 the Lukwakwa groups were heavily defeated by various forces which rallied in support of Lubosi. Lubosi regained the throne and was henceforward called 'Lewanika', 'the conqueror'.

To consolidate his position, Lewanika began by carrying out a thorough and merciless purge of his many enemies, especially those around Sesheke. He then set about more constructive means of binding the kingdom together. Close relations were put in charge of three new provincial councils: in the far south, at Sesheke, and in the north at

Libonta and Kaunga. After the fierce upheavals of the past forty years, Lewanika brought a much-needed stability to human settlement on the central plain by reassessing claims to land rights there. Finally, he set about a deliberate revival of Lozi kingship as it was believed to have existed before the Kololo conquest: to this end, Lewanika made various reforms in royal ceremonial, in military organisation and in the distribution of tribute. He paid special attention to the cults of royal ancestors and thereby affirmed the power of the kingship at the expense of Mbunda diviners; in 1889 he decided to punish, not those charged with witchcraft, but those who brought such charges.

Foreign trade was no less important to Lewanika than it had been to Sipopa and the Kololo kings. Soon after his accession in 1878 he sent a trade mission to Benguela; at the same time he sent ivory down the Zambezi to traders from the south. Lewanika, like Sipopa, keenly appreciated the special value of trade with Westbeech for Lozi external relations, and Westbeech continued to buy ivory from the Lozi until his death in 1888. Early in 1882 Lewanika gave Westbeech a concession to hunt in the Machili valley and by 1886 Westbeech had become a member of one of the royal councils. He and other traders from the south brought large quantities of beads and cloth. A few horses were sold to the Lozi, but the route from the south was too difficult to allow regular horse-trading. Guns continued to reach the Lozi from the south, though there was a ban on their export from British South Africa in 1882–4. We know little of the Lozi arms trade to the south, but it is likely that the emphasis was on quality – on rifles and elephant guns – rather than quantity. The many flintlocks with which the Lozi army was supplied in 1888 may well have come mostly from the west. Mambari and Portuguese traders continued to visit the Lozi capital, and their trade seems to have prospered under Lewanika more than it did under Sipopa. For during the 1880s there was a sharp rise in world demand for wild rubber, which grew on and around the north-western limits of the Lozi empire. Some of this was brought into the Lozi capital for sale to traders from the west, who also began to buy cattle from the Lozi. On the other hand, in 1890 Lewanika formally prohibited the slave trade, for like Mulambwa and Sekeletu before him he valued slaves as labour, not as goods for export. One other commercial reform must be noted. Kololo rulers had claimed sole ownership, as well as monopoly, of the kingdom's ivory. Under Sipopa, this became a major grievance, and Akufuna, during his brief reign in 1884–5, conceded the hunter's right to retain one tusk from each pair. Lewanika upheld this concession, though he continued to monopolise the sale of ivory to foreigners.

Lewanika's achievements in bringing a measure of stability and unity to the Lozi kingdom were not due simply to foreign trade or internal reforms. The prosperity of the kingdom rested in large part upon the exploitation of its empire. The economy of the flood plain was based on the ownership of slaves and cattle. Both had to be imported, whether as tribute or booty, and the demand for both greatly increased in the later nineteenth century. The demand for slaves increased partly because larger areas were put under cultivation. During the Kololo regime, Lozi exiles in the north had been obliged to learn how to cultivate woodland; they also learned the advantages of cassava. After the Lozi restoration, there was a general increase of settlement in the flood plain, and as mounds became scarcer, so people took both to clearing woodland and to draining the plain margins in order to plant both grain crops and cassava. All this called for more manpower (and womanpower) than the Lozi themselves were willing to provide. This demand was aggravated by Lewanika's reforms: there were more and more royal officials to be supported by the products of slave labour. There was also an expansion of transport: more goods were conveyed about the kingdom, whether by head or canoe, and in 1890 thousands of slaves were put to work on a big new canal between the capital and the main channel of the Zambezi. As for cattle, these were needed in order to reward officials, warriors and royal relations. Cattle were loaned out to subject peoples who occupied good pasture, such as groups of Mbunda, Luvale and Totela; and by 1890 cattle were also being sold to traders from the west. So the pressure mounted for new campaigns of plunder and conquest, preferably with the aid of English guns. Besides, the suppression of internal opposition involved Lozi attacks on their neighbours, since Lozi dissidents often took refuge among them. It is in this context that we must now survey the course of events in southern Zambia, and see how far they were shaped by Lozi expansion.

The South: the Tonga and Ila

Around the beginning of the nineteenth century, the inhabitants of the watershed grasslands on the Batoka plateau seem to have enjoyed a measure of peace and prosperity. Their way of life had probably changed little over the past 500 years. They practised mixed farming, though they continued to be skilled hunters and gatherers. They lived in large unfortified villages, centred on enclosures for their herds of cattle; remains of these villages have been recorded south of Zimba, and as far east as Choma. Livingstone passed through this country in 1855 and observed it with a keen archaeological eye:

> Again and again we came to the ruins of large towns, containing the only hieroglyphics of this country, worn millstones, with the round ball of quartz with which the grinding was effected. Great numbers of these balls were lying about, showing that the depopulation had been

the result of war, for, had the people removed in peace, they would have taken the balls with them.[7]

The first cause of this depopulation was a mysterious cattle-raider called Pingola, of whom little is known except that he came from the north-east. Then came Sebituane's Kololo in the 1830s, and after them the Ndebele, who raided as far east as the Lusitu river before retreating south. By 1855 the Toka people between the Victoria Falls and Zimba were paying tribute to the Kololo; further east, fine farming country was uninhabited almost as far as Choma. Beyond this, the people called themselves Tonga; they were independent of the Kololo but had recently dispersed into small settlements in order to spread alarm in the event of invasion. A few leaders exercised quite extensive political authority: one was Mapanza and another was Monze, who seems to have founded a successful rain cult and was also visited by ivory traders.

The borders of foreign domination on the Batoka plateau do not seem to have changed very much during the second half of the century. Neither the Kololo nor their Lozi successors exacted any regular tribute more than a few kilometres east of the Victoria Falls, while the confluence of the Zambezi and Chobe rivers remained the eastern limit of Lozi settlement. In the late 1850s there was probably an Ndebele raid on the Kalomo area, and it was there that Sipopa defeated a 'rebel chief' in about 1866. But on the whole it is likely that between 1860 and 1880 the Tonga on the plateau were left in sufficient peace to re-establish, at least in part, the herds of cattle which had been so gravely depleted earlier in the century. It was civil war, rather than mere appetite for plunder, which prompted Lozi incursions among the Tonga. In 1880 some Tonga in the Choma area almost wiped out a Lozi expedition which had probably been sent to track down the deposed king Mwanawina. Some time after 1885 a Lozi rebel, Sikabenga, took refuge with the Tonga chief Siachitema, north of Kalomo. He then joined forces with some Chikunda who had been driven out of the Zambezi valley. In 1888 Sikabenga attacked Sesheke and then retreated eastwards across the plateau as far as Monze. A Lozi army sent in pursuit contented itself with stealing cattle from Monze, but he meanwhile had called on the Ndebele for help against Sikabenga: the latter was killed by an Ndebele force a few months later. In 1891 and 1893 Ndebele raided the Choma area; in the latter year they carried out a hideous massacre not far north of the Victoria Falls. In face of this Ndebele threat, a Lozi group who had been sent to occupy Toka country promptly turned back and settled instead among the Totela in the upper Njoko valley.

It was, then, the Ndebele rather than the Lozi who proved most troublesome to the plateau Tonga. Lozi raiding was mostly directed further north, to the Ila. By the mid-nineteenth century, Ila political organisation was somewhat more centralised than that of the plateau Tonga. This was due to their more stable pattern of settlement. Around the Kafue flood plain it was possible to concentrate very large herds of cattle in certain areas. Men became both rich and powerful by increasing and distributing their herds, and a few men, such as Shaloba and Mukobela, were acknowledged as leaders of their local communities, in prayer and in war. Nonetheless, the Ila were egalitarians; when such a chief died, most of his cattle were killed and his successor would be another rich man, who might not be a kinsman. Thus no one family could accumulate exceptional wealth and power. Several Ila communities comprised more than a thousand people, but their loyalties were restricted to their immediate neighbours: there was no system whereby Ila communities might combine to resist a common enemy. So despite their reputation for great bravery, the Ila were frequently attacked by invaders organised on a larger scale.

During the early nineteenth century, the western Ila were invaded from both west and north. The Lozi king Mulambwa raided the Ila for cattle at least once. Then came a group of Lozi exiles, who eventually settled at the western end of the Ila plain under one Shezongo. Not far to the north another colony was established by Kaingu, who traced his origins to the Kaonde. Kaingu's village was frequented by Mambari traders on their way east, and both he and Shezongo increased their own followings through trade: they hunted elephant and with the ivory bought slaves as well as cloth from the Mambari. Both colonies adopted many Ila customs, but they kept few cattle and the people were of such mixed origin that the Ila called them Lumbu – foreigners.

Meanwhile, around 1840, Sebituane's Kololo advanced through Ila country before turning west to the Lozi. By the 1850s the Kololo were sending out raiding parties from the upper Zambezi; the Ndebele evidently deterred them from invading the Batoka plateau, and instead they attacked the westernmost Ila. In 1855 Sekeletu seized Kaingu's cattle and probably killed him, then went on eastwards to raid the Lenje of Chipepo, beyond the Lukanga swamp. By 1870 the Ila of Bwengwa, towards the eastern end of the plain, were regarded as tributaries by the Lozi; their refusal of tribute at about this time provoked Sipopa into despatching a 'punitive' raid. In 1875 some Ila visited Sipopa to exchange presents with him, and this was said to be an annual custom. In 1882 Lewanika led an army of several thousands against the Ila; he raided all along the southern edge of the flood plain and eventually returned to the upper Zambezi with 20,000 head of cattle. In 1888 the Lozi who attacked Monze went home by way of the Ila and exacted tribute from Shaloba and Shapela. They did not try conclusions with the redoubtable Sala prophetess Longo (Nashintu), whose magical powers had troubled the Kololo king, Sebituane, many years before, and one Lozi detachment was soundly defeated by the Ila chief Mbeza, who got help from the Tonga chief Mapanza. But in 1889 several Ila visited Lewanika to offer their submission, and a further Lozi raid in 1891, for slaves as well as cattle, persuaded still more Ila that the payment of tribute might be a lesser burden: three Ila parties visited Lewanika in 1892, while Longo too sent him cattle.

The Tonga in the Gwembe valley, along what is now the floor of Lake Kariba, were subject to invasions from three directions: from the Lozi kingdom in the west, the Ndebele in the south and the Chikunda in the east. Most of the Gwembe valley was infested by tsetse, so few Tonga there kept cattle, but they suffered recurrent losses of women and crops. By 1860, and probably long before that, the people in the western part of the valley planted two crops a year: one above the level of the river when in flood, and the other in alluvial soils lower down its banks, when the floodwaters had receded. This system was highly precarious: there was often too little rain for the upper gardens, while the alluvial gardens could be ruined either by too low a flood or by early flooding before the harvest was ready. But in good years the western part of the valley yielded abundant food, and in 1860 there were clusters of dense settlement on both banks. This concentration of people and produce naturally attracted raiders from beyond the valley. At the same time, the Gwembe Tonga were seldom able to mount resistance on a large enough scale to exclude such invaders. In places, the population was thick on the ground, but it was far from united. The Zambezi current flowed too fast to provide easy communication upstream as well as downstream; the river was mostly used to link villages on either bank. As on the plateau to the west, communities in the valley were centred on rain-shrines. In 1860 there were two important leaders among the western Gwembe, Sinamani and Mweemba; but the only real chiefs were in the more open country further east, where Simamba and Sikoongo gained power by trading in ivory and slaves.

During the 1850s, the Gwembe Tonga were raided by both Kololo and Toka. In 1862, Sinamani was paying tribute to the Kololo, but at the same time he was also harassed by Ndebele raiders. In 1874 the Nambiya chief Wankie, who then lived on the Zambezi below the Kalomo gorge, was quite independent of the Lozi; by 1880, they exacted tribute from him, but further east they made only occasional raids, and the villages on the south bank at the western end of the valley paid tribute to the Ndebele. Around 1870, at the mouth of the Kafue, Simamba and Sikoongo used guns to repulse an army of Ndebele, who never again crossed the Zambezi below the Kariba gorge.

Meanwhile, the upper valley was frequented by Chikunda. In 1860, east of Sinamani's, the Zumbo trader Santanna bought slaves as well as ivory. Other traders followed from the east, and by 1875 black 'Portuguese' traders came up the Zambezi as far as Wankie's; in 1877 they bought slaves there with ivory, which Wankie probably resold to white traders from the south. In the same year, one group of black Portuguese took the supplying of slaves into their own hands: the robber-baron Kanyemba devastated the valley for eighty kilometres above the Kariba gorge. Tonga spearmen were no match for Chikunda musketeers, and hundreds of Tonga were killed or enslaved. Trade of a sort seems to have been re-established, for by 1888 one village at the western end of the Gwembe valley had a large number of guns and was able to prevent an Ndebele party from crossing the river. But at the eastern end of the valley many Tonga threw in their lot with the Chikunda and themselves became slave-raiders.

The Impact of Overseas Trade

By 1890, the peoples of Zambia had absorbed two invasions by black South Africans; still more important, they had nearly all been drawn in some way into the world economy. Like other parts of the far interior of Africa, Zambia lay on the last frontiers for the uncontrolled slaughter of elephant and the capture of slave labour. The demand for ivory, and for the fruits of slave labour, now came mostly from Europe and North America. The export of slaves from central Africa was largely a response to the demands of white men for tropical goods produced by slave labour: cotton and sugar in the Americas and the Indian Ocean; cloves in Zanzibar; coffee in Brazil and Angola; cocoa in the Portuguese West African island of Sao Tomé. This was ironical, when so many white men loudly opposed the slave trade. Livingstone himself admitted:

> We are guilty of keeping up slavery by giving increasing prices for slave-grown cotton and sugar. We are the great supporters of slavery – unwittingly often, but truly.[8]

Meanwhile, the demand for slaves within Africa was greatly stimulated by the ivory trade, and it was the demand for ivory in Europe and America – far outstripping the centuries-old demand for African ivory in India – which prompted African and Arab traders to 'open up' the Dark Continent. Slaves were often needed as ivory porters, while they were also employed in the fields and households of ivory traders – whether local chiefs or alien colonists. Sometimes, indeed, villages were razed and their inhabitants taken hostage to compel the production of ivory. The death, disorder and devastation in inner Africa shocked early white visitors, but ultimately whites were responsible. White luxury involved African misery, and an early French traveller in Zambia asked ungallantly:

> O tender-hearted ladies of Europe, as your white hands lightly caress the keyboard of your piano; as you play with your paper knife or the handle of your umbrella; do you suspect what blows, what tears, what sufferings each piece of ivory has cost the wretched black man; can you imagine the horrible crimes and atrocities committed in its name?[9]

Thus events in Zambia in the later nineteenth century were largely, if indirectly, determined by the industrialised societies of the northern hemisphere. And like many other people in the tropical world, Zambia's inhabitants were mostly too poor, too ignorant and too ill-organised to ensure that overseas trade increased rather than diminished their own wealth. Foreigners took out ivory and human beings, and in return provided little more than cloth, beads and third-rate guns. Yet these articles appealed so much to people all over Zambia that they were willing to collaborate in the continued destruction of elephant, and the murderous capture of slaves, whether for use or sale. Thus valuable resources, both human and animal, were squandered for meagre short-term gains.

Some people, of course, gained much more than others. Here and there, as among the Lozi and Bemba, African rulers were able to exploit overseas trade for the purpose of building up their own empires. The Lozi were especially well placed, not only because they already had a quite complex system of local exchange, but because they had access to the outside world in two different directions – both south and west. This made it easier for the rulers of the Lozi kingdom to dictate their own terms to foreign traders. If a king was strong enough to enforce a monopoly of ivory, this could advance, not only his own interests but those of his subjects as against those of his customers. Thus Livingstone reported of the ivory monopoly imposed by the Kololo king Sekeletu:

> Here the Chief is expected to be generous, and, as a father among his children, to share the proceeds of the ivory with his people. They say, 'Children require the guidance of their fathers, so as not to be cheated by foreigners.' This reconciles them to the law. The upper classes, too, receive the lion's share of the profits from the elephant-hunt without undergoing much of the toil and danger.[10]

Much the same can be said of the nationalisation of major industries by the government of modern Zambia.

On the whole, though, it was rare that even a limited group of Africans profited directly from long-distance trade or retained much initiative in conducting it. The Bemba and Lozi terrorised their neighbours, and in between their own spheres of raiding lay a vast region disputed by several powerful invaders: the Ndebele, the Yeke of Msiri, the Ngoni of Mpezeni, the Chikunda of Kanyemba and Matakenya. A fortunate few were laid under tribute and so gained a claim to protection by one of these powers. Those taken captive by the Ngoni were perhaps better off than others in eastern Zambia. The Ngoni valued male prisoners as potential warriors, to expand their own dominions: they were thus – like the Lozi – importers rather than exporters of manpower. But such incorporation within a growing kingdom was very much an exception: most of eastern, central and southern Zambia was a hunting-ground in which the aim of the invader was plunder rather than conquest. For all too many people, participation in overseas trade went no further than seeing their fields and villages overrun by marauders.

There was, indeed, a general rise in violence. Trade multiplied the means and incentives both for enriching a kingdom and for enforcing obedience within it: as the spoils of power increased, so they were the more jealously guarded. And like any other people, African rulers were morally debased by the use of violence for political ends. Like Kanyemba and Matakenya on the Zambezi, Lozi, Bemba and Lunda rulers were guilty of terrible cruelties. To some extent these can be attributed to witchcraft beliefs: war and trade bred new fears and rivalries, which often gave rise to accusations of witchcraft, and this was usually punishable by an extremely painful death. But there is no doubt that mutilation and torture were practised, not only for recognised judicial ends, but also to satisfy private sadistic appetites. And the increasing trade in human beings had an inevitably coarsening effect. The Lozi behaved towards their slaves and subject-peoples with the arrogance to be expected in any society where certain classes of people are regarded simply as factors of production: some Lozi once remarked of slaves at their capital, 'Those are not *people*, they are our dogs.'[11]

It would be a mistake, however, to dismiss the later nineteenth century as a Dark Age of growing violence and degradation. Such a view has indeed been widely held – both by those for whom colonial rule rescued Africans from their own 'savagery' and by those who blame African poverty and weakness on the white men's slave trade. But there is clear evidence that in Zambia, as elsewhere in Africa, the growth of overseas trade had constructive as well as destructive effects. Long-distance trade encouraged the production of goods for local consumption as well as for export. New trade routes linked up older-established networks of local exchange: ironwork, salt or tobacco which used to circulate within, say, a fifty kilometre radius might now be carried much further afield. Besides, there was a new kind of consumer – the long-distance trader. People who spent long periods away from home –

Bisa traders, the Mambari, the East Africans and the white men from the south – depended on trade for subsistence. Thus the production and transport of ivory, slaves, cattle or rubber served to stimulate the production of necessities, such as food, salt and ironwork, as well as the import of 'luxuries', such as cloth, beads or copper wire, which were in any case tending to become necessities.

The impact of long-distance trade was especially marked in the field of food production. In the first place it made possible a kind of agricultural revolution, by stimulating the adoption of American crops. Most of the food crops grown in Africa today were first cultivated, not in Africa, but in the Americas: among these are maize, cassava, sweet potatoes, groundnuts and sugar-cane. These were originally introduced to Africa by the Portuguese, but they were mostly taken inland by African traders and travellers. By the end of the eighteenth century, cassava was common among the Luvale, in the dominions of the Lunda emperor Mwata Yamvo and as far east as Kazembe's eastern borders. By about 1850, if not earlier, all these American crops, and also tomatoes, were abundant in the Lozi flood plain. Further east, at this latitude, cassava was still rare: it was not reported among the Tonga, Lala or southern Bisa, and the Tonga, Ila and Bemba did not begin to adopt it until the end of the nineteenth century or later. Maize and groundnuts, however, were common among the plateau Tonga in 1855, and among the Ila by the end of the century. Maize was available at Kazembe's by 1798; among the Bisa north and east of Lake Bangweulu by 1810; and on the southern borders of Bemba country by 1831. The Bemba king Chitapankwa had abundant maize fields in 1883, though in this he was unusual. Groundnuts were reported among the Bemba in 1867, and sweet potatoes in 1883. A few Bisa also took up the growing of rice, a crop which had originally come to eastern Africa, not from the Americas but from the Arab world.

The adoption of exotic crops tended to increase overall food production, since the new crops could usually be cultivated in addition to rather than instead of the old ones: the land required for maize and cassava was not the same as that best suited to millet, and cassava at least, being a root crop, could be harvested at almost any time of year. Such diversification also reduced the risk of a total crop failure, and hence of famine. Thus the new crops introduced as a result of overseas trade made it easier to produce a surplus of food beyond the requirements of cultivators. This was most noticeable in the upper Zambezi valley, where local conditions favoured an expansion of agriculture in certain areas and where there was a steady demand both from the Lozi ruling classes and from long-distance traders. The Toka and Subiya, for example, had to pay tribute in grain, but they also offered it for sale. In 1875 a Czech traveller noted at Sesheke that

A certain proportion of the ingathering is allotted to the women to dispose of as they please: and to judge from the hard bargains they drove with myself and the white traders, they seem to manipulate their property with considerable advantage to themselves. The men, too, always demanded more for the goods that belonged to the women than they did for their own, saying the wife had fixed the price, and that if they could not obtain it they were to carry the things back again.[12]

In 1886, the same traveller was struck by the eager response of the Toka to the advent of long-distance traders:

If these Matoka hear that no Matabele are in the area and that Europeans have arrived from the south in Panda-ma-Tenka, they rush there with baskets full of fruits on their carrying poles. . . . Or they bring containers made out of pumpkin or so-called calabashes filled with 30 to 40 kg of millet, maize, beans or groundnuts. . . . They ask for calico and glass beads for the objects they bring to exchange. As soon as the exchange is made they force the cloth into the calabashes and hurry home happily to their people where they tell all they have seen in great detail and at great length. This trade is really well organized, and the Matoka like it very much. Often the actual tradesman is accompanied by his brothers as porters who then ask the same in return from him. Many, however, have slaves who have to do the carrying. The Victoria Falls are considered by the natives as the best trading area. Often they bring the cheap cloths they get there further north to the Matoka in order to exchange them for cheap grain with at least 100 per cent profit.[13]

The American food crops were not the only exotic crops to enrich pre-colonial trade: tobacco was also important. We do not know how long tobacco has been grown in Zambia, but it probably reached the region by the same paths of trade which communicated the new food crops. Hemp was grown and smoked all over Zambia, but the available varieties of tobacco mostly flourished only in the hot, moist climates of the main river valleys. Thus for the Gwembe Tonga, and the Senga on the upper Luangwa, tobacco became a major export crop. Livingstone noted that Gwembe tobacco was 'very strong and very cheap . . . the natives come great distances to buy.' Sinamani's people grew large quantities of tobacco, which they made into balls for sale in Lozi country. 'Twenty balls, weighing about three-quarters of a pound each, are sold for a hoe.'[14] Some people, such as the Toka and Ila, smoked their tobacco in finely carved pipes, but it was more commonly taken in the form of snuff, and snuff-boxes as well as pipes were produced for the market.

Metalworking clearly received a new impetus from the expansion of overseas trade. In the first place, there was a new demand for weapons.

Iron spears were needed in order to hunt for elephant and slaves, and, as we have seen, Bemba chiefs paid their iron-workers in imported cloth. Despite the growth of the gun trade from about 1870, spears continued to be widely used: guns were often unreliable and seldom properly maintained, while supplies of ammunition and powder were often irregular. There is indeed much evidence to suggest that in central and eastern Africa spears played a larger part than firearms in the political upheavals of the later nineteenth century. At the same time, it is likely that iron tools became much more common. Livingstone tells a story which clearly shows how long-distance trade, as managed by a powerful kingdom, could promote a modest advance in technology. In the early 1850s, some Mambari traders bought iron hoes near Sesheke and took them on eastwards to a group of Tonga; these 'would not part with children for clothing or beads, but agriculture with wooden hoes is so laborious, that the sight of the hoes prevailed.'[15] Livingstone pointed out that if the Kololo were to supply the Tonga with hoes, they would be able to get Tonga ivory for themselves and also check the export of slaves: the suggestion was adopted, and apparently met with success.

It is also probable that the copper trade expanded in the later nineteenth century. The strictly practical uses of copper remained very limited, though the Kaonde at Kansanshi made bullets from copper which were quite effective. But copper ornaments were highly prized and often seen in the main centres for trade and the exchange of tributary goods. Livingstone noted that Kololo women not only delighted 'in having the whole person shining with butter'; they liked to wear

> large brass anklets as thick as the little finger, and armlets of both brass and ivory, the latter often an inch broad. The rings are so heavy that the ankles are often blistered by the weight pressing down; but it is the fashion, and is borne as magnanimously as tight lacing and tight shoes among ourselves.[16]

It is possible that in the Lozi kingdom the development of trade to the south reduced dependence on African copper industries, for by 1875 the ornaments worn at Sesheke were said to be mostly made from wire imported from South Africa. Such wire may also have been the source for the copper rings worn among the Gwembe Tonga by 1880. But elsewhere in Zambia it would seem that there was an expanding market for the products of African copper mines. In 1855 the Lozi exiles on the Kabompo river received copper (perhaps from the mines on the Dongwe river) from Lukolwe traders who refused to accept ivory but were eager for cloth. The Ndembu who obtained cloth from Mambari traders probably used some of it to pay for the copper which they obtained from Lunda further east. Livingstone noticed that one of Ishinde's relations was obliged by such large bundles of copper rings on his ankles to adopt quite a straddling walk. When I laughed at the absurd appearance he made, the people remarked, '*That is lordship in these parts*'.[17]

By 1867 the leading Bemba chiefs and their wives were also weighed down by leglets of copper wire. These were made from copper bars sold by visiting Yeke traders from Katanga: a few Yeke settled in and around Bemba country, where they made copper wire as well as ironwork and bark boxes. Thus north-eastern Zambia continued to obtain copper from Katanga, even though by this time Kazembe had lost control of the Katanga copper trade. Indeed, it is likely that by this time almost all the African copper traded north of the Zambezi had been produced in Katanga: Africans were still mining copper there in the early twentieth century, whereas the old workings in what is now Zambia appear to have been abandoned many years earlier: the miners had exhausted the payable deposits.

As trade became more far-ranging and diverse, metalwork came to be valued, not only as a consumer good, but as a form of currency. Iron hoes, bars of copper and coils of wire could be exchanged almost anywhere for the goods a trader really wanted, and they were given generally agreed prices in terms of other commodities. The same was true of imported cloth. Salt was too heavy and bulky to serve the same purpose, in spite of its scarcity, but on occasion a long-distance trader might find that the salt trade could advance his own business: in the far north-east, in the 1880s, East African traders often bought ivory and slaves with salt from the Lake Mweru region rather than with imports from the coast.

There are, then, good grounds for supposing that at least in some parts of Zambia there was a marked increase in real wealth during the later nineteenth century. Further research is needed on this subject, but it seems clear enough that the new opportunities presented by the expansion of overseas trade encouraged many people to increase production, not only of goods for export (ivory, slaves, etc.) but also of consumer and capital goods: food, tobacco, ornaments, tools and weapons. Such a conclusion is at least in line with recent research on Tanzania and Rhodesia during this period. Some so-called 'subsistence economies' in tropical Africa were in fact capable of meeting much more than their own immediate needs: they had reserves of land and labour – and commercial enterprise – which could be brought into use once there was a market in which their own products could be exchanged for other goods they wanted – whether these were glass beads from Venice or hoe blades from across a nearby river. It could indeed be argued that the export of wasting assets (people, ivory tusks, wild rubber) did to some extent stimulate agricultural production – a point of special interest at the present time, when Zambia seeks to use copper profits to the same end.

Yet when due allowance has been made for these beneficent side-effects of overseas trade, it remains important to stress that the advances made were very limited and localised. In terms of knowledge and power, there was no fundamental change in the relationship between the peoples of Zambia and the peoples overseas whose markets they supplied. There was, of course, a growing awareness of a wider world; here and there people gained some insight into the mechanisms of price-formation, and African industrial and commercial skills deserve more credit than they have usually received. But in 1890 reading and writing were still almost unknown, and the lack of literacy hampered calculation, communication and the accumulation of knowledge.

Throughout the nineteenth century the underlying conditions of African life were scarcely altered. People remained very much at the mercy of natural forces. In southern Zambia, where rainfall is both less abundant and more erratic than in the north, drought and flood caused periodic famines. Red locusts, from the marshes of Mweru wa ntipa and Lake Rukwa, swept over the north-east in 1827–31 and devastated Lamba country in the 1850s. There were smallpox epidemics in western Zambia throughout the nineteenth century and there was an epidemic in the north-east in 1883. For peoples who cultivated the poorer soils of northern Zambia, disease and warfare may even have been ecologically advantageous, in so far as they checked any increase in the pressure of population on land. Food reserves, stored in pole-and-mud granaries, remained more or less vulnerable to pests and damp, and it was hard to keep much of a surplus against lean years. The greater use of iron tools tended to increase food production, but other advances in technology were unusual. A few men became skilled at repairing the working parts of guns, and by 1893 iron bullets were cast at the Lozi capital. Among the valley Tonga, gun-barrels were forged, while gunpowder was made from nitre and sulphurous wood ash. But such initiatives seem to have been exceptional. In general people still depended on imports for barrels, ammunition and powder. Tsetse fly continued to prevent the introduction of horses in any numbers, or the use of oxen as draught animals; indeed, tsetse encroached into areas deserted by people and cattle as a result of war, or fear of war.

Finally, we must bear in mind the political and cultural diversity of Zambia in the later nineteenth century. There was, of course, a marked expansion in the scale of social and political relations, in so far as people were drawn into the structures of the larger kingdoms, and came within the orbit of long-distance trade. A few rulers could muster armies of several thousand men and could bring influence to bear on subordinates a hundred and fifty kilometres distant, or more. Ideas and skills, as well as goods, circulated widely: people adopted new dances and forms of etiquette as well as food crops, and a few words of Swahili and Portuguese entered their languages. The lines of division between Zambian peoples were less marked than ever before; their political and cultural identities were increasingly merged in wider groupings. Yet there was no single focus for such imitation and assimilation; instead, there were a number of different spheres of influence, which were linked to the outside world by routes which led in all directions. The Lozi kingdom was a meeting-point for influences coming both from Angola and the Atlantic, and from South Africa and Britain. The Chikunda empires drew central Zambia into the orbit of the Portuguese in Mozambique while the Bemba, through their association with Arab and Swahili traders, linked the north-east to East Africa.

Thus in the last years of the nineteenth century the territory that is now Zambia was subject to external influences and pressures from at least four distinct sources. In this respect, Tanzania provides a striking contrast: there, the growth of overseas trade was centred on the Swahili coast and traders began to spread the use of Swahili as a common language throughout the country. This difference in the experience of the two countries during the nineteenth century has been of considerable importance for their more recent history.[18] We must now see why the various spheres of African influence and outside pressure north of the Zambezi were in fact merged in a single territorial unit – the British colony of Northern Rhodesia.

NOTES

1. A small part of Lundazi district was occupied by Magodi and Pikamalaza, followers of Mbelwa.
2. *King Kazembe*, I, 144.
3. D. and C. Livingstone, *Narrative of an Expedition to the Zambesi and its Tributaries* (1865), 502.
4. H. H. Johnston, confidential note enclosed in Johnston to Anderson, 23 March 1893, Foreign Office records 2/54, Public Record Office, London.
5. Livingstone's missionary aims are discussed in Chapter IX.
6. D. Livingstone, *Missionary Travels and Researches in South Africa* (1857), 228.
7. *Missionary Travels*, 548.
8. David Livingstone to Robert Livingstone, 31 May 1859, quoted in George Seaver, *David Livingstone: his Life and Letters* (1957), p. 345.
9. Edouard Foà, *La Traversée de l'Afrique du Zambèze au Congo Français* (Paris, 1900), p. 85.
10. *Narrative*, p. 288.
11. F. S. Arnot, *Garenganze, or, Seven Years' Pioneer Mission Work in Central*

Africa (1889), p. 73. But one such slave, kicked out of a hut, calmly declared, 'Yes, master, I know you think me to be a dog; but, sir, I am not a dog, I am a man.' (ibid., 77).

12. E. Holub, *Seven Years in South Africa* (1881), II, p. 303.

13. E. Holub (tr. C. Johns, ed. L. Holy), *Travels North of the Zambezi* (Manchester, 1975), pp 26–7.

14. *Narrative*, pp. 239, 317.

15. *Missionary Travels*, p. 526.

16. *Missionary Travels*, p. 187.

17. I. Schapera (ed.), *Livingstone's African Journal 1853–1856* (1963), p. 39.

18. See pp. 241 and 246.

IX

The British Take Over
c. 1860 – 1900

As a geographical unit, Zambia was created by the European Partition of Africa in the late nineteenth century. Before we consider why this territory came under British rule, and how its borders were determined, we should briefly consider why it should have come under European rule at all.

The imposition of European rule over most of Africa can be seen as the result of two distinct but converging processes: growing rivalry among the major states of Europe as they became fully industrial powers, and their increasing need for cheap raw materials from the tropical world. Throughout most of the nineteenth century the industrialised world (North America as well as Europe) was able to get what it wanted from tropical Africa without going to the trouble and expense of ruling it. Africans were able to supply such commodities as palm-oil, ivory and manpower at a price that was acceptable to European customers. In the later part of the century, this measure of co-operation began to break down. In the first place, Europeans in West Africa were under increasing pressure to cut their own costs, which meant imposing their own terms of trade on Africans. In the second place, European aims in Africa as a whole were changing fast. White men were no longer content with the scale and variety of exports produced by independent African societies. They wanted raw materials such as cotton and rubber; they wanted minerals, especially gold; and they wanted these things in larger quantities than ever before. To satisfy these demands, it would be necessary to control the use of African labour, and also to build railways.

These new objectives seemed incompatible with African political independence. This was not simply because most whites regarded Africans as primitive savages, incapable of rational behaviour. Such prejudice was indeed an important factor in European policies – and it was on the increase. But it was not mere racism to argue that African political organisation was unfitted for really large-scale exploitation of land and labour. If Africa's mineral and vegetable resources were to be properly 'opened up', capitalists had to be persuaded to invest money in Africa. They would only do so if they could be reasonably sure that white business in Africa was safe from African interference. And even the largest states in tropical Africa seemed too small, or too loosely governed, to provide adequate security for European lives and property.

There were, then, persuasive reasons why white men came to think that tropical Africa should be placed under white rule. But white rule was not in itself enough to meet the needs of individual European nations. At a time of increasing economic rivalry in Europe, governments tended to take more active steps than before to protect the interests of their own traders and manufacturers against those of rival countries. The only sure way for a government to do this in Africa was to control those areas where its own trade and industry were most involved. Besides, governments were not only concerned to defend existing interests in the tropics; they also wished to reserve for themselves areas for possible future exploitation. European trade and influence now reached into most corners of the globe: there were no new continents to be discovered. European expansion had been immensely speeded up by the Industrial Revolution, yet it was now confined within more or less known geographical limits. In such a rapidly shrinking world, claiming large tracts of unexplored wilderness seemed no more than prudent insurance. This anxiety to secure both present and future needs was a major reason why so much of Africa and other parts of the tropical world was shared out among European governments in the late nineteenth century. Besides, the growing competition for tropical empire meant that tropical areas acquired a new value as diplomatic bargaining counters: a European country might seek influence in some part of Africa, not so much for its own sake as to gain a pawn which could be used on the chessboard of European politics. And the scientific and technological advances of the period – especially in tropical medicine, firearms and shipbuilding – meant that Europeans usually had the power to enforce their will in the tropical world.

We can thus see the Partition of Africa, sudden though it was, as a logical consequence of changes in economic relations between the tropics and the industrial West. But the reasons why any one part of Africa was assigned to one European power rather than another must be sought in the history of that particular region and in the case of Zambia the explanation is rather complex. As we saw in the last chapter, this part of Africa was being drawn during the 1880s into a number of different spheres of external influence. In the north-west, there were the Mambari and Portuguese of Angola and the Yeke of Katanga; in the north-east, the Arabs and Swahili of East Africa; in the east, the

Chikunda and Portuguese of the middle and lower Zambezi; in the south-west, the Ndebele. There were also, in the south-west, some British traders, but it was far from obvious in, say, 1885 that most of the vast region between the upper Zambezi and Lake Malawi would shortly pass under British rule. To understand why this happened we must first look more closely at the growth of British interests in this region; we must then look at the wider scene of European interests and rivalries in Africa south of the Equator.

Livingstone and the Missionary Advance

British interest in the country north of the Zambezi was first aroused by David Livingstone's *Missionary Travels and Researches in South Africa*, an account of his great journey across Africa in 1853–6. Livingstone's main purpose in writing this book was to gain support for his own very personal conception of Christian mission work in Africa. Livingstone was a spokesman both of Christianity and of the Industrial Revolution. He had, as a boy in a Lanarkshire cotton-mill, seen the rougher side of modern industry, but he was convinced that the industrial power of Britain and the expansion of British trade were essential to the working-out of the divine plan, which had room for material progress on earth as well as salvation in the life to come. Livingstone was also convinced that Africans would only be persuaded to accept the Christian gospel if their social and economic conditions were improved – which in his view meant learning new skills from European advisers and growing crops for export to Europe. The great obstacle to such progress was the slave trade, but Livingstone was sure that Africans would abandon this once they were given an opportunity to profit by more legitimate trade.

Livingstone had originally hoped that the Kololo kingdom would prove a suitable base for such an experiment. His journey west in 1853–4 proved that the flood plain was too unhealthy and too hard to reach from the west coast; instead, he turned his attention further east, to the Batoka plateau and to the possibility of opening a route to the east coast. It was with this in mind that he set off down the Zambezi in 1856, with a commission from the Kololo king, Sekeletu, to sell a load of ivory for a variety of English manufactures, including a sugar-mill. As he crossed the half-empty plains of the Batoka plateau, Livingstone was impressed by its healthy climate and fertile soils. He continued eastwards to the coast and returned to Britain convinced that the Batoka plateau was the place to begin turning pagan African cultivators into Christian peasants, with the aid of a few carefully chosen white farmers.

Livingstone's appeal for support was warmly received. There was by this time much enthusiasm in Britain for mission projects overseas.

There was also a widespread desire to stop the slave trade: indeed, the British government had been engaged in attempts to suppress the export of slaves from Africa for the past fifty years. But Livingstone's scheme needed money as well as good-will, and in this respect it was the commercial possibilities which counted most. Livingstone asserted that large quantities of cotton could be grown very cheaply on the Batoka plateau, and perhaps elsewhere in the region. It was this point which led the British government to finance a new expedition, in which Livingstone and other experts would begin the work of agricultural and religious instruction. Livingstone himself was appointed a British consul, and he resigned from the London Missionary Society.

In 1858 Livingstone returned to the Zambezi, accompanied by several other Europeans. He now discovered a serious obstacle to his plans for a Batoka mission. On his journey down the Zambezi two years before he had gained the impression that the river was navigable from its mouth to beyond the Kafue confluence. It was only now that he saw for himself the fearsome Caborabassa rapids above Tete. The Zambezi was not quite the broad highway into the far interior which he had imagined. This discovery put paid to Livingstone's chances of further government support for his mission plans. He was reluctant to admit defeat: in 1859 he urged the British government to plant a colony of settlers near the Kafue. But the Prime Minister, Lord Palmerston, acidly remarked:

> I am very unwilling to embark on new schemes of British possessions. Dr L's information is valuable but he must not be allowed to tempt us to form colonies only to be reached by forcing steamers up cataracts.[1]

It was not only Livingstone whose hopes were wrecked on the rocks of Caborabassa: there was also Sekeletu. The Kololo king was sure that if only Livingstone and his wife – Moffat's daughter – would settle on the Batoka highlands the Kololo could settle there too without fear of Ndebele attacks. In 1860 Livingstone revisited Sekeletu, bringing him most of the goods he had ordered four years earlier. Sekeletu gave Livingstone a letter for the British government: 'Sekeletu says to the Lord of the English, Give me of your people to dwell with me, and I shall cut off a country for them to dwell in. . . .'[2] But this plea fell on deaf ears. By this time Livingstone himself had decided that the Shire highlands, south of Lake Malawi, offered the best prospects for the kind of mission he envisaged. Besides, there had been a further setback to missionary ambitions on the upper Zambezi. The London Missionary Society had decided to send out its own expedition to the Kololo. This made its way north from the Cape, and reached the Kololo capital a few months before Livingstone's return in 1860. However this visit was a disaster: the leader, Helmore, his wife and two of their children died at Linyanti. The cause was probably malaria, but his colleague, Price, suspected poison. The Kololo got a bad name, and though they were overthrown in 1864 the political tensions in the region discouraged any further missionary approach to the upper Zambezi for several years.

Thus Livingstone's first two expeditions through what is now Zambia bore no immediate fruit in that area. Indeed, his plans for a mission in the Shire highlands also came to nothing. It was his third and last great expedition, from 1866 to 1873, which really quickened the pace of missionary advance in central Africa; it thereby also revived British interest in the region. Livingstone's last expedition, like his journey across Africa, was simply a journey of exploration: his main objectives were to map the river systems of the interior and report on the continuing spread of the slave trade. He began by going inland from Kilwa and across what is now northern Mozambique to the south end of Lake Malawi. From there he struck north-west, through Chewa, Bemba and Tabwa country, to Kazembe's capital on the Luapula. After a side-trip to Lake Bangweulu, he pushed north, in 1869, into Manyema, in eastern Zaïre, and in 1871 he was 'discovered' by Stanley at Ujiji, on Lake Tanganyika. Stanley urged him to return to England, but Livingstone was now obsessed with the belief that the ultimate sources of the Nile were to be found in what we know to be the upper Zaïre basin. He went south once more, recrossing the route of his outward journey through Lungu country. But by this time he had been far too long without proper medical care. He was terribly weakened by recurrent malaria, and tramping through the swamps around Lake Bangweulu in the rainy season proved too much for him. He died on 1 May 1873, in the village of a Lala headman, Chitambo. Indeed, the expedition had for some time been largely in the hands of two Africans, Susi and Chuma. They now came to a momentous decision: they buried Livingstone's heart at Chitambo's; they embalmed his body; and they carried it, along with his notes and diaries, back to the east coast, whence it was taken by ship to London. On 18 April 1874, Livingstone was buried in Westminster Abbey.

Livingstone's reports on his last wanderings, as they had filtered through to England, and the inspiring story of his death, gave new life to missionary ambitions in Europe and directed increasing attention to central Africa. In 1875-6 two Scottish missions followed in Livingstone's footsteps up the Shire valley. One, from the Church of Scotland, settled in the Shire highlands. The other, from the dissident Free Church, actually called itself 'Livingstonia' and settled at first at the south end of Lake Malawi. In 1881 it moved north up the lake to Bandawe, among the lakeside Tonga. Meanwhile, in 1879, the Livingstonia mission had sent out an engineer, James Stewart, to explore the country further north: he made the first European crossing from the north end of Lake Malawi to the south end of Lake Tanganyika.

In the following year the London Missionary Society, which had advanced inland from the Zanzibar coast, sent an expedition down Lake Tanganyika. In 1887 the L.M.S. opened a mission among the Mambwe, and in 1889 another among the Lungu. But for some years these L.M.S. missions made little impact. They had settled among people who were harassed by slave raiders, especially the Bemba. For this reason they were welcomed as protectors, and their stockaded stations became centres of refuge. Like other missionaries in similar circumstances, the L.M.S. men formed governments of their own. This was less a help than a hindrance; they were seen more as chiefs than as men of religion, and in any case they could not hope to achieve any widespread influence until they left their stockades and penetrated the Bemba, the major power in the region.

Far more important was the missionary advance to the upper Zambezi, from southern Africa. Missionary interest in this remote region, which had lapsed after the Helmore-Price disaster, revived in the late 1870s. The first new approach was made by François Coillard, a French Protestant who began working for the Paris Missionary Society in Basutoland in 1858. Twenty years later he led an expedition north with the aim of opening a mission among the Shona. This was frustrated by the Ndebele; instead, Coillard visited the Ngwato chief Khama, who had already become a Christian. Khama advised Coillard to push on to the Lozi kingdom, for the Lozi spoke the language of their former rulers, the Kololo, and this closely resembled the Sotho language which Coillard spoke fluently. Coillard duly reached Sesheke on the Zambezi. He was not allowed to visit the Lozi capital, for Lewanika had only just succeeded, and the political situation was still confused. But Lewanika had heard enough about missionaries among the Tswana and Ndebele to know that they could be of very practical assistance to an African king. Thus he told Coillard that he would indeed welcome a mission, and Coillard went back south to seek further support.

It was some years before Coillard was able to return, and meanwhile other missionaries from the south had reached the upper Zambezi. In 1880 a Jesuit party visited the valley Tonga, but fever compelled them to withdraw. In 1881 another Jesuit party visited Lewanika, who encouraged them to return with reinforcements. They came back in 1883, but by this time Lewanika had changed his mind for in the previous year he had been visited by a remarkable young Scots missionary, F. S. Arnot. As a child, Arnot had known Livingstone's children, and he early conceived an ambition to follow in the great man's footsteps. He joined a fundamentalist religious movement, the Plymouth Brethren, and came out on his own to South Africa in 1882. Like other white visitors to the upper Zambezi, Arnot needed the support, or at least the approval, of the ivory trader George Westbeech, who exercised great influence as a semi-official commercial agent for the Lozi.[3] Westbeech had been friendly enough to the French and Belgian Jesuits, but Arnot's arrival gave him an unexpected opportunity to promote both British and Protestant influence in central Africa. He thus persuaded Lewanika to admit Arnot, and to exclude the Jesuits when they returned in 1884. This was a crucial decision. Arnot himself left the Lozi in that year, and eventually turned his attention to Katanga, but Coillard finally returned in 1885. Once again, Coillard had arrived at an awkward time: there had been a revolt in the previous year and Lewanika was in exile. But Coillard was backed by Westbeech: the two men were never friends, but what mattered to Westbeech was Coillard's enthusiasm for Britain and the British: his wife was Scottish, and two of his assistants were English. Towards the end of 1885 Lewanika regained his throne, and in October 1886 Coillard was allowed to found a mission at Sefula, not far from the Lozi capital at Lealui.

By 1887, then, a pro-British Protestant mission had gained a foothold in the powerful Lozi kingdom. This was soon to prove of great political significance. There were also, as we have seen, British missions in the Shire highlands, on Lake Malawi, and at the south end of Lake Tanganyika. These were indeed the only Christian missions in what are now Zambia and Malawi. This did not, however, mean that the British government had any desire to control this part of central Africa. It was not entirely unmoved by the missionaries' reports of the continuing slave trade, but British ministers were not yet prepared to commit themselves to an anti-slavery crusade in the far interior. Nor did they consider that Britain had any significant commercial stake in central Africa. They were unimpressed by the fact that most of the white ivory traders who reached the Zambezi from the south were of British origin: their trade was of no national importance, and in any case it was in decline – the elephants had mostly been killed off. Yet within three years Britain had successfully laid claim to most of what is now Zambia and Malawi. To see how this came about we must look at changing European attitudes to the whole of southern Africa.

Rhodes and the Scramble for Southern Africa

The overriding concern of the British government in southern Africa was to retain control of the Cape, which was regarded as essential to British supremacy in the Indian Ocean, and thus in India. So long as this control was not threatened, Britain had no wish to extend its responsibilities northwards. The Boer republic of the Transvaal had regained its independence in 1881, but it seemed unlikely that British interests could be seriously threatened by these white farmers and herdsmen, confined as they were to the far interior. However, the Transvaal would look very different if it managed to secure free access to the sea and it was just this possibility which began to alarm the British in the mid-1880s. Germany annexed South-West Africa in 1884 and seemed ready enough to reach out across the Kalahari to join up with the Transvaal. Such an alliance might form the basis of a powerful and hostile state on the northern frontiers of British South Africa. In order to drive a wedge between the Germans and the Boers, the British sought alliance with Khama, the Christian king of the Ngwato and the most powerful Tswana ruler. Khama welcomed the British as a source of support against the Ndebele, and in 1885 most of what is now Botswana became the Bechuanaland Protectorate.

This was a massive addition to the British empire, but it was not enough, for in 1886 the uneasy balance of forces in southern Africa was upset yet again. Gold was discovered on the Witwatersrand, in the Transvaal. With a revenue from gold-mining, this poor and backward republic might well become a formidable power. The immediate result was to create new local markets for white farmers, and Boers from the Transvaal began to look for better farming land further afield. In 1887 they turned to their old enemies the Ndebele and found their king willing to come to terms: Lobengula's chief worry was the recent alliance of the British with his enemy Khama. Thus Lobengula was now persuaded to sign the Grobler treaty, which gave the subjects of the Transvaal republic special privileges within his kingdom. It was the Grobler treaty which finally scared the British into staking a claim to the country beyond the Limpopo, and by this time the British government had a most valuable ally in southern Africa: the millionaire Cecil Rhodes.

Rhodes came out from England to South Africa to improve his health, but he soon did much more. He moved to the new diamond fields at Kimberley and by 1880, when he was only twenty-seven, he and his partners in De Beers dominated the diamond industry. By 1888, through De Beers, Rhodes had obtained complete control of Kimberley. This wealth enabled Rhodes to pursue still greater power – both financial and political. He wanted to see the British flag fly right across Africa, from the Cape to Cairo; he also wanted to extend his control of Africa's mineral resources. In 1887 he invested heavily in gold mines on the Rand; this venture turned out badly, but Rhodes also had his eye on the goldfields north of the Limpopo. African reef mining had virtually ceased many years before, and although a few whites had tried

mining in the region they had had far too little capital. Rhodes, however, had plenty of capital, and in 1888 he sent off his partner, Rudd, to
negotiate with Lobengula, who as king of the Ndebele dominated the
southern lines of access to the goldfields beyond the Limpopo. This
expedition resulted in the Rudd Concession, which promised Lobengula £1200 a year and 1000 of the most up-to-date rifles. In return,
Lobengula signed away rights to all minerals in his dominion.

With the Rudd Concession in his pocket, Rhodes was able in 1889 to
persuade the British government to grant a charter to the new company
he had formed – the British South Africa Company. This allowed
Rhodes to use the authority of the British government in staking out
claims to African territory at the expense of other European powers.
He could now make treaties with African rulers which would give his
Company powers of administration. Such a charter was a well-establish-
ed technique for extending the British empire. The East India Company
had been given powers of government in the seventeenth century, and
other chartered companies were formed in the late nineteenth century,
in both East and West Africa. Rhodes's charter provided the British
government with the means to exclude potentially hostile European
powers from the high central plateau north of the Limpopo, at no cost
to the British taxpayer. But the actual sphere of the Company's operations was still unclear. The Charter referred to the country north of the
Transvaal and west of the Portuguese possessions, but how far north,
and how far west, was still a matter for international agreement. So
Rhodes now set about collecting treaties with African rulers which
would serve to exclude any European rivals.

In the north Rhodes confronted three European powers: the Portuguese in Angola and Mozambique; the newly formed Congo Free State
of the Belgian king Leopold II; and the Germans in East Africa. The
German question was relatively straightforward. Rhodes's chief concern in this direction was to gain access to Lake Tanganyika, the great
waterway to the north. To this end he arranged for Harry Johnston,
the British consul in Mozambique, to collect treaties in 1889 from
Mambwe, Lungu and Tabwa chiefs between Lakes Malawi and Tanganyika. This was simple enough: the chiefs were glad to accept Johnston's offers of British 'protection' since they were all more or less
harassed by Bemba raiders or East African traders.

King Leopold and the Portuguese presented larger problems. The
bone of contention between Rhodes and Leopold was Katanga. Recent
European visitors to the Yeke king Msiri had drawn attention to the
copper deposits in his country. Leopold himself had no special interest
in these; he was too impatient for quick profits with which to finance his
various military expeditions. At the same time, he had no wish to see
this copper fall into the hands of a rival power and by the end of 1889

Rhodes was also keen to gain possession of Katanga's copper, which – like the northern goldfields – might make up for his losses on the Rand. He was thus disturbed to note the continuing southward expansion of Leopold's Free State from its base on the lower Zaïre.

As for the Portuguese, they believed that as the earliest white colonists in central Africa they had first claim to the interior. They had long hoped to link up their possessions on the east and west coasts. This had been the aim of Lacerda's expedition to Kazembe's in 1798, and the Monteiro–Gamitto expedition in 1831–2. Later ventures north of the Zambezi lent further weight to the view that this was properly a field for Portuguese expansion. In 1854 African agents of the Bihé trader Silva Porto went east from the Lozi capital, through Ila, Lamba and Bisa country, and emerged at Tete, on the lower Zambezi. In 1878 a Portuguese army officer, Serpa Pinto, reached the Lozi from the west coast, hoping to follow the Zambezi down to the east coast, though he was forced instead to go south to South Africa. In 1884–5 two Portuguese naval officers, Capello and Ivens, reached the northern part of the Lozi kingdom from the west; they then visited Msiri, crossed the Luapula and reached the Zambezi at Zumbo.

By this time the Portuguese government was looking anxiously at the expansion of British influence in South Africa, while the Scottish missionaries south and west of Lake Maláwi also seemed to challenge Portuguese claims in central Africa. Thus in the late 1880s Portuguese officials in Mozambique tried to assert their authority both north and south of the middle Zambezi. North of Zumbo, real power still lay with the black warlords, Kanyemba and Matakenya, but they were enlisted as agents of the Portuguese government, and within their spheres of influence several chiefs were induced in 1885–6 to sign treaties of 'homage' to Portugal. This new forward policy met some local opposition: between 1887 and 1890 the Nsenga chief Mburuma waged a guerrilla war against the Portuguese from his base west of Zumbo, and in 1888 he managed, with the help of other chiefs, to enlist 2000 men to lay siege to Zumbo. But the Portuguese strengthened their military posts at Zumbo and the mouth of the Kafue, and in 1890 Zumbo received its first governor. In the following year the Zumbo governor claimed that the Portuguese flag was flown by chiefs among the Lenje, Swaka, Lala and Bisa; he foresaw a great future for gold-mining to the north as well as south of the Zambezi; and he expected thousands of white settlers to exploit the supposedly rich farming country around the middle and lower Kafue. Meanwhile the Portuguese were also staking claims south of the Zambezi. In 1889 they had obtained treaties from several chiefs among the northern and eastern Shona: in return for guns to fight the Ndebele, these Shona chiefs agreed not to make treaties with other Europeans.

Thus by the time Rhodes obtained a charter for the British South Africa Company, he urgently needed to press its claims as far north as possible if he was ever to gain control over the gold and copper of central Africa. In 1890 Rhodes sent out a number of expeditions to forestall the advances of Leopold and the Portuguese. Three of these were concerned to secure territory north of the Zambezi as far as Katanga. All three were instructed to make treaties with chiefs which would grant British aid and 'protection' in return for pledges from the chiefs not to make agreements with any other Europeans. In addition, the treaties were to secure for the Company full rights to all minerals within the chiefs' territories. This was largely a matter of insurance: outside Katanga, Rhodes had no special hopes for mineral wealth north of the Zambezi, but it was as well for the Company to own whatever minerals there were. And though such treaties would be concluded between chiefs and Company agents, each treaty was to specify that it 'shall be considered in the light of a treaty between the said nation and the Government of Her Britannic Majesty Queen Victoria'. With this clumsy clause, Rhodes's profit-seeking company invested itself with all the imperial authority of the British government.

Rhodes failed in fact to obtain Katanga. One of his treaty-makers, Alfred Sharpe, set out from Lake Malawi and managed to reach Msiri's capital at the end of 1890. But Sharpe had no success with the Yeke king, though he signed treaties with the Tabwa chief Nsama, and also with Kazembe on the Luapula, who hoped for British support against Lunda rebels and their ally Msiri. At the same time, Joseph Thomson, the explorer of East Africa, went due west from Lake Malawi as far as the upper Luapula. He was, however, extremely ill; his porters had smallpox; and he eventually turned back without coming anywhere near the Yeke king. Instead, he collected treaties from various chiefs and headmen among the Bisa, Aushi, Lamba, Lenje and Lala: they welcomed Thomson's promises of protection against Ngoni and Chikunda raiders.

Meanwhile, Rhodes had sent yet another agent, Frank Lochner, to the upper Zambezi valley. Lochner's ultimate goal was also Katanga; in fact, he never got there, but he did secure a treaty with the Lozi king Lewanika. The initiative for this came as much from Lewanika as from Rhodes. As always, Lozi foreign policy was dominated by one factor: fear of the Ndebele. Lewanika's great ally against the Ndebele was Khama, the Christian king of the Ngwato. Khama was in no doubt as to the benefits of British protection, which he had accepted in 1885, and Lewanika was inclined to follow his example. He was all the more anxious to do so when he heard about the arms which Lobengula obtained by the Rudd Concession of 1888. Early in 1889 Lewanika got Coillard, the missionary, to write a letter asking for the protection of the

British government. This greatly encouraged Rhodes, though there was a slight complication. In April 1889 Lewanika was visited by Harry Ware, the agent of a South African mining syndicate which was a rival of Rhodes. Ware offered presents of modern rifles and ammunition; the Lozi were much impressed and Lewanika gave Ware an exclusive concession to mine in the country east of the Machili river. However, Rhodes managed to buy this concession from Ware's employers, and meanwhile he had sent Lochner off to the Lozi.

Lewanika was rightly suspicious of Lochner. Unlike other chiefs north of the Zambezi, Lewanika was well aware of the difference between the British government and a private company. He had just made one agreement with a businessman, and he saw no reason to make another. On the other hand, his conduct of foreign relations now owed much to the aid and advice of Coillard, and Coillard was in favour of negotiating with Lochner. The French mission had made a number of enemies among the Lozi; Coillard had come to realise that its future depended on continued protection from Lewanika, and he believed that Lewanika could only survive if he had the support and protection of the British. Coillard was thus inclined to accept Lochner's assurances that what he offered was as good as a treaty with the British government. To many of Lewanika's senior councillors, this was no recommendation; what they saw was a growing alliance between their king and the white men which threatened to strengthen the king at their expense. But they were apparently won over by the sudden appearance of an envoy from Khama – a reminder that Lewanika could call on powerful African assistance in the event of revolt.

After much hesitation, Lewanika finally signed a concession which gave Rhodes's Company mineral rights throughout his kingdom, while the Company undertook to defend the Lozi from outside attacks and to pay Lewanika a subsidy of £2,000 a year in order to arm himself against the Ndebele. The Company also undertook to develop trade, and to build schools and telegraphs. These promises meant a great deal to Lewanika, who for some time had appreciated that such 'modernisation' was essential if his kingdom was to survive the growing competition from both European and African powers. He was not to know that these promises of technical aid, so far from being a special attempt to meet his wishes, were written as a matter of course into all the treaties signed by Rhodes's agents. And even so, Lewanika continued to have doubts about the concession. Soon after Lochner left, Lewanika became convinced that he had been deceived. He now got a trader, George Middleton, to write a letter to the British government repudiating the Lochner concession, and Coillard later wrote asking Queen Victoria to extend her direct protection over Lewanika. But the British government took little notice, and in 1891 it recognised the Company's 'protectorate' over the Lozi kingdom.

Although Rhodes had failed to win Katanga, the concessions obtained for him by Lochner and Thomson at least enabled him to challenge any attempt by the Portuguese to link up their colonies from east to west. But this in itself was not enough: Rhodes wanted his Company's eastern frontier to lie as far to the east as possible. The first step was taken in 1889, when a British protectorate was declared over the Shire highlands. Hitherto, the British government had resisted missionary appeals to keep out the Portuguese, but it quickly gave in when Rhodes offered to pay the costs of administering a protectorate. Together with Johnston's treaties further north, this meant that the British sphere now extended all along the western shore of Lake Malawi. South of the Zambezi, Rhodes's main concern was to gain possession of the gold-bearing areas on the central plateau. For this, the Rudd concession would not suffice, since much Shona country on the plateau lay well outside Lobengula's control. So in 1890 Rhodes sent off the Pioneer Column to occupy the plateau north-east of the Ndebele. Their establishment of Fort Salisbury was a far more effective assertion of authority than the Portuguese treaties with Shona chiefs in the previous year, and it marked the founding of white Rhodesia.[4]

This, then, was how the British eventually staked out claims to exclusive rights over central Africa. They now had to secure the agreement of other European powers. They obtained this through a series of international treaties which largely determined the present borders of Zambia. In 1890 Britain and Germany settled their various differences in Africa by a treaty which included a definition of the frontier between German East Africa and the British sphere: as a result of Johnston's treaties in 1889, this ran more or less directly from the south end of Lake Tanganyika to the north end of Lake Malawi. The same treaty also met the German request for access to the Zambezi from South-West Africa, by allowing them the 'Caprivi Strip' along the Chobe river. This meant that a small part of Lozi territory eventually came under German rule, and for no very good reason, since the Victoria Falls rendered the Zambezi useless to the Germans as an international waterway. But this point may have been overlooked by the diplomats.

In 1891 Britain concluded a treaty with Portugal. This defined the eastern limits of the Company's sphere; it settled what is now the eastern frontier of Rhodesia, while north of the Zambezi it confined the Portuguese to a line running from the lower Luangwa to the Shire Highlands Protectorate. The Portuguese held on to Zumbo, but they had to abandon their claims to the large area west of the Luangwa which had been colonised and terrorised by black Portuguese and Chikunda. In the west, it was confirmed that the Lozi kingdom fell within the

British sphere, though there was a dispute over its western borders which was not resolved for several years.

As for Leopold and Katanga, this question was effectively settled in 1891, when two expeditions working for Leopold reached Msiri's capital. The second expedition had a violent argument with Msiri and one of its members shot him dead. His followers offered no resistance, and Leopold's men found themselves in command of the Yeke kingdom. The British government had never supported Rhodes's claims to Katanga, and in fact the British South Africa Company had already, in 1890, made an informal agreement whereby their border with the Congo Free State was to run eastwards along the Zambesi–Zaïre watershed up to the exit of the Luapula from Lake Bangweulu. This was confirmed in 1894 by a treaty between Leopold and the British government, which further defined the frontier along the Luapula to Lake Mweru and over to Lake Tanganyika. The effect of this border agreement was to create the 'Katanga Pedicle', a long arm of Congo territory which almost bisected the Company's sphere.

The eastern borders of what is now Zambia were a matter for agreement between the Company and the British government. The Scottish missionaries to the west and south of Lake Malawi were unwilling to be governed by the Company, and early in 1891 it was agreed that the British government should be directly responsible for a new Nyasaland Protectorate, including both the Shire highlands and the country between Lake Malawi and its watershed with the Luangwa valley.[5] West of this watershed, the Company was now formally allowed to exercise the rights of government conferred by its Charter.

British Occupation

By the end of 1891 the British South Africa Company had thus gained recognition from other European powers of its right to occupy a specified area north of the Zambezi. But it was another matter to gain recognition from African rulers, or from Arab and Swahili traders. Lewanika had repudiated the Lochner concession, and apart from Sharpe's treaty with Kazembe there was no other agreement with any important chief. The establishment of Company rule beyond the Zambezi would clearly be a major task, and the Company was in no hurry to undertake it, even though European powers expected each other to make good their claims in Africa by 'effective occupation'.

From an economic point of view, the Company's northern territories were not at all promising. It had been the copper of Katanga which had excited Rhodes's interest, and by the end of 1890 it was clear that Katanga had been lost to Leopold of Belgium. The vast area which remained to the Company was valued only for strategic reasons: other

European powers had been kept out of it. So in 1891 the Company assigned temporary responsibility for its northern territories to the Commissioner in Nyasaland, Harry Johnston. This arrangement left the Company free to concentrate its attention in the early 1890s on its territories south of the Zambezi, where the search for a 'second Rand' was becoming increasingly desperate. The appetites both of the Company and of white settlers in the south soon provoked military campaigns which stretched the Company's resources to the limit. In 1893 it fought the Ndebele, and in 1896–7 it had to suppress risings both by the Ndebele and by many of the Shona peoples. Not until it had established control south of the Zambezi did the Company take any major steps to assert its authority further north.

Up to 1896, indeed, most of what is now Zambia was totally unaffected by the fact that, in international law, it now formed part of the British Empire. The Nyasaland Commissioner could do little to meet his obligation to introduce British rule on behalf of the Company. Johnston recruited a small regiment, partly Sikhs from the Indian Army and partly local Africans, but this was preoccupied with a long struggle against slave traders, both on Lake Malawi and in the Shire valley. Johnston confined his efforts in the Company sphere to the far north-east, where there were several slave traders linked to those on Lake Malawi. Johnston dispatched a few British officials to establish stations for the Company near Lake Mweru and Lake Tanganyika, but their armed forces were very small. In 1894 Belgian forces defeated two important Swahili traders north of Lake Mweru, but the British were unable to prevent other traders from importing guns and ammunition. In this situation, despite pleas from anxious missionaries, there could be no question of the British taking on the Bemba, whose chiefs still terrorised the north-eastern plateau. In 1895 one of the officials near Lake Mweru attacked Kazembe (who was supposed by treaty to enjoy the Company's protection), but the expedition was promptly rebuffed.

At the end of 1895 the British South Africa Company resumed responsibility for administering its northern territories, which from 1897 were officially called Northern Rhodesia. The pace of British intrusion began to quicken. The risings in the south in 1896–7 meant that it was still out of the question for the Company to risk war north of the Zambezi, but a few cautious advances were made. These came from two directions. One line of approach followed the traders' and missionaries' route from South Africa to the Zambezi. The Company was now established in Bulawayo, the former Ndebele capital, and this was an advanced base for renewing contacts with the Lozi kingdom. The other line of approach was based on the Nyasaland Protectorate, from which a Company presence had already been established around the northern borders of Bemba country. Further expansion in the north-east, as also in Ngoni country, would continue to depend on bringing men and materials up the Zambezi from the east coast, up the Shire river, and north through Nyasaland.

In the north-east, the Company's policy was to avoid a head-on collision with the fearsome Bemba; instead, it sought at first to weaken them by attacking their East African trading partners. The most power-ful of these was in fact Mlozi, at Karonga, who was defeated by Johnston in 1895 and later hanged. In 1896 Company officials, based on stations between Lakes Malawi and Tanganyika, began to intercept trading caravans as they left Bemba country. Meanwhile, the Bemba, though still the terror of their neighbours, were deeply divided among themselves. This was due partly to their political system, which was largely based on the uncertain ties of kinship, and partly to their trade with the Arabs and Swahili. Their king had no monopoly of trade, and the outlying chiefs had a greater interest in remaining in close touch with traders near their borders than in promotion to the senior chief-tainships in the heart of Bemba country. Moreover, the second most senior chief, whose title was Mwamba, had built up a wide area of influence in the west which rivalled that of the king. The two rulers came into conflict during the reign of Sampa, who succeeded in 1883. Sampa indeed had little of the support from other chiefs which the previous king had enjoyed. He traded with Arabs to the east, and he probably realised that this trade was threatened by the Europeans. But his attempts to keep Europeans out of Bemba country failed. He quar-relled with Makasa, a chief on his northern border, and Makasa decided to strengthen himself by allying with French missionaries of the Catholic White Fathers. These had founded a mission among the nearby Mambwe in 1891, and in 1895 Makasa allowed Bishop Dupont to found Kayambi mission.

Sampa died in 1896. The new Bemba king was a feeble old man, and the real power was Mwamba. Mwamba was anxious to avoid commit-ting himself irrevocably to dependence on Europeans, let alone sub-jection to them; equally, he could not risk provoking a European alli-ance with any lesser chief. So early in 1897 he received Robert Young, a Company official, but did not take him seriously as he brought no presents. However, in September 1897 Young dispersed an Arab strong-hold on the upper Luangwa and chased away a minor Bemba chief who had supported them. This much impressed Mwamba. In 1898 Mwamba fell ill and, hoping for medical aid and perhaps also for mediation with the Company, he summoned Bishop Dupont of the White Fathers, who had visited him the previous year. Dupont, like Young, had gained a local reputation through several acts of skill and bravado, and when Mwamba died in October Dupont was able to take control of his village and prevent the rioting which usually followed a chief's death. Dupont claimed that Mwamba had actually left him his country, but whatever the truth in this Dupont had no chance to become a 'white chief' because Young returned to Mwamba's in November and set up a Company post near by. The only resistance to this rapid occupation of Bembaland came from two border chiefs in the north-west, who were both still involved in the export of slaves and ivory. They were defeated without difficulty in 1898 and 1899.

In 1899 the Company confirmed its control of the north-east by avenging its earlier defeat at Kazembe's. Kazembe seems by this time to have had little support from the Lunda governors; their harsh rule was resented by the various subject tribes, and in any case the area under their control was much less than it had been. In the 1880s the Lunda kingdom had been weakened by Yeke attacks; on one occasion the Yeke had occupied the capital, and Kazembe had only repelled them with the aid of a Bemba force. After Mlozi's defeat in 1895 several Arabs retreated to the Luapula, and Kazembe must have hoped that they would stave off the European advance but in the event they deserted him and fled south into Lamba country. As for the Swahili in Tabwa country, these had decided by 1895 to co-operate with the British rather than risk defeat and the loss of their still considerable ivory trade. Kazembe had heard of Young's exploits among the Bemba, and was ready to make terms with him; but in 1899 the Company decided to deal with Kazembe by calling in a large force from Nyasaland with a machine gun. Kazembe saw that resistance was useless; but he could not bring himself to surrender so he fled across the Luapula into what was now the Congo Free State and only gave himself up in 1900. Once the two great powers of the north-east, the Bemba and the Lunda, had submitted, no other Africans in the area were rash enough to challenge the white man's firearms.

While the British South Africa Company gained control of the north-east, it was also establishing itself in the far west. Its principal strategy here was to make treaties with the Lozi kingdom. It had, of course, already made one in 1890 – the Lochner Concession; but this had been repudiated by Lewanika, and the Company did nothing to fulfil their various obligations to him under it. Yet both Lewanika and the Company had a common interest in coming to terms once again. Lewanika's long-standing fear of the Ndebele began to subside after their defeat in 1893, but he shared with the Company a growing concern at signs of Portuguese expansion from the west.

This concern was reflected in the continued expansion of the Lozi kingdom during the 1890s. Lewanika realised that he was gradually being hemmed in by European powers, and he knew as well as they did that claims to empire would have to be supported by evidence of actual occupation. In the absence of any international agreement safeguarding his dominions he wished to extend the visible signs of his authority as far as possible. In the east Lewanika settled Lozi officials among his Ila and Toka tributaries. At first this proved far from easy, but in 1893 he allowed a group of Primitive Methodist missionaries to settle among the Lumbu, near the western Ila, and this reassured the latter that a Lozi presence would be peaceful. West of the Zambezi, Lewanika had probably levied tribute for several years from the upper reaches of the Kwando, but before 1890 there were very few Lozi officials far to the west of the capital. By 1899, however, there were several Lozi officials among the Mashi people, along the middle Kwando, while cattle from Lewanika's herds had been loaned out to Mbunda on the upper Kwando, and Mbwela on the upper Kwito. In the north, Lewanika came to the aid of his Lunda neighbour Ishinde in 1892, and defeated a minor Luvale chief, Ndungu. This show of strength seems to have induced the Lozi dissidents remaining in Lukwakwa to make their peace with Lewanika. Further east the Lozi had for some time been at odds with the Kaonde chief Kasempa, who was also supplied with guns by Mambari traders. Around 1897 Kasempa defeated an army sent out by Lewanika, but he realised the value of alliance with the Lozi, as the major power in the region; Kasempa began to pay tribute and accepted a Lozi official at his capital.

Thus one response of the Lozi to the pressures of the Scramble for Africa was to join in it themselves. At the same time, Lewanika was busy trying to preserve his empire, and his own position as ruler, by re-opening negotiations with the British. He knew quite enough about European military power – especially after the Ndebele defeat in 1893 – to wish to avoid risking war with his white competitors. He employed Coillard, the missionary, to write letters to the British government complaining that no British official had come to see him since Lochner's departure. Lewanika became especially disturbed early in 1895 when the Portuguese set up a military post near the Luvale chief Kakenge, whom Lewanika regarded as tributary. He was also annoyed that a group of white prospectors had gone without his permission through Tonga and Ila country to the Kafue Hook. He now realised that it was no use hoping for direct protection from the British government; he would have to depend on the British South Africa Company to keep his kingdom free from unwanted Europeans. In July 1895, in a letter to the Company, Lewanika finally acknowledged the Lochner Concession.

By this time the Company was once again responsible for its northern territories. It too was disturbed by the Portuguese advance to the upper Zambezi. It knew – as Lewanika did not – that in 1893 the British government had made a temporary agreement with Portugal whereby the western frontier of the Company sphere should be regarded as following the Zambezi and Kabompo rivers – a line which cut straight through the middle of the Lozi kingdom. Both the British government and the Company were anxious to reach a permanent and more realistic frontier agreement. To achieve this, the British needed to know the true frontiers of the Lozi kingdom, and it would strengthen British claims if the area was clearly under Company control. So in 1896 the British government sent a military officer, Goold-Adams, to ascertain Lozi frontiers, and in 1897 the Company finally sent a Resident, Robert Coryndon, to see that the terms of the Lochner Concession were put into force.

Since 1890, however, both Lewanika and the Company had revised some of their views as to what they wanted from an agreement. In 1898 a new one was made (the Lawley Concession); in 1900 this was ratified by the 'Lewanika Concession'. In some ways, this was rather less favourable to the Lozi than the Lochner Concession, but Lewanika urgently needed a firm basis for dealing with the growing number of Europeans entering his country – traders, hunters, prospectors and missionaries. The Company now gained the right to judge all cases involving white men. It was also allowed to make land grants to white men in Toka and Ila country. It retained rights to all minerals throughout the kingdom with the exception of certain iron mines. The Company reaffirmed its promises to promote trade and education, but the annual payment to Lewanika – which had never been made – was reduced from £2,000 to £850. On the other hand, the new agreements defined for the first time a 'reserved area' from which all mineral prospectors were excluded. This area included most of the country actually occupied by Lozi officials along the upper Zambezi and to the east of it.

This division of the Lozi kingdom into an inner 'reserved area' and a region more open to European enterprise had profound and lasting consequences. Lewanika's motive in requesting a reserved area had simply been to protect the Lozi from the kind of disorder and violence caused by European mining developments south of the Zambezi. In the event, however, it was not white miners but British ideas of government which proved the most immediate threat to Lozi independence. The reserved area quickly acquired a new value as an enclave within which the Lozi managed to retain substantially more autonomy under colonial rule than other peoples in Zambia. On the other hand, the Lozi were gradually deprived of the control they had exercised – and so recently extended – outside the reserved area. Indeed, the new agreements provided no definition of Lozi frontiers and they left the way open for a final settlement between Britain and Portugal in 1905 to which Lewanika took great exception. To the British it might seem that the Lozi, by their treaty-making, had saved their kingdom; to the Lozi, it seemed clear that they had lost an empire.

By coming to terms with the Lozi, Bemba and Lunda, the Company gained authority over a very large part of Northern Rhodesia – and it did so with remarkably little use of force. But its advances in the west and north-east did not suffice to gain access to the country east of the Luangwa river. It was here that the only large-scale resistance to British occupation took place. The leading power in the area were the Ngoni of Mpezeni, who by 1880 had defeated the Chewa of Mkanda and occupied their country. Mpezeni's Ngoni formed a small state of their own, organized on the basis of segments within the chiefly family. The state expanded as the segments increased their numbers by recruiting prisoners of war. Such segments were, as early Ngoni history showed, likely to break off and become independent, as Mpezeni himself had done. For a period, indeed, the expansion of Mpezeni's Ngoni, like that of the Bemba, had a unifying effect; by giving scope to the ambitions of younger men it relieved tension and rivalry at the centre. In due course, however, as with the Bemba, the various parts of the state developed different interests and the power of the paramount declined.

In spite of this, the Ngoni reacted very differently from the Bemba to European intrusion. So far from dividing, they united behind their leaders and went to war with the Europeans. One reason for this was that the Ngoni, far more than the Bemba, Lunda or Lozi, were a warrior society. Fighting was thought to be the only proper occupation for men, and they could not see any future for themselves if war was prohibited. The other main reason for the Ngoni war with the Europeans was that the Europeans themselves saw no alternative to fighting. They were determined to take over Ngoniland, which some believed was rich in gold; they also wanted to recruit Ngoni as labourers for plantations in Nyasaland. Clearly, neither object could be achieved until the Ngoni war-machine was smashed.

The origins of this conflict may be traced back to 1885, when Mpezeni allowed a German, Carl Wiese, to trade and hunt in his country and gave him a large mining concession. Wiese, who had a Portuguese-African wife, gained some influence over Mpezeni and hoped to turn it to the advantage of the Portuguese. Mpezeni refused to make treaties with either Thomson or Sharpe in 1890, but the Anglo-Portuguese agreement of 1891 put paid to Wiese's hopes by placing Mpezeni's country within the British sphere. Instead, Wiese spread stories that Mpezeni's country was rich in gold, and he sold his mining concession there to a new London company. This company, which became the North Charterland Company, sent out prospectors in 1896. Mpezeni allowed them to begin work, but he had no intention of ceasing his raids, let alone of submitting to British rule. Mpezeni himself does not seem to have favoured war with the British, but his son Nsingu, who was the Ngoni war-commander, led a large group who were bent on fighting. They soon had their chance. In 1897 reports reached Nyasaland that the Ngoni threatened the lives of Wiese and an official of the British South Africa Company. The Commissioner in Nyasaland gladly gave the Company military support and early in 1898 the British launched an expedition against Mpezeni. The Ngoni mobilised a large force, and they might have won had they mounted a night attack, but the Ngoni relied on the tactics with which they had so often broken up lesser groups, and these were ineffective against artillery and machine guns. Nsingu was captured and shot, Mpezeni surrendered, and the British took over most of the Ngoni's large herds of cattle, which had themselves mostly been taken in battle.

Once the Company had gained footholds at opposite ends of Northern Rhodesia – in the east and north-east and in the south-west – it was in a position to extend its authority into the middle of the country, between the Luangwa and Kafue rivers. There was here no one predominant ruler, the international frontiers were not in dispute and the Company was content to defer intrusion until it could also establish an administration. Thus throughout the 1890s this region continued to be a happy hunting-ground for traders in search of slaves and ivory. Although the Portuguese had abandoned their claims west of the Luangwa, their black agents Matakenya and Kanyemba were still raiding there in 1893. In 1894 Matakenya died, while Kanyemba gradually succumbed to paralysis, but other adventurers soon appeared to take their place as overlords between the Luangwa and Kafue.

The first of these was an English hunter, Harrison Clark, who had settled north of the Zambezi in the late 1880s. He married a daughter of Caetano Santanna, a 'black Portuguese' who dominated the country west of Feira after the death of his father, Chikwasha, in 1892. In 1896 Clark obtained from Santanna a concession of land, labour and mineral rights; further north, he obtained a similar concession at Algoa, in Lala country, from a former agent of Matakenya. This became the centre of a remarkable, if short-lived, private kingdom. Clark raised a small army, he levied a 'tax' from ivory traders and he made some effort to suppress the slave trade. He exercised influence as far west as the Kafue Flats and the Lukanga Swamp and in 1898 he obtained several concessions from chiefs of the Soli, Sala and Lenje in a vain effort to defend his claims against the British South Africa Company.

Meanwhile, not far to the north, another alien state was being formed by Swahili traders, whose leader, Chiwala, came from Nyasaland. In about 1893 these traders had travelled west from Lake Malawi and settled on the upper reaches of the Luapula river. Here they were able to take advantage of the recent collapse of Msiri's Yeke empire in Katanga. They collected ivory more or less violently among the Lamba, and they sold a number of slaves to Mambari traders from the west. In 1897 Chiwala's Swahili were dislodged by a Belgian force and withdrew southwards to Ndola. They established a new colony, but their trade routes were increasingly obstructed by European advances and when British officials arrived in 1900 Chiwala made no resistance.

Further west, between the headwaters of the Kafue and Zambezi, the Company took longer to assert itself. This region continued to be frequented by Mambari slave traders from Angola until well into the twentieth century. The Portuguese had formally abolished slavery in their African possessions, but it persisted in the form of forced contract labour. There was an acute demand for such labour in the coffee plantations of Angola from the 1870s onwards, and in cocoa plantations on the West African island of Sao Tomé, especially with the rapid growth of the world market for cocoa in the late nineteenth century. Furthermore, porters were needed to carry rubber and ivory to the coast. Much of this labour was bought or seized by Mambari traders among the Luvale, the western Lunda, the Kaonde, Lenje and Lamba. By 1901, the advance of British officials from the middle Zambezi had induced the slavers to retreat to Luvale and Lunda country in the far north-west. Here they remained at large for some years, for this was an imperial no-man's-land, disputed by both British and Portuguese.

Conclusion

To most people in Northern Rhodesia the intrusion of the British South Africa Company did not, at the time, seem an event of great importance. The Company's first officials and soldiers had mostly gained entry by talking to a small number of chiefs. Often they had been welcomed as a potential source of protection against local, African enemies. This was true even among such large kingdoms as those of the Lozi and Kazembe's Lunda. There had been fighting against Mpezeni's Ngoni and lesser actions in and around the Bemba kingdom, but such violence was hardly on a larger scale than the warfare which had become endemic throughout most of the country. The combined result of both talking and fighting was a single sphere of British power and influence far more extensive than that of any of the various African empire-builders who had preceded the British. It took time, however, for this momentous fact to be widely appreciated among the scattered peoples of Northern Rhodesia. At the end of the nineteenth century, it remained to be seen whether the British really would impose a new kind of regime. The full significance of Company rule did not become clear until it had set up a local administration and had begun collecting tax: it was this above all else which first showed the ordinary villager that both he and his chief had a new master.

The 1890s were perhaps most widely remembered, not so much for wars and high politics, as for a series of natural disasters. There was smallpox among the Bisa in 1889, and it may have been this epidemic which afflicted Joseph Thomson's caravan a year later; at any rate the caravan spread smallpox among the Lamba and Swaka. In 1892–3 smallpox spread from the Luvale to the Lozi, Ila and Toka; it was also rife among the Aushi. Then came a cattle disease – rinderpest – from north-east Africa: between 1892 and 1894 cattle, goats and buffalo almost disappeared between Lake Mweru and the north end of Lake Malawi. The rinderpest continued to be carried southwards; it by-passed the Ngoni, but in 1895 it began to kill off both cattle and game among the Ila and Toka, though fortunately it never penetrated the Lozi heartland. Worst of all was the plague of red locusts which ravaged most of southern Africa between 1892 and 1910. By destroying grain crops, locusts caused famine among the Lamba in 1892, the Bemba in 1894 and 1897, the Lozi and Luvale in 1895 and the Gwembe Tonga in 1899. The social consequences of these disasters are hard to assess, but they may well have had some effect on the political changes of the period: it is likely, for instance, that the Bemba famines contributed to the reluctance of their leading chiefs to go to war with the British.

Among a few small groups of people – mainly in the Lozi kingdom and to the north of the Bemba – the Christian gospel began to take root during the 1890s. There were few converts as yet, and the slow progress of the new faith was hardly surprising. Almost all missionaries considered that African life was not only 'primitive' but abysmally wicked. They were horrified not only by slavery and brutal punishments but by polygamy and witchcraft beliefs, while reverence for ancestral spirits seemed little better than idolatry. For an African to become a Christian at that time usually meant a complete break with his or her own family, since missionaries insisted that a Christian life could only be followed within a Christian family or community.

Yet despite this cultural gap, there were forces favouring the missionary cause. The upheavals of the nineteenth century provoked increased dissatisfaction with the dominant religious systems, which were mostly centred on the ancestral spirits of chiefs. In the north-east there was a revival of cults of possession by *ngulu* spirits. Besides, the idea of a High God was by no means new in central Africa, and it became more important as people's horizons were widened beyond their own village and ancestral graves. The movement and mingling of peoples caused by trade and warfare may equally well have increased the appeal of a God who did not confine his concern to any one social group. Moreover, in the Lozi kingdom missionary denunciations of witchcraft beliefs met with royal approval, for witch-finders were among Lewanika's most troublesome enemies. Finally, the mission-aries did more than bring a new faith: they taught reading and writing. Since white men clearly achieved so much with these skills, they attracted a good deal of interest. Lewanika was quick to see the value of training a literate civil service, and this was undoubtedly the main reason why he continued to support Coillard's mission despite the suspicions of many senior Lozi.

Livingstone's hopes for a Christian mission on the Zambezi had of course gone further than this. He envisaged it as a means to economic as well as spiritual and intellectual regeneration. Livingstone's vision was much in Coillard's mind: he, too, strongly believed in the value of material improvement and from an early stage he and his colleagues concerned themselves with technical as well as literary edu-cation. When Coillard arrived at the Lozi capital in 1886 to set up his mission, he found Lewanika thinking deeply about his people's long-term economic prospects. According to Coillard, Lewanika asked him:

> 'What are the riches of a country? The riches of mine is ivory. But ivory diminishes every year; and when all the elephants in the country are exterminated, what shall I do?'

> ... I pointed out to him the fertility of his country, and that if the chiefs would give themselves up to the cultivation of cotton, tobacco, coffee, sugar-cane, etc., they would soon find that it would be an inexhaustible source of riches for them.[6]

This, indeed, had been Livingstone's dream; but it came to nothing. Cash-crops need a market, and neither Coillard nor Lewanika could create one. It was the declining ivory trade which provided what market there was for local crops. The world at large did not want cotton or sugar-cane from the Lozi, or from anywhere else in what is now Zambia: it wanted men. Coillard spoke just as gold was being dis-covered on the Rand. Already, parties of Gwembe Tonga were going to work on the diamond mines at Kimberley, or for white traders among the Ndebele. Westbeech took several men from Pandamatenga to the Rand in 1888; by 1895 the Toka were regular travellers to the mines in the south, and two years later they were joined by some Lozi from Sesheke. This was the answer to Lewanika's question: for his subjects, as for most other people in Northern Rhodesia, the future meant migra-tion, to sell their labour in distant farms, towns and mines.

NOTES

1. Palmerston, memo., 1 October 1859, FO 63/871, Public Records Office, London.

2. Letter of 9 Sept. 1860, in J. P. R. Wallis (ed.), *The Zambezi Expedition of David Livingstone* (1956), 395–6.
3. See p. 133.
4. The name 'Rhodesia' was introduced in 1895; it was officially approved by the British government in 1897.
5. From 1893 to 1907 this was called the British Central Africa Protectorate; it is referred to here simply as Nyasaland.
6. François Coillard (tr. C. W. Mackintosh), *On the Threshold of Central Africa* (1897), p. 222.

X

Mines and Migration
1900 – c. 1950

The imposition of British rule on Northern Rhodesia meant that African villagers were drawn further than ever before into the economy of the world at large. Hitherto, the territory had exported a luxury material – ivory; and labour for use elsewhere in growing tropical crops – mainly sugar, cotton, coffee and cocoa. Under colonial rule, Northern Rhodesia became vastly more important as a source of labour, for its men were needed throughout central and southern Africa to produce gold and copper, two metals which were essential to the industrial world. Then, after nearly forty years of colonial rule, Northern Rhodesia itself became a major supplier of copper. This greatly intensified the territory's interdependence with the rest of the world; it also raised the question of how far wealth from copper might benefit Northern Rhodesia rather than foreign interests.

Meanwhile, the various peoples living within Northern Rhodesia were drawn closer to each other than ever before. This was due partly to their submission to a single government and partly to their growing involvement in mines and towns within the territory. By the 1950s African political pressure had become a major influence on the course of economic and social development. This chapter, therefore, will survey the main outlines of Northern Rhodesia's economic history up to about 1950. The next chapter will examine African reactions to colonial rule, and the white counter-reaction which led to the creation of the Central African Federation in 1953; it will then discuss the economic and political effects of federation and show how Northern Rhodesia came eventually to be transformed by an African nationalist party into the independent state of Zambia.

Company Rule, 1899–1924

The British South Africa Company's territory north of the Zambezi was very much an appendage to its real seat of power in Southern

Rhodesia. Seen from that vantage-point, Northern Rhodesia was simply an awkwardly shaped piece of debris resulting from Rhodes's failure to obtain Katanga. The Company now found itself committed to ruling what amounted to not one but two huge and sprawling territories: one in the west, with communications running south, and the other in the east, with communications running further east, to Nyasaland. In 1899 the Company formally divided the region into two: North-Eastern Rhodesia, with headquarters at Fort Jameson, and North-Western Rhodesia, with headquarters from 1900 at Kalomo, on the Batoka plateau, and then, from 1907, at Livingstone, near the Victoria Falls. In 1905 the border between the two parts was shifted eastwards, from the Kafue river to the 'wasp-waist' between the Katanga Pedicle and the Zambezi. Only in 1911 was the territory reunited to form Northern Rhodesia; this, significantly, was ruled from the southernmost capital, Livingstone.

The Company did little with Northern Rhodesia. Compared with Southern Rhodesia its economic prospects seemed dim. This was ironical, considering what efforts had been made to obtain mining concessions. The Company was the sole owner of mineral rights throughout North-Western Rhodesia, supposedly on the basis of its treaties with the Lozi kingdom and Joseph Thomson's perfunctory agreements among the Lamba. But for many years these rights brought the Company little advantage. Gold deposits soon proved to be insignificant. From 1898, white prospectors examined the surface deposits of copper in Northern Rhodesia; they were frequently guided by local people familiar with the sites of earlier African copper mining. Europeans started some small-scale mining and smelting at Kansanshi and Bwana Mkubwa, and in the Hook of the Kafue. The First World War stimulated the market for base metals: Bwana Mkubwa produced copper from 1916 to 1918, and from 1917 to 1925 the country's principal export was lead, from the open-cast mine at Broken Hill (Kabwe). But these operations were confined to low-grade ores near the surface which were only profitable when prices were high and production costs low. In this land-locked country there were not only the normal technical problems of mining; there was also the expense of transporting raw materials to the coast. In such conditions only large-scale producers would stand much chance of lasting success, but the prospects were too uncertain to attract the necessary investment.

Under Company rule, Northern Rhodesia was economically important less as a source of minerals than as a source of labour for mines elsewhere, and as a link between the mines of Katanga and southern Africa. By 1897 a railway had been built from Kimberley, in South Africa, through Bechuanaland to Bulawayo. In 1902 this was extended eastwards to Beira, on the coast of Mozambique. And in 1904

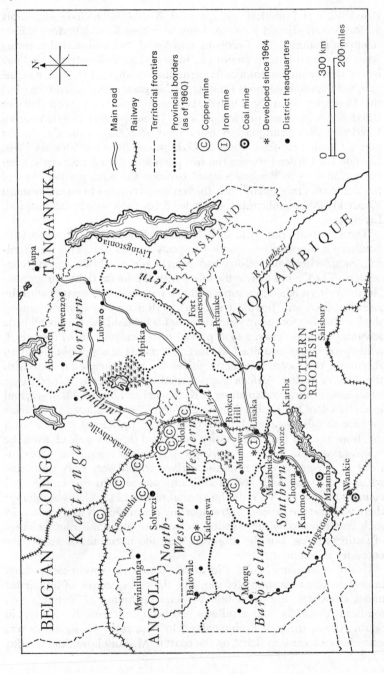

another line from Bulawayo was brought across the Zambezi, on a bridge which spans the chasms just below the Victoria Falls. This line was extended still further northwards, and by 1910 it had reached Elisabethville, the capital of Katanga. European copper-mining there had proved more rewarding than in Northern Rhodesia. Henceforward, the Katanga mines imported coal and coke from a colliery at Wankie, just south of the Victoria Falls, while their copper was exported through the Rhodesias to Beira. (The Benguela railway, from Katanga to the Atlantic, was opened only in 1931.)

Meanwhile, white farmers in Northern Rhodesia were supplying food to the mines in Katanga. In general, Europeans were discouraged from settling in Northern Rhodesia by the prevalence of tsetse fly and malaria but in the more healthy areas the Company sold land to Europeans. From 1903 onwards, white immigrants (mainly Afrikaners from South Africa) began to settle in plateau Tonga country along the railway, which happened to run through a tsetse-free and relatively fertile belt. There they raised maize and beef, for which Katanga provided an expanding market after 1910. A few other white farmers settled in the far north, at the south end of Lake Tanganyika, and also in the east, near Fort Jameson, where from 1914 tobacco was grown for export on a modest scale.

For the Company itself Northern Rhodesia was mainly valuable as a labour reserve for mines in both Katanga and Southern Rhodesia. It had a major stake in the mines of Katanga, since these provided much traffic for the railways which ran through the Rhodesias, and these were owned by the Company. In Southern Rhodesia the Company had a still more direct interest in the mining industry, whether as shareholder or royalty owner, while as the governing power in the territory it taxed mining profits. The Company was thus anxious to see that mines in both Southern Rhodesia and Katanga obtained African labour as cheaply as possible. In Northern Rhodesia it was very well placed to do this, for there it ruled over about a million people and these could be compelled to pay taxes in cash. For nearly all Africans in Northern Rhodesia the only way of obtaining cash was to engage in wage-labour outside the territory; there was very little opportunity to sell local products for cash. There was only a small demand for marketed foodstuffs within Northern Rhodesia and, in any case, the produce of white farmers was given preference. Nor was there much of a market for local crafts: the coming of the railway rapidly exposed African goods to competition from mass-produced wares which despite being imported from overseas were still cheaper than the products of local skills. Finally, there was only a limited demand for African labour within the territory. Some men obtained jobs on the railway, the few small mines, or on white farms; others engaged in government or domestic service but most had to go further afield. Many made their own way south, and some went as far as South Africa.

The migration of Africans from Northern Rhodesia to the labour markets of southern Africa was thus a matter of stark economic necessity: they were not simply moved – as some Europeans supposed – by a primitive instinct for wandering, or by a curiosity to see the 'bright lights' of the towns. These migrants needed cash, and not only to pay tax, but to buy from European stores the imported household goods which were replacing the cloths and pots and hoes once made and bartered in the village. Yet African labour migrants were by no means passive victims of the new cash economy. So far as possible, they chose their employers, for both wages and working conditions varied considerably. In general, mines paid less badly than white farms, for example, but this was mainly because the mines of southern Africa were still extremely brutal, unhealthy and dangerous places. The mines in Katanga, which drew heavily on labour from Northern Rhodesia, were almost as bad as Russian labour camps: between 1913 and 1917 the annual death rate of their African workers ranged from 70 to 140 per thousand, due to gross neglect and malnutrition. The mines in Southern Rhodesia were not much better; until 1923 the annual death rate of Northern Rhodesian workers in these mines was never less than 20 per thousand, while in 1912–13 it was more than 50.[1] In the Transvaal mines wages were somewhat higher than in central Africa, and this had the intended effect of attracting a number of Africans from North-Western Rhodesia. On the other hand, many such workers from tropical Africa died of pneumonia in the unaccustomed cold of winters at this latitude and altitude: this caused a ban in 1913 on their employment in the Transvaal mines.

In view of these varied opportunities and risks, migrant workers from Northern Rhodesia, as elsewhere, tended to shift from job to job; they moved from one mine to another and between the mining industry and other employers, in a continual effort to strike a balance between the lure of money and the fear of death. Such 'feckless wandering' proved to employers that it was not enough simply to induce Africans to work for wages; they had to be forced to go where they did not want to go, and to stay when they wished to leave. This was the purpose of recruitment for contract labour: instead of leaving people to find their own way to work, recruiting agents collected groups of men in or near their home districts and bound them by contract to one employer for a fixed period. Such agents, from both Southern Rhodesia and Katanga, were active in Northern Rhodesia from the early 1900s. The Company, however, soon found that it had to exert some control over the process of recruitment. As the ruling authority in Northern Rhodesia, it had a direct interest in African taxation as a source of revenue as well as an incentive to labour migration. It was therefore important to ensure that Africans who left the territory came back regularly with money to pay their taxes. This was the aim, for example, of the Company's regulations in 1911 whereby Africans recruited for work in Katanga had to be returned after seven months, while part of their pay had to be deferred to the end of their contract. The Company did not stop Africans dying in Katanga, and their wages there were so low that the value of such deferred pay was very small. Nonetheless it represented an important part of the territory's meagre export earnings: in 1912, total domestic exports amounted to only £70,000, which was little more than the total value of deferred pay from Katanga.

To enforce its authority in Northern Rhodesia, the British South Africa Company relied upon a small body of white civil servants. These were at first recruited mainly from Southern Rhodesia and South Africa, though later on preference was given to university graduates from Britain. These officials were dispersed among a number of stations all over the territory: the last important post to be established was Balovale, in the far north-west, in 1908. To assist them, these officials had a small force of African policemen, but they also depended heavily on African chiefs. In theory the chiefs were now little more than policemen, though they were denied appropriate wages. In practice they continued to hold courts for hearing civil disputes among Africans, and the Company administration upheld the traditional rules for chiefly succession, though it also created a number of quite new chieftainships among the Tonga. But the very fact that Company power was so thinly spread meant that local officials often resorted to extreme violence in order to assert their authority. Hut-burning and summary flogging were commonly employed to enforce obedience to demands for tax and labour. It was three especially outrageous cases of such brutality which provoked African resistance to Company rule among the Gwembe Tonga in 1909; the southern Lunda in 1912, and the Luvale in 1923.

Company rule was essentially an instrument for economic exploitation, but this of course was nothing new to the peoples of Northern Rhodesia. The new economic order of the Europeans, founded on a demand for unskilled labour, replaced a variety of African regimes based on raiding or forced labour. It was among these that Company rule involved the most radical break with the past. Initially, the kingdoms of the Bemba, Ngoni and Lozi had been subdued by a mixture of warfare and diplomacy. But their permanent subjection was achieved through a continuous process of economic attrition. The change was perhaps most sudden among the Ngoni of Mpezeni. Hitherto, they had depended heavily on food levies from their neighbours; now they had to support themselves. The Ngoni social system had been underpinned by transfers of cattle, but Europeans seized most of their cattle after the war of 1898. Moreover, Ngoniland was one of the few parts of the country where large blocks of land were alienated from Africans (in this case, to the North Charterland Company). As a result there was acute pressure on the land left for Africans, and men sought wage-employment partly in hopes of feeding better than at home. The Bemba, by contrast, were less immediately affected. They had to go away to work for wages instead of plundering their neighbours, and the wealth and prestige of their chiefs visibly diminished. But they retained almost all their conquests of the previous century, and virtually the only Europeans in their country were a few officials and missionaries – the latter being mostly Catholic White Fathers.

The position of Barotseland (as the British called the Lozi kingdom) was unique. The treaties concluded in 1898 and 1900 set limits to the Company's authority such as existed nowhere else. Although Lewanika's territory was in practice considerably reduced, the Lozi system of government continued for a while to function more or less independently. Lozi chiefs had to collect tax for the Company, but they were the only chiefs to receive a fixed percentage of the taxes paid by their subjects. Moreover, the Lozi gained a head start in education over other Africans in Northern Rhodesia. At first the Company, which had a very limited economic interest in Barotseland, did nothing to provide the various benefits it had once promised Lewanika. Coillard, the missionary, had founded a school, and by 1900 there were several young Lozi who could read and write. But Lewanika wanted a school that was independent of white mission influence. He attempted to achieve this in 1904–5 by bringing in black South African missionaries from the African Methodist Episcopal Church. (This had been founded by Negroes in the USA in 1787 and took root in South Africa a century later.) This scheme was a financial disaster, but it scared the Company into setting up, in 1906, the Barotse National School, which until 1930 was the only school in the country started by government. A further advantage, at least for the Lozi aristocracy, was the existence of a market for Lozi cattle. These had escaped the rinderpest which had swept eastern and southern Africa in the 1890s; they were thus much in demand among white farmers further south who wished to build up new herds. Lozi cattle made an important contribution to Northern Rhodesia's exports until 1915, when a cattle disease imported from Angola put an end to the export of cattle from Barotseland for over thirty years.

In some ways, then, the Lozi struck a better bargain with the Company than any other people in Northern Rhodesia. But this was of course a bargain between the Company and the Lozi ruling class, and it did not protect the latter from the same economic forces which were corroding the authority of Bemba and Ngoni chiefs. Lozi rulers and the Company were in direct competition for the labour of the various subject peoples within the Lozi kingdom. The Lozi had used them to enrich the heart of the kingdom, in the flood plain, but the Company wanted to divert them into European employment. In 1906 slavery and the enforcement of tribute labour were largely outlawed in Barotseland, while recruiting agents from the Rhodesia Native Labour Bureau began work in both North-Western and North-Eastern Rhodesia; meanwhile, Lozi subjects continued to go to South Africa. Thus labour migration from Barotseland steadily undermined the intensive agriculture of the flood plain, which had increasingly come to depend on forced labour, and which had been the basis for the complex Lozi political system. And even though this system was formally protected by treaty, its autonomy was progressively restricted. In 1904 Lewanika abandoned all jurisdiction over Africans outside the 'reserved area' defined in 1898. In 1905 the scope of Lozi criminal jurisdiction was severely reduced. In the same year, the King of Italy settled the dispute between Britain and Portugal over the western borders of the Lozi kingdom by drawing an arbitrary line well to the west of the Zambezi. Lewanika was far from satisfied, and even when this new area was added to the 'reserved area' in 1909 he was obliged to cede all rights to land outside this area. Lewanika was not alone in disputing such encroachments on Lozi power. There was much unrest among the Lozi aristocracy, especially the ambitious and literate younger men, and in 1907 there were rumours of a revolt. By the time Lewanika died, in 1916, this discontent had subsided, but well into the 1920s there was bitter conflict between the British and the new literate, mostly Christian élite headed by Lewanika's son Yeta III and his advisers.

The settlement in 1905 of the border dispute with Portugal opened the way for the last phase of British occupation. For the King of Italy's award not only included part of the Lozi kingdom west of the Zambezi; it also included part of Luvale and Lunda country further up the river. In 1907–8 Company posts were set up at Balovale and Mwinilunga. These finally enabled the Company to bring an end to the slave trade in the far north-west, which had continued to supply labour both for work in Angola and for export to Sao Tomé: by 1912 the last Mambari slavers had disappeared. The Luvale area under British rule was added to Barotseland, in response to Lozi claims that the Luvale had formerly paid them tribute. However, these claims were bitterly contested by the Luvale and eventually, in 1941, they were removed from Lozi overlordship.

The most effective opposition to Company rule came, not from Africans, but from the few European settlers. They resented the Company's restrictive policies concerning rights to land and minerals, which tended to discourage European business and settlement. They also resented the emigration of so much African labour, which forced them to pay higher wages than they wished. But they were far less numerous and powerful than the settlers in Southern Rhodesia, who by 1910 had an elected majority in the legislative council there. North of the Zambezi, white farmers and traders found it much harder to organise and express their complaints. The European population rose from 1500 in 1911 to over 3500 by 1921; a few rich landowners were able to exert pressure on the Company in London, and in 1918 an Advisory Council was created. But this gave the settlers no real power, and by this time they were quarrelling with the Company over Amalgamation.

By 1915 the Company had become anxious to reduce its expenses in Northern Rhodesia, especially as it had to bear the cost of defending the country against German troops from East Africa.[2] Amalgamation with Southern Rhodesia would make administration cheaper and more efficient and some officials argued that amalgamation, by strengthening both territories, would improve the terms on which they might be included in the Union of South Africa, formed in 1910. But at this stage amalgamation was opposed by settlers in both Rhodesias. Those in the south thought it would delay their achieving self-government, while those in the north thought it would drain wealth and labour to the south. Nothing came of this scheme, and by the end of the war the Company was ready to hand over its administrative responsibilities in both countries.

The way was now open to self-government in Southern Rhodesia, which came in 1923. But the settlers in the north still had no wish for amalgamation; they thought they would exert more power if Northern Rhodesia became a Crown Colony with a legislative council. Their claim to such representation was strengthened in 1920 when the Company had to impose an income tax for the first time. In 1924 the Colonial Office took over Northern Rhodesia from the British South Africa Company and instituted a legislative council. This was dominated by officials, but it included five members elected on a franchise which effectively excluded Africans. The Company retained its mineral rights in the north-west; this was thought a minor concession at the time, but it was later to prove enormously profitable to the Company.

Colonial Office Rule: the Early Years

The transfer of Northern Rhodesia to the Colonial Office did not in itself cause any sudden change of direction in the country's affairs. In the short run, at least, it did little or nothing to diminish the influence of southern Africa upon Northern Rhodesia. Britain's main concern was to see that somehow the territory was made to pay its own way: it exported fewer goods than any other British colony except Nyasaland, and it had never managed to balance revenue against expenditure. British thinking – or lack of thinking – on this problem was reflected in the choice of Northern Rhodesia's first Governor. Sir Herbert Stanley had previously served in Southern Rhodesia and South Africa, and he firmly believed that Northern Rhodesia should be developed as a 'white man's country' which could strengthen links between southern Africa and the much smaller communities of white settlers in British East Africa. Under Stanley's guidance the government sought to encourage further European immigration, and it therefore decided to set aside blocks of land which would in effect be available for exclusive European use. This land was mostly situated along the line of rail between Livingstone and Katanga, since in terms of both soil fertility and access to markets this was the most favourable region for farming. The exclusion of Africans from such land would also suit whites by lowering the price of African labour: Africans would find themselves gravely handicapped if they tried to produce crops for sale and would thus have to seek cash through wage-labour.

Africans, then, were to be denied the right to settle in the territory's best land. But if they really were to be kept out they would have to be provided with land where they would be secure against further encroachment. Thus, as in South Africa and Southern Rhodesia, a distinction was made between Crown land, which could be sold, and African reserves, which could not. Between 1924 and 1927 three Reserves Commissions surveyed the three areas where white settlement had already taken place and more was expected. These areas were around Fort Jameson, in the east; around Abercorn, in the far north; and along the railway line. The reserves were duly marked out between 1928 and 1930, and Africans living near, but outside the reserves were mostly forced to move into them.

In all, about 60,000 people were moved; more important, much of the reserve land was unsuited to cultivation and in several reserves there was soon serious overcrowding. Traditional methods of cultivating the generally poor soils of Northern Rhodesia had depended on frequent movement from one patch of land to another to allow soil to recover and trees to grow new branches. Where African cultivators were confined in reserves, such movement was severely restricted: neither soil nor trees were given enough time to regenerate, and it was not long before soil erosion and the destruction of woodland had further reduced the resources for African food production. By the later 1930s, among the Lamba, plateau Tonga and Mambwe, there were serious local shortages of land and therefore of food. The Ngoni and Chewa in the east suffered particularly, since they had already lost much land to the North Charterland Concession. Such hardship was strictly unnecessary,

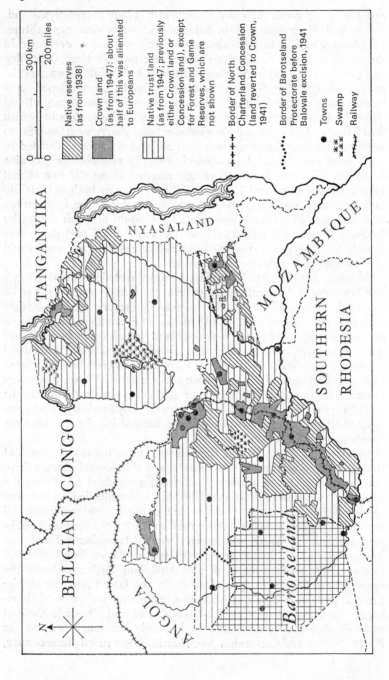

for much of the land next to the reserves remained quite uninhabited: it was meant for a new wave of white farmers, but they never arrived. This empty land soon reverted to bush. Game and tsetse fly flourished there in the absence of people, while reserve land degenerated through excess population. The eventual result, as intended, was to swell the supply of young men from the villages who were willing to work for whites for very low wages.

Thus in one important respect the first five years of Colonial Office rule had a positively harmful effect on the natural resources of Northern Rhodesia and the welfare of its inhabitants. On the other hand there was a real if modest improvement in the country's financial position: in 1928–9 revenue exceeded expenditure for the first time and continued to do so until 1932–3. This partly reflected a slow but steady growth of exports, which doubled in value between 1924 and 1929. Lead-mining at Broken Hill ran into difficulties after 1922, but the production of tobacco increased and it was the main export in 1926–7. Thereafter, the market for Northern Rhodesian tobacco collapsed, but meanwhile Broken Hill had revived, on the basis of zinc and vanadium, which together formed the main export in 1928–30. There was also a revival of mining at Bwana Mkubwa in 1927, and this made copper the country's second most important export from 1927 to 1930.

The Growth of the Copperbelt

These efforts, however, were no more than temporary expedients. Far and away the most important economic development during the 1920s was the discovery of vast deposits of copper, mostly well below the levels reached by existing mines. This discovery had its origins in the last years of Company rule. The expansion of electrical and automobile industries during and after the First World War had greatly increased world demand for copper. Mining financiers began to take a new interest in the copper resources of Northern Rhodesia. First of all there was a massive injection of South African capital at Bwana Mkubwa; it was this which led to its revival in the late 1920s. Meanwhile, large sums were spent on looking for other sources of copper. From 1922 the British South Africa Company began for the first time to allocate vast prospecting concessions to big mining firms. This meant that the latest prospecting techniques, including diamond-drilling, could be applied to a really extensive search for minerals in Northern Rhodesia. Americans led the way in this search, for the USA now led the world in copper production and technology. By 1928 the new style of prospecting, reinforced by expert geologists, had located several huge deposits of copper beneath the woodland around the headwaters of the Kafue. These deposits were mostly ore-bodies of copper sulphide, which in places lay some hundred metres deep. However, the 'flotation' process invented in 1911 for treating sulphides made it possible for a large-scale producer to work them far more profitably than those oxide ores nearer the surface to which mining had hitherto been restricted.

By 1930 four large new mines were being developed on the Copperbelt. Nkana and Nchanga were owned by the Rhodesian branch of the Anglo American Corporation, the colossus of South African mining finance. Roan Antelope and Mufulira were owned by Rhodesian Selection Trust, dominated by American capital. In 1931 Roan Antelope and Nkana went into production. In the same year, the world market for copper collapsed, owing partly to the effects of the world-wide depression and partly to the over-rapid expansion of copper supplies in recent years. For the small mine at Bwana Mkubwa this was a fatal blow; for the new mines it was only a temporary setback. Mufulira began producing in 1933 and in 1934 a refinery was opened at Nkana. The growth of the Copperbelt transformed the foreign trade of Northern Rhodesia; the value of exports increased five-fold between 1930 and 1933, and the contribution of copper rose from 30 per cent to 90 per cent. Further advances were assured by the rearmament programmes of both Britain and Germany and in 1939 Nchanga was brought into production. During the Second World War the Allies made heavy demands on the Copperbelt mines, and by 1945 Northern Rhodesia was firmly established as one of the world's major copper producers, contributing about one-eighth of the non-communist world's total product. The war also enabled Broken Hill to take on a new lease of life: the payable surface deposits were exhausted by 1940, but underground mines had been developed which yielded rich new supplies of lead as well as zinc and vanadium.

The exploitation of the Copperbelt provided a new market within the territory for migrant labour. The skilled labour was supplied by Europeans, many of whom came from South Africa. By 1930 the Copperbelt had been cleared of the chief malaria vector; many of the Lamba inhabitants had been moved to new land; and in 1931 the Europeans on the Copperbelt numbered 4000, as many as the total number of Europeans in the territory in 1924. The unskilled mine labour was mostly supplied by Africans from Northern Rhodesia, especially the Bemba-speaking peoples of the north-east, who already had much experience of mining in Katanga. By 1930, when construction was at its height, there were nearly 22,000 Africans at work on the copper mines, which was over one-third of the total number of Africans employed in Northern Rhodesia. Thereafter the slump intervened, but by 1937 there were almost 18,000, and by 1943, nearly 33,000. The growth of railway traffic provided a further source of employment, while thousands of Africans found work in the market towns next the mines; the

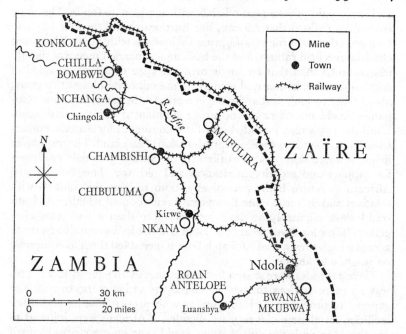

oldest of these, Ndola, became the commercial centre of the Copperbelt.

For many years workers on the Copperbelt continued on the move: they did not settle permanently in towns or mines. This was true of Europeans as well as Africans. Many Europeans returned to South Africa, for example, when conditions seemed more favourable there. Yet their skills were in short supply, and the mining companies boosted the wages of Europeans to induce them to stay on the Copperbelt. On the other hand there was no shortage of unskilled African workers. Most employers throughout Northern Rhodesia continued to pay Africans extremely low wages, on the convenient assumption that they needed money only for paying tax and for buying a few clothes. It was widely supposed that the families of African wage-earners could remain at home in their villages, living off their own produce. Thus, as in other parts of eastern and southern Africa, most employers paid and housed their African workers as if they were all single men.

The mining companies in Northern Rhodesia were a partial exception to this pattern. They could afford to provide better pay and housing than other employers. From the first they housed their workers, both black and white, in segregated compounds and townships which were better supplied and regulated than those in which the employees of other businesses and of government were supervised by understaffed and underpaid government officials with inadequate funds. The mine companies realised that African, like European, workers were likely to be more efficient if they could bring their wives with them. Wives and children received rations, and the housing for married men was slightly less cramped than that for single men. By 1942 the average period of continuous work by married men at Nkana mine was almost two years, about twice as long as that for single men. All the same, the mine companies made no effort to encourage permanent African settlement. Until the 1950s they provided very little housing fit for African workers with children, and few facilities for education of any kind. The companies firmly believed that African workers should look to their fellow villagers for support and security in sickness and old age. They encouraged Africans to return home periodically, both to keep up contacts with relatives and to 'rest': some Europeans even doubted whether Africans could work efficiently at the mines for more than a few years altogether. Thus for many years the mine companies were quite ready to accept a high turnover of African labour if it enabled them to economise on wages and amenities.

These attitudes were shared for a long time by the government. This was no more anxious than other employers to incur the trouble and expense of providing African workers with proper housing and other facilities, let alone social security. Besides, if Africans were induced to cut their ties with the village, they would pose enormous problems if thousands suddenly lost their jobs, as happened during the slump in 1931–3. But the reasons for this official fear of 'detribalisation' lay deeper. Like other colonial governments in eastern and southern Africa, the Northern Rhodesian government regarded settled communities of urban, 'semi-civilised' Africans as a threat to white domination. Most colonial officials had gained their experience in rural areas and believed that there was a single correct path for African social evolution: through tribal institutions, developed in the Africans' rural homelands. During the 1930s the government introduced a policy of 'indirect rule' in rural administration, whereby the powers of chiefs were extended to include not only the administration of justice but the maintenance of 'native treasuries'. It seemed clear that this system could only flourish if migrant workers shared their earnings with their fellow tribesmen and maintained their traditional local loyalties. Thus for both practical and theoretical reasons the government was reluctant to disturb the circulation of migrant labour between village and town.

Despite the general preference among Europeans for cheap, unskilled and highly mobile African labour, there were forces working against this, which instead caused Africans to spend longer periods in employment and thus to become more or less 'stabilised'. In the first

place technological advances meant that for some tasks machines might
be cheaper than unskilled labour. In such cases it might then be necessary to train African workers how to use the machines; this in turn
would mean encouraging them to spend longer periods at work, if the
effort of training was not to be wasted. It is this point which largely
accounts for the difference in labour policy between the copper mines in
Northern Rhodesia and those in Katanga. The latter were mostly
open-cast mines, where from the late 1920s it proved both possible and
economical to use machinery on a large scale. As a result, the Katanga
company, Union Minière, developed a strong interest in forming a
relatively skilled and stable African labour force. From 1927 it began to
enlist workers on three-year contracts, and sought to attract men from
within the Congo or Ruanda-Urundi. They were housed with their
families in decent if modest comfort, and were supplied with limited
social services. In Northern Rhodesia the copper mines were all underground (until 1955), and there was much less scope for mechanisation.
Nonetheless, from the late 1940s onwards the companies there placed
increasing emphasis on mechanisation, partly for technological reasons
and partly because the cost of labour was rising owing to African
pressure for higher wages. Thus the mines in Northern Rhodesia also
began to develop an interest in stabilising at least some African mineworkers so that they could acquire and retain certain skills.

The process of stabilisation was not, however, confined to skilled
African workers. Even by 1940 there were clear signs of a tendency for
unskilled workers to 'stabilise' themselves regardless of European
policies. These policies were based on the theory that the traditional
'subsistence' economies of African villages need not be much affected by
the absence of men in wage-earning employment. In practice, however,
this was simply not true, and many families preferred to take their
chance in the towns rather than starve at home. In spite of low wages
and squalid housing, African workers tended to spend longer periods
in towns – often moving from job to job in search of better conditions –
and less time at home.

By the mid-1940s the growing tendency towards stabilisation of this
kind had become a matter of great concern both to the Colonial Office
and to the Northern Rhodesian government. The latter, unlike the
South African government, lacked the power to keep Africans regularly
on the move through a pass-law system. Eventually, it decided to
follow a new initiative from the Southern Rhodesian government, by
trying to ensure that urban Africans were at least hygienically sheltered
as long as they were actually at work. In 1948, as a belated first step,
the Northern Rhodesian government required all employers to
provide or pay for suitable housing for married workers, and during the
next decade the government substantially increased its expenditure on

African housing. But little of this was adequate for families, and in any case it was still assumed that urban Africans would retire to their villages at the end of their working lives. Thus little provision was made for the needs of Africans in sickness, unemployment or retirement. Besides, any whole-hearted effort at stabilisation, whether by government or business, meant improving not only material conditions but also African skills and education. This would threaten the favoured position of European workers, whom the mining companies especially could not afford to antagonise. Thus social policies continued to be heavily influenced by theories of migrant labour, even though more and more Africans were settling in towns to escape at least from the grim certainties of rural poverty.

A Lop-sided Economy

The development of the Copperbelt was a somewhat mixed blessing. In the long run, it greatly increased the material wealth of the country as a whole. For both Europeans and Africans it created jobs, it increased spending-power and it provided a market for food-producers, and it also yielded tax revenues that helped to pay for a variety of public utilities and services. But these benefits were spread thinly and very unevenly. Within the Copperbelt itself there were vast differences between the material living standards of Europeans and Africans. And if the Copperbelt in general is contrasted with the rest of Northern Rhodesia, it appears throughout its history to have been an island of comparative plenty in a vast sea of rural poverty. Indeed, in some ways, this poverty was actually increased by the growth of the mining industry.

There were, of course, some rural areas which clearly gained from the expansion of mining. Most important were the maize-growing areas along the railway line in the southern and central provinces. In the early 1920s European farmers in these areas were still selling maize and cattle to Katanga, but they were rapidly losing this market to white farmers in Southern Rhodesia. The development of the Copperbelt in the late 1920s at last provided them with a protected home market. By the mid-1930s, maize exports had revived, due to high world prices, while by 1943 the domestic demand, due to the rapid growth of the Copperbelt, exceeded local supplies. Contrary to earlier policy, there was a growing market for African producers, and a few plateau Tonga became large-scale farmers using modern techniques. Some Lamba villagers sold home produce to the mines, as did some Lenje near Broken Hill. The mines of both Northern Rhodesia and Katanga provided new markets for African fishermen: fresh fish, packed in ice by Greek traders, came from Lake Mweru and the Luapula river; dried fish came from the lower Kafue, the Lukanga swamps and Lake

Bangweulu (where the swamp-dwelling Unga had long since produced otter-skins for export).

Elsewhere, however, the only important source of cash income for Africans was money sent or brought home by relatives working for wages. This money was little enough: in the 1930s few villagers handled much more than a pound or two each year. There was thus all the more need for villages to send their young men away to work. Despite the new market for labour created by the copper mines, there continued to be a steady flow of African labour into neighbouring territories. In the later 1920s goldfields were developed near Lupa, in southern Tanganyika; by 1936 these employed well over 10,000 men from Northern Rhodesia, while several thousand had gone further north to work on sisal plantations near the coast. There were also several thousand men from Northern Rhodesia at work in Katanga, though not on the mines: recruitment from Northern Rhodesia for the Katanga mines came to an end in 1931, partly because of the change in mining policy there, and partly because the Northern Rhodesian government wished to ensure a steady supply of labour for the new mines on the Copperbelt. The main market for labour migrants from Northern Rhodesia continued to be Southern Rhodesia, where employment had risen considerably as a result of the expansion of European farming since the beginning of the First World War. The Rhodesia Native Labour Bureau was closed down in 1933, since the depression drastically reduced the demand for labour, but even when demand revived the labour supply was so plentiful that recruiting was unnecessary. By 1936 well over 50,000 men from Northern Rhodesia were at work in Southern Rhodesia. There were also several thousands at work in South Africa, and in 1936 the Transvaal mines were allowed once again to recruit from Northern Rhodesia. Altogether it is likely that by that year as many Africans were employed outside the territory as within it; it is also probable that more than half the able-bodied male population of Northern Rhodesia was working for wages away from home.

The subsistence agriculture of African villages was gravely handicapped by the absence of so many men. In so far as the copper industry gave a new impetus to such migration, it seriously undermined many rural economies. Urban conditions discouraged most married migrant workers from taking wives and children with them, let alone elderly relatives, so that many families were left at home to feed themselves without the aid of their major bread-winner. This caused special hardship in the woodlands of the north-east from which so many Copperbelt miners came. In these regions men were needed to pollard trees and clear the bush, even if women had always done the actual cultivation. Where, as in Mambwe villages, the remaining men were related to one another, it was possible to reduce the impact of labour migration by increased economic co-operation. In Bemba villages, on the other hand, men were usually related only through their wives; villages frequently split up, and long-term co-operation was difficult. Thus not only was there little rural progress; to some extent the condition of the rural population actually declined. Malnutrition was widespread, resistance to disease was lowered, and the efficiency of both rural and urban labour was seriously impaired.

Thus in some areas African poverty was aggravated by a shortage of labour. In others, as we have already noted, poverty was further entrenched by a quite artificial shortage of land. But this was not all; for many years, the territory as a whole suffered from a severe shortage of capital. This seems paradoxical in view of the enormous sums invested in the Copperbelt and the large profits made there after 1935. From this date, the mining industry was indeed Northern Rhodesia's major source of revenue: taxes from the mining industry formed about 45 per cent of the total revenue in 1937 and perhaps as much as 70 per cent in 1939. These revenues were quite large enough to ensure that after 1934 the government never had to show an annual deficit. Yet copper revenues were much less than they might have been. This was due partly to the system of mining royalties and partly to special arrangements for taxing the mines.

The mineral rights throughout the Copperbelt – the rights to search for minerals, mine and own them – belonged to the British South Africa Company. Its legal title to these rights was highly questionable; it certainly owned the mineral rights in Barotseland, but this had never reached within 150 kilometres of the Copperbelt, nor did the dubious treaties collected for the Company among the Lamba by Joseph Thomson refer to any part of the Copperbelt. Nonetheless, the British government acknowledged the claims of the British South Africa Company, and so did the mining companies: they obtained their mining concessions from it, and they duly paid royalties in return. These royalties varied with the price of copper, but they had to be paid whether the companies made a profit or not. Taxation, however, was only levied on the mining companies if, despite the burden of royalties, they did make a profit.

The British South Africa Company was not the only drain on the mineral wealth of Northern Rhodesia; there was also the British government. The headquarters both of this Company and of the mining companies were in London, which meant that they were liable to taxation by the British government as well as the Northern Rhodesian government. By a special arrangement they were taxed only in Britain, at the standard company rate, and only half this revenue was passed on to Northern Rhodesia. Thus in 1936–7, after the Copperbelt had recovered from the slump, the mining companies paid over £300,000 in royalties to the British South Africa Company. From the remaining profits of just over £4,000,000 the governments of Britain and Northern Rhodesia each took in tax £500,000; they also took in tax about £40,000 each from the British South Africa Company's income from royalties. The total levy, in royalties and taxation, on the profits from mining was about 30 per cent, but only 12½ per cent went to the Northern Rhodesian government. In 1939, as copper prices rose, the British South Africa Company drew from the Copperbelt as much, or more, in royalties (about £500,000) as the Northern Rhodesian government did in taxation. And despite the revenue drawn by Britain from the Copperbelt, virtually the only assistance received from Britain by Northern Rhodesia in the 1930s took the form of loans. In 1943 it was calculated that from 1930 to 1940 Britain had kept for itself £2,400,000 in taxes from the Copperbelt, while Northern Rhodesia received from Britain only £136,000 in grants for development.

Thus the prosperity of the Copperbelt was no guarantee of the prosperity of the country as a whole, and the colonial government continued to find it hard to make ends meet. In 1938 the British government sent out Sir Alan Pim, the leading authority on colonial finance, to find ways of reducing government spending in Northern Rhodesia. Pim, however, concluded that, so far from being reduced, government spending should be increased: 'the essential social services are very backward and require to be largely expanded.'³ He argued that despite the rapid expansion of mining the combined burden of royalty payments and British taxation had prevented the colonial government from making any commensurate investment in roads, schools, health services, urban housing, secondary industries and agricultural development. But Pim's report had little immediate effect. In 1939 the Second World War broke out; it served to maintain copper prices but reduced the government's administrative and technical staff, which had just begun to make good the cut-backs imposed during the depression.

The contrast between the wealth generated on the Copperbelt and the poverty of the country at large was clearly reflected in the history of African education. Furthermore this plainly shows that the slow pace of African development was due not simply to shortage of funds but also to deliberate social policy: Africans could not be allowed to compete for jobs held by Europeans. Indeed, the government's financial problems in the 1930s were partly due to its policy (inherited from the Company) of employing whites in jobs which in East and West Africa were done by Africans for far lower wages. It was therefore not surprising that for many years the government was content to leave African education largely in the hands of Christian missions. Owing partly to policy – their main aim, after all, was conversion – and partly to lack of money, the missions concentrated on primary education. By 1931 the government spent £15,000 on assisting selected mission schools, but this was remarkable only by comparison with the neglect of education under Company rule.

After the depression, expenditure on African education rose quite fast, in relative terms: mission subsidies were increased, and several government schools were founded. But the system was extremely wasteful, as very few African children stayed at school long enough to become literate even in their own language. In 1942, of 86,300 who were said to be in school, only 3,000 were in the fifth year and a mere 35 received secondary education. The country's first junior secondary school for African boys, Munali, near Lusaka, had only been opened in 1939. Of the handful who reached the final year of primary education, most become primary school teachers, to give another generation two or three years in school. On the Copperbelt there were by 1944 schools for about half the African children of school age. In 1932 a trades school was started at Lusaka, but in 1948 it only had 70 pupils; besides, plans for giving Africans technical training were a hollow mockery when legislation passed in 1943 prevented Africans from becoming industrial apprentices. It was no great achievement that by 1940 the government spent more on African than on European education: it spent thirty times as much on each white child as on each black child, and this was still true in 1950. After half a century of colonial rule, the educational system in Northern Rhodesia showed all too plainly how far the territory was still an appendage to the white supremacies of southern Africa.

NOTES

1. The influenza pandemic which swept the Old World in 1918 caused the death-rate of African miners to rise in that year to 114 per thousand in Southern Rhodesia, and 206 per thousand in Katanga.
2. In 1918 the German commander General von Lettow-Vorbeck invaded Northern Rhodesia with his force of African guerrillas and met no resistance, but his advance south towards the railway at Broken Hill was cut short by the Armistice.
3. *Report of the Commission appointed to enquire into the financial and economic position of Northern Rhodesia* (Colonial Office no. 145, 1938), p. 347.

XI

The Growth of a Nation
c. 1930 – 1964

Throughout most of the colonial period the political destiny of Northern Rhodesia was far from clear. Even its geographical position was politically ambiguous: it was situated between the territories of southern Africa, dominated by Europeans, and those to the north, such as the Belgian Congo and East Africa, where the colonial governments largely denied white settlers political power and did envisage, however dimly, an eventual transfer of power to Africans. In 1899 the British High Commissioner to South Africa, Lord Milner, argued that the Zambezi was the natural frontier for a future British Africa in the southern part of the continent; the country to the north should become a 'black dependency'. This view was borne out by the very limited scale of white immigration into Northern Rhodesia, and it seemed to be further confirmed when in 1924 Northern Rhodesia, unlike Southern Rhodesia, came under the control of the Colonial Office. Yet the country had been created as an extension of British power in southern Africa; its communications all ran south; and both policies and social attitudes continued to be much influenced by southern examples. This was evident both in the disastrous reserves policy and in the treatment of African wage-labour. Indeed, the growth of the Copperbelt greatly enlarged the scope of southern influences. It attracted white immigrants from South Africa and Southern Rhodesia who were mostly committed to securing European political and economic supremacy for the indefinite future. And though white settlers in Northern Rhodesia remained a far smaller proportion of the total population than in Southern Rhodesia, let alone South Africa, they were vital to the economy and exerted considerable political influence.

By the 1940s most Europeans in Northern Rhodesia felt that their position could best be safeguarded through some form of closer association with the white settler regime in Southern Rhodesia. In 1953 both Rhodesias were joined with Nyasaland in a Central African Federation, and this clearly aligned Northern Rhodesia closer to white southern

Africa than to the 'black dependencies' in East Africa. Ironically, however, it was precisely this attempt to subordinate Northern Rhodesia to
the white south which provoked the rise of a popular African movement
dedicated to overthrowing colonial rule. Indeed, the imposition of
Federation was itself a defensive reaction to the growth of modern
African politics. We must now see how Africans in Northern Rhodesia
joined in common action to improve their own conditions, to challenge
white aspirations and finally to place their country firmly outside the
political orbit of white southern Africa.

Early African Protest

African responses to colonial rule in Northern Rhodesia were inevitably
conditioned by the slow pace of economic and social development. With
so few Africans who could read and write, modern-style politics were
slow to emerge. Significantly, some of the earliest moves towards
political organisation owed much to Africans from Nyasaland. There,
education had advanced much further, and for many years 'Nyasas'
occupied many of those clerical posts and other skilled jobs, mostly in
towns and mines, which were open to Africans in Northern Rhodesia.
But far from the towns, in the remote north-east, a few Northern Rhodesian Africans also obtained an education in Nyasaland. It was these
men who formed the first modern African political association in
Northern Rhodesia.

The centre of this activity was Mwenzo, where the Scottish Livingstonia mission opened a station in 1894. Some of the Africans who
learned their letters at Mwenzo were sent on to the Overtoun training
institute at Kondowe, near the northern end of Lake Malawi, which had
been founded in 1894 by Dr Robert Laws. This institute, which soon
became known simply as 'Livingstonia', had an enormous influence on
the growth of African protest in Northern Rhodesia, and indeed
throughout southern Africa. Students at Livingstonia came from a
variety of backgrounds and rapidly developed a sense of common
identity as Africans. Besides, Laws strongly believed in training Africans
to take a full part in church leadership. He gave his students the
most advanced education then available in central Africa. They were
also encouraged to debate all sorts of current problems, and gained
a very broad perspective on race relations, both in Africa and in the
USA.

In 1904 some of the students from Mwenzo left Livingstonia to begin
work as teachers in their own country. Two years later a new school at
Chinsali, in Bemba country, was placed under one of their Nyasa
colleagues; this was David Kaunda, father of Zambia's first President.
Kaunda and his fellow teachers were naturally proud of their education

and responsibilities, and they were deeply sensitive to European racial-ism, especially the habit of calling all African men 'boys'. Their feelings were well expressed by Donald Siwale, a schools inspector at Mwenzo: 'What we want is fair play and equality because we read in the Bible that every human being is the same.'[1] Thus in 1912 Siwale and Kaunda led the way in forming a Mwenzo Welfare Association to bring African views to the attention of the government.

The Mwenzo association was a bold but rather isolated venture. Unlike similar associations in Nyasaland, it failed to take lasting root. Local Company officials were by no means hostile, but in 1914 the First World War broke out. There was fighting with the Germans near the border; Mwenzo mission was evacuated; and the association dis-solved. It was revived in 1923 but lapsed once again in 1927. During the next few years other welfare societies were formed in rural districts, but these developed as social clubs without any political character. As yet, such groups were still far removed in experience and outlook from the great mass of ordinary villagers. A common interest existed, but there was still no basis for popular participation.

In 1929–31 welfare associations were formed in several towns along the railway line. These were rather more purposeful. They too were mostly confined to small groups of clerks and teachers, among whom former Livingstonia students were prominent. But they made important efforts to protect the interests of ordinary people, and it was easier to do this in the towns than in the sparsely populated countryside. The Ndola association, led by a remarkable Nyasa clerk, Ernest Muwamba, induced the government and the railway to improve facili-ties for Africans. The Livingstone association prevented a compound riot, exposed some outrageous cases of racial discrimination and pro-tested against the recent removal of Africans from land reserved for Europeans along the railway line. The Livingstone association also brought together educated Africans from opposite ends of the territory: both from the Barotse National School and from the schools of the Livingstonia mission and the London Missionary Society in the north-east.

Nonetheless, the influence of these early urban pressure groups remained limited. They did much to create an informed African public opinion, but they could not mount effective concerted action against the central government. An attempt was made in 1933 to form a United African Welfare Association of Northern Rhodesia. This would have been the first territory-wide African organisation, but there was too little determination to follow up this bold idea: when the government refused to recognise it, there seems to have been no reaction. In 1937, among the plateau Tonga, a group of African teachers, chiefs and farmers formed the Northern Rhodesia African National Congress, to protest against land alienation and discrimination against African food-production for the market. In spite of its name, however, the Congress was very much a local group, with essentially local grievances and it did not long survive government disapproval. As yet, the few Africans who had some familiarity with the world of Europeans and of government lacked a cause big enough both to bring themselves together and to draw massive popular support. Details of colonial rule were criticised, but there was still no idea that it should go, as there was, by this time, in West Africa. Popular political leadership first developed, not in the southern towns or in the rural areas, but at the real centre of political gravity, the Copperbelt, in the years after 1935.

African Religious Movements

All the same, Africans throughout Northern Rhodesia were aware that much was wrong with colonial rule: the stresses and strains of labour migration, the consequent weakening of family ties, the decline of chiefs and the increase in rural poverty. The difficulty was to see just how these misfortunes were brought about. Faced with the bewildering complexities of social change, induced by factors beyond their knowledge, let alone control, many Africans sought answers, not in political action but in the realm of the supernatural. For in Northern Rhodesia, as elsewhere in Africa, social tensions and frustrations were commonly ascribed to the action of witches. The government had aggravated these fears by outlawing accusations of witchcraft and the use of the poison ordeal by which chiefs had in the past tested charges of witchcraft. There was thus a widely felt need for new techniques to combat witch-craft. The missions, of course, could offer no help, since they refused to admit the reality of witchcraft. But there was a strong desire to believe that even so the battle against witchcraft could make use of Christianity, or at least elements from it, such as baptism. Besides, the Bible itself greatly strengthened the notion that the world could somehow be released once and for all from the power of evil.

The persistence of the belief in witchcraft, and the search for new ways to attack it, gave rise to a number of witch-finding movements during the first few decades of colonial rule. Some were quite localised, but in 1933-4 most of the east and north-east was swept by the *mucapi* movement, which was introduced from central Nyasaland. This was a time when people were perhaps more than usually eager to clutch at a new hope of deliverance from their troubles. The world-wide depression had thrown many wage-earners out of work, while the 1933 harvest was largely ruined, first by drought and then by locusts; only reserves from the previous year's good harvest prevented widespread starvation. And the methods of the *mucapi* leaders were indeed quite new. They sought to eliminate suspicions and accusations of witchcraft by making people give up all their charms, whether malevolent or merely protective, and by issuing them with a medicine, *mucapi*, which conferred immunity from witchcraft upon the innocent and death to those who attempted witchcraft after taking it. The *mucapi* leaders also showed certain Christian influences; they spoke in sermons of the washing-away of sins and foretold the second coming of their dead founder. Like the popular *mbeni* dances introduced by soldiers returning from Tanganyika after the First World War, the *mucapi* cult induced a feeling of successful adjustment to, and participation in, European custom and belief, but it also offered an answer to a perennial African problem. If only for a short time, the *mucapi* cult provided a means to communal well-being that seemed more effective in colonial conditions than the old communal rituals of chieftainship.

At the same time there were more aggressive innovations in popular religion. In many parts of Northern Rhodesia between the world wars, much enthusiasm was aroused by millenarian preachers who had been influenced, often through the mediation of Nyasas, by the doctrines of the Watch Tower Bible and Tract Society, an American-based organisation also known as Jehovah's Witnesses. These African 'Watchtower' preachers foretold that the end of the world was at hand, and that when it came salvation would be for Africans alone, while Europeans went to hell. Even so, salvation might have to be earned through baptism and by adhering to special moral codes.

Watchtower doctrines were introduced to Northern Rhodesia by home-coming migrant workers. Some, deported from Southern Rhodesia in 1917, made a great impact in the far north-east, which had been forced to supply food and labour for the war in East Africa. Among the Mambwe, such men inspired the growth of a Watchtower community which rejected the authority of chiefs and officials: it was eventually suppressed in 1939. In the Luapula valley, returning migrants formed similar communities from the 1920s. In other rural areas Watchtower preachers generally made a less lasting impression. In 1924–5 they attracted much attention in the east, and in 1925–6 there was a massive response among the Lala to Tomo Nyirenda, a Nyasa who called himself Mwana Lesa, Son of God. But Nyirenda had come not only to preach but to wipe out witchcraft; his methods were drastic, and in 1926 he was hanged for drowning suspected witches. In the early 1930s Watchtower preachers were called in to campaign against witchcraft among the Ila, and also in the far north-west, but their claims soon proved false. In Barotseland, however, Watchtower doctrines did take root during the 1930s, for they made a great appeal to the Wiko peoples who resented Lozi domination.

Meanwhile, several Watchtower communities had been established

in the towns, mostly among African clerks, stores assistants and foremen. These groups were far more literate than their rural counterparts;
they received literature from their original source of inspiration, the
Watch Tower Bible and Tract Society, and in the early 1930s they
developed a church-like organisation for Bible study, prayer and wor-
ship. In 1935 a territory-wide conference of Watchtower supporters was
held in Lusaka (which had just become the new capital of Northern
Rhodesia). For many years the Society itself was not allowed a base in
the territory, since it was viewed with great suspicion by the government; it had urged non co-operation with the war effort in 1914–18, and
though it disclaimed responsibility for African Watchtower movements
it clearly had a subversive influence. In 1931, for example, one Watchtower preacher at Ndola had announced:

> We natives will soon be mixing with the Europeans, sitting down and
> eating food at the same table, and they will shake us by the hand. The
> white men who refuse to mix with us will be told to go home.[2]

On the other hand, it seemed that the best way of checking the spread of
such opinions might be to let the Society itself supervise its followers. In
1936 two white Witnesses from South Africa were allowed to set up a
Society office in Lusaka and over the next two decades the Society
established control over several Watchtower communities, both in the
towns and in the rural north-east.

The Society stressed that its members must prepare for the end of
earthly kingdoms, and it forbade involvement in politics; at the same
time, it strongly deplored civil disobedience. Nonetheless, it was far
more popular than the mission churches. These were slow to train and
ordain African ministers, whereas Witnesses were only indirectly supervised by whites and were left free to organise their own meetings and
religious instruction. Thus the Society offered far more opportunity
than the missions for leadership and full participation in the life of a
Christian community and, unlike the missions, it recognised, or at least
did not deny, the existence of witchcraft, even if it offered no immediate
remedy other than urging people to forswear it. By 1951 it seemed that
the Society's success in Northern Rhodesia accounted for the virtual
absence there of separatist churches.

There were, however, more orthodox ways in which Africans took a
religious initiative. One of the most impressive witnesses to Christianity
in Northern Rhodesia was the Union Church on the Copperbelt. This
was founded in the 1920s by Ernest Muwamba and another Nyasa
clerk trained at Livingstonia, not in reaction against the missions but
simply because there were as yet no missionaries in the area. It was this
African church which provided the first membership of the Ndola
welfare association; it was also the seed-bed of a movement of Christian

union. For in due course it received the co-operation of several Protestant missions, and this co-operation on the Copperbelt eventually
gave rise to what is now the United Church of Zambia. But a number of
Africans followed Muwamba out of the Union Church and into the
African Methodist Episcopal Church. As we have seen, this had flourished for some time in South Africa, and it had collaborated briefly
with Lewanika. In 1928 it was re-introduced to Northern Rhodesia by
John Membe, who was born in the far north-east, received part of his
training as a teacher at Livingstonia, and worked as a clerk in Livingstone. The AME church soon gained support in the towns, especially
among members of welfare associations, and also in parts of the north-
east; it developed its own African leadership, and it is now one of the
major religious groups in the country.

Politics on the Copperbelt, 1935–1949

*These men [white mine-workers] have the idea that the time will come when
Government has finished using us, sucking us like an orange, and there is no
more use for us, we will go.*
                                    South African mineworker on the Copperbelt, 1941[3]
*Improving our country for us, are you? Railways, roads, mines, indeed! For
whose benefit are they? You can take them all away so far as I'm concerned.
What are you leaving us with? A sucked orange!*
                                    Lunda chief, late 1930s[4]

The modern political history of Northern Rhodesia really began in
the late 1930s, when the Copperbelt finally emerged after the depression as the economic heart of the country. The mining towns brought
large numbers of Africans into close association and recurrent conflict
with a small number of dominant Europeans. In this situation, both
sides began to compete in bringing pressure to bear on the government
and the mining companies. It was in the mining towns that popular
African discontent first found effective expression through recognised
leaders. At the same time, the continual movement of workers between
town and country meant that the growth of African political awareness
soon affected the country at large. Moreover, the growth of African
protest gave new urgency to the long-standing problem of Northern
Rhodesia's relationship to Southern Rhodesia, and it was this problem
which dominated political controversy up to the emergence of Zambia
in 1964.

African migrants on the Copperbelt were men of two worlds: they
were still tribesmen, with homes in distant villages, but they were
also workers and townsmen. As tribesmen they continued more or less
to observe traditional law and custom in their relationships with each
other. As workers, however, they were involved in a quite new kind of

situation, in which they were all, at least potentially, united in opposition to their employers and their European fellow-workers. As we saw in the last chapter, both employers and the government tended to regard African workers primarily as tribesmen: transitory visitors to the towns who remained attached to their tribal land and institutions. On the Copperbelt, as in the bush, some form of African participation in administration seemed necessary, but as far as possible this was to follow traditional lines, regardless of the quite different problems of life in the towns. Thus in 1931 when 'Indirect Rule' was being introduced in the rural areas, 'tribal elders' were appointed at the Roan Antelope mine compound and the nearby municipal township, Luanshya. These elders performed a useful function in settling disputes involving tribal custom. But in disputes involving conditions of life and work in the towns they obviously had no authority, either as arbiters or as representatives of African interests. Expertise in tribal custom was no help in dealing with the challenges of European custom and innovation.

In 1935, for the first time, African mineworkers went on strike, first at Mufulira, then at Nkana and Roan Antelope. At Roan, incautious use of the police provoked rioting, and six strikers were killed. Elsewhere, there was very little violence and the strikers soon went back to work. Brief and ineffective though it was, the strike served to show that African mineworkers were already conscious of a common interest and were capable of organising concerted resistance within the urban environment. In the absence of any political organisation, the strikers made use of the mbeni dance societies, which among the Bemba-speaking majority provided a structure of leadership which linked all the mines. The immediate cause of the strike was a plan, partly misunderstood, for revising the assessment of poll tax in favour of rural areas. But the strike crystallised long-standing discontent with living and working conditions. It also exposed the absence of any effective channel of communication between Africans and management: significantly, the tribal elders at Roan were ignored.

This point was duly noted by the Commission of Enquiry which reported on the disturbances. Yet the response of both government and management was to strengthen the 'tribal' character of urban administration rather than seek new and more appropriate forms. In 1937 tribal elders were introduced at Mufulira, and in 1938 Urban Courts, under 'tribal councillors' were set up in the municipal townships. As a channel of communication between Africans and government, Urban Advisory Councils were introduced in 1938, but these were mostly nominated from tribal elders in both mine and municipal compounds, and they were largely forbidden to discuss labour relations. The government was also provoked into setting up a Labour Department in 1940, but to begin with it had no officials on the Copperbelt.

The strike in 1935 showed the potential strength of African miners. And by this time many of them were efficient enough to suggest that before long some at least would be quite capable of taking over jobs reserved for Europeans. The European mineworkers saw this as clearly as anyone, and in 1936 they formed the Northern Rhodesia Mine-workers Union (NRMU) in order to safeguard their interests against their African fellow workers as much as against their employers. In 1940 the NRMU organised strikes at Mufulira and Nkana in protest against the rise in the cost of living brought about by the war, and its wage claims were largely conceded. This success at once stimulated Africans at these mines to stage a strike of their own, and with much greater reason. During the depression, their wages had been reduced and despite the rising cost of living the companies, who by 1940 were making handsome profits, had not even raised wages to their former levels. Basic food rations, housing and medical services were free, but the cash wage was so low that any fall in it was acutely felt. In 1940, the starting wage for Africans underground was 22s 6d for every thirty days of work, whereas in 1929 it was 30s; and surface workers got 12s 6d in 1940 compared with 17s 6d in 1929.

The African strike lasted a week, but came to a bloody end. At Nkana, strikers threw stones at fellow-workers suspected of strike-breaking; soldiers began shooting, and seventeen strikers were killed. Britain sent out a Commission of Enquiry, and as a result wages were slightly increased; more important, they were now classified into three grades, according to responsibility and experience. This was a direct response to the fact that the strike had mostly been led by 'boss-boys' (African foremen in charge of small underground gangs); it was they who felt most keenly the vast difference between African and European wages, as their work was similar to that of several Europeans. Once the wages of boss-boys were placed on a separate scale, their interests tended to diverge from those of other mineworkers, and the chances of further united action diminished. This division within the African labour force was confirmed when in 1942 the Labour Department encouraged boss-boys to form committees on each mine to discuss their problems with management. For mineworkers in general, the only recognised spokesmen were tribal elders. These were now elected at all mines, and renamed 'tribal representatives', but in the sphere of labour relations they were no more representative than they had ever been. The government and most employers refused to admit that Africans had to be regarded as workers and townsmen as well as tribesmen, even though there were now signs in the older towns, such as Broken Hill, that many Africans had lived in town for several years and were as much at home there as in their villages of origin.

The official structure, then, provided only limited opportunities for

Africans to come together and express their views, either as townsmen or as workers. But meanwhile, from 1942, African welfare societies were formed in the mining towns on the Copperbelt. They were led mostly by teachers, clerks and foremen, but they spoke for all kinds of workers, and they were much more effective than the Urban Advisory Councils or the tribal representatives in bringing the problems of mining communities to the attention of the mining companies and the government. The growth of welfare societies on the Copperbelt encouraged migrant workers to revive them in the rural areas. By 1946 there was a network of societies spread over most parts of the territory. This prompted Dauti Yamba, a teacher who had founded the Luanshya welfare society, to convene a meeting in Broken Hill of representatives from all welfare societies in Northern Rhodesia. It was not quite the first time that Africans had met to discuss political problems at a territorial level: an African Civil Servants' Association had been formed in the 1930s, but this was dominated by Nyasas. The welfare societies now formed a Federation of African Societies. Two years later this became the Northern Rhodesia Congress, a forerunner of the nationalist political parties.

The rapid growth of welfare societies provoked the government into providing its own large-scale structures for African political discussion. From 1944, African Regional (Provincial) Councils were formed from among members of Urban Advisory Councils, welfare societies and rural Native Authorities (chiefs and their advisers). In 1946 these provincial councils began to send delegates to a territory-wide African Representative Council, which met more or less annually until its dissolution in 1958.[5] Such councils provided useful platforms for the expression of African opinion. Their more active members were far from being stooges, and some belonged to Congress, including Donald Siwale, founder of the country's first welfare association. The councils frequently criticised political and social conditions; in particular, they forced the government to take note of the unofficial colour bar which pervaded Northern Rhodesia. But none of these councils had more than an advisory role, and like the tribal representatives they were compromised by their semi-official character. Major political and social changes were brought about, not by the councils but by the Africans' own organisations – the Congress, and trade unions.

The welfare societies provided opportunities for common action and for the growth of a new kind of leadership based on experience of town life. But neither they, nor the Urban Advisory Councils, had the power to negotiate effectively with employers on the most fundamental questions – wages and terms of employment: for this, trade unions were needed. The first major step in this direction was the formation in 1943 of an African Shop Assistants' Association on the Copperbelt. African mineworkers, by contrast, were slower to organise. The mine companies were firmly opposed to anything resembling trade unions for Africans; besides, the boss-boys' committees already gave the companies regular contact with some of their most experienced workers. But in 1945 there were well-disciplined African strikes on the railways and at Broken Hill mine. This reinforced the case for allowing African workers some form of negotiating machinery. Early in 1947 the British Labour government sent out a Scottish trade unionist, William Comrie, to help Africans form their own unions.

Within a year the first African trade union in Northern Rhodesia was formed by the shop assistants, and meanwhile Comrie gained support among boss-boys and clerks on the mines. The European miners now tried to attract Africans into their own union, but this only antagonised both Africans and the government and by the end of 1948 there were African unions in all four mines. In 1949 they were amalgamated in the Northern Rhodesia African Mineworkers' Union; this was duly recognised by the mine companies and it soon included more than half the African mineworkers. The first president was Lawrence Katilungu, a senior interpreter at Nkana, who had first worked there in 1936 and had been a boss-boy during the strike in 1940. Other African unions were soon formed on the roads and railways, and in the building trades. The status of all these African unions was protected in 1949 by a government ordinance which confirmed that there was no distinction in law between European and African unions. This was a turning-point in the country's history: the colonial government had at least prevented the possibility of second-class unions for Africans without real bargaining powers, such as existed in South Africa.

Nonetheless, the effectiveness of the Northern Rhodesian unions varied considerably. Building workers, for example, had many different employers, worked in different places, and some lived in compounds outside the municipal townships. They thus found it hard to organise meetings and recognise a common interest as employees. Mineworkers, on the other hand, all lived in the same compound, worked on the same mine, and had a common employer. The strength of this 'unitary structure' was shown in 1952, when mineworkers throughout the Copperbelt went on strike after negotiations for wage increases had broken down. The strike lasted for three weeks; there were no disturbances, and in the end a board of arbitration awarded substantial wage increases, whereby most mineworkers were to earn about 100s per thirty days. The status of the African Mineworkers' Union was dramatically confirmed in 1953 by the abolition of tribal representatives throughout the Copperbelt, at the insistence of more than 80 per cent of the total African labour force on the mines.

The European Challenge

The growth of African organisations on the Copperbelt had a profound effect on the attitudes of Europeans. We have seen that a European miners' union was formed in 1936, largely in response to the growing strength and efficiency of African labour. And in 1930 Europeans had been alarmed by the British government's reminder that in Northern Rhodesia, as in other British colonies to the north, African interests were to be paramount. This, and the fear of African economic and social advance, stimulated Europeans in the 1930s and 1940s to make new efforts to obtain more political power. The Europeans had three main objectives: to gain majority representation in the Legislative Council, to amalgamate the two Rhodesias and thereby throw off control by the Colonial Office, and to end the payment of mining royalties to the British South Africa Company. They succeeded in none of these aims; instead, the first and the last were eventually achieved by Africans. But Europeans undoubtedly did increase their influence on government policy.

The two most important European politicians were Steward Gore-Browne and Roy Welensky. They were elected to the Legislative Council in 1935 and 1938, and later they both received knighthoods. But they came from very different backgrounds. Gore-Browne was an aristocratic ex-army officer with a large estate in Bemba country and influential connections in London. Welensky's father was a South African immigrant from Lithuania; Welensky himself was born in Salisbury, Southern Rhodesia. For a while he was a successful professional boxer; then he became an engine-driver and in 1933 he was elected chairman of the Rhodesia Railwayworkers' Union branch at Broken Hill. The two men thus approached questions of European–African relations from rather different standpoints. Welensky frequently affirmed his support for material improvements for Africans, but he tended to regard the prospect of African political advance with the defensive attitude natural to a white trade unionist. Gore-Browne, on the other hand, felt no such threat to his own vested interests; he stressed that real concessions must be made to African demands and he was one of the first to argue that 'tribal' forms of government were irrelevant for African townsmen.

Despite these differences, there were other issues on which Gore-Browne and Welensky were in close agreement. Both men were impatient with Colonial Office rule, which seemed to limit the opportunities of both Europeans and Africans; indeed, Gore-Browne proposed a scheme for Central African Federation in 1936. And both men strongly resented the loss of so much of the country's wealth in the form of royalties paid to the British South Africa Company and in taxation levied by Britain. In 1948 the royalties may have amounted to as much as £2,000,000. Objections to the Company's legal title to the royalties made no impression on Britain and they were never taken to court. But in 1949 the British South Africa Company was induced to surrender its royalties in 1986, and meanwhile agreed to pay 20 per cent of them to the Northern Rhodesian government; after income tax had been levied, this now received altogether half the value of the royalties each year.

Efforts to secure settler control over the Legislative Council were unsuccessful. In the 1930s settler representation had been increased, and in 1945 a majority of non-official members was created. But this was done by increasing the number of non-officials nominated by the government. One represented farming interests; another, mining interests. Three members represented African interests; one was Gore-Browne, who had done so since 1938. There were still only eight elected members as against nine officials, and in 1948 the African voice was strengthened when the African Representative Council elected two members to sit in the Legislative Council. Thus the prospect of Northern Rhodesia becoming an independent state under white rule still seemed remote, which indeed was hardly surprising, since the Europeans formed less than 2 per cent of the total population.

On the other hand there was considerable progress after 1945 towards the long-term European objective of European domination throughout central Africa, through closer union between the two Rhodesias. In the days of Company rule, Europeans in Northern Rhodesia had feared that amalgamation with Southern Rhodesia would favour the latter's economy, which at that time was much stronger. By the 1940s, however, the development of the Copperbelt had more than redressed the balance and amalgamation, or even federation, seemed to be the only alternative to the eventual development of Northern Rhodesia as an African-controlled territory. Many Europeans in Southern Rhodesia were also in favour of closer union between the Rhodesias. For many years Southern Rhodesia's destiny had seemed to lie in union with South Africa, but in 1948 the South African Nationalist Party came to power. English-speaking settlers had no wish to join a country dominated by Afrikaners who were pledged to reduce its ties with Britain. Moreover, union with the north would mean a greater share, through trade and taxation, in the wealth of the Copperbelt.

Since there was no question of handing over power in Northern Rhodesia to a white minority, Britain had always resisted Rhodesian pressure for amalgamation. On the other hand, there was general support among British political leaders for uniting under a federal government the settler regime to the south and the Colonial Office regimes to the north of the Zambezi, Northern Rhodesia and Nyasaland. The problem was how far Europeans should be allowed to exert power at the federal level. The Labour Government, which took office in 1945, supported Federation in principle, mainly out of fear that Southern Rhodesia would otherwise be absorbed in a potentially hostile South Africa. At the same time, Labour leaders insisted that Federation would have to provide Africans with a real chance of increasing their political power. In 1951, however, Labour gave way to a Conservative government which was more willing to accept mere assurances from Rhodesian settlers that they would in due course share power with Africans. Moreover, the Conservatives were susceptible to pressure for Federation exerted in the City of London by the mining companies and the British South Africa Company.

The Conservatives, like Labour, were searching for some way to reduce and eventually bring to an end British responsibilities in central Africa. It was in 1951 that the Gold Coast achieved self-government, under Nkrumah as Prime Minister, and there was clearly no long-term future for British rule in Africa. But unlike Labour, the Conservatives were prepared to 'decolonise' central Africa by handing over extensive powers to a settler-dominated Federation regardless of African opinion. If the settlers formed a 'partnership' with Africans, so much the better. But the main consideration was that the settlers, not Britain, should have to deal with the massive problems of accommodating African pressure for political and economic advance. Accordingly, in August 1953, the Rhodesias and Nyasaland were joined to form the Central African Federation. Welensky now moved south to take a post in the Federal Cabinet and in 1956 he succeeded Lord Malvern (Godfrey Huggins) as Federal Prime Minister.

The Rise of Congress

The Europeans' drive towards political supremacy had largely been prompted by fears of African advance; but their campaign for amalgamation or federation stimulated Africans to make a counter-bid for political power. Africans in Northern Rhodesia feared any form of union with the south for the same reason that most Europeans welcomed it: such union would strengthen European domination. Africans north of the Zambezi were well aware of European motives in seeking amalgamation, and they sensed that Southern Rhodesia would be the dominant partner. They knew Southern Rhodesia well: many had worked or were still working there, and they had no wish to see its institutions extended to their own territory. In terms of political representation, trade union power, pass-law control and land alienation, Africans in Southern Rhodesia were clearly less well off than in

Northern Rhodesia, even if the social colour bar in the two countries was much the same. Indeed, in Northern Rhodesia, deliberate steps had been taken to increase the land reserved for Africans. In 1938 the reserves in the far north were slightly extended, and in 1941 the government acquired the North Charterland Concession in the Eastern Province. In 1947 most of the unoccupied Crown land throughout the territory was redesignated Native Trust land, in which leases to non-Africans were allowed only in certain circumstances. On the other hand, the remaining unoccupied Crown land was nearly all close to the railway line, and in the late 1940s it began to attract a new influx of European farmers. Closer ties with Southern Rhodesia seemed bound to increase such immigration. Thus, in spite of the creation of Native Trust land, Africans became more and more afraid of losing land to Europeans.

This fear of losing land was widely shared among Africans in Northern Rhodesia. Of all their reasons for opposing amalgamation or federation, this fear carried the greatest emotional force, and it crystallised other fears which were perhaps less easily defined. Land was still of absorbing interest to almost all Africans. The growth of industry on the Copperbelt had done nothing to undermine this interest; rather, indeed, it had strengthened it. Rights to the use of tribal land were still a man's only security against unemployment or old age: this was, after all, not simply the attitude of African workers but the deliberate policy of government and the mining companies. Thus fears of large-scale land alienation alarmed African townsmen no less than their relatives at home in the villages. And in this sphere both looked for leadership to their chiefs, the traditional trustees of tribal land. This unity of African feeling had been expressed in 1937 in testimonies before the Bledisloe Commission, which had investigated the possibilities of amalgamating the Rhodesias. In 1944 a senior Bemba chief raised his voice against amalgamation in the Northern Provincial Council, and from 1950 several chiefs spoke out firmly against plans for federation. In 1953 a petition to the Houses of Parliament against federation was signed by 120 chiefs, including the Bemba and Ngoni paramounts. In the same year the Mambwe paramount was deposed, and leading chiefs of the Aushi and Bisa suspended, for organising resistance to the government in the form of non-compliance with agricultural conservation rules. The government had long insisted that chiefs were the true leaders of their people; now Africans were showing that, on the land question, this was perfectly true, and very awkward for the government.

The campaign for amalgamation, then, gave the first stimulus to an African political awakening throughout the territory; and the protests of chiefs were matched by those of the clerks and teachers who sat in the African Representative Council. But though chiefs and councils could give voice to popular fears and discontent on this issue, they could not themselves organise for political action on a large enough scale to challenge the Europeans. It was above all for this reason that in 1948, at its annual meeting at Munali school, Lusaka, the Federation of African Societies was transformed into an expressly political body, the Northern Rhodesia Congress. The idea of a Congress had been conceived by Dauti Yamba after a visit to South Africa in 1942. The main strength of Congress lay in the towns, and when trade unions were formed several of their members became prominent in Congress. But the welfare societies which had sprung up in several rural areas provided bases on which Congress could build up membership throughout the territory. Thus in 1947 Kenneth Kaunda, a teacher and one of the few graduates of Munali school, had been prominent in the Mufulira welfare society and became a member of the local Provincial Council. In 1949 he returned home to Lubwa, the mission founded by his father in Bemba country, and in 1950 he transformed the local welfare association into a Congress branch.

The growth of Congress was provoked by European ambitions, but its expansion as a popular movement was made possible by patterns of social change within the African community. Munali school was itself a powerful stimulus to the growth of political leadership. Like Livingstonia in earlier years, it enlarged the horizons of young men from many different areas; besides, it was close to the country's capital, and here for the first time, as Kaunda later put it, 'Northern Rhodesia began to make sense to me'. At a popular level, the movement of workers to and from the towns meant that there was a constant flow of news and ideas as well as leadership; such links reinforced the common interest of chiefs and wage-earners in protecting tribal land. Also, in the years immediately after the war, there was a general broadening of outlook among the African population. Many quite uneducated men had served with the Northern Rhodesia Regiment in India, Burma, Palestine or Madagascar. Army service had given them new skills, a new view of Europeans, and a chance to compare experiences with other colonial peoples. Moreover, a special radio service was set up for broadcasting in the main African languages of Central Africa. Its headquarters in Lusaka was refreshingly free from racial prejudice and official paternalism. From 1949, the service sold very cheap receivers ('Saucepan Specials') and it soon had many thousands of African listeners. Most were unable to read English, but the radio enabled them to increase their understanding both of central Africa and of remote but highly relevant events, such as the political advance of Africans in West Africa.

In 1951 Congress was significantly renamed the Northern Rhodesia African National Congress and as President it elected Harry Nkumbula, a former teacher who had studied at Makerere College, Uganda, and also in London, where he had discussed politics with students from other parts of Africa. Nkumbula himself came from Ila country, and he gathered much support for Congress among the nearby plateau Tonga by attacking agricultural conservation rules, which were seen merely as a device for keeping Africans in overcrowded reserves. At the same time Nkumbula and other Congress leaders worked hard to unite the whole territory in a sense of common purpose: opposition to federation. In 1952 a conference of chiefs and Congress delegates in Lusaka set up a Supreme Action Council, with a majority of trade unionists, to plan and if necessary order mass action. In March 1953, at another conference of chiefs and party officials, Nkumbula burned the British White Paper on Federation, announced that the chiefs had determined not to co-operate with a federal government, and called for two days of 'national prayer' in April during which no Africans would go to work.

The plan for 'national prayer' fell through, Federation was introduced despite African protests, and Congress seemed to many to be discredited. Certainly 1953 marks the end of a period in the growth of African nationalism in Northern Rhodesia. It was perhaps inevitable that Congress should fail to prevent Federation; the European pressures in both the Rhodesias and in Britain were too strong. Nonetheless, it is worth looking briefly at the reasons why Congress failed to organise a massive act of African resistance. Its most glaring failure was on the Copperbelt, where African miners, except at Mufulira, completely ignored the call to 'national prayer'. This at first seems puzzling in view of the heavy support for Congress in the African mineworkers' union. But the mine companies' threats of instant dismissal could not easily be disregarded. Furthermore, the union leaders, being more experienced negotiators than the Congress leaders, probably realised that Federation was inevitable. They feared, perhaps, that the prestige of the Union, solidly based on achievements such as the wage increases in 1952, would greatly suffer if it allied itself with Congress in a major defeat.

Federation and the Economy

Federation was seen by most Europeans in Northern Rhodesia as a step towards settler control north of the Zambezi. Instead, ironically, it greatly stimulated the growth of African nationalism in both Northern Rhodesia and Nyasaland. As a result, the Federation collapsed and Africans took over in both countries. Even in the short run, Europeans in Northern Rhodesia were disappointed by federation. Northern Rhodesia remained under the Colonial Office, and there was no significant increase in settler power in the Legislative Council. Their elected membership rose to twelve, but there were now six members representing

African interests, four of whom were elected from the African Representative Council. And at the Federal level, Northern Rhodesia was definitely subordinated to Southern Rhodesia. In the Federal Parliament, out of the twenty-six members elected on a franchise that excluded most Africans, fourteen came from Southern Rhodesia and only eight from the north; there were also two African members for the north, chosen by the African Representative Council. The Federal government dealt with all matters concerning Europeans and economic development, and the preponderance of southern interests in these fields shortly became very clear.

In spite of this the first few years of Federation seemed very promising to Europeans in Northern Rhodesia. African resistance had proved a failure. The Federation attracted both investment and European immigrants, and up to 1956 at least Northern Rhodesia seemed to be doing well. It had certainly entered the Federation on the wave of an economic boom. In 1949 the price of copper rose by nearly a half as a result of the devaluation of the pound sterling. The outbreak of war in Korea in 1950 sharply increased world demand for copper, and between 1950 and 1956 the price of copper rose from £180 to £420 per long ton. This encouraged massive investment in expanding the mines on the Copperbelt to maintain and increase output. The overall effect was to raise the value of minerals produced in Northern Rhodesia from £13,000,000 in 1945 to £50,000,000 in 1950 and £95,000,000 in 1953. In 1956 two new mines, Bancroft (Chililabombwe) and Chibuluma came into production: the latter was largely financed by the U.S. government in order to swell its strategic stockpiles. In 1958 a refinery was opened at Ndola.

The boom in the copper industry created more jobs for Europeans, and for higher pay than ever before. Between 1950 and 1956 the number of whites employed on the copper mines rose from 4500 to about 7000; yet their average annual earnings, including special bonuses, rose from about £1000 to £2300. Moreover, they enjoyed many facilities and amenities, including schools, that were either free or else heavily subsidised. For a time, the material living standards of most daily-paid white mineworkers (more than half the white labour force on the mines) were as high as any in the world for wage-earners. The copper boom also stimulated the growth of service trades, providing more jobs for Europeans. Between 1946 and 1951 the European population of Northern Rhodesia rose from 22,000 to 37,000 and reached 49,000 in 1953. The ratio of Europeans to Africans in that year was thought to be about 1:40, much less than in Southern Rhodesia, where the ratio was 1:13, but more than twice that in 1931. By 1958, the total white population numbered 72,000. Thus when in the same year non-officials obtained a majority in the Executive Council (comprising the Governor and heads of departments), this corresponded to a real growth in the importance of Europeans in Northern Rhodesia. If the economy could be further expanded and diversified, it seemed not inconceivable that Northern Rhodesia might attract enough whites to approach the ratio in Southern Rhodesia.[6]

This spectacular economic advance, however, was unbalanced. Copper alone could not guarantee the country's prosperity; it was necessary to develop agriculture and secondary industries. It was easy for Europeans to come north from South Africa, make a 'killing' on the Copperbelt and return home when copper prices and wages fell, as they did in 1956. But in the long run European prosperity was bound up with that of Africans. Rich as it was, the European community still offered too small a market to stimulate much expansion of trade and industry and, thus, European employment. If Europeans were to continue to enter the country as managers, supervisors and businessmen, they would have to depend on African as well as European buying power. This would mean creating more jobs for Africans by developing new industries; it would also mean raising African wages and increasing African production of food and cash-crops. This point was appreciated by a number of Europeans, but there were formidable obstacles to such development. Some were due to the environment – the scarcity of land for high-yield production, or the sparseness of the African population. But there were also political obstacles.

The dominant position of Southern Rhodesia in Federal politics meant that it also gained the greatest economic benefits from Federation. Salisbury, the capital of Southern Rhodesia, was also the Federal capital, and it became the business headquarters of the Federation. Africans in Northern Rhodesia bluntly called it 'Bamba Zonke' (take all) and this attitude was shared by many Europeans. Hopes for economic progress in Northern Rhodesia were also set back by the decision in 1955 to build a hydro-electric power station at Kariba, on the Zambezi. This decision overturned a recent agreement to build a power station on the lower Kafue river, which would have been much more economical and also more profitable for Northern Rhodesia. Moreover, the flooding of the Zambezi above Kariba meant that in 1958 30,000 people on the north bank, who had never been consulted, were forcibly resettled. Many suffered great hardship, but in Salisbury this seemed to matter little when Kariba created 'the biggest man-made lake in the world' and provided a spectacular advertisement for Federation. Besides, the power station, a highly strategic point, was sited on the south bank, thus symbolising the predominance of Southern Rhodesian interests in Federal planning.

This predominance was also expressed in Federal financial policy. All income tax from the three territories went into a Federal pool, from which the Northern Rhodesia government received less than one-fifth, while almost two-thirds went to the Federal government. This concentrated its expenditure in Southern Rhodesia, where it greatly assisted the expansion of secondary industries. Southern Rhodesia thus obtained great benefit from Northern Rhodesia's taxation of profits and royalties from the Copperbelt. This was ironic, since Britain had just ceased to take a share of tax paid by the mining companies, which had recently moved their headquarters to central Africa. And the fiscal dominance of Southern Rhodesia was a far greater burden than that of Britain had been. In 1959 the Northern Rhodesia Minister of Finance, a British civil servant, publicly complained of the grossly unequal distribution of wealth between the territories. By then, Northern Rhodesia had suffered a net loss of more than £50 million to the rest of the Federation and by 1963 this had increased to £97 million. A further disadvantage of Federation for Northern Rhodesia was that it could no longer determine its own rate of income tax. This meant that it could not do anything to reduce the massive flow of mining dividends and royalties out of the country. Between 1953 and 1963 these amounted after tax to £260 million – far more than the recurrent expenditure of the colonial government during this period. Little of this enormous sum was reinvested in Northern Rhodesia: instead, much of it went to finance development in Southern Rhodesia and South Africa.

In Northern Rhodesia, then, the economic arguments for Federation seemed more and more doubtful. If most Europeans continued to support it, this was mainly on political grounds, as a protection against the spectre of black government. As for the Africans, they had of course no reason to favour Federation on political grounds. Some did make certain economic and social gains, but these were limited and belated. African production of cash-crops – mainly maize and groundnuts – which hitherto had been limited, rose considerably, owing to improved communications and agricultural extension services. But this only affected a few areas in the Central and Southern Provinces, within easy reach of the towns. Besides, the relative gains were slight, since Europeans in the same areas were able, with more capital and experience, to make much more rapid progress, and in the Central Province there was a rapid increase in European settlement on Crown land. The major stimulus to European farming was the rapid expansion after 1945 of the Commonwealth market for Virginia tobacco: by 1960 production from the railway line areas far exceeded that from the Eastern Province, once the main centre for this crop. However, growing this type of tobacco was difficult for illiterate and inexperienced farmers and few Africans were able to share in the tobacco boom. In 1960 Europeans still sold over twice as much farm produce as Africans, and over the greater part of the country there had been no perceptible progress in the rural economy. The obstacles were indeed great, but the necessary changes could certainly not be effected by a government lacking any popular support.

Thus most villagers in Northern Rhodesia continued to depend for cash on wage-employment. The opportunities for this did not increase much under Federation: indeed, it marked an end to the rapid pace of earlier expansion. Between 1946 and 1953 the number of African wage-earners in Northern Rhodesia almost doubled, due mainly to the growth of government employment in administration, public utilities and social services. This was made possible by a growing revenue from the mining industry: the value of copper sales multiplied more than sevenfold between 1946 and 1953. The number of wage-earners increased most sharply just after the Korean war began to boost the price of copper, and this coincided with the first-fruits of the 20 per cent share in copper royalties which the government had obtained in 1949. Under Federation, however, this expansion of the African labour force came in effect to a halt. In 1953 there were nearly 270,000 Africans in employment, but there was a sharp fall in 1954, and the 1953 level was not reached again until 1957 when a prolonged decline set in. Yet the adult male population continued to grow as part of a long-term growth in population made possible by improved famine relief measures, hygiene and medical care: by 1960 the total population was about three million. Furthermore, Africans from Northern Rhodesia had to face competition in the labour market from other territories: in the 1950s there were probably about 40,000 such immigrant workers. Thus a large number of men continued to seek work outside Northern Rhodesia: in 1956, there were well over 40,000 in Southern Rhodesia.

The lack of real growth in the Northern Rhodesian labour market between 1953 and 1960 was due to a number of factors. The copper boom came to an end in 1956 when prices suddenly fell and with them the value of copper sales. Meanwhile, the cost of labour was rising. The average real earnings of all African workers during this period probably increased by a half; this reflected the growing bargaining-power of labour as a result of trade unions, and also its increased efficiency. But the shortage of new jobs can also be attributed in part to the financial effects of Federation. Southern Rhodesia attracted the lion's share of foreign investment, while the heavy drain of government revenue from Northern Rhodesia to the rest of the Federation restricted the government's ability to increase employment, whether by expanding its own staff or by providing utilities, such as new roads, which would encourage other employers. Furthermore, the loss of revenue to the Federation restricted the government's capacity to finance welfare services for urban Africans. There was certainly some increase in government spending on African welfare, especially housing, but it was much less than it might have been and it was unimpressive compared with Federal spending on services for Europeans.

It would, however, be misleading to discuss the fortunes of Africans in Northern Rhodesia under Federation without noting that the mineworkers were a special case. Directly or indirectly, most people depended heavily on government spending, both for jobs and welfare services: they were thus much affected by Federal fiscal policies. The mineworkers, however, were more or less insulated from the economic effects of Federation: their fortunes were largely determined by changes within the mining industry. Unlike most other industries in the territory, it was able to make major changes in the balance it struck between the use of cheap unskilled labour and the use of machinery operated by skilled or semi-skilled labour. By 1960 African mineworkers had developed into a relatively small, highly productive and well-paid 'labour aristocracy' within the total labour force. Between 1953 and 1960 copper production rose by a half, yet the African labour force on the copper mines hardly increased at all. This was made possible by technical changes which diminished the need for unskilled labour: new methods of drilling had been introduced from 1946, and in 1955 Nchanga mine began producing copper from a colossal open-cast pit operated by enormous mechanical shovels.

The reason why the mine companies reduced their dependence on unskilled African labour was that it was becoming much more expensive. Pressure on the companies from the African mineworkers' union ensured that African employees, as well as Europeans, shared in the proceeds of the copper boom: between 1952 and 1960, the average real earnings of African mineworkers in Northern Rhodesia were more than doubled. This placed them well ahead of mine labour elsewhere in southern Africa: in 1960 their wages were 37 per cent above those of African mineworkers in the Belgian Congo, 56 per cent above those in South Africa, and more than twice those of mineworkers in Southern Rhodesia. Moreover, between 1949 and 1960 the gap between European and African mineworkers' earnings on the Copperbelt was reduced from a ratio of 28:1 to 11:1 and it was mainly the substantial improvements in the wages for African mineworkers which brought about a general rise in wage levels: unions in other industries were able to take mine wages as a starting-point in negotiations, even if the average wages of mineworkers continued to be more or less double that of other workers in Northern Rhodesia.

The rising cost of African labour induced the mine companies during the Federal years to allow African progress in other spheres. Like the government, the companies continued to encourage African workers to retire to the rural areas once they ceased to be wage-earners. Nonetheless, both Rhodesian Selection Trust (RST) and Anglo American made substantial improvements in African housing and adult education: they now wished to retain their more skilled and experienced African employees as long as possible, since as labour became more expensive it became increasingly wasteful to replace it with untrained newcomers. Furthermore, the rising cost of labour, both black and white, induced the mine companies to economise in the use of expensive European labour by giving Africans some of the jobs hitherto reserved for Europeans. In 1946 the European mineworkers' union had protected their jobs from African competition through a 'closed shop' agreement with the mine companies, but in 1955 both Anglo American and RST persuaded the European mineworkers to accept a new agreement which opened to Africans a number of hitherto 'reserved' jobs.

This was an important, if modest, step towards abolishing the industrial colour bar which had so long prevailed on the mines. Ironically it was made possible by a slackening of British interest in the Copperbelt. From 1939 to 1944, and again from 1947 to 1953, Northern Rhodesia's copper was sold by 'bulk-buying' agreements to the British government. These agreements assured Britain of adequate supplies of this highly strategic raw material, for both military and industrial use, despite the world shortages of copper during and after the Second World War. At the same time these agreements meant that Britain had an overriding interest in undisturbed production on the Copperbelt. The main threat to this came from the European trade unionists, since their skills were irreplaceable, so Britain was not prepared to risk any action which might antagonise them. In principle, of course, the British government was firmly opposed to any form of colour bar in its colonies, but on the Copperbelt this principle had to give way to arguments of national self-interest. When bulk-buying ended in 1953, the white mineworkers could no longer, as it were, hold Britain to ransom, and the companies could at last negotiate free of external constraints.

The gradual advancement of Africans in the copper industry was by no means an isolated development. In 1958, against strong opposition from the Europeans in the Legislative Council, the government enabled Africans to become industrial apprentices. From 1960 Africans on the railways could be trained as firemen and engine drivers, although they were still excluded from the workshops. Thus at the lower levels of industry Africans were at last beginning to make some headway. However the training of Africans for more senior posts, whether in industry or administration, continued to be grossly neglected. A major key to full African participation in industry was technical education but this was a Federal responsibility. Not until 1962 was the Copperbelt Technical Foundation opened to Africans after years of pressure from the few Africans in the Federal Parliament.

Education, indeed, was one field in which Federal policies affected all Africans, whether villagers, mineworkers, or other wage earners. Whereas European education was a Federal responsibility, African education was a territorial responsibility, and it duly suffered from Northern Rhodesia's unequal share in Federal wealth. There was certainly a real effort at progress: between 1953 and 1960 the proportion of government revenue devoted to African education was doubled, and the financial gulf between the European and African systems was much reduced. But even in the latter year ten times as much was spent on education for each white child in school in Northern Rhodesia as for each black child in school. If the two systems are measured against the total European and African populations, twenty times as much was spent on Europeans as on Africans. Besides, the main emphasis in African education continued for some years to be on primary schools, which remained extremely wasteful. After 1958 secondary schools were given greater attention, but in 1960 they had only 2500 pupils. As for higher education, this had scarcely begun. Only one African school, Munali, had a sixth form to prepare boys for university entrance and only three girls were sent to a sixth form in Southern Rhodesia. In 1957 the Federal government opened a multi-racial University College at Salisbury, in Southern Rhodesia. Hitherto, Africans from Northern Rhodesia had had to go for higher education to East or South Africa, but by 1960 there were twelve at Salisbury, and another forty or so on government scholarships at other places. This was an important step forward, but compared to the record of other, less wealthy British colonies it had come pitifully late.

The backwardness of African education was perhaps the most convincing proof to Africans in Northern Rhodesia that European talk of 'partnership' was sheer hypocrisy: how could Africans be partners unless they were taught to take part in running their own affairs? Even where, as on the Copperbelt, a few concessions were made to Africans, most Europeans were still reluctant to admit any Africans as social, let alone political, equals, while the gap between European and African earnings was still vast and bitterly resented. And, the Federal political structure certainly did not encourage hopes that any substantial power would be conceded to Africans in the near future. Thus most Africans in Northern Rhodesia continued to oppose Federation, and some now began to work towards a new objective; the creation of an independent state based on majority rule.

The Emergence of Zambia

In the first few years of Federation African political progress was slow. Popular enthusiasm for the African National Congress subsided after its failure to prevent Federation, and it took time for new strategies and objectives to emerge. This temporary loss of political purpose was reflected in the rapid growth between 1954 and 1958 of a new religious movement in Bemba country, the Lumpa Church, founded by Alice Lenshina. Lenshina herself was moved by a genuine, if ignorant, religious feeling, and she was more concerned to eradicate witchcraft than Federation. But for a few years the Lumpa Church attracted support from a great many people, both in the north-east and on the Copperbelt, who needed some form of organisation in which they could feel free of European domination. Significantly, the Lumpa Church gained little or no support in areas where Jehovah's Witnesses were strong.

The Congress was also weakened by its disagreements with the African Mineworkers' Union. The immediate reason was the union's 'betrayal' of Congress in 1953 when it ignored the Congress call for a work stoppage. The underlying reason, however, was perhaps that the AMU, unlike Congress, represented compact and closely knit groups of men bound together both by work and residence. Congress found it hard to obtain any direct control over mineworkers, who tended to look to the union for the solution of nearly all their problems. This tension was exposed in 1954 when the AMU refused to co-operate in a Congress boycott of European butchers' shops where the colour bar was especially vicious. The conflict was further complicated by the division of union strength in 1955, when African clerks and foremen gained the approval of the companies for a separate Mines African Staff Association.

By 1958 Congress had revived and once again had a network of branches over most of the country. The resurgence of Congress in the late 1950s was partly a response to economic stress. As we have seen, the price of copper fell sharply in 1956 and for two years the value of copper sales was well below its previous level. Between 1957 and 1962 jobs in construction industries fell from 66,000 to 24,000, and losing jobs also meant losing the right to free housing. At the same time there was increasing continuity in local political leadership, since there was a growing number of African workers, especially on the Copperbelt, who were staying in towns for several years at a time. There was also an influx of new leaders into Congress, as more young men emerged from secondary schools and obtained further education abroad. Some of these young men, such as Sikota Wina, a son of a former chief minister of the Lozi paramount, or Simon Kapwepwe, a friend of Kaunda's from Lubwa, were committed to the idea of creating an independent African state. This aim, they believed, could only be achieved by refusing to compromise in any way with the Federal political system. They dedicated themselves to uniting Africans, and any Europeans who cared to listen, in a sense of belonging to a new nation to be called Zambia.

This ideal was most lucidly expressed by Kenneth Kaunda, who had been Secretary-General of Congress since 1953. Nkumbula, the Congress President, was less clearly committed to this radical approach. In 1958 Nkumbula agreed to take part in elections based on a new constitution for Northern Rhodesia, which allowed the vote to about 25,000 Africans. This concession did not impress the radicals, who decided to boycott the election. As a result, there was a major split in Congress. Kaunda, Kapwepwe, Sikota Wina and others formed a new party, the Zambia African National Congress (ZANC). Nkumbula retained much support in the Southern Province in which his home area lay. Elsewhere, however, Africans mostly gave their support to the new ZANC, especially in the north and east, from which so many people went to work on the Copperbelt. In 1959 a state of emergency was declared in Nyasaland and Southern Rhodesia, following the unfounded rumours that the Nyasaland African Congress was about to launch a 'murder plot' against Europeans. As a result, the ZANC was banned and several of its leaders gaoled, but this repression only stiffened African resistance. Following further secessions from the ANC, a new party was formed, the United National Independence Party (UNIP). In January 1960, Kaunda was released from gaol; he was greeted as a popular hero and took over the leadership of UNIP.

By this time the British government realised that there would have to be rapid constitutional advance in Northern Rhodesia, and it also seemed increasingly doubtful whether the Federation could be held together. Not only was the African pressure against it rising fast in Northern Rhodesia and Nyasaland; in Southern Rhodesia, where many Europeans had always opposed any form of union with the north, there was growing white support for the Dominion Party, which aimed at a fully independent Southern Rhodesia. And in Northern Rhodesia, as we have seen, there were powerful economic reasons why at least the more far-sighted Europeans were ready to see the end of Federation. Thus in 1961 the Colonial Office proposed a constitution for Northern Rhodesia which would make possible an African majority in the legislature, even though this was bound to lead before long to Northern Rhodesia seceding from the Federation. Under pressure from the Federal Prime Minister, Sir Roy Welensky, Britain revised this plan in favour of the Europeans. But this concession provoked UNIP to stage a campaign of civil disobedience throughout the northern and eastern parts of the country. This campaign involved a good deal of violence, against government property rather than Europeans, despite Kaunda's personal belief in non-violence. It was amply justified, however, for in

1962 the constitution was revised once again, and this time UNIP agreed to participate.

In the election of October 1962 UNIP and the old Congress (ANC) between them won over 80,000 votes – two-thirds of the total; they gained a majority of seats and their leaders took over a number of government departments. The Federation was now doomed and it was finally broken up at the end of 1963. Early in 1964 another election was held, based on universal adult suffrage. This gave UNIP a decisive majority. Kaunda now became Prime Minister of an all-UNIP government with full control of internal affairs, except for defence. Constitutionally, the way was now clear to full independence and this was arranged for October. But the triumphant force of African nationalism faced two major sources of resistance, and these were not European but African.

The relationship of Barotseland to the nationalist movement was complicated by the fact that it was a 'protectorate within a protectorate', with its own treaty relationship to Britain. The Lozi paramount was enticed into supporting Federation by promises that Barotseland would become an independent state. The younger Lozi, however, had no sympathy with this idea; they knew that Barotseland had no economic future on its own. UNIP won massive Lozi support in the elections in 1962 and 1964 and eventually the paramount agreed reluctantly to the full integration of Barotseland with the rest of the country.

More difficult was the problem posed by the Lumpa Church. From about 1958 this had begun to lose much of its support, but in its home area in the north-east there was a hard core of believers who opposed any outside interference with their affairs, whether from the colonial administration or from African politicians. UNIP, however, was committed to obtaining total support from the whole country; not to support UNIP was to declare oneself an enemy of the new nation, Zambia. The conflict between the Lumpa Church and UNIP was peculiarly bitter, since the centre of Lumpa strength was also a UNIP stronghold; indeed, the church had originated in a split from the Lubwa mission where Kaunda and Kapwepwe were educated and where they had taught for a time. By mid-1964 Lumpa defiance of government authority had reached a point where an explosion was inevitable; in the event, a war broke out in which over 700 people were killed. As a result, the Lumpa Church was banned and its surviving leaders, including its founder, Alice Lenshina, were detained indefinitely. Many Lumpa followers took refuge in the Congo, at Mokambo, just across the border from Mufulira.

There was still one other adversary with which the new African government was anxious to come to terms before Independence. This was the British South Africa Company. The Zambian leaders were determined to gain possession of the Company's mineral rights, and with them the whole of the hugely profitable royalties from the Copperbelt. Since 1950 the Northern Rhodesian Government had in effect enjoyed roughly a half-share in these royalties, but since these were first paid the Company had by 1964 taken out of the country a net total of £70 million. In 1963 alone its net royalties were £6 million, which was twice the current budget for African education. The government now mounted a skilful public relations campaign, and for the first time assembled all the evidence which proved that the Company had never in fact had any legal right to these royalties. At the same time, the government was careful to allay fears that it might be bent on the expropriation of foreign-owned interests. The final stages of negotiations were accelerated by the advent of a Labour government in Britain which then seemed eager to assist the new regime. On the evening before Independence Day, behind a tea-tent at a garden party on the lawns of Government House, the chairman of the British South Africa Company agreed to surrender its mineral royalties in return for token payments of £2 million apiece by the British government and the nascent Zambian government. Thus the latter finally sealed up a major leak in the country's economy and took formal possession of its greatest material asset.

The new state of Zambia came into being on the following day, 24 October 1964: the date, which is United Nations Day, symbolised Zambia's commitment to the ideals of the United Nations Charter. Zambia chose to become a Republic within the British Commonwealth: Kaunda became Head of State as well as chief executive. The only other head of state to attend the Independence celebrations was Julius Nyerere, President of Tanzania; his presence affirmed the two leaders' determination to pull Zambia away from the white south and closer to the independent black north. After years of colonial exploitation and neglect, the country could at last take a hand in shaping its own destiny. After years of humiliating subjection to the colour bar, Africans had successfully asserted their own dignity as human beings. Against so many expectations, they had achieved political emancipation, both from Britain and from the white supremacies. But this victory was only the beginning of a new struggle.

NOTES

1. Donald Siwale, 'Autobiographical Sketch', *African Social Research* 15 (June 1973), 366.
2. A. Kasambala, quoted in Sholto Cross, 'The Watch Tower Movement in South Central Africa, 1908–1945' (Oxford D.Phil. thesis, 1973), 355.

3. M. S. Visagie (Labour Party member for Nkana), 17 December 1941, in Legislative Council Debates, vol. 41, col. 372.
4. Quoted in R. J. B. Moore, *These African Copper Miners* (1948), p. 103.
5. Similar councils were set up in Nyasaland at the same time, and there was a model for the territorial council in the South African Native Representative Council, formed in 1936.
6. There was also a rapid growth of the small Asian community, who were mostly traders: they numbered just over 1000 in 1946, 2500 in 1951, and 8000 in 1960.

XII

Ten Years of Independence
1964 – 1974

Independence in Zambia was one of the last episodes in the decolonisation of British Africa; it also marked the beginning of a new phase in the struggle to liberate southern Africa from white domination. In the first place the Zambian government sought to give greater meaning to political independence by striving also for economic independence. This of course has been the ambition of many new states in the 'Third World', where so often decolonisation has scarcely affected their subordination to capitalist interests overseas. But in Zambia this problem was peculiarly acute. For one thing, the country's economy was quite exceptionally dependent: that is to say, its capacity to trade with the rest of the world depended almost entirely on its production of one commodity – copper. Thus the fortunes of Zambia were very largely at the mercy of world demand for copper, and this was far from predictable. Moreover, under colonial rule the country had had little stake in, let alone control over, the copper industry: this was essentially an autonomous enclave of foreign business. But what made Zambia's economic dependence especially trying was the fact that it meant dependence on the white supremacies of southern Africa. In 1964 Zambia had to rely on Rhodesia, South Africa or Mozambique for nearly all its communications with the outside world, for much of its trade, for skilled manpower and for employment for many of its citizens. This dependence on the white supremacies clearly had to be challenged if political independence was not to be a sham.

Thus one way in which Zambia engaged in struggle with the white south was to minimise its own economic links to the south. Meanwhile, Zambia took a leading part in efforts to extend the frontiers of African political and military power south of the Zambezi. The independent government lost no time in giving support to African guerrilla movements in Portuguese Africa and Rhodesia. As a result Zambia found itself in the front line of conflict between black and white Africa. This in turn gave added significance to Zambia's efforts to increase its economic freedom of action and to maintain political stability within its own borders. It also made Zambia a crucial test-case for the merits of African government. Since Zambia is at odds with the white south on moral as well as economic grounds, it has been of great importance that Zambia should show the world that African rule can be not only stable but non-racialist, law-abiding and democratic. Zambia's political behaviour since independence has thus itself been a major factor in the struggle for freedom in southern Africa. The country has of course been under severe strain, both from without and within, and there have been serious infringements of liberty. Nonetheless, Zambia has so far maintained a balance between central authority and personal freedom which compares favourably with countries more fortunately placed. The problem is that this balance is precariously based and the country remains dangerously dependent: the economy is still dominated by copper, which aggravates the divisions between rich and poor, while Zambia's political welfare still owes almost everything to the continuing leadership of Kenneth Kaunda.

The Break with the South

The British South Africa Company's surrender of its mineral rights on the eve of Independence Day was a major step towards the economic independence of Zambia. Yet the country remained firmly tied to the economy of southern Africa. In particular, it was heavily dependent on its links with Rhodesia. All Zambia's coal and coke came from Wankie, while much of its power came from the Kariba hydro-electric station on the south bank of the Zambezi. Besides, Zambia was land-locked, and its main lines of access to the sea ran through Rhodesia. Its oil came up through Rhodesia from Beira, in Mozambique, while Rhodesia Railways carried Zambia's copper out to Beira, via Bulawayo and Salisbury. These links with Rhodesia were soon a source of grave embarrassment to Zambia, for Rhodesia became not merely an unfriendly but an actively hostile neighbour.

The Central African Federation had been broken up by the rise of black nationalism north of the Zambezi, but it was also undermined by the growth of white nationalism in Southern Rhodesia. The Federal Party regime there had given way at the end of 1962 to the Rhodesian Front; this made no pretence at 'partnership' and aimed to make the country an independent state under white rule. In April 1964 Ian Smith became Prime Minister and began to threaten a unilateral declaration of independence (UDI) if Britain would not voluntarily concede it to the white minority. On 11 November 1965, Smith finally announced UDI. The British government – still the sovereign power in Rhodesia – declined to use force against the rebels and instead mounted

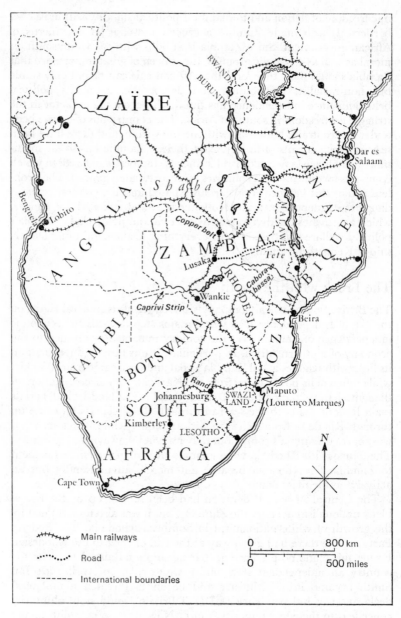

an international campaign of economic sanctions, in the foolish belief that the country could swiftly be isolated and the regime undermined from within. But Rhodesia's links with the outside world were also Zambia's, so that sanctions designed to isolate Rhodesia would also isolate Zambia. Thus Zambia had good reason to object to a policy of sanctions, as indeed Kaunda did when visiting London just after Independence. In the Zambian view, the only effective strategy against Rhodesia would be an armed invasion. But since the United Nations agreed to apply sanctions, however partial and ineffective, Zambia did its best to comply: indeed, in some respects it had little choice.

The first major sanction to affect Zambia was the closure of the oil pipeline from Beira to Rhodesia in December 1965. This made little difference to Rhodesia, which simply turned to South Africa, but it was a body-blow to Zambia. At first oil was flown into the country at vast expense. Then it was hauled in over 1500 miles of dirt road from the Tanzanian port of Dar es Salaam. Finally, in 1968, a new pipeline was opened, running from Dar es Salaam to the Copperbelt; it was built by Italians, after Britain had refused to help. Meanwhile, Zambia sought to reduce its dependence on Rhodesia for exporting copper. There was limited scope for doing this, but after a few months of hasty improvisation a new transport pattern emerged. Half Zambia's copper continued to go south to Beira, but the rest went north: a quarter by road to Dar es Salaam, and a quarter along the Benguela railway, through the Congo and Angola to the port of Lobito on the west coast.

This process of re-routing was given a further boost early in 1973 when Smith tried to retaliate against Zambia for allegedly launching guerrilla incursions into Rhodesia. He closed the border between the two countries to all traffic except for copper; this traffic was valued by Smith as a major source of foreign exchange. But Kaunda promptly called Smith's bluff: he simply stopped all shipments of copper through Rhodesia. Smith then reopened the border, but in vain; Zambia pressed ahead with plans to dispense with imports from Rhodesia and to ship out all its copper by the northern routes. Half went out by road to Dar es Salaam (this was now an excellent tarmac highway), and half went out west to Lobito. Within a few months various countries had contributed £20 million to a UN fund to help Zambia meet its massive new bills for road transport.

By this time, Zambia had reduced its trade with Rhodesia to a minimum. In 1964 Rhodesian products accounted for 40 per cent of total imports; by 1966 they were 20 per cent and by 1971 only 5 per cent. This last figure mostly represented power from Kariba and coke from Wankie for the mine smelters. For its coal, however, Zambia was by now virtually self-sufficient. Early in 1966 a coal mine was opened at

Nkandabwe, in Southern Province; this closed in 1969, but by this time the vast open-cast coal mine at near-by Maamba had gone into production; in 1973 this produced nearly a million tonnes of coal and it should last beyond the end of the century. Maamba cannot supply coke, and after the Rhodesia border closure Zambia imported this from overseas, but the copper smelters were mostly converted to heavy fuel oil. Meanwhile Zambia greatly increased its own sources of power. In 1972 a hydro-electric station built by a Yugoslav firm was opened on the lower Kafue and by 1974 Zambia relied on Rhodesia for only one-third of its power requirements. Another power station was being built by an Italian firm at the north end of the Kariba dam; this was expected to make Zambia self-sufficient in power in 1976.

Within ten years of Independence, then, Zambia snapped almost all its economic links with Rhodesia. It also managed to reduce its dependence on South Africa, despite Vorster's 'enlightened' efforts to draw black Africa further into South Africa's commercial orbit. In 1964 South Africa accounted for 20 per cent of Zambia's imports; by 1973, this had dropped to 11 per cent. This was partly due to the Rhodesian border closure, which compelled South African goods to be shipped expensively by sea and thence through Angola, but it was mainly due to long-standing efforts both to tap alternative sources and to replace imports by local manufactures.

It is in this context that the Tanzam railway financed by China is especially significant. The idea of a railway from the Copperbelt to the coast of Tanzania was discussed by Kaunda and Nyerere in 1963; not only did it hold out hope of freeing Zambia from its southern transport links, it could also stimulate the economic development of vast and neglected areas in both Zambia and Tanzania. But although surveys were made the results were discouraging: to Western powers the scheme made no economic sense and they offered no aid. However, the People's Republic of China did take an interest; it made a survey in 1967–8, and in 1970 building began at Dar es Salaam, with teams of skilled Chinese and African labour gangs. Progress was rapid, and the railway was linked up to the Copperbelt in 1975.

The Tanzam railway will certainly alleviate Zambia's transport problems. It should be able to carry out most of Zambia's copper, providing the East African ports can handle it. It is convenient for Japan, which by 1970 was Zambia's best customer. It may even fulfil the hope of promoting development in backward areas along the route. But for the Chinese the railway was an attractive way of increasing their trade with Africa. In 1970 China agreed to make an interest-free loan, split equally between Zambia and Tanzania, to cover the total cost of the project, £167 million. But this was not an advance in cash; China was very short of foreign exchange and in any case was looking for opportunities to expand markets for its own manufactures, including those of its infant heavy industries. So the railway agreement provided that China would make half the loan in the shape of equipment, such as rails and rolling-stock. This left the local costs, which were mainly those of buying materials in Africa and paying the wages of African workers. Since these had to be paid in local currencies, of which China had little, China persuaded Tanzania and Zambia to buy Chinese goods in local currencies: from 1970 to 1977 both countries had to buy about £8 million worth of Chinese goods every year. All this, however, was simply trade to enable the loan to be made at all; the loan must still be repaid. The repayment is spread out over thirty years, beginning in 1983, but the medium of payment is restricted: the money must be returned to China either in a third-party currency, or in the proceeds obtained by Zambia and Tanzania from their exports to China. For Zambia, of course, this means copper, for which as a young industrial power China's needs are increasing fast: in 1970 it became Zambia's sixth-best customer. Thus the old links between Zambia and the white south are rapidly being replaced by new links with the Far East.

The State and the Economy

The redirection of Zambia's trade routes was a very expensive operation: in spite of international aid, it cost the country many millions of pounds and contributed to the rapid inflation of recent years. This burden was tolerable only because the government drew great wealth from the copper mines. To some extent, this was a matter of luck – and misery elsewhere: Zambia's first five years of independence were boom years for copper, due partly to the massive demand from the USA for munitions in Vietnam. From 1964 to 1969 copper prices rose on average by 7 per cent each year; a new mine, Chambishi, came into production in 1965; and Zambian copper production rose from 632,000 to 747,000 tonnes. This made Zambia the third-largest producer in the world. At the same time, however, the Zambian government took various steps to increase its share of copper profits, and during this five-year period its revenues from copper increased fivefold. The break-up of Federation at the end of 1963 had meant that the then Northern Rhodesian government, which in effect had been paying the rest of the Federation more than half of its total copper revenues, now kept them all. In July 1964 the income tax on copper was raised from 40 per cent to 45 per cent of profits, and in October, as we have seen, the government obtained the royalties, which amounted to $13\frac{1}{2}$ per cent of the value of copper produced. In April 1966 a special export tax was levied on the copper industry, to yield 40 per cent of the amount by which each tonne of copper was sold for more than £300 on the London Metal

Exchange, and during the next three years prices there frequently rose above £500.

Until 1969 the Zambian government disclaimed any intention of nationalising the copper industry: it was reluctant to risk undermining the confidence of investors, and besides, Kaunda asserted that the industry was simply 'too big' to handle. By contrast with the lean years of colonial rule, Zambia was doing very well out of the copper industry: the net result of the various tax changes was to yield the government roughly three-quarters of the total profits made by the mining companies, which by international standards was a very substantial proportion. Nevertheless, the arguments for some form of nationalisation seemed to increase with time. Since the country depended so heavily on the copper industry, the government was bound sooner or later to want a major share not only in its profits but also in shaping mining policy. The main issue at stake here was further investment in the industry. The government sought this for reasons of both economic and social policy. More investment could increase output, which would help protect the industry from any fall in prices and could also increase employment. The companies, however, had done little to develop new mines, since the royalty payments and export tax (which were unrelated to profits) discouraged them from any venture which was not bound to yield an immediate profit. Instead, most of their own share of profits was being distributed in the form of dividends. So in 1969 Kaunda set about nationalising the copper industry. The first step was a national referendum in June, which enabled Parliament to remove an 'entrenched' clause in the constitution whereby the government was prevented from acquiring private property by compulsory order. This reform, and also the recent example of copper nationalisation in Chile, encouraged Kaunda two months later to make a major speech at Matero, outside Lusaka, in which he proposed a comprehensive new formula for sharing out Zambia's copper wealth.

First, Kaunda met the companies' objections to the existing tax system by replacing royalty and export tax with a single mineral tax of 51 per cent on gross profits. On the remaining 49 per cent, the government continued to levy income tax at 45 per cent. This brought the total tax on mining profits to 73 per cent; as it happened this was roughly the existing level, but there was now more incentive for expansion. Second, the government appropriated all mining rights in the country. The reversion of the British South Africa Company's mineral rights had transferred its royalties to the government, but it left the mining companies in full possession of mining rights which Rhodes's company had granted them 'in perpetuity'. Besides, there were other vast areas where mining rights had been assigned to various companies who were not mining at all. The compulsory reversion of all mining rights now gave the government the power to issue mining licences on condition that they were productively used; it also increased the government's ability to direct new mining investment to some of the more backward rural areas. The third, and perhaps most important, of the Matero reforms was the government's acquisition of a 51 per cent share in the ownership of the copper mines. The details were settled in negotiations with the companies; the government arranged to buy its majority holding by paying the companies out of its own dividends over the next 8 to 12 years. The government had no wish, as yet, to run the mines itself, and it undertook to pay the companies for continuing management and services. After 1969 state control over the copper industry was still further increased. In 1973 the government paid over £80 million to the companies to redeem the bonds issued for its 51 per cent holding. In August 1974 the government took over responsibility for management and sales from the Anglo American group; a similar agreement with the RST group followed in February 1975.

We must now consider how the Zambian government used its substantial stake in the mining industry. One major aim of nationalisation had been to stimulate expansion in the industry. Five years later this was still rather limited. Except for the coal mine at Maamba the government did not itself develop any important new mines. In 1970 the copper-mining companies opened a new copper mine at Kalengwa, in the far north-west, and in 1971 they reopened Bwana Mkubwa; meanwhile an iron mine had been opened at Nampundwe, west of Lusaka. But the prospects for developing these mines were at once overcast by a dramatic fall in copper prices: in 1970 they averaged £748 per tonne; in 1971, £444; and in 1972, only £428 – barely enough to cover the cost of production and marketing. They revived at the beginning of 1973, and transport problems that year pushed them steadily upwards. By April 1974 the price had rocketed up to £1400, but in the second half of the year it fell back to below £500. Such wild fluctuations made a lottery of any long-term planning. An essential first step towards stabilising copper prices would be agreement between Zambia and its fellow-members of CIPEC, the organisation of copper-exporting countries set up in 1967, but the military coup in Chile in 1973 created a political obstacle to such agreement. Thus the resources available for mining development were less than was hoped for at Matero. In any case, a fairly conservative attitude to development prevailed since in practice the companies retained effective control over mining policy: indeed, it has been strongly argued that they got the best of the bargain after Matero.

The fluctuations in the price of copper also gave great urgency to the question of how far the Zambian government had used its copper revenues since Independence to reduce its dependence on copper in the long run. Some progress was certainly made: in 1969 copper accounted for 49 per cent of the gross domestic product and 68 per cent of government revenue, whereas in 1973, when copper production, prices and taxation were at much the same levels, copper accounted for only 29 per cent of the gross domestic product and 28 per cent of government revenue. Clearly there had been a considerable increase in other forms of production in Zambia. The main factor in this was the rapid expansion of power and coal supplies, prompted by UDI, but manufacturing industries also grew. The end of Federation slackened the hold of Rhodesian industry on the Zambian market, while UDI gave a further boost to import substitution. Zambian manufacturing tripled in value between 1964 and 1968; thereafter, growth was much slower, though the 1973 border closure provided a new stimulus as it increased the transport costs of goods imported from or through South Africa. Zambia now produces explosives for the mines, copper wire, glass, and chemical fertiliser; there is also a textile mill and a car assembly plant. However, such enterprises are handicapped by high labour and transport costs and it is hard for their products to compete with imported goods, let alone find markets in other countries; besides, Zambia is still committed to buying large quantities of goods from China. The economic viability of Zambian manufacturing industries is masked by state participation, through the Industrial Development Corporation (INDECO); this has cushioned them against early adversities, but it may not work to the long-term advantage of the Zambian consumer.

Agriculture made rather uncertain advances after Independence. Zambia's capacity to produce food for the market is clearly of great importance: by 1974, almost one-third of the total population (which was over 4½ million) lived in towns. Yet food imports had doubled in value since 1964; they amounted to 40 per cent of the total value of marketed foodstuffs. Commercial production of maize, the staple food of town-dwellers, almost tripled between 1964 and 1972, but this progress has been very erratic. In 1970 the country was humiliated by having to import maize from Rhodesia, and the prospects for maize remain obscure. In 1973 Zambia suffered its worst drought for forty years, while in 1974; heavy rains at the worst possible time caused a disease which ruined much of the crop and compelled heavy inroads into stockpiles. Sugar production has been more continuously successful: up to 1960 the country imported all its sugar, but it may well be exporting it before long. Commercial production of vegetables, groundnuts, pigs and poultry has more or less doubled since 1964, while egg production has increased fivefold; these are all fields in which small-scale African farmers have been able to make a sizeable contribution. On the other hand, dairy farming has declined since 1964, and a good deal of beef is still imported; here, as in the production of Virginiaflue-cured tobacco, the departure of several European farmers since Independence has had a marked impact.

Overall, indeed, the agricultural record is disappointing. In most respects Zambia is still a long way from being assured of permanent self-sufficiency. In theory it could well be a net exporter of foodstuffs, since it can easily afford to increase productivity through improved techniques. But so far such progress has been rather limited. Perhaps the most obvious gain is that in 1974 the government began to expropriate much valuable but unused land from absentee owners and thus helped to bring it into production. The government has certainly spent enormous sums on agricultural development, but these have largely been wasted. Schemes to help villagers produce for the market have been vitiated by over-reliance on complex machinery, such as tractors; inadequate technical training; inefficient marketing; and the gross mismanagement of credit facilities. All this has tended to discourage ordinary people from staking their future livelihood on the vagaries of the agricultural market; instead, many people have left the land altogether and have become urban consumers.

It seems clear, in fact, that for too long the government failed to take the measure of the agricultural problem. Farming in Zambia, in contrast to some other parts of Africa, is mostly handicapped by natural disadvantages (especially infertile soils and inadequate water supplies) which can only be overcome by the application of sophisticated modern skills on a fairly large scale. This situation has been aggravated by the movement of terms of trade against the Zambian farmer: real prices for agricultural products have been steadily falling owing to the continuous rise in the cost of consumer and capital goods needed by farmers: the real price of maize has fallen by two-thirds over the past twenty years. All these factors have placed a very high premium on efficient production. As a result commercial agriculture is dominated by about 400 large-scale farmers, most of whom are still expatriates. Otherwise, the market is mostly supplied by smaller-scale African farmers who have the experience and temperament to make farming a business. These are mainly concentrated in three areas: in the Southern Province, where African commercial farming began between the wars; in the Central Province, where skilled African immigrants from Rhodesia have had a considerable 'demonstration effect'; and in the Eastern Province, where many Africans gained insight into modern farming methods while working for Europeans, either locally or in Rhodesia. Elsewhere, however, there has been very little change. The woodlands of the north-east are still cultivated by the traditional methods of *citemene* ash-planting; politicians may disapprove, but so far they have no better answer to offer than the early Company officials who vainly tried to abolish this 'wasteful' system in 1907.

One vital field for import-substitution has been high-level man-power. At Independence Zambia was still almost wholly dependent on highly paid white foreigners, not only at professional and managerial levels but right across a range of supervisory, technical and clerical jobs. This dependence, which clearly had grave political as well as economic disadvantages, has been diminished as a result of the rapid growth of African education. In 1963 there were less than 100 Zambians with university degrees and less than 1000 with secondary-school certificates – a point reached by Uganda in 1955 and by Ghana in 1943. Within the first few years of Independence the government opened 100 secondary schools all over the country: in 1971 they enrolled over 54,000 students. The secondary schools have provided teachers for the rapidly expanding primary school system; they have also provided students for the University of Zambia. This was founded in 1965 and within a few years included schools of law, science, humanities, medicine and education, together with an extra-mural department. Two thousand students were enrolled in 1971.

This expansion of education has naturally taken time to produce results in terms of Zambian employment. Throughout the 1960s there seemed to be as many foreigners in the country as ever, due partly indeed to the new demands for teachers. However, the total number of non-Africans fell from 87,000 in 1963 to 58,000 in 1972. By 1966 all the permanent secretaries of government departments were Zambians. Zambians now predominate in the civil service and the various para-statal organisations, while an increasing number are qualifying as secondary-school teachers. In the army, the first Zambian commander-in-chief was appointed in 1970, and all army officers are now Zambians. The most glaring needs for qualified Zambians are in agriculture and the mining industry, especially now that the state has a majority interest in the latter. Schools of agriculture and of mines were finally opened at the University in 1973; these will provide Zambian graduates for management and senior technical staff. Meanwhile, Zambian mineworkers have taken over many jobs formerly reserved for Europeans, whose resistance was belatedly undermined by the coming of political independence. There are also several hundred secondary-school leavers in training schemes for the mines, though there are still over 4000 white foreigners in the copper industry and it will continue to rely on white experts for several years.

So far, we have seen what progress Zambia has made towards self-reliance in material wealth and human skills. In relation to the white south Zambia's position has greatly improved. No longer is it simply a peripheral backward region, valued only as a source of labour and copper. The economy has been substantially diversified and the country now produces much of what it once had to import. Admittedly, copper still provides about 95 per cent of total foreign exchange earnings; in this sense, Zambia is still entirely dependent on the copper industry. But the outward flow of foreign exchange has been checked, both by import-substitution and by curbing the flow of profits from mining. In important respects, Zambia is richer than it was at independence.

This increase in national wealth, however, has been unequally distributed. Such inequality is no longer mainly a matter of race. Most whites are still comparatively rich, and most Africans are still very poor, but this is no longer due to a colour bar. Several steps have been taken to close the economic gap between foreigners and Zambians. Education and training have opened up to black Zambians a whole new range of highly paid jobs. White pay-levels had tended to be high in order to attract foreign skilled labour in the absence of skilled Africans; where Zambians have taken over from foreign whites, these pay-levels have largely persisted. On the Copperbelt, where racial tension was always most acute, African mineworkers secured a massive pay rise in 1966; this soon led to a general rise in wage levels. In 1968 the 'Mulungushi reforms' sought to encourage the emergence of African businessmen by restricting retail trade outside the towns and small building contracts to Zambian citizens; to help them, the government took a majority share in various retail stores and building supply firms and, to offset expected losses, the government also took a majority interest in two big breweries. In 1969 wholesale trade was also restricted to Zambian citizens and by 1972 the restriction on retail trade had been extended to the towns. Some expatriate traders stayed on by taking out Zambian citizenship, but many others, especially Asians, have been displaced.

Thus the Zambian economy is no longer so sharply divided on racial lines as it once was. Instead, there is a deepening rift within the black population. To a large extent this is a division between town and country. The overwhelming predominance of the copper industry has meant that economic development has continued to be concentrated around the Copperbelt and the towns along the railway line down the middle of the country. The purely commercial objections to rural development away from the railway line are obvious enough. The sparseness of human settlement over much of the country has always been a major deterrent to providing the services – roads, schools, medical care – which would make possible radical economic change. Since independence some progress has been made in these fields. But as we have seen, the government has had little success in its efforts to bring about a popular revolution in agriculture. Over much of the country the economy is still one of 'sub-subsistence': many villagers still depend on cash or goods from relatives in towns. Infant mortality is still shockingly high: in 1969, one in three Zambian children died under the age of five, while in 1974 40 per cent of children surveyed by an FAO team in Copperbelt and Southern Provinces suffered permanent mental retardation due to malnutrition. Nevertheless, the population continues to grow very fast, perhaps almost 3 per cent per year. There are now primary and secondary schools all over the country, but children who reach them acquire new ambitions which increase their dissatisfaction with rural conditions. Primary education is still highly literary; it has not, as in Tanzania, been remodelled to develop rural skills. Thus many of the most active and intelligent young people go off to seek their fortunes in the towns.

So the drift to the towns which worried many colonial officials in the 1940s continues to be a central feature of the country's economy: since 1964 the urban population has increased by 8 per cent per year. This migration presents the government with a bigger problem than ever before. Wage employment has expanded steadily since Independence, but not nearly fast enough to absorb the new immigrants. The steep rise in wage levels since 1966 has prompted employers to use machines rather than labour where possible. The 1969 census showed 400,000 Zambians in employment, but there were probably well over 80,000 seeking work in or near towns. And few of those lucky enough to get jobs can in fact be called well paid. By African standards, the 50,000 mineworkers are certainly well paid: in 1971 their average wage was not far short of £1000 per year. But this was about twice as much as that of other industrial workers and nearly five times as much as that of agricultural workers. And since 1970 inflation (which has of course been partly caused by wage increases) has reduced the great majority of wage-earners to a bare subsistence level.

There is thus not only a grossly unequal division of wealth between town and country; there are also great contrasts of wealth and poverty within the towns. A privileged minority of Zambians now live in formerly all-white suburbs, where spacious bungalows stand in large gardens along tree-lined avenues. Others live in more modest comfort in mine or municipal compounds, where there have been commendable efforts to provide adequate family housing. The Zambian government, unlike the colonial government, has accepted that many town-dwellers have come to stay: a rapidly growing number, indeed, have never lived anywhere else. Many people have built their own homes in official 'site-and-service' schemes. All the same, an alarming number of both workers and job-seekers have had to improvise shacks in technically illegal squatter settlements without basic utilities.

The great inequalities in Zambian society are perhaps largely inevitable, given the facts of geography and the country's continuing dependence on copper. Nevertheless they have been aggravated by development policies which in effect give to those who already have.

The new manufacturing industries have reduced dependence on imports, but some, such as the car assembly plant and the textile mill, supply consumer goods which only a small minority of Zambians can afford; indeed, the textile mill now imports synthetic materials rather than buy more cotton from Zambian farmers. Such anomalies reflect the continuing influence of the various multi-national corporations which have gone into business with INDECO. There is, after all, no quick return to be made from investment in industries which might benefit the countryside rather than the towns, and the urban poor rather than the emerging black middle class. For some time to come such investment would yield social rather than economic dividends; the government has an interest, but only now is it beginning to take a lead.

Liberation in Southern Africa

Zambia's success in largely detaching itself from the economies of white southern Africa enabled it to play a significant part in attempts to extend African political power south of the Zambezi. In 1964, before Independence, representatives of African political parties in Angola, Mozambique, Rhodesia and South-West Africa (Namibia) were allowed to open offices in Lusaka. This concentration of 'freedom-fighters' immediately exposed Zambia to the possibility of attack from several directions. At Independence, Zambia was largely surrounded by more or less hostile powers. Three were bent on maintaining white supremacy. Bechuanaland, which had a minimal frontier with Zambia on the Zambezi, did not become independent until 1966, and even then its foreign policy was severely constrained by its economic dependence on South Africa. Zaïre (then called the Congo) still had massive internal problems, and in any case Zambia's dependence on transit across the Katanga Pedicle still provided a bone of contention between the two states. In Malawi, Dr Banda had decided that the country was far too poor to be able to challenge either the economic or political power of the white supremacies on which its economy depended; besides, Zambia had antagonised Banda by sheltering many of his political opponents. Thus in 1964 only Tanzania could be counted a friendly neighbour. In 1965 South Africa placed an airbase in the Caprivi Strip, within easy striking distance of Zambia, and in the same year Rhodesia's UDI created a new military threat. By 1967 African guerrillas were invading Rhodesia from Zambia, and South Africa sent militarised police to support Rhodesian forces on the southern banks of the Zambezi.

This military confrontation worried the Zambian government, whose own armed forces (still under white commanders) were very small: at the break-up of the Federation, Rhodesia was deliberately given the lion's share of its military assets in a vain attempt by Britain to stave off UDI. Kaunda had no wish to risk war with South Africa; instead, he wanted to see if Zambia's quarrel with Rhodesia could be separated from the much larger question of who should rule South Africa. At the same time the South African government was also most reluctant to come to blows with Zambia; not simply because this might draw in Communist powers but because South Africa's long-term aim was to transform hostile black African states into compliant and dependent trading partners. Lesotho and Swaziland provided models; so did Malawi, which opened diplomatic relations with South Africa in 1967, and it was hoped that Zambia might yet be induced to follow suit. As a result there was a brief exchange of letters between Kaunda and Vorster in 1968, but such contacts led nowhere. In the following year Zambia and Tanzania took a leading part in formulating the 'Lusaka Manifesto' signed by thirteen African countries. This was a statement of policy towards southern Africa: the signatories stressed their rejection of racialism of any kind and their preference for achieving liberation from white rule by non-violent means.

> We would prefer to negotiate rather than destroy, to talk rather than kill. We do not advocate violence; we advocate an end to the violence against human dignity which is now being perpetrated by the oppressors of Africa. If peaceful progress to emancipation were possible, or if changed circumstances were to make it possible in the future, we would urge our brothers in the resistance movements to use peaceful methods of struggle even at the cost of some compromise on the timing of change. But while peaceful progress is blocked by actions of those at present in power in the States of Southern Africa, we have no choice but to give to the peoples of those territories all the support of which we are capable in their struggle against their oppressors.[1]

The conditions for peaceful negotiations were not, of course, met, and Zambia remained committed to supporting armed struggle. In 1970 it strengthened its own capacity to deter invasion by acquiring a few jet fighter aircraft from Yugoslavia; later, it obtained a small British ground-to-air missile system. In October 1971, after South African troops had been killed by landmines in the Caprivi Strip, Zambia claimed that South Africans had entered Zambia in pursuit of guerrillas. In January 1973 there were landmine explosions in Zambia at Kazungula, opposite the Strip, and Namibian guerrillas later killed four black South African soldiers in the Strip; in the same year there were similar incidents further down the Zambezi involving Rhodesian forces. Meanwhile, Zambia had provided support for guerrillas of the MPLA, who gained control of parts of eastern Angola; this provoked several bombing attacks by the Portuguese on Zambian territory, especially in 1966–8.

Much the most important guerrilla activity, however, took place in Mozambique. By 1968 Frelimo forces based on Tanzania had occupied much of north-eastern Mozambique. They then launched a new offensive in Tete province; this was based on eastern Zambia. In 1969 work began on a great hydro-electric project at Caborabassa, on the lower Zambezi. South Africa was heavily involved in this, and it was an obvious target for guerrillas. The Portuguese thus concentrated their forces around Caborabassa, but as a result lost much of the rest of Tete province. Then in 1973, with the closure of the Rhodesia–Zambia border, Zambia stopped using the Beira railway. This encouraged Frelimo to extend its war still further southwards and attack this major line of communication between the Portuguese coast and interior. Malawi now felt itself increasingly isolated from its white allies. It had opened diplomatic relations with Zambia in 1970 and now began discussing possible transport links with Zambia. But the Frelimo advance had far greater repercussions. It was above all the failure of the Portuguese army to contain, let alone defeat, Frelimo which brought about the *coup d'état* in Lisbon in April 1974. The military officers who replaced the forty-year-old dictatorship were convinced that Portugal could no longer hope to retain the African empire which it had founded over four centuries earlier. By the beginning of 1975 arrangements had been made to transfer both Angola and Mozambique to African governments by the end of the year.

The retreat of the Portuguese transformed the whole power situation in southern Africa. No longer was Zambia an almost isolated salient of independent black Africa; instead, it was Rhodesia which now found itself largely surrounded by more or less hostile territory. South Africa's military support for the illegal Rhodesian regime had been rooted, not simply in racialist fellow-feeling but in the hope that Rhodesia, together with the Portuguese territories, could serve as buffers to protect South Africa from the southward advance of black nationalism. Once the Portuguese had admitted defeat, Rhodesia's strategic value evaporated, for it now became completely dependent on South Africa. Smith's last-ditch attempt to preserve 'Christian civilisation' was now a liability, since it merely provoked continuing guerrilla activity uncomfortably close to South Africa. It would suit South Africa far better to see Rhodesia quietly ruled by a 'moderate' black government. Thus towards the end of 1974 South Africa renewed contacts with Zambia in an attempt to co-ordinate pressure on the Smith regime to open the way to majority rule in Rhodesia. There was even a meeting in Lusaka between Kaunda, Nyerere, Seretse Khama of Botswana and Rhodesian officials.

This astonishing turn of events seemed at first to promise fulfilment of Kaunda's earlier hope that the problem of Rhodesia could be separated from that of southern Africa as a whole. But the obstacles were still formidable. Smith and the Rhodesian Front stubbornly resisted pressure for change from both Zambia and South Africa. Besides, the possibility of maintaining this unlikely partnership was complicated by Zambia's other commitments. Botswana was building an all-weather road to link it to Zambia by way of a new pontoon at Kazungula. This would do much to free Botswana from its dependence on South Africa for external communications; it might even encourage Botswana to take a fuller part in supporting African guerrillas. Thus South Africa challenged the existence of a common frontier between Botswana and Zambia. At the same time Zambia was committed to support for the freedom struggle in Namibia. In 1971 the World Court finally declared illegal South Africa's occupation of this former League of Nations mandate. In 1974 the United Nations appointed a Commissioner for Namibia, Sean MacBride, to collaborate with the South-West Africa Peoples' Organisation (SWAPO) in forming a government in exile. Zambia had urged the United Nations to take this step as early as 1970, and in 1975 a Namibian institute for research and administrative training was set up in Lusaka. But by April 1975 South Africa had shown no sign of willingness to negotiate with SWAPO; its only plans were for the creation of isolated and powerless 'Bantustans'.

Unity and Freedom

Despite these major uncertainties, it was clear that Zambia's strategic position had improved considerably since Independence: after ten difficult years the country had begun to reap some reward from its resolute, and very costly, defiance of the southern white supremacies. This defiance was of course only possible because throughout these ten years Zambia enjoyed a sufficiently stable government to pursue a consistent policy of its own. This stability, however, was rather precarious. In Zambia, as in other new states, it proved hard to sustain the unity engendered by the struggle to overthrow colonial rule. National unity seemed essential, not only to confront the tasks of economic development but to counter internal subversion and external attacks. But it was not at all easy to give substance to the UNIP rallying-cry 'One Zambia, One Nation'. As we have seen, economic inequality has in important respects increased since Independence. This inequality was not only a matter of class distinction; some parts of the country are richer than others, and this aggravated the regional rivalries which are commonly referred to as 'tribalism'. At the same time the economic break with the south contributed to inflation and shortages of consumer goods; these perhaps especially alienated the more wealthy and articulate town-dwellers. There was thus considerable scope for hostile foreign powers to exploit internal disaffection for their own ends. In these circumstances it was scarcely surprising that the Zambian government became increasingly authoritarian in its search for unity, even though this tendency provoked further unrest.

The regional divisions in Zambia have deep roots in history. This is not to say that they are in any narrow sense 'tribal' divisions. Of all the various pre-colonial political units, only the Lozi kingdom had continued to be an important focus for resistance to the central government. Politicians and journalists are fond of saying that Zambia has seventy-two tribes, but this statement, based on the stereotypes of colonial officials, is both meaningless and irrelevant. What is significant is the fact that the country comprises at least nine different language groups, and although these all belong to the Bantu family few people are fluent in more than two. English is still understood by only a small minority and there is no African common language such as Tanzania enjoys in Swahili. Instead, four main languages have become common languages for different parts of the country: Bemba, Nyanja, Tonga and Lozi.

The prevalence of these four common languages is essentially a by-product of colonial economics. It was usually when people came to work in mines and towns, whether inside the country or elsewhere, that they first began to be aware of a common identity with people speaking languages closely related to their own, or who at any rate came from the same part of the country. And the patterns of labour migration tended to reinforce this growing sense of regional identity. We have already noted that at the end of the nineteenth century the territory comprised several different spheres of commercial influence, facing out towards Angola, East Africa, the lower Zambezi and South Africa. The imposition of colonial rule created the possibility of a political centre for these various spheres, but it did not create any one economic centre. Early patterns of labour migration linked the Lozi and other western peoples to Southern Rhodesia and South Africa; the Tonga and the eastern peoples to Southern Rhodesia; and the Bemba-speaking peoples of the north-east to Katanga. When the Copperbelt was developed in the late 1920s and 1930s, this attracted many Bemba-speakers who had already worked in Katanga. In 1964 nearly half the African workers on the copper mines came from either Northern or Luapula Provinces, while only 2 per cent came from Barotse Province and less than 1 per cent from Southern Province. Thus the economic heart of the country was dominated by Bemba-speakers from the north-east.

These patterns of migration profoundly influenced the growth of nationalism in Northern Rhodesia. When UNIP took over the struggle against Federation in 1960 it owed much of its mass support to Bemba-speakers: most of them had spent their working lives entirely within the territory and many of them were concentrated within a few towns where party organisation was relatively easy to develop. In the Southern Province, by contrast, very few people had worked on the Copperbelt and in any case the African National Congress had retained a large following in the south. In the west there had been very little popular involvement in the economic and political mainstream. Labour had long flowed south to Livingstone and Rhodesia. This pattern was intensified when in 1940 agents of the Witwatersrand Native Labour Association ('Wenela') began recruiting in Barotseland and the north-west for the South African mines. In the general elections before Independence, UNIP did receive much support in Barotseland, but this was partly due less to solidarity with the emerging nation than to a temporary alliance of interests between UNIP, which wished to abolish the Lozi monarchy, and Lozi dissidents who wished to reform it.

At Independence, then, Zambia was still far from being one nation. One source of disaffection did withdraw from the political arena: once universal suffrage had arrived, there was clearly no future for any sort of European political party. In the 1964 election the ten 'reserved' seats had been won by an all-white party, but nearly a third of the white voters had voted for UNIP, and the reserved seats were abolished without fuss soon after Independence. White attitudes did not, of course, change overnight; there was plenty of support on the Copperbelt for Rhodesia's UDI, and several whites were imprisoned or deported for racialist behaviour or subversive activities. In 1966 President Kaunda dismissed seventeen white police officers on security grounds. But there was no concerted attempt at subversion among the white mining staff on whom the country still depends. It was the various African sources of opposition which gave the government most cause for concern.

The UNIP government which took control of Zambia at Independence was deliberately composed of leaders from almost all parts of the country: only the north-west was unrepresented in the Cabinet. Nonetheless, UNIP itself was widely regarded by the ANC as essentially a 'Bemba' party, while ANC in turn was seen by many people in UNIP as a 'Tonga' party. In one sense, ANC posed no real threat to UNIP: it had only ten out of seventy-five seats, and its MPs seldom provided any serious criticism of specific government policies. But the persistence of ANC as the dominant party in the south challenged UNIP's claim to embody the whole Zambian nation, while ANC laid itself open to the charge of collusion with hostile foreign powers. At the local level there continued to be violent clashes between the youth wings of both parties, and these aggravated the pressure within UNIP for transforming Zambia into a one-party state, such as existed elsewhere in Africa.

Meanwhile, UNIP itself was increasingly torn by conflict. The struggle for power between black and white had given way to competition between African politicians for senior posts in the central government. Veterans of the freedom struggle had to be rewarded by jobs in government, even though many were quite unsuited to administrative work. To advance their claims, UNIP leaders naturally tended to seek support in those regions where they were best known and understood. It is mainly for this reason that political competition in Zambia (as indeed in other nations, new and old) has taken on a 'tribal' character. The 'tribes' in question do not represent any units of social organisation, past or present; they are formed by the main lines of linguistic division within the great majority of the population who speak no English. At the same time these linguistic divisions have been intensified and complicated by regional lines of economic inequality, real or imagined. It is inevitable that ambitious politicians, dependent on popular election, should exploit (or be thought to exploit) these regional ties and grievances to their own advantage. And since politics at the centre are dominated by regional rivalries, illiterate villagers in the remoter and more backward regions are naturally ready to believe that their continuing poverty is due not to basic economic problems but simply to discrimination by the government in favour of other regions at the expense of their own.

The erosion of UNIP's precarious position as the one truly national party began as early as 1966, when two Lozi-speaking M.P.s formed a new opposition group, the United Party. This rapidly gathered popular support in western Zambia at UNIP's expense, for in the same year the government banned Wenela from recruiting labour in Zambia for South Africa. This was an important element in the government's strategy for detaching itself from the white south, but it suddenly removed a major source of income from Barotseland and the north-west, where in any case poor soils and distance from the railway inhibited economic development. Moreover, since UDI, the Smith regime made it increasingly difficult for Zambians to obtain work in Rhodesia: this mostly affected Barotseland, Southern Province and Eastern Province. The UNIP party elections in 1967 both exposed and provoked bitter 'tribal' rivalries, and since then Kaunda has repeatedly reshuffled the Cabinet in an attempt to hold such rivalries in check, even at the expense of efficient administration. In 1968 a 'Unity in the East' movement briefly challenged 'Bemba domination', while six people were killed on the Copperbelt in fighting between UNIP and the UP. As a result the latter was banned, but its members were welcomed into the ANC. Towards the end of the year a general election was held: ANC took most of the seats in Barotseland (since renamed Western Province) and altogether won twenty-three seats; UNIP won eighty-one.

In 1969 yet another source of opposition began to crystallise. The Vice-President, Simon Kapwepwe, resigned, and soon afterwards claimed that his fellow Bemba-speakers were being 'persecuted'. He then withdrew his resignation, but over the following year he lost his political offices. In August 1971 a group of UNIP dissidents on the Copperbelt formed the United Progressive Party (UPP); Kapwepwe was soon revealed as its leader and he resigned from UNIP. Support for the UPP partly reflected growing unemployment due to the cut-back in business investment which followed the end of the copper boom in 1970. Most of the UPP activists, except for Kapwepwe himself, were promptly detained without trial. Early in 1972 the UPP was banned and still more of its members were detained, including Kapwepwe. He and most of his colleagues were released early in 1973, but meanwhile Zambia had become a one-party state.

Many UNIP members pointed to the unhappy record of party fission and conflict since independence as proof that the existence of rival political parties was in itself a major cause of conflict and violence. Hitherto, Kaunda had been reluctant to introduce a one-party state as an act of policy; he hoped that UNIP might simply win all seats at the polls. Instead, UNIP was losing votes. So in February 1972 a National Commission was appointed to formulate a new, one-party constitution, and the kernel of this was approved by Parliament, which thus inaugurated Zambia's Second Republic.

Elections under the new constitution were held in December 1973. President Kaunda was re-elected for a third term of office, though 20 per cent of the voters opposed him. All Parliamentary candidates belonged to UNIP, but most seats were contested. Three Cabinet ministers and six junior ministers lost their seats. Most of the new MPs were under forty, and the new Cabinet included several younger ministers with considerable administrative experience. Under the new constitution strategies for national political development were the responsibility of the UNIP National Executive Committee, which included many veteran nationalist politicians. Nonetheless, the main burden of government appeared to have shifted to a new generation of leaders. At the same time it must be noted that only 39 per cent of the electorate voted in 1973, as against 77 per cent in 1968. This apathy may have been due partly to the absence of rival parties, but it may well reflect widespread discontent, due to increasing poverty in both town and country. In these circumstances it seemed clear that regional rivalries would continue to flourish, whether within the framework of UNIP or outside it.

In view of the great contrasts of wealth and poverty within Zambia it may seem surprising that political competition has not been based on class differences rather than regional rivalries. But few Zambians as yet see their interests in terms of economic class. The continued presence of relatively wealthy European and Asian minorities encouraged black Zambians to perceive a common interest in removing these immigrant minorities from the best-paid jobs. The rapid expansion of education and the rapid advancement of the more qualified Zambians promoted a sense of an open society, in which inherited status and privilege count for little or nothing. Nor are the great multitude of poverty-stricken villagers exploited by landlords or moneylenders: these are confined to a few pockets of commercial farming and to the towns. Villagers might indeed complain of the relative prosperity of the areas along the railway line, but many have shared in this prosperity by working in towns or living off relatives there. Quite realistically, they are unlikely to complain of urban wealth in itself; rather, they question the way in which it is spread between the various outlying provinces.

Within the towns the trade unions do provide a possible focus for class-based politics; in 1971 they comprised about half of all wage-earners. But the position of the unions is highly ambiguous. The large pay rises in 1966 consolidated the position of mineworkers as a 'labour aristocracy' as contrasted with the poorer wage-earners and the unemployed. The mineworkers enjoy a rather special relationship with the government, due to their strategic importance for the economy and the government's own dominant share in mine-ownership since 1969. The need for industrial peace on the mines has given rise to a series of compromises between the government and the leaders of the mineworkers' union.[2] The latter have often seemed more responsive to government than to their own rank and file, but mineworkers continue to look primarily to their union to further their interests, which are now not so much to improve their position in relation to whites as to maintain their privileged position in relation to other black workers. Neither UNIP nor any other party could serve this purpose, since any party seeking victory at the polls, even on a regional basis, has been obliged by arithmetic to appeal to both urban and rural poor. Thus UNIP continues to receive very limited support in the mine compounds and in this sense mineworkers have remained largely outside the national political arena.

One further reason why class plays so small a part in Zambian politics is simply that ideologies of class conflict have scarcely begun to take root. Few Zambians are at all familiar with socialist theory or practice, and those few belong to the small group of educated English-speakers. They have far more in common with the rest of this relatively wealthy élite than with any significant section of the 'masses', and it need hardly be said that the rapid growth of State control in the economy reflects not socialism but nationalism. Nor can one point to the growth of any homespun socialism: workers who know no English cannot address the nation at large, and failing this they are liable to be trapped in the regional politics of 'tribalism'. The fact that Tanzania is one of the very few African countries with a Socialist ruling party owes much to its possession of a national language, Swahili.

Zambia does have a national political philosophy which claims to be socialist in principle. This is 'Humanism' which was first presented to the nation in 1967 in the form of a pamphlet by President Kaunda. The immediate inspiration for this was doubtless the Arusha Declaration earlier that year by Kaunda's friend Julius Nyerere, but there is no very close resemblance between Tanzanian socialism and Zambian Humanism. Both are grounded in a commitment to the freedom and dignity of the individual, but their approaches to social problems are very different. Kaunda identifies Humanism with 'African democratic socialism', but he condones private property and seeks to avoid, rather than precipitate, class conflict. He acknowledges the danger that economic differentiation could lead to class-formation and conflict, but he argues that this can be prevented if everyone works for a 'Man-centred society' in which human relations are valued above material possessions.

This theory is rooted, not in socialist doctrines, but in Kaunda's own Christian beliefs and the ideals of mutual respect and co-operation which he sees as characteristic of pre-industrial African society. Such a vision of a classless and socialist 'traditional' Africa is also an important element in Nyerere's thinking, and the communal values of village life are undeniably more humane, if not indeed more 'civilised', than those of large-scale industrial societies. But in practice even 'traditional' Africa was subject to economic forces, both internal and external, which undermined such 'primitive socialism'. The historical record shows all too plainly that by the nineteenth century much of Zambian society was anything but Humanist, and in the latter part of the twentieth century Zambia is further removed than almost any other African country from the conditions in which a small-scale agrarian socialism might flourish. Instead, Humanism has to reckon not only with the growth of an industrial working class, but with the emergence of a highly materialistic African middle class whose life-style is naturally modelled on that of the free-spending Europeans it has partly displaced. Ironically, it is precisely this class – which includes the politicians, civil servants and teachers – that is charged with propagating the anti-materialistic doctrines of Humanism. Such people have been ready enough to accept Humanism in so far as this has meant making Zambians masters in their own homes. But they are no more willing than any other privileged group to make material sacrifices which might at least symbolically diminish the gulf between rich and poor, and set an example of frugality to the rest of the nation. A 'Leadership Code' was introduced under the 1973 Constitution to limit the wealth of holders of public office, but its effectiveness has yet to be tested.

Thus the approach towards a 'Man-centred society' appears to be obstructed by class interests even though Humanism does not explicitly challenge them. However it would be wrong to conclude from this that Humanism is simply a naïve and romantic statement of personal belief, irrelevant to real political problems. In common with the ideologies proclaimed by other leaders of new states it must be understood as an attempt to strengthen the sense of nationhood after the initial anti-colonial impetus has subsided. Efforts to develop a 'national culture' in Zambia have been complicated by the fact that at the popular level this is bound to take a number of local forms, which are potentially 'tribalistic'. Humanism, however, has offered a moral centre for the nation: by imparting a sense of ethical purpose to the difficult years after Independence, Humanism contributed to the growth of a single moral community and helped to sustain respect for the aims of government, if not always its performance. And in so far as Humanism seeks to be a unifying influence, it is bound not to give explicit support to any one economic class. Given the dependence of the State and the economy on the skills of a relatively rich minority, it is sound practical politics to adopt an ideology that is diffuse rather than divisive. In the short run, at any rate, nationalism in Zambia is probably incompatible with socialism. In the long run, the survival of the nation (as opposed to the State) may well depend on a move towards socialism: if Humanism continues to transcend class divisions it is unlikely to inspire any radical steps towards economic equality, and the moral community of Zambia may well split up into two nations of rich and poor.

It must in any case be acknowledged that the maintenance of national unity in Zambia has owed much less to ideology than to political action. Zambia's cornerstone is not Humanism but its author, Kenneth Kaunda. He alone among Zambian politicians is seen as a truly national figure. Others, however unfairly, are identified with some regional interest. Kaunda is Zambian, yet belongs to no Zambian 'tribe': he was born and raised in Bemba country, but his parents came from Nyasaland. This fact has given Kaunda a unique authority. It is reinforced by his obvious dedication, his passionate hatred of racialism and his remarkable endurance under enormous pressure. But Kaunda's moral qualities should not obscure his talents as a politician. His exercise of power, as in the series of nationalisation measures or Cabinet reshuffles, has revealed a subtle awareness both of popular feeling and of the constraints within which he must work. Kaunda indeed remained the one fixed point in a continually shifting political scene. He thereby became increasingly independent of the Cabinet and has taken many key decisions on his own, confining his consultations to a small circle of personal advisers. Meanwhile, he responded to growing regional tensions within UNIP by taking increasing power within the party into his own hands: in 1969 he became Secretary-General and dissolved the elected central committee.

The rapid growth of presidential power raises the question whether this has been a threat to civil liberties: in view of this trend towards autocracy, what claim has Zambia to be called a democracy? Both at the national and local level, representative government is based on British forms and procedures. Powers of legislation and control of expenditure are vested in an elected Parliament and elected urban and district councils. The electoral system itself has worked remarkably well, despite the illiteracy of most voters; at the same time illiteracy has severely restricted public knowledge of national politics and in any case Parliament has scarcely been a forum for major debates and decisions on national issues, while few members have been at all sensitive to the hardships of the vast majority of their constituents. The relative insignificance of Parliament is due partly to economic circumstances: it is not a meeting-place for conflicting economic interests, while up to 1970 at least the high level of government revenues obscured the need to argue over economic priorities. But the preponderance of UNIP in Parliament has further confirmed Parliament in its role as a discussion club rather than a potential challenge to government. The 1973 general election proved, as in Tanzania, that even in a one-party state it is quite possible for voters to exercise a real power of choice, but it is a choice between politicians, not policies, and even then the President, as Secretary-General of UNIP, can do much to determine the range of choice before the voter.

The limited powers of the legislature to control the executive make it all the more important that the judiciary should be independent. By and large, the rule of law has been upheld; judges have not been dismissed and justice has not been perverted to political ends. Some quite senior politicians and civil servants have been convicted of corruption and the judgements have been respected. But the record is not untarnished: this is scarcely to be expected in a country subject to the internal tensions and external pressures which have troubled Zambia since Independence. When Rhodesia declared UDI, the emergency regulations inherited from the colonial regime were promptly enforced over the whole of Zambia, and they have since been renewed by Parliament every six months: in effect, they allow preventive detention indefinitely without trial, at the President's sole discretion. This power of detention (which is possessed by most governments in Africa, whether black or white), has been used sweepingly against political opponents; for much of 1972 there were over 200 detainees. Some UPP members were grossly ill-treated by the police, though the courts awarded damages against the police. In 1973 many people from Western Province were detained, including the former leader of the United Party, Nalumino Mundia, who was held without trial for several months. In the same year, when introducing the one-party constitution, Parliament followed the government in rejecting several safeguards for civil liberties which had been proposed by the constitutional commission.

There has also been tension between UNIP and the judiciary. Until 1969 the Bench was entirely white and this very fact was sometimes seen as a direct challenge to the party, some of whose junior officials supposed UNIP to be above the law. The need to appease grass-roots sentiment within the party has occasionally led the President to use his prerogative of mercy in favour of UNIP members convicted of criminal offences arising from 'political' activities. Resentment of the judiciary reached a climax in 1969 when a High Court judge set aside a magistrate's punishment of two Portuguese soldiers who had strayed across the Angolan border. The President protested against the judge's decision and this in turn provoked the resignation of this judge, another judge and the Chief Justice (a Zambian citizen of Irish origin). This collision suggested to many Zambians that the rule of law is essentially a white man's law; since then, such suspicions have been allayed by the appointment of several black Zambians to the Bench. But in March 1974 the courts awarded substantial libel damages to Kapwepwe against the state-owned radio and television services, and both daily newspapers; this judgement provoked UNIP to seek to outlaw such claims by ex-detainees.

There can be no doubt that Zambia is a more tolerant society than was Northern Rhodesia. The various forms of colour bar and segregation which deformed the country under colonial rule were gradually broken down in the last few years before Independence. Nor has white racialism simply been replaced by black racialism. Inevitably racial tension has persisted in some quarters; there are still some whites from Rhodesia and South Africa whose attitudes are distinctly primitive, and racial feeling was easily inflamed in the atmosphere of near-siege following UDI. But there were remarkably few violent incidents, and Zambian leaders preserved their commitment to non-racialism, both on moral grounds and because whites at least were still essential to the economy. Asians have fared less well; under colonial rule they had been prominent in both wholesale and retail trade, and when these were reserved to Zambian citizens by the reforms of 1968-70 many were forced out of business, along with some whites and non-Zambian Africans. However, there was no general expulsion of Asians and in 1972 President Kaunda was quick to deplore the mass deportation of Asians from Uganda. Zambian citizenship is open to all races, and most non-Africans who have adopted it have prospered.

Zambia's capacity for toleration was most severely tested, not by racial tensions but by various forms of African dissent. As we have seen, there were violent collisions between UNIP and rival political parties, and the latter have now been outlawed. There are also two religious movements which have challenged the government. The leader of the Lumpa Church, Alice Lenshina, has never been tried, but she has been kept in detention, or under restriction, ever since her followers clashed with the government in 1964. The church is still banned, but between 1968 and 1971 most of those who had fled to Zaïre returned to Zambia and many settled in the towns where the church probably survives 'underground'. Jehovah's Witnesses are a much more numerous body: there may be as many as 100,000 in Zambia, and the proportion of Witnesses to total population is said to be higher there than in any other country. They are, moreover, heavily concentrated in one area, Luapula Province, which is also an important source of support for UNIP. The Witnesses refuse to vote, to sing the national anthem or salute the national flag, and this has provoked the wrath of local UNIP branches: during the election campaign in 1968 and the referendum campaign in 1969, clashes between UNIP and Witnesses caused widespread arson and violence. There has been pressure to ban their Society; this would almost certainly be quite impracticable, but their freedom to hold meetings and preach from door to door has been severely restricted.

The press in Zambia has enjoyed more freedom than in most African countries, but critical comment on national affairs is confined to English-language newspapers with a limited circulation. The *Times of Zambia*, which until 1975 was owned by a multi-national corporation, Lonrho, sells about 65,000 copies. Its first Zambian editor published outspoken criticisms of political leaders and policies, but in 1972 the President secured his dismissal, and in 1975 the paper was taken over by UNIP. One other source of dissent is the University. Few students have felt much solidarity with UNIP, and in 1971 many claimed that the government was not protesting firmly enough against French arms sales to South Africa. Following marches and demonstrations the President (as Chancellor) temporarily closed the University and deported two white lecturers.

Considering the grave handicaps of its colonial heritage, and the exceptional strains under which it has laboured since Independence, Zambia has in practice remained a remarkably free society. But it is clear that this freedom is dangerously dependent on the President's good will. Constitutionally he has the power to curb it drastically. As in many other new states there is a very delicate balance between political freedom and the stability of central government. Each depends on the other, but the President is essential to both. As yet, national institutions do not provide an effective counterpoise, whether as a force for national unity or as a guardian of liberty. Now that Zambia is a one-party state it might be expected that UNIP (like TANU in Tanzania) should improve upon earlier efforts to function, not simply as an election machine but as an agency for promoting economic development and civil education at the grass roots. As yet, however, it is doubtful whether it enjoys either sufficient expertise or public confidence to assume such a creative role. Advances in education should improve the quality of leadership, administration and public debate in the coming years: on the other hand, the aspirations of Humanism are confronted by a widespread mood of materialistic cynicism and even demoralisation. Excessive drinking is common among all sections of Zambian society, and it is partly responsible for the very high rate of road accidents, in which many talented Zambians have been killed. The economy continues to depend on the price of copper; since 1973, high oil prices have been a major constraint on development, and there is every likelihood that economic inequality will continue to increase, thus aggravating existing lines of social tension. When national unity is thus precariously based, the possibility of a *coup d'état* cannot be altogether discounted. The army has deliberately been kept small (it numbers about 5000), but the government has not always been fully in control of army operations, and nine senior officers had to be dismissed in 1973.

*   *   *   *

It is too early to see Zambia's first ten years of independence in historical perspective. The country has certainly made great progress in tackling some of the problems which faced it in 1964, but others loom as large as ever. At the end of 1974, it seemed just possible that major tensions in Zambia's external relations might be relaxed and that the country might thus obtain a breathing-space in which to concentrate its resources on further social and economic development. Events in 1975, however did not encourage such hopes. At the end of the year the prospects for ending white rule in Rhodesia by negotiation still seemed uncertain. Meanwhile, Angola was independent but its rival nationalist parties were at war. The MPLA were supported by arms and men from the USSR and Cuba, but they were challenged in the south by troops from South Africa.

Quite apart from its ominous wider implications, the fighting in Angola meant that Zambia could no longer use the Benguela railway to export copper. The new Tanzam railway was only a partial answer, since the East African ports were still a major bottleneck. There was thus a powerful incentive for Zambia to re-open the border with Rhodesia and once again export copper by rail to Beira. Besides, three years of blockade on the Zambezi had cost Zambia a net total of £120 million – a quite disproportionate share of the burden of implementing United Nations policy on Rhodesia. At the same time, Zambia's imports cost more than ever before, due to high oil prices. Yet Zambia's earnings from copper remained very meagre; copper prices remained very low, despite new efforts at international co-operation to stabilise them at levels acceptable to producers as well as consumers. In confronting the white supremacies, Zambia now argued from a position of economic weakness rather than strength. The cause of Zambian independence, in the broadest sense, still faces formidable obstacles.

NOTES

1. Fifth Summit Conference of East and Central African States, *Manifesto on Southern Africa* (Lusaka, 1969), 3–4.
2. In 1965 the African Mineworkers' Union was renamed the Zambian Mineworkers' Union and in 1967 the Mineworkers' Union of Zambia. The European Mineworkers' Union was dissolved in 1964 and by 1966 white miners had moved over to contract terms of service.

Appendixes

1. The Copper Industry in Pre-colonial Central Africa

African copper production was restricted by several factors. The right to mine for copper was jealously controlled by local chiefs. Mining took place only in the dry season, when the main tasks of cultivation were completed. But the most important constraint on production was the simple technology available. Soft rock was dug out by iron-headed picks. Harder rock was broken up by fire-setting: the rock was heated and then split by pouring cold water over it. But only the richest ore was removed: it was closely followed along its narrow seams, leaving intact the harder surrounding rock. Thus workings tended to be long, deep and narrow cuttings, sometimes little wider than a man. Seams were usually followed downwards at an incline, which rendered ladders unnecessary. In the absence of pumps, the depth of a cutting was limited by the water-table. Light could be provided by firing clumps of straw, but pit-props were seldom used. Men did the actual digging, but the dirt and ore were lifted to the surface in bark buckets by a chain of women. Women and children washed the broken ore by shaking it in baskets in a nearby stream.

The ore was then taken away for smelting. The furnaces might be some distance from the mine for they were most conveniently located near supplies of hardwood for making charcoal. For each operation, two furnaces were needed: one for the initial smelting, and another for refining. Smelting methods varied a good deal, and the following account is based on Kaonde practice.

A furnace about 40 cm high was quickly constructed from ant-hill clay over a hollow dug out of the ground. This was filled with ashes, and charcoal was then piled up to cover the hole near the foot of the furnace into which a draught-pipe was inserted. Bellows were then used to pump air into the draught-pipe to start the fire. When the charcoal was seen to glow, the ore was placed on top and then covered with more charcoal. Within three hours or so most of the impurities would have been burnt away. The furnace was then broken down, the charcoal was scattered and the liquid copper rapidly solidified into lumps. These were introduced into the second furnace which was built over a clay pot filled with ashes and heated in much the same way as the first. When the copper had liquefied again it ran down into the clay pot and could then be tipped into a mould. Once it had set in the mould it was ready to be carried off to a smith, or offered for sale.

Such copper was remarkably pure: a Kaonde spearhead was found on assay to be 98·68 per cent copper. Nonetheless, Kaonde methods of extraction seem to have been less efficient than those practised by peoples further north. The Sanga sometimes built tall furnaces as much as 1·7 m high, to smelt large quantities of ore: these were fired by several draught-pipes and bellows. They also built smaller permanent furnaces, from which the copper flowed out through channels leading into cross-shaped moulds. The Yeke, who conquered the Sanga in the nineteenth century, built furnaces about 70 cm high which were fired by natural draught, except in the last stages. These could receive up to 45 kg of ore at a time and this normally averaged 40 per cent copper. After the initial smelting this amount of ore yielded about 11 kg of metal, which thus represented 60–70 per cent of the copper content of the ore: the wastage, in other words, was 30–40 per cent. Unfortunately, we have no comparable figures for copper production by other people but it is probable that Yeke methods were more efficient than others in central Africa: higher temperatures could have been reached in their large natural-draught furnaces, thus improving the recovery of copper from ore.

There were other regional differences and specialities. Refined copper was cast in moulds to form ingots of various shapes and sizes. The most common in the last century was a small St Andrew's cross, about 15 cm across and weighing 0·2 kg. Such ingots were then melted down by smiths to be reworked into ornaments and, more rarely, tools or weapons. One type of copper-working was especially important – wire-drawing. This was the first stage in making the anklets and brace-lets which became so popular in the later nineteenth century. It was a highly skilled craft, and wire-drawers were comparatively rare, though the Sanga and their Yeke conquerors acquired reputations as specialists. A 15 cm copper ingot was heated in the fire of a forge and hammered out by a team of several men to a length of over 6 m. This bar was then elongated into a thick wire 15 m long, by fixing it in a post and using a lever to pull it through an iron drawplate. This thick wire was then tied round a post and again pulled through a drawplate: the process was further repeated, until the wire was less than 0·5 mm thick. It could then be rolled round a core of wood fibre to form a bracelet.

2. Colonial Administrators and Governors

BRITISH SOUTH AFRICA COMPANY: ADMINISTRATORS

NORTH-WESTERN RHODESIA	NORTH-EASTERN RHODESIA
1900–7 R. T. Coryndon	1900–7 R. E. Codrington
1907–8 R. E. Codrington	1907–9 L. A. Wallace
1909–11 L. A. Wallace	1909–11 L. P. Beaufort

NORTHERN RHODESIA

1911–21 L. A. Wallace
1921–4 F. D. P. Chaplin

COLONIAL OFFICE: GOVERNORS

1924–7 H. J. Stanley
1927–32 J. C. Maxwell
1932–4 R. Storrs
1934–8 H. W. Young
1938–41 J. A. Maybin
1941–8 E. J. Waddington
1948–54 G. K. Rennie
1954–9 A. E. T. Benson
1959–64 E. T. Hone

Bibliography

This bibliography is intended both as a guide to further reading and as a list of the main secondary sources on which this book is based. In Chapters VII–IX I have also drawn here and there on primary sources (mainly early European travellers) which are only acknowledged in footnotes where they are actually quoted. This is not the place for a list of such sources, but it is perhaps worth stressing how useful it would be to have an anthology of source-material for Zambian history, on the same sort of lines as Thomas Hodgkin's *Nigerian Perspectives* (second edition, 1975).

I have divided the following bibliography into two parts. In the first, entries are listed under the chapter headings of this book. For Chapters I–IX they are listed in approximately the order in which reference is made to them within each chapter; for Chapters X–XII the entries are arranged by topic. Books and articles which are mainly concerned with one particular group of people are listed separately in an 'Ethnic Bibliography', against an alphabetical list of peoples. Finally, I have given some information about aids to the study of history in Zambia: bibliographies, serial publications (such as periodicals) and guides to historical source-material.

The place of publication is given only for books not published in London. Books and articles marked with an asterisk include bibliographies of special value for Zambian history.

Chapter I: The Natural Setting

DAVIES, D. H. (ed.), *Zambia in Maps* (1971)

REEVE, W. H., *The Geology and Mineral Resources of Northern Rhodesia* (Bulletin of the Geological Survey, no. 3: Lusaka, 1963. Vol. I text; vol. II maps)

MENDELSOHN, E. (ed.), *The Geology of the Northern Rhodesian Copperbelt* (1961)

PHILLIPSON, D. W. (ed.) *Mosi-oa-Tunya: a handbook to the Victoria Falls region* (1976)

TRAPNELL, C. G., *The Soils, Vegetation and Agriculture of North-Eastern Rhodesia* (Lusaka, 1953)

TRAPNELL, C. G., and CLOTHIER, J. N., *The Soils, Vegetation and Agriculture of North-Western Rhodesia* (Lusaka, 1957)

ALLAN, William, *The African Husbandman* (Edinburgh, 1965). The author was formerly Director of Agriculture in Northern Rhodesia and much of the book is concerned with this country.

*KAY, George, *A Social Geography of Zambia* (1967)

Chapters II–IV: Archaeology: The Stone Age and Iron Age

CLARK, J. D., *The Prehistory of Africa* (1970)

PHILLIPSON, D. W., 'The Late Stone Age in sub-Saharan Africa' in J. D. Clark (ed.), *The Cambridge History of Africa*, vol. I (in press)

CLARK, J. D., *The Stone Age Cultures of Northern Rhodesia* (Claremont, S. Africa, n.d. [1950])

PHILLIPSON, Laurel, 'Survey of the Stone Age Archaeology of the Upper Zambezi Valley: I. The Northern Part of the Valley', *Azania*, X (1975), 1–48

CLARK, J. D., *Kalambo Falls Prehistoric Site*, vol. II (Cambridge, 1974). This covers the Later Stone Age and the Iron Age; the earlier Stone Age remains will be treated in vol. III. Vol. I was concerned with geology, palaeoecology and stratigraphy.

PHILLIPSON, D. W., *The Prehistory of Eastern Zambia* (Nairobi 1976)

PHILLIPSON, D. W., 'The prehistoric sequence at Nakapapula rock-shelter, Zambia', *Proceedings of the Prehistoric Society*, XXXV (1969), 172–202

GABEL, C., *Stone Age Hunters of the Kafue* (Boston, 1965)

FAGAN, B. M., and VAN NOTEN, F., *The Hunter-Gatherers of Gwisho* (Musée Royal de l'Afrique centrale, Annales, LXXIV: Tervuren 1971)

PHILLIPSON, D. W., 'The Chronology of the Iron Age in Bantu Africa', *Journal of African History*, XVI (1975), iii, 321–42

PHILLIPSON, D. W., 'Archaeology and Bantu Linguistics', *World Archaeology*, 8, i (1976), 65–82.

PHILLIPSON, D. W., 'The Early Iron Age in Zambia: regional variants and some tentative conclusions', *Journal of African History*, IX (1968), ii, 191–211

MILLER, Sheryl F., 'Contacts between the Late Stone Age and the Early Iron Age in Southern Central Africa', *Azania*, IV (1969), 81–90

PHILLIPSON, D. W., 'Zambian Rock Paintings', *World Archaeology*, III (1972), 313–27

PHILLIPSON, D. W., *Prehistoric Rock Paintings and Engravings of Zambia* (Livingstone, 1972). An illustrated exhibition catalogue

PHILLIPSON, D. W., 'The Early Iron Age Site at Kapwirimbwe, Lusaka', *Azania*, III (1968), 87–105

PHILLIPSON, D. W., 'Excavations at Twickenham Road, Lusaka', *Azania*, V (1970), 77–118

PHILLIPSON, D. W., 'Early Iron Age Sites on the Zambian Copperbelt', *Azania*, VII (1972), 93–128

MILLS, E. A. C., and FILMER, N. T., 'Chondwe Iron Age Site, Ndola, Zambia', *Azania*, VII (1972), 192–145

BISSON, M. S., 'Kansanshi: a prehistoric coppermine in north-western Zambia', *Archaeology*, XXVII (1974), iv, 242–47

BISSON, M. S., 'Kansanshi Mine and the Iron Age in North-Western Zambia', *Zambia Museums Journal* (in press)

PHILLIPSON, D. W., 'Iron Age History and Archaeology in Zambia', *Journal of African History*, XV (1974), i, 1–25. This discusses the 'Luangwa' and 'Lungwebungu' pottery traditions.

DANIELS, S. G. H., 'A note on the Iron Age material from Kamusongolwa Kopje, Zambia', *South African Archaeological Bulletin*, XXII (1967), 142–50

VOGEL, J. O., 'The Shongwe Tradition', *Zambia Museums Journal*, 3 (1972), 27–34

VOGEL, J. O., *Kamangoza*, Zambia Museum Paper no. 2 (Nairobi, 1971)

VOGEL, J. O., *Kumadzulo*, Zambia Museum Paper no. 3 (Lusaka, 1971)

VOGEL, J. O., *Simbusenga*, Zambia Museum Paper no. 4 (Lusaka, 1975)

VOGEL, J. O., 'Kabondo Kumbo and the Early Iron Age in Victoria Falls Region', *Azania*, X (1975), 49–75

VOGEL, J. O., 'The Mosiatunya Sequence', *Zambia Museums Journal*, 4 (1973), 105–52

VOGEL, J. O., 'The Iron Age Pottery of the Victoria Falls Region', *Zambia Museums Journal* (in press)

VOGEL, J. O., 'The Kalomo Culture of Southern Zambia: some notes towards a reassessment', *Zambia Museums Journal* 1 (1970), 77–88

FAGAN, B. M., *Iron Age Cultures in Zambia, I: Kalomo and Kangila* (1967)

FAGAN, B. M., and PHILLIPSON, D. W., 'Sebanzi: the Iron Age sequence at Lochinvar, and the Tonga', *Journal of the Royal Anthropological Institute*, XCV (1965), ii, 253–94

FAGAN, B. M., PHILLIPSON, D. W., and DANIELS, S. G. H., *Iron Age Cultures in Zambia, II: Dambwa, Ingombe Ilede and the Tonga* (1969)

PHILLIPSON, D. W., and FAGAN, B. M., 'The date of the Ingombe Ilede burials', *Journal of African History*, X (1969), ii, 199–204

FAGAN, B. M., 'Early Trade and Raw Materials in South Central Africa', *Journal of African History*, X (1969), i, 1–13; reprinted in R. Gray and D. Birmingham (eds.), *Pre-Colonial African Trade* (1970), 24–38

GARLAKE, P. S., *Great Zimbabwe* (1973)

BISSON, M. S., 'Copper currency in central Africa: the archaeological evidence', *World Archaeology*, VI (1975), iii, 276–92

Chapter V: The Peoples of Zambia

There is no reliable and comprehensive ethnographic or sociological survey of Zambia, despite the wealth of available material. The first three items listed below provide more or less useful introductions.

MITCHELL, J. Clyde, 'The African Peoples', in W. V. Brelsford (ed.), *Handbook to the Federation of Rhodesia and Nyasaland* (Salisbury, 1960), 117–82. A straightforward survey for the layman by a leading social anthropologist who was formerly Director of the Rhodes-Livingstone Institute for Social Research, Lusaka.

COLSON, Elizabeth, and GLUCKMAN, Max (eds.), *Seven Tribes of British Central Africa* (1951; reprinted Manchester, 1962). This includes essays on the Lozi, Plateau Tonga, Bemba and Mpezeni's Ngoni; the editors were both formerly Directors of the Rhodes-Livingstone Institute.

BRELSFORD, W. V., *The Tribes of Zambia* (Lusaka, 1966). This is a compilation, by a former colonial official, of 'tribal' histories as collected by officials and missionaries. It is not a work of historical scholarship and should be used with caution: the numerous uncritical accounts of 'tribal migrations' tend to take it for granted that tribes are clearly defined groups which have existed since time immemorial.

VANSINA, Jan (tr. H. M. Wright), *Oral Tradition* (1965; Penguin Books, 1973)

DE HEUSCH, Luc, *Le roi ivre, ou l'origine de l'état* (Paris, 1972). An analysis of myths of origin among the Bemba, Lamba, Lunda, Luba and other central African peoples, in terms of the structural anthropology of Claude Lévi-Strauss.

DOUGLAS, Mary, 'Matriliny and Pawnship in Central Africa', *Africa*, XXXIV (1964), iv, 301–13

CAMPBELL, D., 'A Few Notes on Butwa', *Man*, XIV (1914), 76–81

RANGER, T. O., 'Territorial Cults in the History of Central Africa', *Journal of African History*, XIV (1973), iv, 581–97

SCHOFFELEERS, M., 'The Chisumphi and Mbona Cults in Malawi: a comparative history': paper for the Conference on the History of Central African Religious Systems, Lusaka, 1972.

Chapter VI: The Growth of Chieftainship

HENIGE, D. P., *The Chronology of Oral Tradition* (Oxford, 1974). A sceptical analysis of king-lists and genealogies both in Africa and in other parts of the world.

VANSINA, Jan, 'The Bells of Kings', *Journal of African History*, X (1969), ii, 187–97

MILLER, J. C., 'The Imbangala and the Chronology of Early Central African History', *Journal of African History*, XIII (1972), iv, 549–74

*VANSINA, Jan, *Kingdoms of the Savanna* (Madison, 1966), especially chapters 1 and 3.

REEFE, T. Q., 'A History of the Luba Empire to *c.* 1885', Ph.D. thesis, California (Berkeley), 1975

*LANGWORTHY, H. W., *Zambia before 1890* (1972). This is based on a series of short radio talks; half the chapters are focused on the histories of the main kingdoms.

WHITE, C. M. N., 'Ethnohistory of the Upper Zambezi', *African Studies*, XXI (1962), i, 10–27

Chapter VII: The Expansion of Trade

*ROBERTS, A. D., 'Pre-colonial Trade in Zambia', *African Social Research* 10 (1970), 715–46

ST JOHN, C., 'Kazembe and the Tanganyika-Nyasa Corridor, 1800–1890', in R. Gray and D. Birmingham (eds.), *Pre-Colonial African Trade* (1970), 202–230

SUTHERLAND-HARRIS, N., 'Zambian Trade with Zumbo in the Eighteenth Century', in R. Gray and D. Birmingham (eds.), *Pre-Colonial African Trade* (1970), 231–42

MUDENGE, S. I., 'The Rozvi Empire and the Feira of Zumbo', Ph.D. thesis, London, 1972

NEWITT, M. D. D., *Portuguese Settlement on the Zambesi* (1973)

ALPERS, E. A., *Ivory and Slaves in East Central Africa* (1975). This is specially concerned with the trade of the Yao.

CUNNISON, I. G., 'Kazembe and the Portuguese', *Journal of African History*, II (1961), i, 61–76

CHILDS, G. M., *Kinship and Character of the Ovimbundu* (1969; first published as *Umbundu Kinship and Character*, 1949). This includes several perceptive and well-documented passages on the history of the Ovimbundu.

Chapter VIII: African Intruders

*OMER-COOPER, J. D., *The Zulu Aftermath* (1966). A useful overall survey of the various migrations prompted by the expansion of the Zulu.

OMER-COOPER, J. D., 'Aspects of political change in the nineteenth-century Mfecane', in L. Thompson (ed.), *African Societies in Southern Africa* (1969), 207–29

ROBERTS, A. D., 'The History of Abdullah ibn Suliman,' *African Social Research*, 4 (1967), 241–70

ROBERTS, A. D., 'Tippu Tip, Livingstone, and the Chronology of Kazembe', *Azania*, II (1967), 115–31

VERBEKEN, A., *Msiri roi de Garenganze* (Brussels, 1956)

ROBERTS, A. D., 'Nyamwezi Trade', in R. Gray and D. Birmingham (eds.), *Pre-Colonial African Trade* (1970), 39–74

LANGWORTHY, H. W., 'Swahili Influence in the Area between Lake Malawi and the Luangwa River', *African Historical Studies*, IV (1971), iii, 575–602

ROBERTS, A. D., 'Firearms in north-eastern Zambia', *Transafrican Journal of History*, I (1971), ii, 3–21

NEWITT, M. D. D., *Portuguese Settlement on the Zambesi* (1973)

*ROBERTS, A. D., 'Pre-Colonial Trade in Zambia', *African Social Research*, 10 (1970), 715–46

Chapter IX: The British Take Over

JEAL, Tim, *Livingstone* (1973: paperback ed. 1975). This is a very serviceable biography, but there is still room for a scholarly study which would take full account both of the African scene and of the British social and intellectual background.

HANNA, A. J., *The Beginnings of Nyasaland and North-Eastern Rhodesia, 1859–1895* (Oxford, 1956)

SAMPSON, Richard, *The Man with a Toothbrush in his Hat* (Lusaka, 1972). A short biography of George Westbeech.

*CLAY, Gervas, *Your Friend, Lewanika* (1968). A well-documented biography by a former colonial official.

LOCKHART, J. G., and WOODHOUSE, C. M., *Rhodes* (1963)

OLIVER, Roland, *Sir Harry Johnston and the Scramble for Africa* (1957)

AXELSON, Eric, *Portugal and the Scramble for Africa* (Johannesburg, 1967)

ISAACMAN, Allen, *The Tradition of Resistance in Mozambique* (1976)

ROTBERG, R. I., *Joseph Thomson and the Exploration of Africa* (1971)

STEPHENSON, J. E., *Muhammedan Early Days in the Copperbelt of Northern Rhodesia*, National Archives of Zambia, Occasional Paper no. 1 (Lusaka, 1972)

BRELSFORD, W. V., *Generation of Men: the European Pioneers of Northern Rhodesia* (Salisbury, 1965)

*SAMPSON, Richard, *They came to Northern Rhodesia* (Lusaka, 1956). An alphabetical list of people (mostly white) who had entered the territory by the end of 1902.

Chapters X–XI: The Colonial Period

1. GENERAL WORKS

*GANN, L. H., *The Birth of a Plural Society* (Manchester, 1958). A study of Northern Rhodesia between 1894 and 1914.

*GANN, L. H., *A History of Northern Rhodesia: early days to 1953* (1964). This is a massive survey, full of interesting material, but its usefulness is diminished by the totally inadequate index.

GELFAND, M., *Northern Rhodesia in the Days of the Charter* (Oxford, 1961). This includes two chapters on the territory's medical services under Company rule and a chapter on the control of human trypanosomiasis.

POLLOCK, N. H., *Nyasaland and Northern Rhodesia: Corridor to the North* (Pittsburgh, 1971). This study of the period 1889–1924 was mostly written in 1948 and takes little account of more recent research; it has a few useful pages on early colonial economic history.

DAVIS, J. MERLE (ed.), *Modern Industry and the African* (1933; second edition 1967). This comprises reports by members of a commission set up by the International Missionary Council to study the economic, social and religious effects of the growth of the Copperbelt.

*GRAY, Richard, *The Two Nations: Aspects of the Development of Race Relations in the Rhodesias and Nyasaland* (1960). A study of economic and social history between 1918 and 1953; the main emphasis is on Southern Rhodesia.

HALL, Richard, *Zambia: 1890 to 1964. The Colonial Period* (1976). A revised version of a book published in 1965, with special emphasis on African politics, which the author wrote while editing the country's leading newspaper.

CLEGG, Edward, *Race and Politics: Partnership in the Federation of Rhodesia and Nyasaland* (1960). Primarily a study of Northern Rhodesia from the 1930s onwards; like the next three books on this list, it is highly critical of Federation.

MASON, Philip, *Year of Decision: Rhodesia and Nyasaland in 1960* (1960). A survey of Central Africa since the imposition of Federation in 1953; the author was the first Director of the Institute of Race Relations.

LEYS, Colin and PRATT, R. C. (eds.), *A New Deal in Central Africa* (1960). This collection includes studies by the editors of the origins of Federation as well as essays on its political, social and economic effects.

FRANKLIN, Harry, *Unholy Wedlock: the Failure of the Central African Federation* (1963). The author was formerly a civil servant and politician in Northern Rhodesia; see below under (5) Biography and Memoirs.

2. POLITICS

(a) General studies

KEATLEY, Patrick, *The Politics of Partnership* (Penguin Books, 1963). A lengthy study of British rule in Central Africa by a very experienced journalist.

DAVIDSON, J. W., *The Northern Rhodesia Legislative Council* (1948). A short but admirable historical study.

HAILEY, Lord, *Native Administration in the British African Territories, Part II* (1950). Chapter 6 (pp. 75–168) is devoted to Northern Rhodesia. . .

DATTA, K., 'Indirect Rule in Northern Rhodesia 1924–1953', Ph.D. thesis, London, 1976.

SLINN, Peter, 'The Northern Rhodesia mineral rights issue, 1922–1964', Ph.D. thesis, London, 1974.

SLINN, Peter, 'Commercial Concessions and Politics during the Colonial Period: the Role of the British South Africa Company in Northern Rhodesia, 1890–1964', *African Affairs*, LXX (1971), 365–84.

COOK, John, 'The Influence of Livingstonia Mission upon the Formation of Welfare Associations in Zambia 1912–1931', in T. O. Ranger and J. Weller (eds.), *Themes in the Christian History of Central Africa* (1975).

*ROTBERG, R. I., *The Rise of Nationalism in Central Africa: the making of Malawi and Zambia 1873–1964* (Harvard and London, 1966). This is mainly valuable for the period between 1930 and 1953.

HENDERSON, Ian, 'The origins of nationalism in East and Central Africa: the Zambian case', *Journal of African History*, XI (1970), iv, 591–603.

MULFORD, David, *The Northern Rhodesia General Election, 1962* (Nairobi, 1964).

*MULFORD, David, *Zambia: the Politics of Independence, 1957–1964* (1967).

(b) Industrial Politics

*BERGER, Elena L., *Labour, Race and Colonial Rule: the Copperbelt from 1924 to Independence* (Oxford, 1974).

EPSTEIN, A. L., *Politics in an Urban African Community* (Manchester, 1958). An outstanding study of the growth of African politics in Roan Antelope mine compound and Luanshya township.

HENDERSON, Ian, 'The Limits of Colonial Power: Race and Labour

Problems in Colonial Zambia, 1900–1953', *Journal of Imperial and Commonwealth History*, II (1974), iii, 294–307.

HENDERSON, Ian, 'Early African Leadership: the Copperbelt disturbances of 1935 and 1940', *Journal of Southern African Studies*, 11 (1975), 83–97.

HENDERSON, Ian, 'Labour and Politics in Northern Rhodesia, 1900–1953', Ph. D. thesis, Edinburgh, 1972.

HOOKER, J. R., 'The Role of the Labour Department in the Birth of African Trade Unionism in Northern Rhodesia', *International Review of Social History*, X (1965), 1–22.

MWENDAPOLE, M. R. (ed. Robin Palmer), *A History of the Zambian Trade Union Movement to 1968* (forthcoming). Memoirs of a trade union leader.

ZELNICKER, S., 'Changing Patterns of Trade Unionism: the Zambian Case, 1948–1964', Ph.D. thesis, California (Los Angeles), 1970.

(c) *Local Studies*

CAPLAN, G. L., *The Elites of Barotseland, 1878–1969: a political history of Zambia's Western Province* (1970). The title is misleading; this is really a study of relations between the Lozi and the central government.

SHALOFF, S., 'The Kasempa Salient: the tangled web of British–Kaonde–Lozi relations', *International Journal of African Historical Studies*, V (1972), i, 22–40.

MEEBELO, Henry S., *Reaction to Colonialism: a Prelude to the Politics of Independence in Northern Zambia, 1893–1939* (Manchester and Lusaka, 1971). This is concerned with the north-east, and especially with the Bemba.

MUNTEMBA, Maud, 'The Evolution of Political Systems in South-Central Africa, 1894–1953', M.A. thesis, Zambia, 1973. A study of traditional authorities in the Southern and Central Provinces.

DIXON-FYLE, MCSR, 'Politics and agrarian change among the plateau Tonga of Northern Rhodesia, 1924–1963', Ph.D. thesis, London, 1976.

3. *ECONOMICS*

(a) *General Studies*

*BALDWIN, R. E., *Economic Development and Export Growth: a Study of Northern Rhodesia, 1920–1960* (Berkeley and Los Angeles, 1966). A short but valuable analytical study by an economist.

BARBER, W. J., *The Economy of British Central Africa* (1961). Largely concerned with Southern Rhodesia.

BETTISON, D. G., 'Factors in the determination of wage rates in Central Africa', *Rhodes-Livingstone Journal*, 28 (1960), 22–47.

DEANE, Phyllis, *Colonial Social Accounting* (Cambridge, 1953; reprinted Hamden, Conn., 1973). A study of the measurement of wealth in Northern Rhodesia and Nyasaland, with special emphasis on rural conditions.

HAZLEWOOD, A., 'The Economics of Federation and Dissolution in Central Africa' in A. Hazlewood (ed.), *African Integration and Disintegration* (1967), pp. 185–250.

HINDEN, Rita, *Plan for Africa* (1941). A critical study of economic change in Northern Rhodesia and the Gold Coast, written for the Fabian Colonial Bureau.

KESSEL, N., 'The mineral industry and its effects on the development of the Zambian economy 1945–70', Ph.D. thesis, Leeds, 1971.

KUCZYNSKI, R. R., *Demographic Survey of the British Colonial Empire*, (1949), II, 402–521. Specially valuable for its detailed and sceptical analyses of statistics for (Northern Rhodesia) labour migration.

PIM, Sir Alan, *Report of the Commission appointed to enquire into the financial and economic position of Northern Rhodesia* (Colonial no. 145: 1938). This is still the best general study of the territory's economic history between the two World Wars.

POTTS, D. L., 'The Development of the Zambian Copper Economy, 1928–1970', M.A. thesis, Sheffield, 1970.

(b) *Agriculture, land policy and the rural economy*

ALLAN, William, *The African Husbandman* (Edinburgh, 1965). Much material on Northern Rhodesia.

BOHANNAN, P., and DALTON, G. (eds.), *Markets in Africa* (Evanston, 1962). Includes M.P. Miracle, 'The Copperbelt – Trading and Marketing' (pp. 698–753); E. Colson, 'Trade and Wealth among the Tonga' (pp. 601–16); and R. I. Rotberg, 'Rural Rhodesian Markets' (pp. 581–600: this is in fact concerned with Northern Rhodesia). The essay by Miracle was reprinted in the paperback selection from *Markets in Africa* (same editors: New York, 1965), pp. 285–341.

HARKEMA, R. C., 'The Production and Geographical Distribution of Tobacco in Zambia', *East African Geographical Review* (April 1972), 51–64.

HAVILAND, W. E., 'Economic Development of the Tobacco Industry of Northern Rhodesia', *South African Journal of Economics*, XXII (1954), iv, 375–84.

*HELLEN, J. A., *Rural Economic Development in Zambia, 1890–1964* (1969).

JOKONYA, T., 'East Luangwa 1895–1947: A Study of the Colonial Land Policy in the Eastern Province of Zambia', Ph.D. thesis, Sussex, 1973.

KAY, George, *Changing Patterns of Settlement and Land Use in the Eastern Province of Northern Rhodesia* (Hull, 1965).

LOMBARD, C. S., *The Growth of Co-operatives in Zambia, 1914–71*, Zambian Papers no. 6 (Lusaka and Manchester, 1971).

MAKINGS, S. M., *Agricultural Change in Northern Rhodesia/Zambia 1945–1965* (Stanford, 1966: reprint from *Food Research Institute Studies*, VI (1966), ii, 195–247).

PALMER, Robin (ed.), *Zambian Land and Labour Studies I*, National Archives Occasional Paper no. 2 (Lusaka, 1973). Includes essays on land policy and commercial farming in Northern Rhodesia.

PALMER, Robin, and PARSONS, Neil (eds.), *The Roots of Rural Poverty: essays on the development of underdevelopment in southern central Africa* (in press). Includes essays on the agricultural history of Barotseland and on economic change in Kabwe rural district.

RANGER, T. O., *The Agricultural History of Zambia*, Historical Association of Zambia, paper no. 1 (Lusaka, 1971). A brief summary of, and comment on, the books by Allan and Hellen listed above.

WHITE, C. M. N., 'Factors determining the content of African Land Tenure Systems in Northern Rhodesia', in D. Biebuyck (ed.), *African Agrarian Systems* (1963), pp. 364–72.

See also entries in the 'Ethnic Bibliography' under Bemba, Ila, Lala, Lozi, Luapula, Luvale, Mambwe, Tonga, Unga.

(c) *Labour*

ARMOR, M., 'Migrant Labour in the Kalabo district of Barotseland', *Bulletin of the Inter-African Labour Institute*, IX (1962), 5–42.

HOLLEMAN, J. F., and BIESHEUVEL, S., *White mine workers in Northern Rhodesia, 1959–60* (Leiden, 1973).

MITCHELL, J. CLYDE, 'Wage Labour and African Population Movements in Central Africa', in K. M. Barbour and R. M. Prothero (eds.), *Essays on African Population* (1961), 193–248.

MOORE, R. J. B., *These African Copper Miners* (1948). A short but very perceptive and vivid account by a missionary-anthropologist who died early in his career in 1943.

OHADIKE, P. O., *Development of and Factors in the Employment of African Migrants in the Copper Mines of Zambia 1940–66*, Zambian Papers no. 4 (Lusaka and Manchester, 1969).

van ONSELEN, Charles, 'Black Workers in Central African Industry: a critical essay on the historiography and sociology of Rhodesia', *Journal of Southern African Studies*, I, ii (April 1975), 228–46.

van ONSELEN, Charles, *Chibaro: African Mine Labour in Southern Rhodesia, 1900–1933* (1976).

PERRINGS, C., 'Black Labour in the Copper Mines of the Belgian Congo and Northern Rhodesia, 1911–1941: industrial strategies and the evolution of an African proletariat', Ph.D. thesis, London, 1976.

268   A HISTORY OF ZAMBIA

(d) *Mining*

*BANCROFT, J. A., *Mining in Northern Rhodesia* (1961). Mainly a study of the development of mines in which Anglo American had a major interest: Broken Hill, Bwana Mkubwa, Nchanga, Nkana, and Bancroft (Konkola). The author, an eminent Canadian geologist, organised a major campaign of mineral exploration in Northern Rhodesia between 1927 and 1930.

BRADLEY, K., *Copper Venture: the discovery and development of Roan Antelope and Mufulira* (1952). A short popular account.

COLEMAN, F. L., *The Northern Rhodesia Copperbelt, 1899–1962* (Manchester, 1971). A short technological study; one chapter is devoted to Nchanga mine.

GEORGE, F., and GOUVERNEUR, J., 'Les Transformations techniques et l'évolution des coefficients de fabrication à l'Union Minière du Haut-Katanga de 1910 à 1965', *Cultures et Développement*, II (1969–70), 53–100.

GOUVERNEUR, J., *Productivity and factor proportions in less developed countries* (Oxford, 1971). A study of the former Belgian Congo, with special reference to Union Minière.

GREGORY, Theodore, *Ernest Oppenheimer and the Economic Development of Southern Africa* (1962). The authorised history of the Anglo American Corporation; see chapter 7, 'The Northward Expansion', pp. 384–489, for Northern Rhodesia.

HERFINDAHL, O. C., *Copper Costs and Prices, 1870–1957* (Baltimore, 1959).

MOODY, C. E., and KESSEL, N., 'Productivity Change in Zambian Mining', *South African Journal of Economics*, XL (1972), i, 61–71. Covers the period 1954–1966.

PRAIN, Sir Ronald, *Copper: the anatomy of an industry* (1975). An account for the non-specialist, by the former chairman of Roan Selection Trust.

4. *SOCIAL HISTORY*

(a) *Education*

COOMBE, T., 'The Origins of Secondary Education in Zambia' [1928–1939], *African Social Research*, 3 (1967). 173–205; 4 (1967), 283–315; 5 (1968), 365–405.

PARKER, F., 'African Education in Zambia (formerly Northern Rhodesia): a partial bibliography of magazine articles, 1925–1963', *African Studies Bulletin* [U.S.A.], X, iii (December 1967), 6–15.

SNELSON, P. D., *Educational Development in Northern Rhodesia, 1883–1945* (Lusaka, 1974).

WINCOTT, N., 'Education and Urban Development in Zambia', in B. Pachai *et al.* (eds.) *Malawi Past and Present* (Blantyre, 1971), 137–60. An essay on Northern Rhodesia.

(b) *Religion*
BOLINK, P., *Towards Church Union in Zambia* (Franeker, Netherlands, 1967). A history of the United Church of Zambia and its component parts in the Livingstonia Mission of the Church of Scotland, the London Missionary Society, the Paris Evangelical Society and the Methodist Missionary Society.

CROSS, Sholto, 'A prophet not without honour: Jeremiah Gondwe', in C. Allen and R. W. Johnson (eds.), *African Perspectives* (Cambridge, 1970). Study of a Watch Tower community near Luanshya.

CROSS, Sholto, 'The Watch Tower Movement in South-Central Africa, 1908–1945', D.Phil. thesis, Oxford, 1973.

CROSS, Sholto, and RANGER, T. O. (eds.) *The Problem of Evil in Eastern Africa* (forthcoming). Includes essays by S. Cross on Watch Tower and T. O. Ranger on the *mucapi* cult.

GARVEY, Brian, 'The Development of the White Fathers' Mission among the Bemba-speaking Peoples, 1891–1964', Ph.D. thesis, London, 1974.

MARWICK, Max (ed.), *Witchcraft and Sorcery* (Penguin Books, 1970). Includes essays on anti-witchcraft movements among the Bemba (by Audrey Richards) and Chewa (by Marwick).

RANGER, T. O., and WELLER, J. (eds.), *Themes in the Christian History of Central Africa* (1975). Includes essays by A. Hastings on John Membe, T. O. Ranger on the Mwana Lesa movement and J. Weller on Bishop Alston May.

ROBERTS, A. D., 'The Lumpa Church of Alice Lenshina', in R. I. Rotberg and A. A. Mazrui (eds.), *Protest and Power in Black Africa* (New York, 1970), 513–68. Reprinted as a pamphlet, Lusaka, 1972.

*ROTBERG, R. I., *Christian Missionaries and the Creation of Northern Rhodesia, 1880–1924* (Princeton, 1965).

STONE, W. V., 'The Livingstonia Mission and the Bemba', *Bulletin of the Society for African Church History*, II (1968), iv, 311–22.

TAYLOR, J. V., and LEHMANN, D., *Christians of the Copperbelt* (1961). Mainly concerned with Protestant missions and churches; includes studies of the Union Church; Jehovah's Witnesses; and the Lumpa Church.

WELLER, J. C., *The Priest from the Lakeside: the story of Leonard Kamungu of Malawi and Zambia, 1877–1913* (Blantyre, 1971). Short biography of the African priest who established a mission for the U.M.C.A. at Msoro, in the Luangwa valley.

WELLER, J. C., 'Msoro Mission under Leonard Kamungu and his successors, 1911–1923', in D. B. Barrett (ed.), *African Initiatives in Religion* (Nairobi, 1971), 35–49.

ZIYAMBE, Ruth, 'The African Methodist Episcopal Church in Zambia: Afro-American Mission and African Independent Church', Ph.D. thesis, Northwestern University, 1975.

(c) *Urban Studies*

BROWN, Richard, 'Anthropology and Colonial Rule: the Case of Godfrey Wilson and the Rhodes-Livingstone Institute, Northern Rhodesia', in T. Asad (ed.), *Anthropology and the Colonial Encounter* (1973), 173–97.

EPSTEIN, A. L., *Politics in an Urban African Community* (Manchester, 1958). Roan Antelope mine and Luanshya.

HARRIES-JONES, Peter, 'The Tribes in the Towns', in W. V. Brelsford, *The Tribes of Zambia* (Lusaka, 1966), 124–46.

HARRIES-JONES, Peter, *Freedom and Labour: mobilization and political control on the Zambian Copperbelt* (Oxford, 1975). Based on research in Luanshya, 1962–5; chapter 1 (pp. 23–41) is a fascinating auto-biographical account by Mrs Foster Mubanga of the role of women in the rise of UNIP at the local level.

HEISLER, H., *Urbanisation and the Government of Migration: the Inter-relation of Urban and Rural Life in Zambia* (1974). Mainly a study of the colonial administration of labour; it is curiously naïve and unnecessarily obscure.

MITCHELL, J. CLYDE, *The Kalela Dance*, Rhodes-Livingstone Paper no. 27 (Manchester, 1956). Classic analysis of 'tribalism' in Luanshya in 1951.

MITCHELL, J. CLYDE (ed.), *Social networks in urban situations* (Manchester, 1969). Includes essays by A. L. Epstein on Ndola, 1955–6; B. Kapferer on the electro-zinc plant at Kabwe mine, 1964–5; D. M. Boswell on Lusaka, 1964; P. Harries-Jones on Luanshya, 1964.

POWDERMAKER, Hortense, *Copper Town: Changing Africa* (New York, 1962). Impressions of African life and thought in Luanshya, 1953–4.

ROTHMAN, N. C., 'African Urban Development in the Colonial Period: a Study of Lusaka, 1905–1964). Ph.D. thesis, Northwestern, 1972

SAMPSON, Richard, *So this was Lusaakas* (Lusaka, 1960; second edition 1971).

TURNER, Arthur, 'A History of Broken Hill, Northern Rhodesia', Ph.D. thesis California (Los Angeles), 1975.

WATSON, Sir Malcolm, *African Highway: the Battle for Health in Central Africa* (1953). Accounts by various authors of anti-malaria campaigns on the Copperbelt, which were supervised by Watson from 1929 to 1950.

WILSON, Godfrey, *An Essay on the Economics of Detribalisation in Northern Rhodesia*, Rhodes-Livingstone Papers nos. 5 and 6 (Livingstone, 1941; Manchester 1968). Classic study of Africans in Broken Hill, by the first Director of the Rhodes-Livingstone Institute.

(d) *Miscellaneous*

BRELSFORD, W. V., *The Story of the Northern Rhodesia Regiment* (Lusaka, 1954).

CLIFFORD, W., *Crime in Northern Rhodesia*, Rhodes-Livingstone Communication no. 18 (Lusaka, 1960).

DOTSON, F. and L., *The Indian Minority of Zambia, Rhodesia and Malawi* (New Haven, 1968).

HALL, Barbara (ed.), *Tell me, Josephine* (1964). A selection from the advice column of the *Zambia Mail*.

RANGER, T. O., *Dance and Society in Eastern Africa* (1975). A study of *mbeni* societies.

5. *BIOGRAPHY AND MEMOIRS*

BRADLEY, Kenneth, *The Diary of a District Officer* (1943; fourth ed. 1966). Fort Jameson, 1938.

FRAENKEL, Peter, *Wayaleshi* (1959). African broadcasting in Northern Rhodesia, 1952–1957.

FRANKLIN, Harry, *The Flag-Wagger* (1974). The author served as a colonial official in Northern Rhodesia from 1928 to 1952 and introduced the 'Saucepan Special' radio.

HATCH, John, *Two African Statesmen: Kaunda of Zambia and Nyerere of Tanzania* (1976)

KAUNDA, Kenneth, *Zambia shall be free: an autobiography* (1963).

MACPHERSON, Fergus, *Kenneth Kaunda of Zambia: the Times and the Man* (Lusaka, 1975). A long biography based on interviews, private papers and party records as well as public archives.

MORRIS, Colin, *The Hour after Midnight* (1961). A Methodist minister's account of religion, race and politics in the Copperbelt and Lusaka, 1956–60.

MUSHINDO, P. B., *The Life of a Zambian Evangelist*, Institute for African Studies, Communication no. 9 (Lusaka, 1973). The author, who died in 1972, was ordained as a minister at Lubwa mission in about 1940 and was later a member of the African Representative Council.

SHORT, Robin, *African Sunset* (1973). Memoirs of a colonial official, opposed to both Federation and African nationalism.

SIWALE, Donald, 'Autobiographical Sketch', *African Social Research*, 15 (June 1973), 362–73.

WELENSKY, Sir Roy, *Welensky's 4000 Days: the Life and Death of the Federation of Rhodesia and Nyasaland* (1964). There are two biographies of Welensky, both by journalists: Don Taylor, *The Rhodesian* (1955); Garry Allighan, *The Welensky Story* (Cape Town, 1962).

Chapter XII: Independent Zambia

1. *GENERAL WORKS*

HALL, Richard, *The High Price of Principles: Kaunda and the White South* (revised edition, Penguin, 1973).

HALL, Richard, and PEYMAN, Hugh, *The Great Uhuru Railway: China's Showpiece in Africa* (1976)

KAY, George, *A Social Geography of Zambia* (1967).

PARKIN, David (ed.), *Town and Country in East and Central Africa* (1975). Includes essays on Zambia by E. Colson and T. Scudder, M. Kashoki, P. Ohadike and J. van Velsen

*PETTMAN, Jan, *Zambia: Security and Conflict* (1974).

SIMONIS, H. and U. E. (eds.), *Socioeconomic Development in Dual Economies: the example of Zambia* (Munich, 1971).

2. *POLITICS*

BATES, Robert H., *Unions, Parties and Political Development: a Study of Mineworkers in Zambia* (New Haven, 1971).

GOOD, Robert C., *UDI: the international politics of the Rhodesian rebellion* (1973).

KAUNDA, Kenneth, *A Humanist in Africa: letters to Colin M. Morris* (1966).

KAUNDA, Kenneth, *Zambia: Independence and Beyond* (1966), Speeches, ed. C. Legum.

KAUNDA, Kenneth, *Letter to my Children* (1973).

MEEBELO, Henry S. (ed.), *Main Currents of Zambian Humanist Thought* (Lusaka, 1973).

*TORDOFF, William (ed.), *Politics in Zambia* (Manchester, 1974). Essays by the editor, R. Molteno, T. Rasmussen, I. Scott, A. Gupta, R. L. Sklar. Molteno's essay 'Cleavage and conflict in Zambian politics' is a perceptive discussion of the relative importance of 'class' and 'tribe'.

3. *ECONOMICS*

(a) *General*

ELLIOTT, Charles (ed.), *Constraints on the economic development of Zambia* (Nairobi, 1971).

MARTIN, Antony, *Minding their own Business: Zambia's Struggle against Western Control* (1972).

YOUNG, Alastair, *Industrial Diversification in Zambia* (New York, 1973).

NZIRAMASANGU, M. T., 'The copper export sector and the Zambian economy', Ph.D. thesis, Stanford, 1973.

(b) *Agriculture*

BUNTING, A. H. (ed.), *Change in agriculture* (1970). Includes essays by K. R. M. Anthony on the plateau Tonga, and W. Allan on African farming in Zambia.

KAY, George, 'Agricultural progress in Zambia' in M. F. Thomas *et al.* (eds.), *Environment and land use in Africa* (1969, 1972), 495–524.

LOMBARD, C. S., and TWEEDIE, A. H. C., *Agriculture in Zambia since Independence* (Lusaka, 1973).

(c) *Demography*

BATES, R. H., and BENNETT, B. W., 'Determinants of the rural exodus in Zambia: a study of inter-censal migration, 1963–1969', *Cahiers d'études africaines*, XIV (1974), iii, 453–99.

JACKMAN, M. E., *Recent Population Movements in Zambia; some aspects of the 1969 census*, Zambian Paper no. 8 (Lusaka and Manchester, 1973)

(d) *Labour*

BURAWOY, Michael, *The Colour of Class on the Copper Mines: from African Advancement to Zambianization*, Zambian Paper no. 7 (Lusaka and Manchester, 1972)

KAPFERER, Bruce, *Strategy and Transaction in an African factory* (Manchester, 1972). Social relationships between African workers in an Indian-owned clothing factory in Kabwe, in 1965–1966.

(e) *Mining*

BOSTOCK, Mark, and HARVEY, Charles (eds.), *Economic Independence and Zambian Copper: a Case Study of Foreign Investment* (New York, 1972). Includes essays on the role of the British South Africa Company (P. Slinn) and prospecting and mining (A. Drysdale) as well as on the nationalisation of the copper industry.

FABER, M., and POTTER, J. G., *Towards Economic Independence; papers on the nationalisation of the copper industry in Zambia* (Cambridge, 1971).

SKLAR, Richard L., *Corporate Power in an African State* (Berkeley and Los Angeles, 1975). Relations between the government and the mining groups.

4. *MISCELLANEOUS*

MUSONDA, Kapelwa [pseudonym], *The Kapelwa Musonda File* (Lusaka, 1973). Articles by the satirical columnist of *The Times of Zambia*.

MWANAKATWE, John, *The Growth of Education in Zambia since Independence* (Lusaka, 1968). The author was Minister of Education, 1964–7.

MYTTON, Graham, *Listening, Looking and Learning: Report on a National Mass Media Audience in Zambia, 1972–3* (Lusaka, 1974).

OHANESSIAN, Sirarpe (ed.), *Language in Zambia* (forthcoming).

Appendix 1 : The Copper Industry in Pre-colonial Central Africa

*BANCROFT, J. A., *Mining in Northern Rhodesia* (1961), chapter 2.

PHILLIPSON, D. W., 'Prehistory of the Copper Mining Industry in Zambia', *South African Mining and Engineering Journal* (1968), 1332–39 (reprinted from *Horizon* [Ndola], April 1968).

CHAPLIN, J. H., 'Notes on Traditional Smelting in Northern Rhodesia', *South African Archaeological Bulletin*, XVI (1961), no. 62, 53–60.

GREVISSE, F., 'Notes ethnologiques relatives à quelques populations autochthones du Haut-Katanga: extraction des minerais et des rochers', *Bulletin du Centre d'Etudes des Problèmes Sociaux Indigènes*, XXXII (1956), 177–87.

Ethnic Bibliography

AMBO

STEFANISZYN, B., *Social and Ritual Life of the Ambo of Northern Rhodesia* (1964).

BEMBA

RICHARDS, Audrey I., *Land, Labour and Diet in Northern Rhodesia* (1939). Based on fieldwork among the Bemba in 1930–33; by the first professional anthropologist to work in Northern Rhodesia.

*ROBERTS, A. D., *A History of the Bemba* [to 1900] (1973). Includes material on the histories of the Bisa, Lungu, Mambwe and Tabwa.

EPSTEIN, A. L., 'Military Organisation and the Pre-Colonial Polity of the Bemba of Zambia', *Man* (n.s.), X (1975), 199–217.

WERNER, Douglas, 'Some Developments in Bemba religious history', *Journal of Religion in Africa*, IV (1971), i, 1–24.

See also MEEBELO, GARVEY, as listed on pp. 265, 269.

BISA

MARKS, Stuart A., *Large Mammals and a Brave People: Subsistence Hunters in Zambia* (Seattle, 1976). Study of the Valley Bisa, between the two Luangwa game reserves.

CHEWA

LANGWORTHY, H. W., 'Conflict among rulers in the history of Undi's Chewa kingdom', *Transafrican Journal of History*, I (1971), i, 1–23.

LANGWORTHY, H. W., 'Chewa or Malawi Political Organization in the Precolonial Era', in B. Pachai (ed.), *The Early History of Malawi* (1972), 104–22.

MARWICK, M. G., *Sorcery in its social setting: a study of the Northern Rhodesian Cewa* (Manchester, 1965).

SCHOFFELEERS, J. M., 'The Meaning and Use of the Name Malawi in Oral Traditions and Precolonial Documents', in B. Pachai (ed.), *The Early History of Malawi* (1972), 91–103.

GOBA

LANCASTER, C. S., 'The Economics of Social Organisation in an Ethnic Border Zone: the Goba (Northern Shona) of the Zambezi Valley', *Ethnology*, X (1971), iv, 445–65.

ILA

SMITH, Edwin W., and DALE, Andrew M., *The Ila-Speaking Peoples of Northern Rhodesia* (1920; reprinted New York, 1968). This classic of African ethnography was written by a missionary and a government official.

FIELDER, R. J., 'The role of cattle in the Ila economy', *African Social Research*, 15 (June 1973), 327–61.

FIELDER, R. J., 'Social change among the Ila-speaking peoples of Northern Rhodesia, with particular reference to their relations with the Primitive Methodist mission', M.A. thesis, Manchester, 1965.

KAONDE

MELLAND, F. H., *In Witch-bound Africa* (1923). An ethnographic account of the Kaonde; the author was an official at Kasempa from 1911 to 1922.

CHIBANZA, S. J., 'Kaonde history', *Central Bantu Historical Texts*, I. Rhodes-Livingstone Communication no. 22 (Lusaka, 1961), 41–114.

JAEGER, Dick, 'A general survey of the historical migration of the Kaonde clans from southern Congo into Zambia', *Tropical Man* (Leiden), IV (1971), 8–45.

LALA

MUNDAY, J. T., 'Kankomba', *Central Bantu Historical Texts*, I. Rhodes-Livingstone Communication no. 22 (Lusaka, 1961), 1–40.

LONG, Norman, *Social Change and the Individual* (Manchester, 1968). A study of a Lala chiefdom by a social anthropologist, focused on tobacco farming and the local importance of Jehovah's Witnesses.

LAMBA

DOKE, C. M., *The Lambas of Northern Rhodesia: a study of their customs and beliefs* (1931), By a South African Baptist missionary.

LOZI

GLUCKMAN, Max, *Economy of the Central Barotse Plain*, Rhodes-Livingstone Paper no. 7 (Livingstone, 1941; Manchester, 1968).

GLUCKMAN, Max, *The judicial process among the Barotse of Northern Rhodesia* (Manchester, 1955; second edition, 1967). The second edition includes a 'Reappraisal' and also an account of changes between 1947 and 1965.

GLUCKMAN, Max, *The ideas in Barotse jurisprudence* (Yale, 1965; second edition, Manchester, 1972).

MAINGA, Mutumba, *Bulozi under the Luyana Kings* [to 1900] (1973). The author of this academic history is herself a Lozi.

HERMITTE, Eugene, 'An Economic History of Barotseland, 1800–1940', Ph.D., Northwestern University, 1974

See also under CAPLAN, p. 265; CLAY, p. 262.

LUNDA (of Kazembe) and Luapula peoples

CUNNISON, Ian, *The Luapula Peoples of Northern Rhodesia* (Manchester 1959). A study of Kazembe's kingdom by a social anthropologist, with special emphasis on historical awareness and tribal identity.

CUNNISON, Ian (tr. and ed.), *Historical Traditions of the Eastern Lunda*, Rhodes-Livingstone Communication no. 23 (Lusaka, 1962). The official history of Kazembe, as recorded in 1942.

CUNNISON, Ian, *History on the Luapula*, Rhodes-Livingstone Paper no. 21 (Cape Town, 1951).

LUNDA (Ndembu)

TURNER, V. W., *Schism and Continuity in an African Society: a study of Ndembu village life* (Manchester, 1957).

SCHECTER, R., 'A History of the Lunda-Ndembu of Kanongesha from oral traditions', Ph.D. thesis, Wisconsin, 1973.

LUVALE

WHITE, C. M. N., 'The Balovale Peoples and their historical background', *Rhodes-Livingstone Journal*, 8 (1949), 26–41.

WHITE, C. M. N., *A Preliminary Survey of Luvale Rural Economy*, Rhodes-Livingstone Paper no. 29 (Manchester, 1959).

WHITE, C. M. N., *An Outline of Luvale Social and Political Organisation*, Rhodes-Livingstone Paper no. 30 (Manchester, 1960).

WHITE, C. M. N., 'Clan, Chieftainship and Slavery in Luvale Political Organisation', *Africa*, XXVII (1957), i, 59–73.

PAPSTEIN, R., 'A History of the Luvale Peoples of North-Western Zambia', Ph.D. thesis, California (Los Angeles), forthcoming.

MAMBWE

WATSON, William, *Tribal Cohesion in a Money Economy* (Manchester, 1958). A study of the Mambwe of Northern Rhodesia, with special reference to their adjustment to the effects of labour migration.

NGONI

BARNES, J. A., *Politics in a changing society: a political history of the Fort Jameson Ngoni* (Cape Town, 1954; Manchester, 1967).

RAU, William, 'Mpezeni's Ngoni of Eastern Zambia, 1870–1920', Ph.D. thesis, California (Los Angeles), 1974.

NSENGA

APTHORPE, R. J., 'Problems of African History: the Nsenga of Northern Rhodesia', *Rhodes-Livingstone Journal*, 28 (1960), 47–67.

SOLI

ARGYLE, W. J., 'The society and polity of the Basoli of Northern Rhodesia', D.Phil. thesis, Oxford, 1962.

FAGAN, B. M., 'A collection of nineteenth century Soli ironwork from the Lusaka area of Northern Rhodesia', *Journal of the Royal Anthropological Institute*, XCI (1961), ii, 228–50.

TONGA (Plateau)

COLSON, Elizabeth, *The Plateau Tonga of Northern Rhodesia: Social and Religious Studies* (Manchester, 1962).

COLSON, Elizabeth, *Marriage and the Family among the Plateau Tonga of Northern Rhodesia* (Manchester, 1958).

COLSON, Elizabeth, 'A Note on Tonga and Ndebele', *Northern Rhodesia Journal*, I, ii (1950), 35–41.

See also DIXON-FYLE, p. 265.

TONGA (Valley or Gwembe)

COLSON, Elizabeth, *The Social Organisation of the Gwembe Tonga* (Manchester, 1960).

COLSON, Elizabeth, *The Social Consequences of Resettlement* (Manchester, 1971).

SCUDDER, Thayer, *The Ecology of the Gwembe Tonga* (Manchester, 1962).

REYNOLDS, Barrie, *The Material Culture of the Peoples of the Gwembe Valley* (Manchester, 1968).

MATTHEWS, T. I., 'The traditional history of the Tonga-speaking people of the middle Zambezi valley', Ph.D. thesis, London, 1976.

UNGA

BRELSFORD, W. V., *Fishermen of the Bangweulu Swamps*, Rhodes-Livingstone Paper no. 12 (Livingstone, 1946).

Aids to the Study of History in Zambia

1. BIBLIOGRAPHIES

There are only four comprehensive subject bibliographies of Zambia:

GUERNSEY, T. D., 'Bibliography of Northern Rhodesia: part III, Geology', *Northern Rhodesia Journal*, II, iii (1954), 26–33.

JONES, Ruth, *South-East Central Africa and Madagascar: General, Ethnography, Linguistics and related subjects* (Africa Bibliography Series: International African Institute, 1961).

PHILLIPSON, D. W., *An Annotated Bibliography of the Archaeology of Zambia* (Lusaka, 1968).

DERRICOURT, R. M., *Supplementary Bibliography of the Archaeology of Zambia, 1967–1973* (Lusaka, 1975).

There is a bibliography, by W. V. Brelsford and G. Clay, of works published on Northern Rhodesia up to 1924, but this was offered only as an amateurs' reading list; it is inaccurate and by no means comprehensive. See *Northern Rhodesia Journal*, I, vi (1952), 20–27; II, ii (1953), 28–36; V, iv (1964), 398–400.

Academic publications on Zambia are listed comprehensively in the quarterly *International African Bibliography* published for the International African Institute. Two research bulletins regularly list recently-published work in archaeology and history, and also provide brief accounts of research in progress:

Archaeologia Zambiana (National Monuments Commission, P.O. Box 124, Livingstone).

History in Zambia (research bulletin of the Historical Association of Zambia, History Subject, University of Zambia, P.O. Box 2379, Lusaka).

2. SERIALS

Articles about Zambia and its history appear from time to time in the following journals:

Journal of African History; Azania (Journal of the British Institute in Eastern Africa, Nairobi); *South African Archaeological Bulletin; Zambia Museums Journal; Transafrican Journal of History* (Nairobi); *African Social Research* (formerly the *Rhodes-Livingstone Journal*, 1944–1965); *African Affairs* (formerly the *Journal of the Royal African Society*); *Journal of Local Administration Overseas* (formerly the *Journal of African Administration*); *Journal of Modern African Studies; Africa.*

In addition to such academic journals, there are a variety of other periodicals with useful historical material. The *Northern Rhodesia*

Journal (1950–65) is specially valuable for reminiscences by officials and white settlers. Economic and mining affairs are discussed in *Optima*, the magazine of the Anglo American Corporation. The other big mining group, Roan Selection Trust, used to publish *Horizon*, a monthly magazine which carried illustrated articles both about the mines and about social and economic developments throughout the country. Its place has been taken by *Z Magazine*, published by the Ministry of Information. *African Development*, a monthly published in London, regularly devotes special issues to Zambia's economic affairs.

3. *SERIES*

National Monuments Commission: *Annual Reports.*
National Archives of Zambia: *Occasional Papers* (1972–).
Rhodes-Livingstone Museum: *Occasional Papers* (1948–60).
Zambia Museum Papers (1970–).
Rhodes-Livingstone *Papers* and *Communications* (1938–65).
Institute of African Studies, University of Zambia: *Zambian Papers* and *Communications* (1966–).
Historical Association of Zambia: *Papers* (1971–).

4. *GUIDES*

PHILLIPSON, D. W., *National Monuments of Zambia: an illustrated guide* (Lusaka, 1972).
GRAHAM, I. M., and HALWINDI, B. C., *Guide to the Public Archives of Zambia, vol. I, 1895–1940* (Lusaka, 1971).

Index